YOUTH SOCCER

A COMPLETE HANDBOOK

Eugene W. Brown, Ph.D., Editor
Youth Sports Institute
Michigan State University

Library of Congress Cataloging in Publication Data:

BROWN, EUGENE W., 1946-

YOUTH SOCCER: A COMPLETE HANDBOOK

Cover Design: Gary Schmitt

Art: Craig Gosling, Linda Kilbert, Dave Anderson

Executive Editor: I. L. Cooper

Production Manager: Joanne Cooper

Project Coordinator: Jan Edmondson

Library of Congress Catalog Card number: 88-70145

ISBN: 0-697-14837-8

Printed in the United States of America by Brown & Benchmark, 2460 Kerper Boulevard, Dubuque, IA 52001.

10 9 8 7 6 5 4 3 2 1

The Publisher and Author disclaim responsibility for any adverse effects or consequences from the misapplication or injudicious use of the information contained within this text.

YOUTH COACHING SERIES

The Youth Coaching Series of books were written to provide comprehensive guides for coaches, parents, and players participating in youth soccer, baseball, football, softball, and basketball.

Developed by the Youth Sports Institute of Michigan State University, these books meet the guidelines established for youth coaches by the National Association for Sport and Physical Education.

Books in the Series:

YOUTH BASEBALL
A Complete Handbook (ISBN: 14844)
Skills and Strategies (ISBN: 15196)
Rules of Play (ISBN: 15197)
Effective Coaching (ISBN: 15198)
Training and Conditioning (ISBN: 15199)

YOUTH BASKETBALL
A Complete Handbook (ISBN: 15183)
Organizing for the Season (ISBN: 15185)
Rules of Play (ISBN: 15186)
Individual Basketball Techniques (ISBN: 15187)
Basic Strategies (ISBN: 15188)
Methods for Effective Coaching (ISBN: 15189)
Sports Medicine and Training (ISBN: 15190)

YOUTH FOOTBALL
A Complete Handbook (ISBN: 15191)
Skills and Strategies (ISBN: 15192)
Effective Coaching (ISBN: 15193)
Conditioning and Training (ISBN: 15194)
Rules of Play (ISBN: 15195)

YOUTH SOCCER
A Complete Handbook (ISBN: 14837)
Organizing for the Season (ISBN: 15201)
Methods for Effective Coaching (ISBN: 15202)
Rules of Play (ISBN: 15203)
Individual Techniques for Soccer Field Players (ISBN: 15204)
Individual Techniques for Soccer Goalkeepers (ISBN: 15205)
Basic Strategies of Soccer (ISBN: 15206)
Sports Medicine and Training (ISBN: 15207)

YOUTH SOFTBALL
A Complete Handbook (ISBN: 15200)
Skills and Strategies (ISBN: 16417)
Rules of Play (ISBN: 16418)
Effective Coaching (ISBN: 16420)
Conditioning and Training (ISBN: 16419)

Also available: Program for Athletic Coaches Education (PACE), a program specifically designed by the Youth Sports Institute for interscholastic coaches. (ISBN: 14827)

For more information or to order books in the Youth Coaching Series:
    Call: 1-800-338-5578
    Write: Order Department
        Brown & Benchmark
        2460 Kerper Blvd., P.O. Box 539
        Dubuque, IA 52001

For information on discounts for youth sports groups, contact:
    Brown & Benchmark
    701 Congressional Blvd., Suite 340
    Carmel, IN 46032
    (317) 573-6420

Table of Contents

Introduction ix
Preface xiii
Contributors xv
Keys to Symbols xvi

Section I Organizing for the Season

CHAPTER 1   ROLE OF THE COACH 1
Introduction 1
Goals for the Coach 3
Summary 4

CHAPTER 2   PLANNING FOR THE SEASON 5
Introduction 5
Why Play? 5
Developing a Season Plan 6
Summary 17
Supplements 18

CHAPTER 3   WORKING EFFECTIVELY WITH PARENTS 31
Introduction 31
Content of a Parents' Orientation Meeting 32
Getting Parents to Attend an Orientation Meeting 37
Organizing the Parents' Orientation Meeting 38
Follow-ups on the Parents' Orientation Meeting 38
Summary 39
References 39
Suggested Readings 39
Supplements 41

CHAPTER 4   LEGAL LIABILITIES 53
Introduction 53
Legal Duties 53
Coaching Responsibilities 57
Summary 63
References 64

Section II Methods for Effective Coaching

CHAPTER 5   PLANNING EFFECTIVE INSTRUCTION 67
Introduction 67
Clearly Communicating the Content to be Learned 68
Continually Evaluating the Performance of Players 68
Using a Systematic Model for Instruction 71
Applying Guidelines for Effective Instruction 74
Planning Effective Practices 74
Summary 78
Supplements 79

CHAPTER 6   MOTIVATING YOUR PLAYERS 99
Introduction 99
Why Young Athletes Participate in Soccer 99
Why Young Athletes Drop Out of Soccer 100
How to Help Motivate Your Players 102
Dealing with Competitive Stress 108
Appropriate Use of Team Trophies, Medals, and Other Awards 109
Summary 113
References 114
Suggested Readings 114

CHAPTER 7   COMMUNICATING WITH YOUR PLAYERS 115
Introduction 115
Sending Clear Messages 115
Being a Good Listener 117
Summary 118
Suggested Readings 118

CHAPTER 8   MAINTAINING DISCIPLINE 119
Introduction 119
Plan for Sound Discipline 119
Summary 124
References 124

CHAPTER 9   DEVELOPING GOOD PERSONAL AND SOCIAL SKILLS 125
Introduction 125
Personal and Social Skills 126
Summary 137
References 138
Suggested Readings 138

CHAPTER 10   EVALUATING COACHING EFFECTIVENESS 139
Introduction 139
What Should be Evaluated? 140
Who Should Evaluate? 140
What Steps can be Used to Conduct an Evaluation 141
Summary 146
Supplements 148

Section III Youth Soccer Rules of Play

CHAPTER 11   SOCCER RULES OF PLAY 155
Introduction 155
Laws of Play 156
Summary 182
References 182
Suggested Readings 182

CHAPTER 12   GLOSSARY OF SOCCER TERMS 183
Introduction 183

Section IV Individual Techniques for Soccer Field Players

CHAPTER 13   KICKING 209
Introduction 209
Individual Techniques 214
Progression for Teaching Kicking 229
Supplements 232

CHAPTER 14   RECEIVING AND CONTROLLING 243
  Introduction 243
  Individual Techniques 245
  Progressions for Teaching Reception and Control 262
  Supplements 265

CHAPTER 15   DRIBBLING AND MAINTAINING CONTROL 269
  Introduction 269
  Individual Dribbling Techniques 271
  Progressions for Teaching Individual Dribbling Techniques 273
  Individual Techniques to Maintain Control of the Dribble 274
  Progressions for Teaching Techniques to Maintain Control of the Dribble 283
  Summary 283
  Suggested Readings 283
  Supplements 285

CHAPTER 16   HEADING 297
  Introduction 297
  Individual Techniques 299
  Developmental Concerns 305
  Recommended Progressions for Teaching Heading 306
  Summary 307
  Suggested Readings 307
  Supplements 308

CHAPTER 17   THROW-IN 317
  Introduction 317
  Individual Techniques 320
  Progression for Teaching the Throw-In 322
  Common Errors in Technique and Their Corrections 324
  Supplements 326

CHAPTER 18   DEFENSIVE TECHNIQUES 329
  Introduction 329
  Individual Techniques 330
  Summary 339
  Supplements 340

Section V Individual Techniques for Soccer Goalkeepers

CHAPTER 19   GOALKEEPING 349
  Introduction 349
  Individual Techniques 365
  Summary 380
  References 380
  Suggested Readings 380
  Supplements 381

Section VI Basic Strategies of Soccer

CHAPTER 20   TACTICS OF PLAY 393
  Introduction 393
  Four Fundamental Principles of Offense 394
  Four Fundamental Principles of Defense 405
  Relationships Between Offensive and Defensive Play 414
  Teaching the Fundamental and Individual Tactics of Offense and Defense to Youth Players 415
  Special Defensive Tactics 417
  Methods of Defensive Play 425
  System of Play 429

Set Plays (Restarts) 436
Common Tactical Errors and Their Corrections 453
Summary 455
Supplements 459

Section VII Sports Medicine and Training

CHAPTER 21   CONDITIONING YOUTH SOCCER PLAYERS 473
Introduction 473
Energy Production Systems 473
Use of the Energy Systems in Soccer 476
Muscular System 477
Use of the Muscular System in Soccer 479
Methods for Conditioning 483
Summary 487
Suggested Readings 488
Supplements 489

CHAPTER 22   NUTRITION FOR SUCCESSFUL PERFORMANCE 513
Introduction 513
Proper Diet 514
Meal Patterns 523
Weight Loss and Weight Gain 526
Summary 528
References 528
Suggested Readings 529
Supplements 530

CHAPTER 23   PREVENTION OF COMMON SOCCER INJURIES 531
Introduction 531
Injury Prevention Techniques 532
Summary 538
References 538
Suggested Readings 538

CHAPTER 24   CARE OF COMMON SOCCER INJURIES 539
Introduction 539
Medical Information 540
Emergency Procedures 540
Provide First Aid 543
Common Medical Problems in Soccer 545
Maintaining Appropriate Records 557
Summary 558
References 558
Suggested Readings 559
Supplements 560

CHAPTER 25   REHABILITATION OF COMMON SOCCER INJURIES 563
Introduction 563
General Procedures 563
Summary 566

Index 567

INTRODUCTION

The success of any youth soccer program depends on the quality of adult leaders who instruct and guide the players. Most of the direct contact between adults and children in a youth soccer program occurs in coach-player relationships. Youth soccer coaches should be chosen with the greatest care and provided with many educational opportunities to grow as models, teachers, counselors, and friends of young athletes.

The success that you and your players achieve will depend largely on the choices that you make as a coach.

Despite an organization's best efforts to recruit and educate its coaches, there is usually a shortage of qualified individuals to fill numerous coaching vacancies. The dilemma that faces league administrators in such situations is to: 1) reduce the number of teams or 2) persuade reluctant volunteers to accept the responsibilities of being a coach. In most programs, the latter course of action is attempted first, generally with considerable success. However, solving one problem by filling vacancies with inexperienced, unqualified coaches often creates other problems that will require attention. *Youth Soccer* provides solutions to the problems associated with educating youth soccer coaches.

Educating its coaches is one of the soundest investments a youth soccer program can make.

From an organization's perspective, the education and guidance of its inexperienced coaches is essential. Similarly, adults who volunteer to coach should strive to become more knowledgeable about the many aspects of coaching.

Youth Soccer consists of seven sections, each of which are available as separate handbooks, specifically written to meet the educational needs of beginning and intermediate-level coaches. Even veteran coaches who have acquired much of their knowledge about soccer from previous experiences are likely to find this volume helpful. The use of this volume will benefit coaches and athletes alike because its orientation suggests that the success of the season is determined largely by the extent of the participants' growth, rather than exclusively by the record of games won or lost.

The content of this volume is based on the belief that youth soccer programs should exist for the benefit of the players. All sections in this volume include material that is essential for coaching youth soccer, with each addressing a separate theme. Individual sections can "stand alone" as handbooks, even though some of them refer to other sections. Similarly, individual chapters within a section may be read separately. Therefore, coaches may choose to read sections or chapters that cover materials in which they are most deficient.

Many of the chapters contain practical information in the form of supplements. These supplements include practice drills and games, forms for record keeping, handouts, worksheets, forms for medical records, guidelines, lists of coaching objectives, and forms for planning instruction. Much of this material can be reproduced.

INDIVIDUAL SECTIONS

Sections I and II

Section I (Organizing for the Season) and Section II (Methods for Effective Coaching) contain the sport science coaching methodology materials. These sections were written by experts, based upon translations of up-to-date research findings. Coaches must have an understanding of the contents of these sections before they begin their seasons.

Section III

The rules of play and glossary of terms are contained in Section III. The rules include suggested modifications for youth play that may be implemented to make the game more compatible with the developmental characteristics of youth soccer players. In addition, the chapter on rules of play contains flowchart tables to assist coaches, and possibly referees, in developing a better understanding of the many contingencies associated with the 17 Laws of the Game. This material, together with the glossary of terms, should help coaches, referees, players, and parents develop an insightful understanding of the terminology and structure of the game.

These handbooks were written for beginning and intermediate-level coaches. However, advanced coaches may also find the material to be enlightening.

Sections IV and V

Section IV contains separate chapters on each of the individual techniques for field players: kicking, receiving and controlling, dribbling and maintaining control, heading, throw-in, and defensive techniques. The individual techniques for goalkeepers are included in Section V. In both Sections IV and V, the soccer techniques are described and analyzed by authors with many years of experience as players and coaches and professional education in the biomechanical analysis of sport techniques.

Both sections include sequential illustrations of skillful youth soccer players performing the individual techniques of field players and goalkeepers.

Other features of the chapters on techniques include:

- listings of key elements and common errors of performance,
- progressions for coaching,
- sample drills and games,
- performance variations, and
- suggestions for the specific age and ability levels at which these techniques should be emphasized.

Section VI

Section VI (Basic Strategies of Soccer) contains a systematic approach to the presentation of the tactics of play. The four fundamental principles of offense (penetration, support, mobility, and width); the four fundamental principles of defense (delay, depth, balance, and concentration); and the relationships between offensive and defensive principles are presented in an organized fashion. Additionally, individual and team tactics employed in achieving the fundamental principles of offense and defense are described and illustrated.

Section VI also includes instruction on how to teach the fundamental principles and tactics of play to youth players. The concepts of systems of play are presented in a step-by-step approach that includes information on systems of play, team formation, and advantages and disadvantages for several team formations. Offensive and defensive concepts associated with six set play situations—kickoff, goal kick, penalty kick, corner kick, free kick, and throw-in—are described and accompanied by informative figures that could be photocopied and used as handouts.

Section VII

Section VII (Sports Medicine and Training) contains soccer-specific material on physical conditioning, nutrition, and sports medicine. The chapter on conditioning contains fundamental information on the energy production and muscular systems of the body, as well as the principles of training, as a basis for the development of interval, circuit, and weight training programs specific for soccer. Examples of training programs are accompanied by forms for record keeping. The chapter on nutrition covers the topics of proper diet, meal patterns, and weight loss and gain and their relationships to successful performance in soccer. Sports medicine is covered in the chapters on prevention, care, and rehabilitation of common soccer injuries. The chapters devoted to sports medicine include techniques for injury prevention, procedures for emergency and first aid, and guidelines for rehabilitation of injuries. An understanding of this material is essential for coaches at all levels.

PREFACE

In the United States, there is rapid growth in the number of young athletes seeking to participate in soccer. Unfortunately, the pool from which volunteer coaches must be recruited does not contain a sufficient number of persons with either soccer playing or coaching experiences. Therefore, there is a need to recruit and educate adults who are willing to assume the responsibilities of being soccer coaches. In an attempt to meet the educational needs of volunteer coaches in the state of Michigan, the Youth Sports Institute has conducted approximately 25 soccer clinics per year over the past 10 years. During this time, we have also reviewed existing soccer materials to judge their utility. From our experiences, we have concluded that:

1. It is becoming increasingly difficult to directly meet the growing number of requests for in-service training.

2. Existing educational materials are incomplete with reference to the beginning and intermediate-level coach.

This book was written to alleviate these problems by providing supplemental materials to coaches who have access to workshops and as pre-service education for persons who must coach without a formal educational session. It is our intent that, through a wide distribution of these materials, we can more broadly meet the educational needs of volunteer coaches in order to enhance the quality of experiences provided to young athletes.

This manuscript represents the second publication by the Youth Sports Institute, under the guidance of its director, Dr. Vern Seefeldt, that is written as a sport-specific book for educating volunteer coaches. Some of the generic materials from our first text, *Fundamentals of Ice Hockey*, have been revised and incorporated into this text. Therefore, gratitude is extended to Paul Vogel, editor of the hockey manual, as well as the other authors, who initiated what is planned as a series of sport-specific books from the Youth Sports Institute.

Sincere appreciation is also extended to the many people who contributed in one way or another to the writing of this book—the youth and collegiate soccer players, especially Brant, Cullen, and Kimberly Brown, who patiently permitted me to coach them and occasionally get in a scrimmage or two while I was developing ideas about the game of soccer; Byeong Hwa Ahn and Bob Jarema, who assisted with the high-speed cinematography of our skilled subjects (Cullen Brown, Tim Cansfield, David Jarema, and Mike Rosenbaum) from which sequential drawings of individual techniques were generated; the many coaches who, as colleagues or attendees at our clinics, exchanged ideas in helping me understand their sport-specific needs; Nancy Seefeldt, who helped with the formatting of this text; Judy Polechonski, who was primarily responsible for the typing of the manuscript; the many educational experts and coaches who reviewed our materials; and Gary Williamson, who contributed to the writing of this text as well as served as a willing listener and consultant as we discussed the many aspects of coaching youth soccer players. Finally, I would like to thank my wife, Jean, for her support and patience—who, on only a rare occasion, would say to me, "Soccer, is that all you can think about?"

Eugene W. Brown
Editor

CONTRIBUTORS

Joe Baum, M.A.
Head Men's Soccer Coach
Department of Intercollegiate Athletics
Michigan State University

Eugene W. Brown, Ph.D.
Youth Sports Institute
Michigan State University

Martha Ewing, Ph.D.
Youth Sports Institute
Michigan State University

Deborah Feltz, Ph.D.
Youth Sports Institute
Chair, Department of Physical Education and
  Exercise Science
Michigan State University

Jeanne Foley, Ph. D.
Department of Physiology
Michigan State University

Elaina Jurecki, R.D., M.S.
Clinical Pediatric Nutritionist
Medical Center
University of California, San Francisco

Rich Kimball, M.A.
Head Men's Lacrosse Coach
Department of Intercollegiate Athletics
Michigan State University

Annelies Knoppers, Ph.D.
Coordinator of Second Women's Ecumenical
  Synod/Conference
Netherlands

Wade Lillegard, M.D.
Department of Family Practice
Madigan Army Medical Center

Bernard Patrick Maloy, J.D., M.S.A.
Department of Sports Management
University of Michigan

Vern Seefeldt, Ph.D.
Director, Youth Sports Institute
Michigan State University

Paul Vogel, Ph.D.
Youth Sports Institute
Michigan State University

Gary Williamson, M.A.
Baton Rouge Soccer Association

KEYS TO SYMBOLS

O   Offensive player

⊙   Offensive player with ball

O ●   Offensive player taking a restart

X   Defensive player

X⊣   Defensive player marking an opponent

xxxx   Defensive wall of 4 players

△   Cone (Pylon)

⟶   Direction of player's movement

– – –→   Direction of kicked ball (pass or shot)

⌇⌇⌇→   Direction of player's movement while dribbling the ball

⊗   Coach

ORDER OF EVENTS

1   First Event

2   Second Event

3   Third Event

4   Fourth Event

5   Fifth Event

etc

Two offensive players; player 1 is dribbling the ball and player 2 is moving diagonally without the ball.

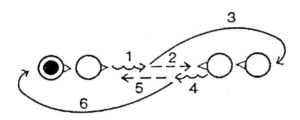

The player with the ball at the front of the one line dribbles toward the second line, passes the ball to the first player in the second line, and runs to the back of the second line. The player receiving the ball dribbles it back toward the first line, passes it to the new head of the line, and runs to the back of the first line. This activity is repeated several times.

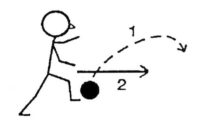

The player punts the ball into the air, then runs after it.

C   Center

L   Left

R   Right

I   Inside

W   Wing

F   Forward

HB Halfback

FB Fullback

G   Goalkeeper

ST Stopper

SW Sweeper

Section I
ORGANIZING FOR THE SEASON

ROLE OF THE COACH

Paul Vogel

QUESTIONS TO CONSIDER
- What are the primary roles of a youth soccer coach?
- What benefits does soccer offer participants?
- What potential detriments can occur in the presence of inadequate adult leadership?
- What principal goals should a coach seek to achieve?

INTRODUCTION

For young people participating in a soccer program, the quality and subsequent benefits of their experience is determined largely by their coach. Strong leadership during practices, games, and special events encourages each young person to nurture and develop individual strengths physically, psychologically, and socially. Poor or weak leadership not only inhibits such growth, it actually undermines a youth's existing strengths in these areas.

While it's impossible to provide a totally beneficial experience, as a soccer coach it is your responsibility to ensure that the benefits gained by each youth far outweigh the detriments. To accomplish this, you must know what these benefits and detriments are, and you must set reasonable coaching goals.

Possible Benefits for Participants

The numerous benefits for youth include:

- developing appropriate skills,

- developing physical fitness,

- learning appropriate conditioning techniques that affect health and performance,

- developing a realistic and positive self-image,

- developing a lifetime pattern of regular physical activity,

- developing a respect for rules as facilitators of safe and fair play,
- obtaining enjoyment and recreation, and
- developing positive personal, social, and psychological skills (e.g., self-worth, self-discipline, teamwork, goal-setting, self-control).

Many players achieve significant benefits in at least some of these areas depending on the frequency, duration, and intensity of participation and the quality of coaching leadership.

Many significant benefits can be
gained in youth soccer.

Possible Detriments for Participants

Players are likely to benefit from a soccer program when the coach sets appropriate objectives in the areas of skill, knowledge, fitness, and personal/social development. If, however, the coach sets inappropriate goals or teaches poorly, detriments may result.

To fully understand the value of a good coach, contrast the benefits listed previously with these possible detriments for the participant:

- developing inappropriate physical skills,
- sustaining injury, illness, or loss of physical fitness,
- learning incorrect rules and strategies of play,
- learning incorrect conditioning techniques,
- developing a negative or unrealistic self-image,
- avoiding future participation in activity for self and others,
- learning to misuse rules to gain unfair or unsafe advantages,
- developing a fear of failure,
- developing anti-social behaviors, and
- wasting time that could have been made available for other activities.

When incorrect techniques and negative behaviors are learned by young athletes, the next coach must perform the difficult and time-consuming task of extinguishing these behaviors.

To maximize the benefits and minimize the detriments, you must understand your role as a soccer coach and provide quality leadership.

The benefits of participation relate directly to the
quality of leadership.

As a coach, it is important to:

1) effectively teach the individual techniques, rules, and strategies of the game in an orderly and enjoyable environment;

2) appropriately challenge the cardiovascular and muscular systems of your players through active practice sessions and games; and

3) teach and model desirable personal, social, and psychological skills.

Winning is also an important goal for the coach and participants but it is one you have little control over because winning is often contingent on outside factors (e.g., the skills of the opposition, calls made by officials). If you concentrate on the three areas mentioned above and become an effective leader, winning becomes a natural by-product.

The degree of success you attain in achieving these goals is determined by the extent to which you make appropriate choices and take correct actions in organizing and administering, teaching and leading, and protecting and caring.

Organization and Administration

Effective coaching relies heavily on good organization and administration. Organization involves clearly identifying the goals and objectives that must be attained if you are going to create a beneficial experience (with few detriments) for the participating youths. Steps necessary to organize the season so it can be efficiently administered include:

- identifying your primary purposes as a coach,

- identifying goals for the season,

- selecting and implementing the activities in practices and games that lead to achievement of the objectives, and

- evaluating the effects of your actions.

Specific information, procedures, criteria, and examples necessary to effectively complete these steps are included in Chapter 2, Chapter 5, and Chapter 10.

Teaching and Leading

Teaching and leading are the core of coaching activity. Principles of effective instruction such as setting appropriate player expectations, using clear instructions, maintaining an orderly environment, maximizing the amount of practice time that is "on task," monitoring progress, and providing specific feedback are included in Chapter 5. This chapter gives you many insights into how you may effectively teach your players. Other important information for teaching and leading young athletes includes motivating your players, communicating effectively, maintaining discipline, and developing good personal and social skills. Coaching guidelines for each of these areas are included in Section II.

The only real control you have over winning and/or losing is the manner in which you plan and conduct your practices and supervise your games.

Because of the influence you have as "coach," your players will model the behaviors you exhibit. If you respond to competition (successes and failures), fair play, officials' calls, and/or spectators' comments with a positive and constructive attitude, your players are likely to imitate that positive behavior. If, however, you lose your temper, yell at officials, or bend and/or break rules to gain an unfair advantage, your players' actions are likely to become negative. When what you say differs from what you do, your players will be most strongly affected by what you do. Negative behavior by players can occur even if you tell them to "be good sports and to show respect to others" and then ignore this advice by acting in a contrary manner. In essence, "actions speak louder than words" and you must "practice what you preach" if you hope to positively influence your players' behavior.

Protecting and Caring

Although coaches often eliminate the potential for injury from their minds, it is important for them to (a) plan for injury prevention, (b) effectively deal with injuries when they occur, and (c) meet their legal responsibilities to act prudently. The information on legal liabilities in Section I, and conditioning youth soccer players, nutrition for successful performance, and prevention, care, and rehabilitation of common soccer injuries in Section VII, provides the basis for prudent and effective action in these areas.

SUMMARY

Your primary purpose as a youth soccer coach is to maximize the benefits of participation in soccer while minimizing the detriments. To achieve this, you must organize, teach, model, and evaluate effectively. Your players learn not only from what you teach but from what you consciously or unconsciously do. You're a very significant person in the eyes of your players. They notice when you're organized and fair, are a good instructor, know the rules, are interested in them or in the win/loss record, know how to control your emotions, know how to present yourself, and treat others with respect. The choices you make and the actions you take determine how positive the experience is for them.

PLANNING FOR THE SEASON

Paul Vogel

QUESTIONS TO CONSIDER
- Why should planning for the entire season precede day-to-day planning?
- What steps should a coach follow when organizing for the season?
- What skills, knowledges, aspects of fitness, and personal/social skills should be included as objectives for the season?
- How should the season be organized to be most effective from a coaching-learning point of view?

INTRODUCTION

Planning for the season involves two basic tasks. First, coaches must select the content that will be the focus of instruction during the season (objectives that involve physical skills, sport-related knowledges, fitness capacities, and personal/social skills). Second, these desired outcomes should be organized into a plan from which practices, games, and other events can be efficiently managed.

What follows provides reasons why season planning is useful and gives you steps necessary to develop a season's plan as well as examples of season objectives. Materials and examples are also provided at the end of this chapter for completing your season plan.

WHY PLAN?

Coaches agree that teaching the skills, rules, and strategies of soccer are among their primary responsibilities. Most coaches would also agree that improving the physical condition of the players, promoting enjoyment of the game, teaching good sportsmanship, and attempting to avoid physical and psychological injury are also outcomes they wish to achieve. Many coaches, however, fail to recognize the importance of planning to accomplish these goals.

> *Achievement of goals and objectives*
> *requires effective planning.*

Organized practices are vital to maximizing the benefits of soccer. Disorganized practices often result in players failing to obtain desired skills, knowledge, fitness, and attitudes and often contribute to injuries and inappropriate skills. Organizing your season and planning your practices prior to going on the field can result in the following benefits:

- efficient use of limited practice time,

- inclusion of season objectives that are most essential,

- appropriate sequence of season objectives,

- directing practice activities to the season's goals and objectives,

- reduction of the time required for planning,

- enhanced preparation of the team for competition,

- improved ability to make day-to-day adjustments in practice objectives, and

- deterrent to lawsuits involving coaches' liability.

DEVELOPING A SEASON PLAN

Use these three steps to develop a season plan:

- identify the goals and objectives of the season;

- sequence the season objectives into the pre, early, mid, and late portions of the season; and

- identify practice objectives.

The relationship of these three steps to fulfilling your "role as the coach" and to evaluating the "outcomes" you desire your players to achieve is illustrated in Figure 2-1.

Identify Goals and Objectives for the Season

Your primary role is to maximize the benefits for your players while minimizing the potential detrimental effects of participation. This alone provides the basis for identifying the specific goals and objectives for your coaching effort. You will affect your players either positively or negatively in each of the following areas:

- physical skills (kicking, receiving and controlling, dribbling and maintaining control, heading, throw-in, defensive techniques, and goalkeeping),

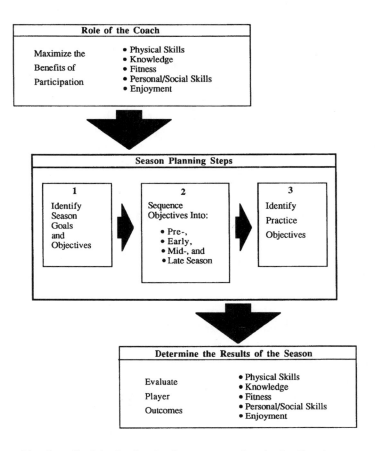

Figure 2-1. *A coach's role as it relates to planning the season and evaluating the players.*

- knowledge (rules, tactics, training techniques, terminology, nutrition, and safety),

- fitness (muscular strength, endurance, flexibility, aerobic fitness), and

- personal/social skills (feelings about soccer, motivation, discipline, sportsmanship, and other character traits).

By thinking of these four broad areas of player outcomes as goals (i.e., to develop physical skills, knowledge, fitness, and appropriate personal/social skills), you are taking the initial step toward fulfilling your major role of "maximizing the benefits" of participation in soccer and "minimizing the potential detrimental effects of participation" by clearly specifying the objectives for the season.

Although the identification of goals is an important first step, it is the selection of specific objectives within each goal area that provides the direction necessary to organize the season and plan effective practices.

● Selection of Skill Objectives

Supplement 2-1 (Individual Techniques for Field Players) and Supplement 2-2 (Individual Techniques for Goalkeepers) provide you with lists of objectives for each physical skill area. By reviewing the individual techniques listed, you can select objectives that are best for your players. To help with this task, appropriate objectives for players at three levels of play (beginning, ages 6-9; intermediate, ages 10-13; and advanced, ages 14 and over) are suggested. Note that a detailed description of each of these individual techniques, including key elements and common errors in their performance, as well as progressions for teaching, can be found in Sections IV and V. The key elements of performance are the bases for assessing player performance and for focusing your coaching efforts. This information should be reviewed if you do not have a good understanding of these individual techniques.

● Selection of Knowledge Objectives

Cognitive outcomes (e.g., knowledge of rules, strategies, and information related to physical conditioning) are important for your players. When you select information that you want your players to know, it is important to identify that knowledge as an objective. Rules pertaining to "offside" and "fouls," how to warm up and cool down, what to eat for a pre-game meal, and exercises to avoid are all important objectives because they can influence a player's performance. Several cognitive and tactics objectives have been identified for you in Supplements 2-3 and 2-4. You may wish to add to, delete from, or alter the objectives on these lists as you determine those that are most appropriate for your team. By identifying these objectives, it is more likely that they will be taught at specific times during the season and at an appropriate level of understanding.

● Selection of Fitness Objectives

Generally, your primary concern for athletes in the 6-13 age range should be to develop physical skills, knowledge, and appropriate personal/social skills. This is not to suggest that conditioning is unimportant. It is, however, the studied opinion of many coaches and specialists in growth and development that the specific training designed to promote high levels of sport-related fitness should receive a lower priority at this age. For highly skilled soccer players 14 years of age and older, a gradually increasing emphasis should be placed on conditioning the muscular and energy production systems. Part of the reason for this recommendation is that when young athletes train for skilled performance, they also obtain conditioning stimuli that are sufficient to cause the body to adapt to the fitness demands associated with learning and performing soccer skills. As players become highly skilled, conditioning becomes a more important factor for enabling more frequent, more intense, and more enduring application of their abilities. Supplement 2-5 includes an overview of fitness objectives you may wish to include in your season plan for older players who are also highly skilled.

For younger players, fitness should be a by-product of learning the physical skills.

• Selection of Personal and Social Skill Objectives

A primary objective in the season plan should be to have all players feel increasingly better about their abilities as the season progresses. This should occur not only in the areas of physical skill, knowledge, and fitness, but should also include character qualities such as persistence, self-control, tolerance, respect for authority, encouragement of teammates, concentration on the task, commitment to best efforts, and cooperation. Athletes need guidance (modeling, direction, encouragement, gentle rebuking, etc.) to develop such attributes. When achieved, these personal and social qualities contribute to performance in athletic and non-athletic situations. Moreover, unlike opponents, officials, and/or the "breaks of the game," these qualities are within the control of individual players. The opportunity for individual control has been strongly linked to motivation, and motivation is strongly linked to performance.

Coaches are responsible for developing socially desirable skills in their players.

As a coach, perhaps your most important and lasting contribution is helping your players improve their feelings of self-worth and socially desirable qualities of character. By focusing on controllable qualities such as "effort" versus uncontrollable "outcomes," which are often dependent on others (e.g., an official's call, a "lucky" bounce, the ability of another team), you have a unique opportunity to make a significant and lasting contribution to the personal character of your athletes.

Contributing to team membership is another worthy objective that coaches should set for every player. Athletes, especially those who engage in team sports such as soccer, must learn to overcome the natural tendency to blame others for a loss or even a bad performance. Players must be taught that their role is to play as well as they can and to think, do, and say those things that can help their teammates do the same. The team will only be as good as its weakest link. Often, an otherwise excellent team performs at a mediocre level due to the dissension created by "putting others down," making excuses, or transferring blame to others.

Coaches should reward effort when they review the accomplishments of the team.

Included in Supplement 2-6 is a listing of several personal and social skill objectives that you may want to incorporate into your season plan. This listing may be modified and made specific to your players.

Sequence Objectives Into Pre, Early, Mid, and Late Portions of the Season

Once you have identified season objectives for your team, they can be listed on the worksheet provided in Supplement 2-7. While the list may need to be revised as the season unfolds, the objectives should become the basis of your planning for the season.

Categorize the listed objectives into goals you want to achieve in the pre-, early-, mid-, and late-season (see Figure 2-2). Some objectives may be emphasized throughout the season, whereas others may be emphasized in only one division of the season. Photocopy Supplement 2-7 and use it to complete this step of your season plan.

Deciding what objectives should be achieved in the pre-, early-, mid-, and late-season is the basis for all subsequent planning.

● **Preseason Objectives**

If preseason activity is possible, it can save you valuable practice time. Many of the objectives pertaining to knowledge of the rules and strategies and some of those involving conditioning can be all, or partially, achieved before formal practice even begins.

Objectives appropriate for the preseason involve skills, knowledge, fitness capacities, or personal/social skills that can be achieved independently (all or in part) by the player in a safe and efficient manner before the initiation of formal practices. This could include learning the basic rules, infractions and penalties, and strategies; obtaining appropriate equipment; and developing strength and aerobic fitness.

● **Early-season Objectives**

The early-season should be devoted to determining how well your players have mastered the fundamental and/or prerequisite objectives you have selected and to teaching, reteaching, or practicing those objectives. Objectives appropriate for the early-season should contain abilities that are prerequisite to attaining other identified objectives. For example, players must be able to dribble before they can be expected to dribble and shoot. This attention to the sequence of skills is particularly important for the inexperienced player, who should spend more time on learning skills typically placed in the early-season division. In addition to objectives associated with physical skills, early-season objectives should include logistical and organizational concerns, safety, strategy, discipline, fitness, socialization, rules of play, and team rules. These are all essential in preparing players for early-season games and to provide a foundation for the rest of the season.

SEASON PLAN WORKSHEET

Coach: **Season:**

Goal Areas	Objectives	Season Division Pre	Early	Mid	Late
Physical Skills	Inside of foot kicks				
	low drive		X	X	
	lofted ball			X	X
	Instep kicks				
	low drive		X	X	
	lofted ball			X	X
	Outside of foot kicks				
	low drive			X	X
	Etc.				
Knowledge	Laws of the game				
	field of play	X	X		
	start of play	X	X		
	ball in/out of play	X	X		
	throw-in	X	X		
	Tactics				
	team formation		X	X	X
	Etc.				
Fitness	Flexiblity				
	neck	X	X	X	X
	shoulder	X	X	X	X
	hip/spine	X	X	X	X
	Etc.				
Personal/Social	Personal				
	best effort		X	X	X
	listening		X	X	X
	Social				
	cooperation		X	X	X
	fair play		X	X	X
	Etc.				

Figure 2-2. An abbreviated example of a season plan for young soccer players.

- ## Mid-season Objectives

Mid-season objectives should continue to focus on teaching individual techniques. However, a large share of practice time should be devoted to refining these techniques within the context of game-like drills and controlled scrimmages. Time should be spent combining individual techniques (e.g., receiving the ball, then shooting it) and integrating these techniques with game strategy. Many of the cognitive, fitness, and personal and social objectives established for the early-season should continue to be emphasized during the mid-season.

- ## Late-season Objectives

Late-season objectives should be focused on the maintenance and refinement of early- and mid-season skills, and refinement of the team's offensive and defensive play. A greater portion of practice time should be spent on small-sided games, game-like drills, and controlled scrimmages. Practices should be organized so fitness levels are maintained and emphasis continues on cognitive and personal and social skills.

Generally, you should focus on single skills in the early-season, skill combinations in the mid-season, and combinations of both within systems of play in the later portion of the season. There are no hard and fast divisions among these three phases of the season (in fact, they should blend or overlap through good transitions). However, you should have them clearly in mind as you view the entire season in terms of what you wish to accomplish and the time in which it must be done.

Identify Practice Objectives

As you place objectives into season divisions and adjust the number of weeks assigned to each division, you will likely find that you have chosen to cover more than your available practice time allows. A good guide in such situations is to devote enough time to the cumulative instruction and practice of each objective so the majority of players are able to make significant improvements on most of the objectives included in the season plan. Merely exposing your team to the individual techniques of the game, without spending sufficient time for them to be learned, results in frustration for you and the players. Your players must receive sufficient instruction, practice, and feedback to master the objectives at an appropriate level of performance for use in a game situation. Accordingly, select, teach, and practice only the objectives that are essential to the game at your team's level of play. You can always add objectives to your plan as it is implemented, but you cannot recover time wasted on objectives that are not achieved or that are inappropriate for your players' level of development.

*Select, teach, and practice the key objectives
that are essential to your team.*

Generally, the allotment of time to physical skill objectives should be based upon the following instructional sequence and distributed across several practices. You should allow time:

1. to introduce the objective—tell the players what you want them to learn and why it is important,

2. for the players to try the individual techniques and for you to determine their levels of performance,

3. for you to teach the key elements of the individual techniques and for players to practice these elements, and

4. for skill refinement and automation such that an individual technique can be used in game situations.

The time allotment to fitness, cognitive, and personal and social objectives may not be as structured as the allotment for physical skill objectives. Fitness goals may be achieved along with practice of individual techniques in drills and scrimmages. Similarly, some cognitive and personal and social objectives may be concomitantly attained during the practice of physical skills. However, some of these objectives may need practice time specifically devoted to them.

Integrating your chosen objectives into a season calendar (see Figure 2-3) will give you a master plan of everything you need to manage your coaching activities. The season calendar converts your plans to practice outlines. The daily entries on the calendar provide a guide from which specific practice plans can be developed. Supplement 2-8 provides a blank reproducible worksheet that you can use to develop a master plan of practices. The following list includes examples of entries that can be included on a calendar.

Example of Entries for a Season Calendar

- Registration dates and deadlines

- Date team roster is distributed

- Sign-up date for practice times and fields

- Dates and times for coaches' education meetings

- Equipment distribution dates and times

- Date and time for parents' orientation meeting

- Dates and times for league meetings

- Sequential numbers designating practices (e.g., #1 designates first practice)

- Practice objectives and time allocations

- Game days and times

- Tournament dates

- Dates and times for special events

The most important part of developing a season calendar is the decision you make about what objectives to include and how much practice

SEASON PLANNING CALENDAR

Coach _____ Team _____ Weeks _____

S	M	T	W	T	F	S
	Coaches' education meeting 7:00–10:00 (High School)		Team rosters distributed, sign-up for practice times/fields 7:00–8:00 (Rec Office)			
	Parents' orientation meeting 7:00-8:30 (Elementary School Rm. 101)					

Figure 2-3. Example of a season planning calendar.

SEASON PLANNING CALENDAR

Coach _____ Team _____ Weeks _____

S	M	T	W	T	F	S
		Practice #1 :01 Overview of practice :09 Team rules and organization :05 Warm-up Review and evaluate: :23 dribbling :23 kicking :23 receiving and controlling :05 Cool down/team talk :01 Handouts: team rules, practice and game schedule, and rules of play		**Practice #2** :01 Overview of practice :10 Review rules of play :05 Warm-up Review and evaluate: :10 throw-in :10 heading :15 defensive techniques Practice: :11 dribbling :11 kicking :11 receiving and controlling :05 Cool down/team talk :01 Handouts: team formation, positional play, and set plays		**Practice #3** :01 Overview of practice :05 Review rules of play :05 Warm-up :20 Review and evaluate goalkeeping skills :25 Practice individual techniques: dribbling, kicking, receiving and controlling, throw-in, heading, and defensive techniques :14 Small group games and tactics (1v2 & 2v2) :05 Cool Down :15 Chalk talk: team formation, positional play, and set plays (kick-off, goal kick, and corner kick)
		Practice #4 :01 Overview of practice :05 Warm-up :29 Practice set plays: kick-off, goal kick, and corner kick :20 Practice individual techniques: field play and goal keeping :15 Small group games and tactics (2v2 and 2v3) :05 Cool down :15 Chalk talk team formation, positional play, and set plays (throw-in, free kick, penalty kick, and drop ball)		**Practice #5** :01 Overview of practice :05 Warm-up :35 Practice set plays: throw-in, free kick, penalty kick, and drop ball :15 Practice individual field player techniques (passive pressure) :14 Practice individual goalkeeper techniques :15 Small group games and tactics (2v3 and 3v3) :05 Cool down/team talk		**Practice #6** :05 Warm-up :20 Practice individual field player techniques and combinations of techniques (moderate pressure) :20 Practice defensive and goalkeeper techniques (moderate pressure :15 Small group games and tactics (3v3 and 3v4) :25 1/2 field scrimmage (review team formation, positional play, and set plays) :05 Cool down/team talk

Figure 2-3, continued.

SEASON PLANNING CALENDAR

Coach _____ Team _____ Weeks _____

S	M	T	W	T	F	S
		Practice #7 :01 Overview of practice :05 Warm-up :20 Practice individual field player techniques and combinations of techniques (full pressure) :20 Practice defensive and goalkeeper techniques (full pressure) :15 Small group games and tactics (3v4 and 4v4) :24 1/2 field scrimmage (review offensive and defensive tactics and set plays) :05 Cool down/team talk		**Practice #8** :01 Overview of practice :05 Warm-up :30 Review set plays for offense and defense (kick-off, goal kick, corner kick, throw-in, free kick, penalty kick, and drop ball) :15 Review team strategy and positional responsibilities :34 Controlled scrimmage with another team :05 Cool down/team talk		Game #1 vs. Tigers 1:30 p.m. (Middle School Field #3)

Figure 2-3, continued.

16

time you devote to each objective on a practice-by-practice basis. Using your season plan worksheet, select an appropriate number of objectives listed in the early-season that you wish to include in your first practice and enter them in the space labeled "practice #1" on your season calendar. This process should be repeated for your second, third, and subsequent practices through the early-, mid-, and late-season divisions.

> *The two most important decisions in planning the season are deciding what objectives to teach and how much time you should spend teaching them.*

You will spend less total time planning for your season and practice if you use the approach suggested here than if the task is done practice-by-practice throughout the season. This process will also help you verify which skills you believe are most important as you run out of available practice time and are forced to either omit objectives from your plan or find other ways to achieve them outside of the normal practice time. In addition to the good feeling and confidence that comes with completing a season calendar, you will have developed the base necessary to systematically change your plans as unexpected events develop. More importantly, you will know before the mid to late portions of the season whether in your initial plan you assigned too much or too little time to some of your early-season objectives. A completed plan that has been implemented and refined is also an invaluable resource for next year's coaching assignment or as a guide for new coaches coming into the program.

SUMMARY

Your role as a coach can be best filled through the leadership and instruction you provide in practice and game situations. Clearly, those coaches who are most effective in helping their players acquire the necessary physical skills, knowledge, fitness, and personal and social skills are those who have clear objectives and who organize to achieve them. Organization of the season by selecting and then teaching objectives in a proper order, and for an appropriate amount of time, is a major step toward helping players acquire the benefits of soccer.

OBJECTIVES FOR FIELD PLAYERS
Individual Techniques

Level of Player* Approximate Age*	Suggested Emphasis		
	Beginning 6-9 yrs.	Intermediate 10-13 yrs.	Advanced 14 yrs. and up
Kicking			
Inside of the foot kicks			
ground ball			
low drive	X	X	X
half volley			
low drive		X	X
lofted ball		X	X
swerved ball		X	X
air ball			
low drive	X	X	X
lofted ball	X	X	X
swerved ball		X	X
Instep kicks			
ground ball			
low drive	X	X	X
lofted ball	X	X	X
"chip"		X	X
swerved ball		X	X
half volley			
low drive		X	X
lofted ball		X	X
swerved ball			X
air ball			
low drive	X	X	X
lofted ball	X	X	X
swerved ball			X
side volley			X
front scissors			X
overhead scissors			X
over the shoulder scissors			X
Outside of the foot kicks			
ground ball			
low drive	X	X	X
half volley			
low drive			X
lofted ball			X

Level of Player* Approximate Age*	Suggested Emphasis		
	Beginning 6-9 yrs.	Intermediate 10-13 yrs.	Advanced 14 yrs. and up
Outside of the foot kicks (cont.)			
swerved ball			X
air ball			
low drive			X
lofted ball			X
swerved ball			X
Heel pass (back-heel)		X	X
Toe kick		X	X
Receiving and Controlling			
Sole of the foot			
rolling ball		X	X
half volley		X	X
Inside of the foot			
rolling ball		X	X
redirecting forward		X	X
"touch and turn"		X	X
"out the back door"		X	X
half volley			
redirecting forward		X	X
"touch and turn"			X
"out the back door"			X
air ball			
redirecting forward		X	X
"touch and turn"			X
"out the back door"			X
Outside of the foot			
rolling ball		X	X
half volley		X	X
air ball		X	X
Instep		X	X
Inside of the thigh		X	X
"touch and turn"			X
Top of the thigh		X	X
Chest		X	X
"touch and turn"			X
"over the top"			X

Level of Player* Approximate Age*	Suggested Emphasis		
	Beginning 6-9 yrs.	**Intermediate 10-13 yrs.**	**Advanced 14 yrs. and up**
Head			
redirecting forward		X	X
"touch and turn"			X
"over the top"			X
Dribbling and Maintaining Control			
Dribbling			
inside of the foot	X	X	X
outside of the foot	X	X	X
instep	X	X	X
Controlling			
slowing the pace			
hooking the ball with the inside of the instep	X	X	X
hooking the ball with the outside of the instep	X	X	X
applying pressure to the top of the ball with the sole of the foot	X	X	X
increasing the pace			
inside of the foot	X	X	X
outside of the foot	X	X	X
instep	X	X	X
changing direction (turning the ball)			
inside of the foot	X	X	X
outside of the foot	X	X	X
sole of the foot	X	X	X
shielding			
inside of the foot	X	X	X
outside of the foot	X	X	X
Feinting			
body feints		X	X
ball feints			X
body and ball feints			X
Heading			
Heading while on the ground			
forward heading	X	X	X
sideward heading		X	X

Level of Player* Approximate Age*	Suggested Emphasis		
	Beginning 6-9 yrs.	Intermediate 10-13 yrs.	Advanced 14 yrs. and up
Heading (cont.)			
backward heading		X	X
Heading while in the air			
jump heading forward		X	X
jump heading sideward			X
jump heading backward			X
dive heading			X
Throw-in			
Stationary throw-in			
side straddle	X		
forward-backward straddle	X	X	
Approach run and throw-in	X	X	X
Defensive Techniques			
Marking			
player in possession of the ball	X	X	X
player not in possession of the ball	X	X	X
Tackling			
front block tackle	X	X	X
pivot tackle		X	X
side tackle	X	X	X
slide tackle			
bent leg			X
hook			X

*Note that "Beginning," "Intermediate," and "Advanced" does not always correspond with the age range given. Coaches should use this classification system as an approximation, adjusting the emphases to meet their players' ability and maturation levels.

OBJECTIVES FOR GOALKEEPERS
Individual Techniques

Level of Player* Approximate Age*	Suggested Emphasis		
	Beginning 6-9 yrs.	Intermediate 10-13 yrs.	Advanced 14 yrs. and up
Fundamentals of Goalkeeping			
Ready position	X	X	X
Positioning	X	X	X
Narrowing the angle on a breakaway	X	X	X
Supporting the defense	X	X	X
Shot stopping			
catching	X	X	X
punching and deflecting	X	X	X
Diving (see Diving Saves)			
Individual Techniques			
Distribution			
bowled ball	X	X	X
sling throw	X	X	X
baseball throw		X	X
punt	X	X	X
drop kick		X	X
goal kick	X	X	X
Saves (catches, punches and deflections)			
Scoop saves			
standing	X	X	X
low air ball	X	X	X
waist-high air ball	X	X	X
chest-high air ball	X	X	X
kneeling	X	X	X
half-kneeling	X	X	X
Overhand saves			
chest-high	X	X	X
head-high	X	X	X
above head	X	X	X
jump save		X	X
Diving saves			
rolling ball	X	X	X
low air ball		X	X
medium-high air ball		X	X
high air ball			X

Level of Player* Approximate Age*	Suggested Emphasis		
	Beginning 6-9 yrs.	**Intermediate 10-13 yrs.**	**Advanced 14 yrs. and up**
Diving Saves (cont.)			
forward diving			X
back diving punch or deflection			X
drop dive		X	X

*Note that "Beginning," "Intermediate," and Advanced" does not always correspond with the age range given. Coaches should use this classification system as an approximation, adjusting the emphases to meet their players' ability and maturation levels.

KNOWLEDGE OBJECTIVES

Level of Player Approximate Age	Suggested Emphasis*		
	Beginning 6-9 yrs.	Intermediate 10-13 yrs.	Advanced 14 yrs. and up
Laws of the Game			
the field of play	X		
the start of play	X		
ball in and out of play	X		
method of scoring	X		
offside	X	X	
fouls and misconduct	X	X	X
free kick	X	X	
penalty kick	X	X	
throw-in	X		
goal kick	X		
corner kick	X		
Prevention of Injuries			
equipment and apparel	X	X	X
field conditions	X	X	X
structural hazards	X	X	X
environmental hazards	X	X	X
use of appropriate techniques	X	X	X
contraindicated exercises	X	X	X
overuse injuries	X	X	X
Conditioning			
energy production system			X
muscular system			X
principles of training			X
methods for conditioning			X
warm-up/cool-down procedures	X	X	X
Nutrition			
proper diet	X	X	X
vitamins and minerals			X
water intake	X	X	X
ergogenic aids			X
steroids			X
meal patterns	X	X	X
weight control	X	X	X
Soccer Terminology	X	X	X
Other Knowledge Objectives			

*Note that these knowledge objectives must be taught. It should not be assumed that young athletes will have learned these just by playing soccer.

TACTICS OBJECTIVES

Level of Player Approximate Age	Suggested Emphasis*		
	Beginning 6-9 yrs.	Intermediate 10-13 yrs.	Advanced 14 yrs. and up
Team formations	X	X	X
Zone defense	X	X	X
Man-to-man defense		X	X
Combination defense		X	X
Set plays (restarts) on offense and defense			
kickoff	X	X	X
goal kick	X	X	X
penalty kick	X	X	X
corner kick	X	X	X
free kick	X	X	X
throw-in	X	X	X
drop ball	X	X	X
Fundamental Principles and Individual Techniques—Offense			
penetration	X	X	X
support			
depth	X	X	X
wall pass	X	X	X
checking run	X	X	X
overlapping run		X	X
cross-over run		X	X
mobility			
blind side run	X	X	X
diagonal run		X	X
width			
positioning off the ball	X	X	X
dummy run		X	X
Fundamental Principles and Individual Techniques—Defense			
delay			
goal-side marking of the ball	X	X	X
recovering run	X	X	X
pressuring the ball	X	X	X
jockeying	X	X	X
shepherding		X	X
depth			
covering	X	X	X
supporting	X	X	X
switching		X	X

Level of Player Approximate Age	Suggested Emphasis*		
	Beginning 6-9 yrs.	**Intermediate 10-13 yrs.**	**Advanced 14 yrs. and up**
balance			
diagonal coverage	X	X	X
shifting toward the ball	X	X	X
concentration			
compactness	X	X	X
overloading	X	X	X
funneling	X	X	X
Special Defensive Tactics			
offside trap		X	X
defensive wall		X	X

*Note that these tactics and strategy objectives must be taught. It should not be assumed that young athletes will learn these just by playing soccer.

FITNESS OBJECTIVES

Level of Player Approximate Age	Suggested Emphasis*		
	Beginning 6-9 yrs.	Intermediate 10-13 yrs.	Advanced 14 yrs. and up
Energy Production			
aerobic capacity			X
anaerobic capacity			X
aerobic/anaerobic capacity			X
Muscular Fitness (strength, endurance, and power)			
neck			X
shoulder			X
upper arm			X
lower arm			X
wrist			X
abdominal			X
hip/spine			X
low back			X
groin			X
upper leg			X
lower leg			X
ankle			X
Muscular Flexibility			
neck			X
shoulder			X
trunk			X
hip			X
ankle			X
Other Fitness Objectives			

*Note that progress is made in many of these fitness objectives at the beginning and intermediate levels of play. This development should occur concomitantly through carefully planned practice sessions designed to enhance physical skills. The "X's" in this chart suggest that coaches should not plan "fitness only" drills for their team until the players have reached approximately 14 years of age and are at the advanced level of play.

PERSONAL AND SOCIAL OBJECTIVES

Level of Player Approximate Age	Suggested Emphasis		
	Beginning 6-9 yrs.	**Intermediate 10-13 yrs.**	**Advanced 14 yrs. and up**
Personal			
best effort	X	X	X
initiative	X	X	X
persistence	X	X	X
responsibility	X	X	X
self-discipline	X	X	X
following directions	X	X	X
listening	X	X	X
Social			
respect for authority	X	X	X
leadership	X	X	X
respect for others	X	X	X
fair play	X	X	X
cooperation	X	X	X
appropriate winning behavior	X	X	X
appropriate losing behavior	X	X	X
tact	X	X	X
encouragement of teammates	X	X	X
respect for rules	X	X	X
sport-related etiquette	X	X	X
respect for property	X	X	X
Other Personal and Social Objectives			

SEASON PLAN WORKSHEET

Coach: **Season:**

Goal Areas	Objectives	Season Division			
		Pre	**Early**	**Mid**	**Late**

SEASON PLANNING CALENDAR

Coach _____ Team _____ Weeks _____

S	M	T	W	T	F	S

3

WORKING EFFECTIVELY WITH PARENTS

Martha Ewing, Deborah Feltz, and Eugene W. Brown

> QUESTIONS TO CONSIDER
> - How can I obtain the information and help needed from parents to do a good job?
> - What is my responsibility to the parents of the players on my team?
> - How can I avoid the negative influence some parents have on a team or program?
> - What are the responsibilities of the players and their parents to this program?

INTRODUCTION

Support and assistance from parents can be very helpful. Some parents, however, through lack of awareness, can weaken the effects of your coaching, reducing the benefits soccer can provide to their children.

These negative influences can be minimized if you tell the parents:

- how you perceive your role as the coach,

- the purpose and objectives of the soccer program, and

- the responsibilities they and their children have in helping the team run smoothly.

> *Some parents, through lack of awareness, can weaken the effects of your coaching.*

The most effective way of communicating the purposes and needs of your program is through a parents' orientation meeting. A parents' orientation meeting can be used to:

- teach parents the rules and regulations of soccer so they understand the game,

- provide details about the season, and

- provide a setting for collecting and distributing important information.

At the parents' orientation meeting, you have the opportunity to ask for their assistance and discuss other items that are specific to the team. A meeting for parents is also an excellent way for them to get to know you and each other. A face-to-face meeting and a few short remarks go a long way toward uniting coaches and parents in a cooperative endeavor that benefits the players. Many potential problems can be eliminated by good communication that begins before the first practice.

CONTENT OF A PARENTS' ORIENTATION MEETING

Parents usually have a number of questions concerning their child's soccer program. With proper preparation and an outlined agenda, you should be able to answer most questions. A sample agenda is provided. This agenda can be supplemented with items you and/or the parents believe to be important.

Sample Agenda
Parents' Orientation Meeting

1. Introductions

2. Goals of the team and program

3. Understanding the sport of soccer

4. Dangers and risk of injury

5. Emergency procedures

6. Equipment needs

7. Athletes' responsibilities

8. Parents' responsibilities

9. Season schedule

10. Other

Each agenda item and its relationship to the soccer program is explained in the following paragraphs.

Introductions

Parents should be informed about who administers the soccer program. They should become acquainted with the coaches and the parents of the other players. As the coach, you should introduce yourself, briefly describing your background, coaching experience, and reasons for coaching.

The parents should also introduce themselves, identify where they live, and perhaps indicate how long their children have been involved in the program and the objectives that they have for their child's involvement in soccer. Learning who the other parents are makes it easier to establish working relationships for specific tasks and to initiate sharing of responsibilities (e.g., carpooling and bringing refreshments to games).

Finally, the purpose of the meeting should be explained to communicate important information about each agenda item. If handouts are available, they should be distributed at this time. We suggest that at least one handout, an agenda, be distributed to provide order to the meeting, a sense of organization on your part, and a place for parents to write notes.

Information about the players and their families should be collected (see Supplement 3-1—Team Roster Information). A team roster and telephone tree (see Supplement 3-2) could be compiled from the information collected, then typed and distributed to each of the families at another time.

Goals of the Team and Programs

The goals of the sponsoring organization, as well as your personal goals, should be presented. Parents then will be able to judge whether those goals are compatible with their beliefs regarding what is appropriate for their child. Goals that have been identified by young soccer players as most important are:

- to have fun,
- to improve skills and learn new skills,
- to be on a team and to make new friends, and
- to succeed or win.

Most educators, pediatricians, sport psychologists, and parents consider these to be healthy goals that coaches should help young athletes achieve. Parents should be informed of the primary goals of the team and of the amount of emphasis that will be placed on achieving these goals.

Parents should be informed
of the primary goals of the team.

Other areas that should be addressed are your policies on eliminating players, missing practices, and recognizing players through awards. You may be asked to answer many questions about how you will function as a coach. Some examples are:

- Will players be allowed to compete if they missed the last practice before a game?
- Will players be excluded from contests or taken off the team if they go on a two-week vacation?
- Will players receive trophies or other material rewards?
- How much emphasis will be placed on rewards?

- Are the rewards given only to good performers or are they given to all participants?

Chapter 6, Motivating Your Players, in Section II discusses the issue of appropriate use of awards. You may wish to comment on several points explained in this chapter as you address this issue.

Understanding the Sport of Soccer

Many times spectators boo officials, shout instructions to players, or contradict the coach because they do not know the rules or strategies of soccer. This is particularly true if the rules of play have been modified for younger age groups. Informing parents about basic rules, skills, and strategies may help those who are unfamiliar with soccer and will prevent some of this negative behavior.

The information may be presented in the form of a film, brief explanation, demonstration of techniques, and/or rule interpretations. In addition, parents could obtain copies of Section III—Youth Soccer Rules of Play—to learn more about the rules of the game. If you'd rather not use the meeting to cover this information, you could invite parents to attend selected practice sessions where a demonstration and/or explanation of positions, rules, and strategies will be presented to the team.

Dangers and Risk of Injury

Parents should be told what they can expect in terms of possible injuries their child may incur in soccer. As noted in Chapter 4, Legal Liability, failure to inform parents of potential injuries is the most frequent basis for lawsuits involving coaches and players.

Tell them, for example, that generally the injuries are confined to bruises, but that there is a possibility for broken bones, torn ligaments, and other serious injuries. Supplements 3-3 and 3-4 provide information on types and sites of injuries in youth soccer. This information should be reviewed with the parents. Let them know if a medical examination is required before their child's participation. If so, what forms or evidence of compliance is acceptable, to whom must it be provided, and when it is due.

Parents should be told what they can expect in terms of possible injuries in youth soccer.

Tell the parents what will be done to prevent injuries and assure them that the playing/practice area and equipment will be checked to help keep players safe and free from exposure to hazards.

Lastly, the program's policy of accident insurance should be described. Inform parents if the program maintains athletic accident coverage or whether parents are required to provide insurance coverage for injuries that happen during their child's athletic participation.

Emergency Procedures

Have the parents provide you with information and permission necessary for you to handle an emergency. The Athlete's Medical Information Form (Supplement 3-5) and Medical Release Form (Supplement 3-6) were designed for these purposes. You should have the parents complete these forms and keep them with you at all team functions. These forms will provide you with information to guide your actions in an emergency.

Equipment Needs

Explain what equipment the players need and where it can be purchased. You may also want to offer advice on the quality of particular brands and models and to indicate how much parents can expect to pay for specific items.

If an equipment swap is organized, tell them where and when it will be held. A handout describing proper equipment should be provided. Supplement 3-7 provides a list and guidelines for the selection of soccer equipment. This supplement could be reproduced and used as a handout to the parents for properly outfitting their child.

Athletes' Responsibilities

The "Bill of Rights for Young Athletes,"[2] reminds adults that the child's welfare must be placed above all other considerations. Children and their parents must realize, however, that along with rights, they must meet certain responsibilities. Young athletes must be responsible for:

- being on time at practices and games with all of their equipment,
- cooperating with coaches and teammates,
- putting forth the effort to condition their bodies and to learn the basic skills, and
- conducting themselves properly and living with the consequences of inappropriate behavior.

These responsibilities should be discussed so parents may help reinforce them at home.

Parents' Responsibilities

Parents of young athletes must assume some responsibilities associated with their child's participation on the soccer team. This should be discussed at the parents' orientation meeting. Martens[1] has identified a number of parental responsibilities. You may wish to cover all or a portion of the following responsibilities in the parents' orientation meeting.

- Parents should learn what their child wants from soccer.

- Parents should decide if their child is ready to compete and at what level.

- Parents should help their child understand the meaning of winning and losing.

- Parents are responsible for disciplining their child and ensuring that their child meets specific responsibilities for participating on the soccer team.

- Parents should not interfere with their child's coach and should conduct themselves in a proper manner at games.

Parents should also be sensitive to fulfill the commitment they and their child have made to the team. This often requires that parents displace other important tasks in order to get their child to practice on time, publicly support the coach, encourage players to give their best effort, reward players for desirable efforts, and participate in the social events of the team.

Children and their parents must assume certain responsibilities.

If called upon, parents should be willing to assist the coach to carry out some of the many tasks required to meet the needs of the team. If you, as the coach, can anticipate and identify tasks that you will need assistance with, these should be presented to the parents at the orientation meeting.

It is surprising how many parents will volunteer to help you if the tasks are well-defined. See Supplement 3-8 for a description of some qualifications required of assistants and some possible responsibilities. You may not be able to anticipate all the tasks. However, by developing an expectation of shared cooperation at the orientation meeting, parents who are not initially called upon for assistance are more likely to provide help as the need arises.

One conflict that sometimes arises results from parents falsely assuming your responsibility as coach. They may attempt to direct the play of their child and/or others during practices and games. This type of action by a parent undermines your plans for the team. It may also create a conflict in the mind of the athlete as to which set of instructions to follow.

You must inform parents that their public comments should be limited to praise and applause and that you will be prepared to coach the team. There are many ways to coach young athletes and different strategies that can result in success. You should inform parents that, if they disagree with your coaching, you will be open to their suggestions when they are presented in private.

Season Schedule

Fewer telephone calls and memos will be needed later in the season if you prepare and distribute a schedule of events for the season at the orientation meeting. The most efficient way to provide parents with the entire season schedule is with a handout.

The schedule should inform the parents about the length of the season; the dates, sites, and times when practices and games will be held; lengths of practices and games; number of games; number of practices; and other events for the season. Maps and/or instructions about where team events are to occur are often helpful.

GETTING PARENTS TO ATTEND AN ORIENTATION MEETING

After you have received your team roster and, if possible before the first practice, you should make arrangements to schedule a parents' orientation meeting. If you do not personally have a large enough space to accommodate the parents, a room in a neighborhood school usually can be scheduled free of charge for an orientation meeting.

Before scheduling the time and date for the meeting, the parents should be asked about the times that they could attend. This information, as well as items of parental concern for an agenda, can be obtained through a telephone conversation with the parents. Once the time and date have been determined, the parents should be notified about this information by telephone or brief letter.

If a letter is sent, the agenda for the meeting could be included. If possible, this notification should occur about two weeks before the meeting and should be followed by a courteous telephone reminder on the night before the meeting.

In your communication with the parents, you should stress the importance of the meeting and the need for each family to be represented at the meeting.

ORGANIZING THE PARENTS' ORIENTATION MEETING

If you are well-prepared and organized, conducting a parents' orientation meeting will be an enjoyable and useful event. Before the meeting, you should complete the agenda and write down key points you plan to communicate under each item. Next, assemble the handouts that will be distributed at the meeting. At the very least, the handouts should include an agenda for the parents to follow.

Other suggested handouts and forms for distributing and collecting information include: information on common soccer injuries, medical examination form (if provided by your program), accident insurance form and information (if provided through your program), athletic medical information form, medical release form, description of proper equipment, list of team assistants and responsibilities, season schedule, telephone tree, and player and parent roster. The items in Supplements 3-1 through 3-8 are suitable for duplication (permission is granted) and could be distributed at the orientation meeting.

FOLLOW-UPS ON THE PARENTS' ORIENTATION MEETING

After having conducted the parents' orientation meeting, you should contact the families who were unable to attend and briefly inform them about what was discussed. They should be given the handouts that were distributed at the meeting, and you should collect whatever information is needed from them. Once your records are completed, you may compile additional handouts (e.g., telephone tree).

Keep the lines of communication open between yourself and the parents.

No matter how many questions you answer at the parents' orientation meeting, it will not solve all of the problems. Thus, it is important to keep the lines of communication open. You should indicate your willingness to discuss any problems that were not discussed at the first meeting. This might be done with a telephone call or at a conference involving the coach and parent, or the coach, parent, and athlete. Immediately before or after a practice is often an appropriate time to discuss major issues with parents. You could even have another meeting for parents midway through the season to provide an update on the team's progress, to discuss any problems, or to listen to parents' comments. By inviting parents to talk with you, they will become a positive, rather than a negative, influence on the players and the team.

SUMMARY

Parents can be an asset to your program, but some parents can have a negative influence on your program. Communicating to parents about how you perceive your role as the coach, the purpose of the soccer program, and the responsibilities that they and their children have to the soccer program can minimize these negative influences. The most effective way to communicate this information is through a parents' orientation meeting. The time and effort you put into developing a well-organized meeting will save you considerably more time and effort throughout the season.

In a parents' orientation meeting, you have the opportunity to explain to parents that they have responsibilities to you and the team, such as deciding if their child is ready to compete, having realistic expectations, disciplining, and not interfering with coaching and playing. Children's responsibilities of promptness, cooperation, commitment, and proper conduct can also be outlined for parents.

In addition, other agenda items can be discussed and information can be gathered at a parents' orientation meeting that may make your job run more smoothly throughout the season. Be sure to discuss such items as danger and risk of injury, equipment needs, emergency procedures, and the season schedule.

The agenda items outlined in this chapter may not cover all the issues you need to address with the parents of your players. Therefore, you must organize a specific meeting that meets the needs of your team.

REFERENCES

1. Martens, R. (1978). *Joys and sadness in children's sports*. Champaign, IL: Human Kinetics Publishers.

2. Martens, R. and Seefeldt, V. (Eds.). (1979). *Guidelines for children's sports*. Reston, VA: AAHPERD.

SUGGESTED READINGS

Agre, J.C. & Krotee, M.L. (1981). Soccer safety—Prevention and care. *Journal of Health, Physical Education, Recreation and Dance* 52(5), 52-54.

American College of Sports Medicine, American Orthopaedic Society for Sports Medicine & Sports Medicine Committee of the United States Tennis Association (1982). *Sports injuries—An aid to prevention and treatment*. Coventry, CT: Bristol-Myers Co.

Estrand, J. & Gillquist, J. (1983). Soccer injuries and their mechanisms: A prospective study. *Medicine and Science in Sports and Exercise* 15(3), 267-270.

Foley, J. (1980). *Questions parents should ask about youth sports programs.* East Lansing, MI: Institute for the Study of Youth Sports.

Jackson, D. & Pescar, S. (1981). *The young athletes health handbook.* New York: Everest House.

McCarroll, J.R., Meaney, C. & Sieber, J.M. (1984). Profile of youth soccer injuries. *Physician and Sportsmedicine* 12(2), 113-115, 117.

Micheli, L.J. (1985). Preventing youth sports injuries. *Journal of Health, Physical Education, Recreation and Dance* 76(6), 52-54.

Mirkin, G. & Marshall, H. (1978). *The sportsmedicine book.* Waltham, MA: Little, Brown, & Co.

Smodhaka, V.N. (1981). Death on the soccer field and its prevention. *Physician and Sportsmedicine* 9(8),101-107.

TEAM ROSTER INFORMATION

Player's Name	Birth Date	Parents' Names	Address	Phone #'s Home/Work
1.	/ /	_____	_____	___/___
2.	/ /	_____	_____	___/___
3.	/ /	_____	_____	___/___
4.	/ /	_____	_____	___/___
5.	/ /	_____	_____	___/___
6.	/ /	_____	_____	___/___
7.	/ /	_____	_____	___/___
8.	/ /	_____	_____	___/___
9.	/ /	_____	_____	___/___
10.	/ /	_____	_____	___/___
11.	/ /	_____	_____	___/___
12.	/ /	_____	_____	___/___
13.	/ /	_____	_____	___/___
14.	/ /	_____	_____	___/___
15.	/ /	_____	_____	___/___
16.	/ /	_____	_____	___/___
17.	/ /	_____	_____	___/___
18.	/ /	_____	_____	___/___

TELEPHONE TREE

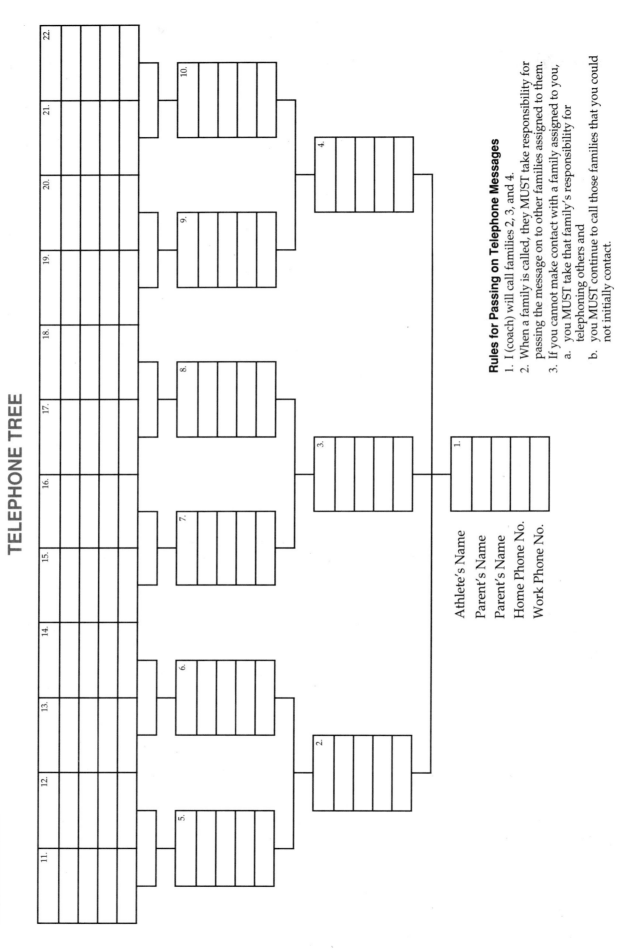

Athlete's Name

Parent's Name

Parent's Name

Home Phone No.

Work Phone No.

Rules for Passing on Telephone Messages

1. I (coach) will call families 2, 3, and 4.
2. When a family is called, they MUST take responsibility for passing the message on to other families assigned to them.
3. If you cannot make contact with a family assigned to you,
   a. you MUST take that family's responsibility for telephoning others and
   b. you MUST continue to call those families that you could not initially contact.

Supplement 3-2

RULES FOR CONSTRUCTING A TELEPHONE TREE

1. Put your name (coach)/family at the trunk of the tree.

2. In boxes 2, 3, and 4, enter information for families who are likely to
   be available to receive telephone messages.

3. Fill in the remaining boxes in order until all athletes are listed.

TYPES OF INJURIES IN YOUTH SOCCER[1,2]

	Report 1[a]		Report 2b	
Age of athletes	**11 to 18 years**		**8 to 18 years**	
INJURIES	**NO.**	**%**	**NO.**	**%**
Contusion	306	36	44	27
Sprain and Strain	174	20		
Fracture	29	4	22	25
Skin abrasion/blister	336	39		
Sprain			47	13
Strain			17	10
Concussion			5	3
Other	13	2	41	23
Total	858	101	176	101

[a]Types of injuries reported to have occurred to 25,000 boys and girls who participated in a highly competitive international youth tournament consisting of 2,987 games.

[b]Types of injuries reported to have occurred over a four-month period to 4,018 boys and girls who participated in practices and games in a state youth soccer association.

References

1. Nilsson, S., & Roaas, A. (1978). Soccer injuries and adolescents. *American Journal of Sports Medicine* 6(6), 358-361.

2. McCarroll, J.R., Meaney, C., & Sieber, J.M. (1984). Profile of youth soccer injuries. *The Physician and Sportsmedicine* 12(2), 113-115, 117.

SITES OF INJURIES IN YOUTH SOCCER[1,2]

Age of athletes	Report 1[a] 11 to 18 yrs.		Report 2[b] 5 to 15 yrs.		15 and over	
SITES	No.	%	No.	%	No.	%
Head and face	54	10	4,304	11	6,983	12
Trunk	37	7				
Trunk and shoulders			2,491	7	6,700	12
Upper extremities	80	15				
Arms and hands			11,709	31	8,087	14
Lower extremities	351	68				
Legs and feet			19,154	51	34,119	61
Other			110	<1	219	<1
Total	522	100	37,768	100	56,108	100

[a]Sites of injuries reported to have occurred to 25,000 boys and girls who participated in a highly competitive international youth tournament consisting of 2,987 games.

[b]Sites of injuries estimated to have occurred, based upon projections from injuries treated in selected U.S. hospital emergency rooms in 1980.

References

1. Nilsson, S., & Roaas, A. (1978). Soccer injuries and adolescents. *American Journal of Sports Medicine* 6(6), 358-361.

2. Rutherford, G., Miles, R., Brown, V. & MacDonald, B. (1981). *Overview of sports related injuries to persons 5-14 year of age*. Washington, D.C.: U.S. Consumer Product Safety Commission.

ATHLETE'S MEDICAL INFORMATION

Athlete's Name:_____ Athlete's Birthdate: _____

Parents' Names:_____ Date: _____

Address: _____

Phone No's.: _____ _____ _____

           (Home)   (Work)   (Other)

Who To Contact In Case of Emergency (if parents cannot be immediately contacted):

Name: _____ Relationship: _____

Home Phone No: _____ Work Phone No: _____

Name: _____ Relationship: _____

Home Phone No: _____ Work Phone No: _____

Hospital Preference: _____ Emergency Phone No: _____

Doctor Preference: _____ Office Phone No: _____

MEDICAL HISTORY*

Has your child, or did your child, have any of the following?

A. General Conditions:	Circle One		Circle One or Both		B. Injuries:	Circle One		Circle One or Both	
1. Fainting spells	Yes	No	Past	Present	1. Toes	Yes	No	Past	Present
2. Headaches	Yes	No	Past	Present	2. Feet	Yes	No	Past	Present
3. Convulsions/epilepsy	Yes	No	Past	Present	3. Ankles	Yes	No	Past	Present
4. Asthma	Yes	No	Past	Present	4. Lower legs	Yes	No	Past	Present
5. High blood pressure	Yes	No	Past	Present	5. Knees	Yes	No	Past	Present
6. Kidney problems	Yes	No	Past	Present	6. Thighs	Yes	No	Past	Present
7. Intestinal disorder	Yes	No	Past	Present	7. Hips	Yes	No	Past	Present
8. Hernia	Yes	No	Past	Present	8. Lower back	Yes	No	Past	Present
9. Diabetes	Yes	No	Past	Present	9. Upper back	Yes	No	Past	Present
10. Heart disease/disorder	Yes	No	Past	Preser t	10. Ribs	Yes	No	Past	Present
11. Dental plate	Yes	No	Past	Present	11. Abdomen	Yes	No	Past	Present
12. Poor vision	Yes	No	Past	Present	12. Chest	Yes	No	Past	Present
13. Poor hearing	Yes	No	Past	Present	13. Neck	Yes	No	Past	Present
14. Skin disorder	Yes	No	Past	Present	14. Fingers	Yes	No	Past	Present
15. Allergies	Yes	No	Past	Present	15. Hands	Yes	No	Past	Present
Specify: _____			Past	Present	16. Wrists	Yes	No	Past	Present
_____			Past	Present	17. Forearms	Yes	No	Past	Present
16. Joint dislocation					18. Elbows	Yes	No	Past	Present
or separations	Yes	No	Past	Present	19. Upper arms	Yes	No	Past	Present
Specify: _____			Past	Present	20. Shoulders	Yes	No	Past	Present
_____			Past	Present	21. Head	Yes	No	Past	Present
17. Other: _____			Past	Present	Specify: _____				
					22. Others: _____			Past	Present
					_____			Past	Present

*Please explain on the back of this sheet any "yes" responses that have present implications for my coaching your child. Also, describe proper first aid requirements, if appropriate.

When did your child last receive a tetanus booster? _____
(Date)

Is your child currently taking any medication?   Yes   No   **(Circle One)**

If yes, describe medication, amount, and reasons for taking. _____

_____

_____

Does your child have any adverse reactions to medications: Yes   No   **(Circle One)**

If yes, which medications and what are the reactions? _____

_____

_____

Has a physician placed any restrictions on your child's present activity?   Yes   No   **(Circle One)**

If yes, explain. _____

_____

_____

Does your child have any existing and/or past medical or emotional conditions that require special concern and attention by a sports coach?   Yes   No   **(Circle One)**

If yes, explain. _____

_____

_____

	Signature	Date
Athlete:	_____	
Parent or guardian:	_____	_____
Parent or guardian:	_____	_____

MEDICAL RELEASE FORM

I hereby give permission for any and all medical attention necessary to be administered to my child in the event of an accident, injury, sickness, etc., under the direction of the people listed below until such time as I may be contacted. My child's name is _____ .
This release is effective for the time during which my child is participating in the _____ soccer program and any tournaments for the 19____/19____ season, including traveling to or from such tournaments. I also hereby assume the responsiblity for payment of any such treatment.

PARENTS' NAMES _____

HOME ADDRESS _____
| Street | City | State | Zip |

HOME PHONE _____ WORK PHONE _____

INSURANCE COMPANY _____

POLICY NUMBER _____

FAMILY PHYSICIAN _____

PHYSICIAN'S ADDRESS _____ PHONE NO. _____

MY CHILD'S KNOWN ALLERGIES _____

_____

_____

In case I cannot be reached, either of the following people is designated:

COACH'S NAME _____ PHONE NO. _____

ASS'T COACH OR OTHER _____ PHONE NO. _____

SIGNATURE OF PARENT OR GUARDIAN _____

SUBSCRIBED AND SWORN BEFORE ME THIS DAY OF _____, 19_____

SIGNATURE OF NOTARY PUBLIC _____

GUIDELINES FOR SELECTING
SOCCER EQUIPMENT
Field Players and Goalkeepers

1. Ball

- Balls used in youth play are made in different sizes (3, 4, and 5). The size 3 is the lightest and smallest. A 5 is a full-size ball used for adolescent and adult competition.

- Balls vary in their design and construction. Currently, the standard ball has 32 panels with an inflatable bladder. The materials used for the panels include plastic, synthetic leather, and leather. These panels may be glued to an inner shell or sewn together. A good quality synthetic leather ball with either glued or sewn panels is recommended for youth play. The glued panel ball costs less and tends to have a longer life than the sewn panel ball, but it is not as easily controlled and tends to "sting."

- All players should have a ball of their own that they bring to each practice session and use at home.

2. Shin guards

- Shin guards vary in size. They should not inhibit running by extending beyond the ankle and knee joints.

- Shin guards vary in their design and construction. They should conform to the contour of the lower leg to dissipate the force of a direct blow. They should also be constructed of materials that provide good force-absorbing qualities.

- All youth soccer players should wear shin guards throughout all practices and games.

3. Shoes

- Shoes are the most important piece of personal equipment for a soccer player.

- Shoes should be purchased to fit and not to be grown into.

- Gym shoes, multi-cleated molded shoes, and shoes with screw-in cleats are permissible. The multi-cleated molded shoes are recommended as a versatile shoe for all levels of youth play.

4. Mouth guards

- It is recommended that field players and goalkeepers wear a molded mouth guard throughout all practices and games.

- A mouth guard protects a player's teeth.

- A mouth guard may dissipate the shock of a blow to the head and may reduce the chance for, or severity of, a concussion.

Goalkeepers

1. Goalkeeper gloves

- Goalkeeper gloves are not essential. However, they provide the goalkeeper with better control of a kicked ball and protect the hands.

- Goalkeeper gloves may be purchased by the team and shared by those who play the goalkeeper position. Or, the gloves may be personally purchased by players who have a keen interest in the goalkeeper position.

2. Goalkeeper shirt

- According to the rules of play, a goalkeeper's shirt must be different in color than the shirts of the field players and opposing goalkeeper.

- A goalkeeper's shirt usually consists of a snug-fitting shirt with full-length sleeves and built-in elbow padding.

- Standard elbow pads worn either under or over an activity shirt is a good alternative to an "official" goalkeeper shirt.

3. Goalkeeper pants

- Goalkeeper pants come in shorts, three-quarter length, and full-length pants with feet stirrups. The seat, hip area, and knees (if full-length pants) have built-in padding.

- Standard knee pads worn with a few layers of shorts, sweat pants, and/or full-length tights provide a good alternative to "official" goalkeeper pants.

4. Goalkeeper helmet

- A goalkeeper helmet consists of a foam rubber molded shell, with an open face region, which fits over the head and is held in place with a chin strap.

- Most goalkeepers do not wear a helmet. However, the helmet does provide protection to regions of the head other than the face.

- It is recommended that a goalkeeper helmet should be part of the equipment assigned to or purchased by a youth team and that it should be worn by goalkeepers during practices and games.

5. Athletic supporter with cup

6. Athletic bra

Descriptions of Team Assistants
and Their Responsibilities*

Assistant coach—aids the coach in all aspects of coaching the team during practices and games.

Team manager—keeps game statistics, completes line-up cards, and makes arrangements for practice sites and times; works approximately one hour per week.

Team treasurer—collects fees from players, identifies sponsors, maintains financial records; works approximately five hours at the beginning of the season and a few hours throughout the remainder of the season.

Team doctor/nurse/paramedic—establishes a plan to respond to possible emergencies for each practice and game site, prepares and updates a medical kit, assists the coach in responding to injured players by providing first aid, collects and organizes completed medical history forms and reviews these with the coach, maintains records of completed on-site injury reports and completes a summary of season injuries, delegates other parents to bring ice to games for initial care of certain injuries; works approximately five hours at the beginning of the season and approximately a half-hour per week throughout the remainder of the season. Note that only a certified medical doctor, nurse, or paramedic should assume some of these defined responsibilities. See Section VII, Chapter 24, Care of Common Soccer Injuries, for more details.

Team social coordinator—plans team party and team social functions; works approximately three hours near the end of the season.

Team refreshments coordinator—contacts parents to assign them the shared expense and responsibilities of providing refreshments at all games (see Section VII, Chapter 22, Nutrition for Successful Performance); works approximately two hours.

Team secretary—prepares and duplicates handouts, types, sends out mailings; works approximately five hours.

Others—

---

* Note that these are only suggestions for assistants and responsibilities. The way you organize your team may result in the need for different and/or additional assistants.

4

LEGAL LIABILITIES

Bernard Patrick Maloy and Vern Seefeldt

QUESTIONS TO CONSIDER
- In terms of legal liability, what are the coaching duties?
- Against which risks to their players are coaches responsible for taking reasonable precautions?
- Do children who participate in youth sports assume the risk of their own injuries?
- What influence does the age and maturity of the athletes have upon the legal responsibilities of the coach?
- Do coaches' legal responsibilities to their players extend beyond the field of play?
- Are coaches responsible for informing players, parents, and guardians about the risks and hazards inherent in sports?
- What legal responsibilities do coaches have to their players when coaches delegate duties to assistants?

INTRODUCTION

It is inevitable that the role of a coach is expanded beyond that of mere instructor or supervisor when it comes to working with youth sports. Because coaches are the most visible administrators to players, parents, and officials, they are expected to handle anything from correcting player rosters to fitting equipment on the field, from assuaging parents' feelings to arranging player transportation. While these duties may tax the limits of a coach's patience, they remain very important areas of responsibility.

LEGAL DUTIES

Coaches are subject to certain terms of legal liability. However, it would be wrong to assume these legal duties were created by the courts to be imposed on the coaching profession. They are the time-honored, recognized obligations inherent to the coaching profession. Thus, they should be termed coaching responsibilities (see Chapter 1, Role of the

Coach). These are responsibilities expected of a coach regardless of pay and regardless of whether the coaching is performed for a school, a religious organization, or a youth sports association.

Where Does Coaching Responsibility Begin?

The primary responsibility of coaches is to know their players. In that regard, it is always important to remember that young athletes are children first, athletes second. The degree of responsibility that coaches owe to their teams is measured by the age and maturity of their players. The younger and more immature a player, the more responsibility a coach bears in regard to the instruction, supervision, and safety of that child (see Section VII, Chapter 23, Prevention of Common Soccer Injuries). Additionally, the coach is expected to be aware of any physical or mental handicap that a player may have and must know how to recognize emergency symptoms requiring medical attention (see Section VII, Chapter 24, Care of Common Soccer Injuries). A coach in youth sports must always bear in mind that:

- nine-year-olds participating in organized sport activities for the first time require more instruction and attention than teenagers with playing experience;

- a 10-year-old child should not be expected to behave, on or off the playing field, any differently than other 10-year-old children;

- all children with special needs or handicaps must be identified; and

- a plan for the emergency treatment of children with special needs and those who sustain injuries should be devised.

As will be discussed, coaches do not have to guarantee the safety of their young players. However, they are responsible for taking reasonable precautions against all foreseeable risks that threaten their players. Coaches must realize that those precautions are not measured by what they may have thought was reasonable, but rather by what was reasonable according to the age and maturity of the players.

Do You Know How to Coach?

The volunteer coach is the backbone of many organized youth activities. Nevertheless, despite good intentions, some degrees of qualifications and certification are necessary for responsible coaching. Therefore, in addition to personal athletic experience and background, coaches should attend programs and seminars on the development of athletic skills, youth motivation, and emergency medical treatment. A coach's responsibility begins with an understanding of current methods of conditioning (see Section VII, Chapter 21), skill development (see Sections IV and V), and injury prevention and care (see Section VII, Chapters 23 and 24).

> *Coaches have certain responsibilities that they may not transfer to assistant coaches, parents, or league officials.*

In many cases, a youth sports league or association will offer classes, materials, or advice on skill development and injury prevention and care. Generally, those associations require some certification or recommendation regarding coaching background, skills, and experience before an applicant is permitted to coach youth sports. Coaches must avail themselves of instructional programs or other information helpful for coaching youth sports. In other words, coaches are responsible for their own incompetencies. A youth sports coach should create a competency checklist:

- Does the youth sports association certify its coaches?

- Does the association require coaches to attend coaching clinics and emergency medical programs?

- Do you know how to identify the necessary individual athletic skills based on size, weight, and age?

- Do you know of any agencies that will help identify those skills?

- What steps should you take to become certified in first aid treatment?

> *Knowledge of your coaching incompetencies is the first step toward seeking a corrective solution.*

Coaches must be able to recognize their limitations. Acknowledging that skills, youth motivation, and medical treatment may be different today than when you played is the first step toward becoming a responsible coach.

Where Do Your Coaching Duties Lie?

As noted, youth sports coaches are many things to their teams, parents and guardians, and supporters. Coaching responsibilities extend to areas beyond the playing field. The responsibilities require the same effort and devotion as do the on-field duties and may include:

- league or team fund-raising activities;

- assisting during registration periods;

- talking to interested players and their parents about the league and its athletic and social goals;

- providing or planning team transportation to and from practices and games;

- attending league or association meetings;

- buying, selecting, or maintaining equipment;
- maintaining locker rooms and athletic fields; and
- supervising players during pre-practice and post-practice periods.

What Misconceptions Do Many Coaches Have?

There are two common misconceptions regarding youth sports. The first is that children participating generally assume the risk of their own injury; the second, that the role of the coach is severely limited by legal liability.

The legal defense of assumption of risk as it applies to sports is very specific. An athlete assumes the risk of injury from dangers inherent to the sport itself. In other words, it is recognized that injuries occur, especially in contact sports, from activities on the playing field. Some examples would be:

- the collision of two players chasing a ball on the playing field; or
- the injury of a player on the field resulting from a non-intentional foul.

Many risks confronting athletes are not inherent to the sport; rather they are the result of improper instruction, supervision, or equipment. For example, young athletes do not assume the risk of injury from:

- protective equipment or pads that are defective or have been poorly fit; or
- lack of instruction in athletic skills.

The interpretation of "assumption of risk" is complicated when it is applied to youth sports because young athletes require careful supervision regarding their own welfare. The concept that young athletes must assume the responsibility for their injuries sustained in practices or games must be contrasted with whether or not the coach or other adult supervisors were negligent in their instruction and supervision of the activity. In such a comparison it is unlikely that responsibility for "assumption of risk" will serve as a viable excuse.

When an injury occurs in youth sports, the coach's responsibility is considered a much greater factor than the "assumption of risk" by the player.

Fortunately, most coaches inherently understand the limitations involved in "assumption of risk." The motivation for many youth coaches is the involvement of their own children in sports. And, like most parents, those coaches accept injury as a natural risk of the sport, but they will not tolerate an injury resulting from lack of proper skill development or poor equipment.

Youth sport coaches should concern themselves less with whether adhering to these responsibilities is good legal protection, and more with the thought that their actions represent the standards expected of youth sport coaches. Actually, the areas of expertise legally required of coaches can serve as measures of qualifications and certification. Youth sport leagues and conferences realize that coaches must adhere to legal principles of liability not merely to protect the league and the coach from costly litigation but also to ensure that children continue to participate in athletics. It is very doubtful that parents would continue to support youth sports if it were plagued by poor coaching, lack of supervision, or poor medical treatment procedures. In short, these imposed responsibilities are good business practices for youth sports.

COACHING RESPONSIBILITIES

As a youth soccer coach you have many responsibilities beyond teaching your players the skills of the game. Your coaching responsibilities are: providing proper instruction, providing reasonable supervision, warning of hazards and risks, providing competent personnel, preventing and caring for injuries, providing safe equipment, and selecting participants. Each of these responsibilities are discussed in subsequent sections.

Providing Proper Instruction

A coach must teach the physical skills and mental discipline or attitude required to play soccer (see Sections II, IV, and V). You must enhance the development of those skills while reducing the chance of injury. Specifically, volunteer coaches, who represent that they can teach the sport or activity, must be aware of the rules of safety and know how to teach the proper methods of conditioning. For example, when young players are injured, coaches should be prepared to competently assess whether:

- the conditioning or skill drills are realistic for players of young or immature years;

- video, film, or written materials, in addition to on-field instruction, would improve instructional techniques;

- the players are taught the correct way to wear equipment;

- all the players, starters, and substitutes have been given the same amount of time, instruction, and practice on the correct methods of play, conditioning, and the rules;

- conditioning techniques and skill drills are current;

- coaching methods are accurately evaluated by the league;

- parental comments and concerns have been integrated into the coaching instruction;

- provision has been made in coaching instruction for learning disabled and mentally or emotionally handicapped children who participate; and

- criticism or comments regarding coaching instruction are met with a positive response.

The foregoing list consists of some expectations a parent or guardian has of a coach. While those expectations impact heavily on liability, they more accurately serve as guidelines by which youth sports coaches can evaluate their instruction. Again, a youth sports coach must remember that the age and immaturity of the players are key factors to instructional techniques. The coach must be sensitive to the outside environment in which a young player lives, as well as the sports environment created by the coach. Only then can you ensure a youngster the full benefit of your instruction (see Chapter 1).

Providing Reasonable Supervision

A coach is responsible for the reasonable supervision of the players. There is little question that this responsibility starts on the field of play during all practices and games. Again, the scope of this responsibility depends on the age and maturity of the players. The younger the player, the greater the degree of responsibility a coach must take for the player's safe supervision.

In youth sports, a coach's supervisory responsibility may extend to times and places other than the field of play. In some instances, this may include managing parents or guardians and supporters as well as the players and assistant coaches. A coach's checklist of potential supervisory functions should question:

- Is there a supervisor available for a reasonable time before and after practice?

- Have parents or guardians advised who will pick up their children after practices and games?

- Who is assigned to remain with the players until all have been called for, according to instructions provided by parents or guardians?

- How are parents or guardians notified of practice and game times, dates, and places?

- Who is responsible for player transportation to and from games?

- Are substitute players supervised off the field during games?

- Are players allowed off the field during practice for bathroom or other personal comforts? If so, how are those players supervised?

Many youth sports leagues or associations will have a rule that coaches are responsible for the behavior of team parents, guardians, and fans. Such a rule becomes very important in those instances where a coach disagrees with a referee's decision, or where parents believe their child has been slighted on the field during play, or off the field from lack of play. Coaches have to recognize that their conduct can incite parents, guardians, and supporters. A coach must ask:

- Have team and league rules regarding parental involvement, the rules of play, and rules regarding team participation been communicated to parents and guardians?

- Do parents and guardians know your coaching philosophy and team goals?

- Have the team and parents and guardians been notified that only the coach is permitted to discuss a decision with a referee?

The coach's role in supervision off the field of play can be made easier by a parents' orientation meeting at the start of the season (see Chapter 3). The parents have a right to know what to expect of the coach. Also, the meeting prepares parents to become actively involved with other parents in stopping any unruly conduct. Again, the supervisory responsibility starts with coaches who conduct themselves in the spirit of good sportsmanship. It also includes a coach's support of game officials in order to defuse angry parents, guardians, supporters, or players.

Warning of Hazards and Risks

A coach is responsible for informing players, parents, and guardians about the risks and hazards inherent to the sport. Obviously, it is not expected that coaches will dissuade parents and guardians from permitting their youngsters to participate. By the same token, a coach's experience and knowledge is critical to assure parents and guardians that the greatest possible care will be taken for the well-being of their children.

The age and maturity of the players plays a major role in the degree of risk from playing soccer. Older, more experienced children may face a greater risk of injury from soccer simply due to the more sophisticated style of play. However, those children and their parents and guardians already should be fairly well-versed in the risks of soccer. Therefore, they don't need the same information and assurances as parents and guardians whose children are younger and have never participated.

The coach must inform athletes and parents of the potential dangers inherent in playing youth soccer.

The youth league or association may provide information regarding sports hazards, but the responsibility to warn parents and athletes remains a very important coaching duty (see Section VII, Chapter 23). Therefore, a coach would be well-served to provide parents, guardians, and players with as much information and materials as possible regarding soccer at registration, as well as during the season. The coach must be prepared to instruct or advise:

- how many injuries his or her teams with similar age and experience have suffered, and what types of injuries occurred;

- what types of equipment, clothing, or shoes are not recommended or permitted for play;

- how equipment should properly fit;

- what written, video, or audio materials are available that will instruct parents and guardians about the sport and its risks;

- what style, conduct, or manner of play is to be avoided due to the likelihood of injury to the player or an opponent;

- what conduct or manner of play is not permitted under the rules; and

- whether the field and facilities have been inspected for hazards and determined to be safe for play.

Hosting a parents' orientation meeting prior to the first game is an excellent way to describe your role in the prevention and care of their children's injuries.

Providing Competent Personnel

We have already examined the coach's responsibility to provide quality instruction. Also, we have examined many of the attendant roles and duties that coaches must provide with that instruction. In many cases, the sheer numbers of players and responsibilities demand that a coach have some assistance. It is not unusual for a coach to delegate some of those coaching or supervisory duties to assistant coaches or parents (see Supplement 3-8). However, the coach must ensure that the people who are assisting are competent. Obviously, having a responsible coach is of little value if the players are subject to the directions of incompetent assistants. Therefore, in a coach's absence, an assistant coach or aide must be able to provide the same responsible instruction and supervision as the players and parents expect from the head coach. It is wise, then, for a coach to learn:

- whether the league or association certifies assistant coaches;

- what policies the league or association has regarding the use of parents for supervision, transportation, or instruction;

- whether assistant coaches have any hidden past regarding child abuse, or other conduct that constitutes a threat to children;

- whether assistant coaches or parents who agree to transport players have suspect driving records;

- whether there is any reason to suspect an assistant's or aide's coaching competency; and

- whether teenagers may be qualified as assistants with coaching and supervisory duties.

It is a coach's responsibility to determine whether assistant coaches and team aides are qualified to step into the coach's shoes.

Preventing and Caring for Injuries

There are few areas that demand as much attention as the prevention and care of injuries (see Section VII, Chapters 23, 24, and 25). It is not uncommon to find many youth sports programs conducting practices in contact sports without qualified medical personnel or knowledgeable athletic trainers readily available. In those instances, the first attendant to an injured player is usually the coach or teammates. The coach's responsibility is to recognize when immediate medical treatment is required and to ensure that assistant coaches and teammates do not attempt to touch, move, or help the injured player. Obviously, that can be a very confusing task because the majority of injuries will be minor.

Many problems in the initial care of athletic injuries might be solved if coaches were required to qualify as emergency medical technicians, or to have some type of comparable training in first aid and health care. In the absence of those qualifications, however, coaches must use their best discretion, based on experience. Obviously, those deficiencies are compounded in youth sports where most of the coaches are volunteers.

In addition to recognizing when emergency medical help is needed, a coach must be able to recognize symptoms of ongoing problems. If a player has a disease, diabetes for instance, the coach has the responsibility for checking with the player's parents about medication, learning how to recognize the symptoms of shock or deficiency, and what type of emergency treatment to request.

A coach must also be aware of the effects a conditioning program may have on players (see Section VII, Chapter 21, Conditioning Youth Soccer Players). For instance, if practices are conducted during hot weather, a coach should provide ample water (see Section VII, Chapter 22, Nutrition for Successful Performances), change the time of practice to early morning or late afternoon, learn the symptoms of heat stroke or exhaustion, and learn how to provide for immediate care (see Section VII, Chapter 24, Care of Common Soccer Injuries).

It's impossible to categorize all the areas of concern for injuries that a coach may face. However, there are precautions that you can take to ensure that your responsibilities have been reasonably met:

- attend league-sponsored programs dealing with athletic injuries;
- check with local health authorities, local hospitals, coaching associations, or emergency medical personnel to find programs that address emergency medical care;
- implement a plan to provide immediate emergency medical care at the practice field;
- implement a plan for the immediate notification of parents or guardians in case their child is seriously injured;

- do not attempt unfamiliar care without emergency medical competency or ability;

- identify players with specific medical handicaps before the season and prepare reasonable emergency plans in case of sudden illness;

- do not permit players who have suffered injuries requiring medical attention to play or participate until their return to practice and competition has been approved by a physician; and

- notify parents or guardians of any minor injuries occurring to, or complaints by, their children.

It is wise to document the circumstances of a serious injury (see Section VII, Chapter 24, Care of Common Soccer Injuries). In many cases, a written report shows that coaches have reasonably met their responsibility. Such a report is also helpful to medical personnel in the subsequent treatment of the injury. The documentation should include:

- a record of all facts surrounding the injury including who, when, and where the injury occurred, and the injured player's responses;

- a list and description of the equipment involved, if any;

- a list of those who witnessed the injury; and

- a record of actions taken in response to the injury prior to the arrival of medical personnel.

When completed, provide copies of the injury report to the attending physician, the medical response personnel, and the league or association. Be sure to keep a copy for your own files.

Providing Equipment

A coach must take reasonable care to provide the team with proper and safe equipment (see Supplement 3-7). You should know the various types and brands of equipment, master the proper maintenance procedures, and learn to outfit players properly and safely. Generally, you are not responsible for equipment defects unless you're directly involved in the manufacture of equipment. However, you are expected to know whether or not the proper equipment is being used, if it's defective, and to ensure that defective equipment is not distributed to players. A coach must take reasonable care to:

- select or recommend the proper equipment for the sport;

- select or recommend specific types of equipment for specific uses;

- properly fit players;

- verify that old equipment has been properly reconditioned or recertified for use;

- disallow players who are not properly equipped and dressed to participate in practices or games;

- have knowledge of league or association rules regarding proper dress and equipment;

- instruct players and parents on the proper maintenance of sports equipment in their possession;

- utilize a written inventory for reporting and tracking the repair of damaged equipment; and

- become aware of manufacturers' recommendations and warnings.

Selecting Participants

A soccer coach is obligated to protect the health and safety of players during practices and games. The potential for injuries to occur in soccer is reduced when players are matched according to size, age, and playing experience. Injuries that occur when players are mismatched in terms of body size and playing experience are more likely to be viewed as the result of irresponsible teaching and supervision rather than as an inherent risk of playing soccer. Coaches should protect players by following these guidelines:

- Never permit an injured athlete to compete in practices and games;

- Never allow athletes who are out of condition to participate in drills, scrimmages, or games;

- Never place players in drills, scrimmages, or games in which there is the potential for mismatches in physical conditioning, chronological age, and/or skill level.

SUMMARY

A youth sports coach cannot guarantee a child's safety. Legally, a coach is responsible for reasonably foreseeing risks and hazards to the players.

For example, if a youth sports group uses a field that has permanent benches close to the sidelines, or is fenced by standard chain link fencing with the open barbs sticking up rather than down, a coach should recognize the foreseeable risks to players and supervise, instruct, and/or warn of those dangers.

Some consider this foreseeability factor as a legal precept. However, it is predicated on knowledge and experience of the sport or activity. Therefore, its true application is not in legal theory but in the real world of sports.

REFERENCES

Berry, R., & Wong, G. (1986). *Law and business of the sports industries.* (Vol. II pp. 227-302, 320-341). Dover, MA: Auburn House.

Clement, A. (1988). *Law in sport and physical activity.* (pp. 27-61). Indianapolis, IN: Benchmark Press.

Maloy, B. (1988). *Law in sports: Liability cases in management and administration.* Indianapolis, IN: Benchmark Press.

Responsibility is also Part of the Game. *Trial,* 13, 22-25, January, 1977.

Schubert, G., Smith, R. & Trentadue, J. (1986). *Sports law.* (pp. 220-231). St. Paul, MN: West Publications.

Seefeldt, V. (1985). Legal liability. In P. Vogel & K. Blase (Eds.), *AHAUS associate coaches manual: Fundamentals of coaching youth ice hockey* (pp. 167-174). East Lansing, MI: Institute for the Study of Youth Sports.

Wong, G. (1988). *Essentials of amateur sports law.* (pp. 336-350). Dover, MA: Auburn House Publishing Co.

Section II

METHODS
FOR EFFECTIVE COACHING

5

PLANNING EFFECTIVE INSTRUCTION

Paul Vogel and Eugene W. Brown

QUESTIONS TO CONSIDER
- What four steps can coaches use to systematically instruct their players?
- What guidelines for instruction should be applied to ensure effective instruction?
- What are the features of an effective practice plan?
- What are the characteristics of a good drill?

INTRODUCTION

Effective instruction is the foundation of successful coaching. This is particularly true when you are coaching players in the six- to 16-year-old age range. Successful results in competition are directly related to the quality of instruction that players have received during practices. Effective instruction requires:

- clear communication of "what" is to be learned (objectives which represent physical skills, rules, strategies, and/or personal-social skills),

- continual evaluation of players' performance status on the objectives selected,

- use of a systematic method of instruction,

- application of guidelines for effective instruction, and

- evaluation and alteration of instruction in accordance with the degree to which players obtain the desired objectives.

CLEARLY COMMUNICATING
THE CONTENT TO BE LEARNED

The results (or outcomes) of effective instruction can be grouped into three areas.

- Physical—individual techniques and conditioning
- Mental—rules, strategies, positional responsibilities
- Social—personal and social skills

Clearly stated objectives are a prerequisite to effective instruction.

To provide effective instruction, you must identify the teaching objectives for each of these three areas. Players do not learn skills merely through exposure and practice. Rather, they must have specific feedback revealing what they are doing correctly and, equally as important, what they are doing incorrectly. Specific feedback cannot be communicated to your players unless the skill to be learned and its key elements of performance are clearly specified and understood by the coach. By using the suggestions and procedures outlined in Section I, Chapter 2, Planning for the Season, you can be confident that the objectives you include are appropriate for your players. Application of the steps explained in Section I, Chapter 2, also results in a systematic plan (preseason to late-season) for covering the objectives you select. This type of season plan provides a solid base from which effective instruction can occur.

CONTINUALLY EVALUATING
THE PERFORMANCE OF PLAYERS

As a coach, it is important to evaluate your players' ability based on the objectives you have selected. Their current status on these objectives determines the instructional needs of the team. The evaluation should include physical, mental, and social content because deficiencies in any one area may preclude successful participation in the sport. For example, the highly skilled soccer player who lacks motivation may be a liability rather than an asset to the team because of the poor example set for teammates. Also, knowledgeable players who understand the rules and strategies of the game but who lack the skills and fitness to perform as team members must also be evaluated and taught to improve their deficiencies.

> *To conduct effective practices, you must continually*
> *assess players' needs.*

The physical, mental, and attitudinal abilities of players new to the program or team are usually unknown. Even when accurate records are available from the previous season, considerable changes will normally occur in the abilities of returning players. This results in your knowing very little about many of your players. Accordingly, more time may need to be spent on evaluation of player abilities at the beginning of the season. However, player evaluation must also occur, skill by skill, practice by practice, throughout the entire season. As needs change, there should be corresponding changes in your instructional emphasis.

Assessment of Physical Needs

● **Performance Assessment**

Assess physical skills by carefully observing your players while they participate in individual and small group drills, scrimmages, and/or games. Descriptions of individual techniques, their key elements, and common errors of performance are presented in Sections IV and V. You must have this information to properly evaluate your players.

In addition to knowledge about how individual techniques of soccer are performed, the following visual evaluation guidelines should be helpful to you in making accurate observations and assessments about physical performance.

- Select a proper observational distance.
- Observe the performance from different angles.
- Observe activities in a setting which is not distracting.
- Select an observational setting that has a vertical and/or horizontal reference line.
- Observe a skilled reference model.
- Observe slower moving body parts first.
- Observe separate key elements of complicated skills.
- Observe the timing of performance components.
- Look for unnecessary movements.
- Observe the full range of motion.

● **Fitness Assessment**

Evaluating the fitness of your players requires two levels of assessment; namely, the aerobic and anaerobic energy systems. Precise physiological abilities are difficult to determine because they often require sophisticated measurement apparatus, take a lot of time, and the results are often confounded by players' skill and experience. Due to these complexities, your assessment of fitness should be at a more practical level. For the most part, you should compare individual players with their teammates on the characteristics of energy and muscular systems fitness that are explained in Section VII, Chapter 21, Conditioning Youth Soccer Players. When skill, size, and maturity levels are judged to be similar between players and one is more (or less) fit than the others on a given attribute, you can assume a differential on that attribute. You can then instruct the underdeveloped player on how to make changes. Similarly, when a player cannot keep up with teammates on a series of drills that require either maximum effort or longer, sustained effort, it is prudent to assume that one or both of the energy systems is inadequately trained.

Assessment of Cognitive Needs

Knowledge of strategy, rules, positional responsibilities, and set plays can be evaluated during drills, scrimmages, and games by noting the response of your players to situations that require a decision prior to action. By clearly communicating what you want the players to know in certain circumstances, and then asking questions and observing how they react, you can learn what they know and what skills and knowledge they can appropriately apply.

Assessment of Personal/Social Needs

An assessment of social needs, though subjective, is not difficult. Informally converse with your players and observe their interactions with other team members during practices, games, and informal gatherings to determine what needs exist. Strengthening the personal/social weaknesses of your players, however, may be more difficult than enhancing their performance of individual physical techniques and their knowledge about the game.

As skilled performance is contingent on learning the key elements of each skill, the modification of a negative or interfering attitude requires you to correctly analyze the underlying problem. Ask yourself, the parents, or the player why the behavior in question is occurring. This may require some probing. Often the problem is not related to soccer. The fact that you care enough about the individual player to invest some time and energy may be all that is needed to reverse or eliminate a negative quality that could become an individual and team burden. Based upon the information obtained, generate a specific strategy for modifying the behavior. The information in Chapters 6 through 9 will help you identify strategies for dealing with important personal/social skills.

Evaluating the status of players in the physical, mental, and attitudinal areas of performance is necessary in order to obtain insight about how to conduct practices that match your players' needs. Whether your players are performing at low, moderate, or high levels, they can all improve with good instruction.

USING A SYSTEMATIC MODEL FOR INSTRUCTION

Although there are many ways to instruct young soccer players, the following approach has proven both easy to use and effective in teaching and/or refining skills.

1) Get the attention of the players by establishing credibility.

2) Communicate precisely what needs to be learned.

3) Provide for practice and feedback.

4) Evaluate results and take appropriate action.

Step 1: Establish Credibility

Players must direct their attention to the coach before instruction can occur. To encourage this, arrange the players so that each one can see your actions and hear your instructions. Choose where you stand in relation to the players so that you avoid competing with other distractions. Often it is a good strategy to have the players seated or kneeling on the ground in front of you as you begin.

Immediately establish the precedent that when you speak, important information is being communicated. Point out that the team cannot maximize its practice opportunity when several people are talking at once.

Establish and maintain the precedent that when you speak, important information is being communicated.

As you begin your instruction, establish the need for competence on a particular physical skill or ability by relating it to some phase of successful team and/or individual play. An excellent way to gain your players' attention and motivate them to want to learn the individual techniques is to mention how a local, regional, or national level player or team has mastered the skill and has used it to great advantage. The objective of your introductory comments is to establish the idea that mastery of this skill is very important to individual and team play and that the key elements of its execution are achievable.

The next, and perhaps even more important, task is to clearly establish in the minds of the players that they need to improve their ability on this skill. This can be accomplished with the following steps:

1) Briefly describe the new skill and then let them try it several times in a quick paced drill.

2) Carefully observe their performance and identify their strengths and weaknesses. (Use the key elements of the skill as a basis for your observations.)

3) Call them back together and report your observations.

This approach will allow you to point out weaknesses in performance on one or more key elements that are common to many, if not all, of the players. Using this approach will enhance your credibility and motivate the players to listen to and follow your instructions. Also, your subsequent teaching can be specifically matched to the needs (weaknesses) you observed. Of course, if in observing, you determine that your players have already achieved the desired skill level, then you should shift your focus to another skill. This might mean moving on to the next phase of your practice plan.

Step 2: Communicate Precisely What Needs To Be Learned

When you and your players know their status (strengths and weaknesses of their performance) on a particular skill, you have created an environment for teaching and learning. Because individuals learn most efficiently when they focus on one aspect of a skill at a time, it is important to communicate precisely the one key element you want an individual, pair, group, or team to concentrate on. Demonstrate the key element, and explain it, so that all players know exactly what they are trying to achieve.

Individuals learn most effectively by focusing their practice efforts on one clearly understood element of skilled performance.

When your players are at two or three different levels of ability, you may want to establish two or three instructional groups. This can be accomplished by using the following three divisions:

- Early Learning—focus on learning the key elements of the skill in a controlled situation

- Intermediate Learning—focus on coordination of all key elements in common situations

- Later Learning—automatic use of the skill in game-like conditions

Step 3: Provide for Practice and Feedback

Organize your practice time and practice activities to provide players with:

1) as many repetitions (trials) as possible within the allotted time (minimize standing in lines); and

2) specific, immediate, and positive feedback on what they did correctly and then on what they can do to improve (follow this with some form of encouragement to continue the learning effort).

Repetitions and feedback are essential to players' achievement and are therefore fundamental to effective coaching. You can expect a direct relationship between the gains in players' performances and the degree to which you find ways to maximize these two dimensions of instruction. John Wooden, UCLA basketball coach of fame, was found to provide over 2,000 acts of teaching during 30 total hours of practice, of which 75 percent pertained directly to skill instruction. This converts to more than one incidence of feedback for every minute of coaching activity!

Repeated trials and specific feedback on what was right, followed by what can be improved and an encouraging "try again," produces results.

Feedback can be dramatically increased by using volunteers and/or the players themselves as instructional aids. When instruction is focused on one key element of performance and the important aspects of performing the skill have been effectively communicated to the players, they are often as good (and sometimes better) at seeing discrepancies in a partner's performance as some adults. Thus, working in pairs or small groups can be very effective in increasing both the number of trials and the amount of feedback that individuals get within a given amount of practice time. Also, by providing feedback, players are improving their mental understanding of how the skill should be performed.

Step 4: Evaluate Results and Take Appropriate Action

Evaluation of player performance must occur on a continuing basis during practices and games. This is the only valid means to answer the question, "Are the players achieving the skills?" If they are, you have two appropriate actions to take:

1) Enjoy it. You are making an important contribution to your players.

2) Consider how you can be even more efficient. How can you get the same results in less time or how can even more be achieved within the same time allotment?

If the players are not achieving the instructional objectives, it is important to ask, "Why?" Although it is possible that you have players who are very inept at learning, this is seldom the case. First, assume that you are using inappropriate instructional techniques or that you simply did not provide enough instructional time. Go through the instructional factors related to effective planning, motivating, communicating, and discipline in this section, and possibly conditioning in Section VII, to determine which of the guidelines or steps were missed and/or inappropriately implemented. Then alter your subsequent practices accordingly. Steps for how to complete this type of evaluation are described in more detail in Chapter 10, Evaluating Coaching Effectiveness. Continuous trial, error, and revisions usually result in improved coaching effectiveness, which then translates into increased achievement by the players. In instances where you cannot determine what to alter, seek help from a fellow coach whose teams are consistently strong in the physical skills that are causing your players difficulty. This is an excellent way to obtain some good ideas for altering your approach.

APPLYING GUIDELINES FOR EFFECTIVE INSTRUCTION

As you provide for practice and feedback to your players (Step 3 of the instructional model illustrated earlier), you may wish to use some of the guidelines for instruction that have been found by recent research to be effective in improving student learning. Nine guidelines for effective instruction are named below and described in more detail in Supplement 5-1.

1. Set realistic expectations.

2. Structure instruction.

3. Establish an orderly environment.

4. Group your players according to ability.

5. Maximize on-task time.

6. Maximize the success rate.

7. Monitor progress.

8. Ask questions.

9. Promote a sense of control.

PLANNING EFFECTIVE PRACTICES

If practices are to be effective, they must be directed at helping players meet the objectives defined in the season plan. Objectives are best achieved by using appropriate instructional methods. Instruction is both formal (planned) and informal (not planned) and can occur during practices, games, and special events. Virtually any time players are in your presence, there is potential for teaching and learning.

All coaches, even those who are highly knowledgeable and experienced, are more effective teachers when they organize and plan their instruction. This does not mean that unplanned instruction should not be used to assist your players in learning more about soccer. In fact, unplanned events that occur often present ideal opportunities to teach important skills. By capitalizing on temporary but intense player interest and motivation, a skilled coach can turn an unplanned event into an excellent learning opportunity. For example, an opponent's passing attack may prove so effective during a game that your defensive players become highly motivated to learn the defensive tactics necessary to stop such an attack. Often these "teachable moments" are unused by all but the most perceptive coaches.

Features of an Effective Practice

Scheduled practice sessions usually constitute the largest portion of contact between you and your players. Each practice session requires that you select both the content of instruction and its method of presentation. To do this effectively and efficiently, each of your practice plans should:

- be based upon previous planning and seasonal organization (see Section I, Chapter 2, Planning for the Season),
- list the objectives which will be the focus of instruction for that practice,
- show the amount of time allotted to each objective during the practice,
- identify the activities (instructional, drill, or scrimmage) that will be used to teach or practice the objectives,
- identify equipment and/or special organizational needs, and
- apply the guidelines for effective instruction (included in Supplement 5-1).

An effective practice combines the seasonal plan, assessment of your players' abilities, instruction, and an evaluation of practice results. The evaluation portion should be retained even if it means changing future practices to meet the needs of players that may have been unanticipated. The features of a good practice plan are outlined in Table 5-1. Not all of the features are appropriate for every practice you conduct. There should be a good reason, however, before you decide not to include each feature.

Table 5-1. *Features of an effective practice.*

FEATURES	•	COACHING ACTIVITY
Practice Overview	•	Inform the team about the contents and objectives of the practices (e.g., important new skills, positional play, new drills) to motivate and mentally prepare them for the upcoming activity.
Warm-up	•	Physically prepare the team for each practice by having them engage in light to moderate aerobic activity sufficient to produce slight sweating. Follow this by specific stretching activities.
Individual skills and drills	•	Review and practice objectives previously covered.
Small group skills and drills	•	Introduce and teach new objectives.
Team skills and drills	•	Incorporate the individual and small group drills into drills involving the entire team.
Cool-down	•	At the end of each practice, use activities of moderate to light intensity, followed by stretching, to reduce protential soreness and to maintain flexibility.
Team talk	•	Review key points of practice, listen to player communications, make announcements, and distribute handouts.

Format and Inclusions in a Practice Plan

Several ingredients that should be included in a practice plan are: the date and/or practice number; the objectives and key points, drills and/or activities; amount of practice time devoted to each objective; equipment needs; and a place for evaluation. The date and/or practice number are helpful to maintain organizational efficiency. The objectives are the reason for conducting the practice and, therefore, must be clearly in mind prior to selecting the activities, drills, games, or scrimmage situations you believe will develop player competence. The key points of each objective you desire to have your players achieve must be clearly in mind. It also helps to have the key points written prominently on your plan or drill notes. Supplement 5-2 provides an example plan written to cover the objectives of practice #5 on the season calendar included in Section I, Chapter 2 (Planning for the Season). In order to communicate the essential features of a practice plan to many readers, this example contains far more narrative than is necessary for most coaches. You need to record only information that will be needed at some later date. Accordingly, phrases, symbols, key words, and other personalized communications will substitute for the more extensive narrative included in the example. A full-sized copy of the practice plan form which you can reproduce is included in Supplement 5-3.

• Practice Time

Allotting time for each objective during practices is a difficult but important task for the coach. Sufficient practice time results in the majority of your players making significant improvement on each objective. Although these changes may not be noticeable in a single practice session, they must occur over the season. Assigning too little time results in players' exposure to individual techniques but often little change in performance. Keep in mind, however, that practice time must be distributed across several objectives (and/or drills or activities within the practice of a single objective) to keep players' interest high. This is particularly true for younger players who tend to have short attention spans and thus need frequent changes in drills or activities.

• Instructional Activities

The selection and implementation of instructional activities, drills, or games should constitute most of each practice session. Players' achievements are directly related to your choices and actions in these important areas. Instructional activities should be conducted in accordance with the guidelines presented in Supplement 5-1. Because most practices are composed largely of drills, you should follow the same guidelines in Supplement 5-1, and develop your drills to include these important features:

- have a meaningful name
- require a relatively short explanation
- provide an excellent context for mastering an objective
- match skill, knowledge, or fitness requirements of soccer
- keep players' "on task time" high
- are easily modified to accommodate skilled and unskilled players
- provide opportunity for skill analysis and feedback to players

Drills should be written on file cards or paper. It is also helpful to organize them according to objective, group size (individual, small group, team), possession (offensive and defensive), and position (goalkeeper, fullback, midfielder, or forward). When you find a good drill, classify it and add it to your collection. A format for collecting drill information is provided in reproducible form in Supplement 5-4.

• Equipment Needs

The equipment needed to conduct a drill or activity should be recorded on the practice plan. It is very frustrating to realize after you have explained and set up an activity or drill for your team that the necessary equipment is missing. Therefore, after you have planned all the activities for your practice, review them and list essential equipment needed.

- **Evaluation**

The evaluation/comment portion of the practice plan can be used to highlight ways to alter the practice to accommodate players at unexpected skill levels, or to note changes that should be made to improve the plan. It also provides a place for announcements or other information that needs to be communicated to your players.

SUMMARY

Effective instruction is the foundation of successful coaching. It requires practices which include clear communication of what is to be learned, a continuous evaluation of players' performance on the objectives of the practices, a systematic method of instruction, and the use of guidelines for instruction which have been associated with player achievement.

Systematic instruction includes: a) establishing credibility; b) providing precise communication of what needs to be learned; c) providing many practice trials and specific, immediate, and positive feedback; and d) evaluating the achievement of your players. Use of the guidelines for effective instruction (realistic expectations, structured instruction, order, grouping, maximizing time, success, monitoring and providing a sense of control) in combination with systematic instruction will maximize the results of your coaching effort.

GUIDELINES FOR EFFECTIVE INSTRUCTION

> QUESTIONS TO CONSIDER
> - What are the nine guidelines for effective instruction?
> - How can setting realistic expectations for your players influence their achievement?
> - How can you coach players of different ability levels on the same team?
> - When players are attempting to learn new things, what success rate motivates them to want to continue to achieve?

Introduction

This supplement provides an overview of nine guidelines for effective instruction. As you plan your practices, this list should be reviewed to help maximize your coaching effectiveness. The nine guidelines are:

1. Set realistic expectations.

2. Structure instruction.

3. Establish an orderly environment.

4. Group your players.

5. Maximize on-task time.

6. Maximize the success rate.

7. Monitor progress.

8. Ask questions.

9. Promote a sense of self-control.

1. Set Realistic Expectations

The expectations that coaches communicate to their players can create a positive climate for learning that will influence their achievement.[7] Clear, but attainable, objectives for performance and expenditure of effort for all players on your team will facilitate achievement. As stated in a recent review,[3] the reasons associated with this occurrence may be related to the following ideas.

In comparison to athletes for whom coaches hold high expectations for performance, the athletes perceived to be low performers are:

- more often positioned farther away from the coach;
- treated as groups, not individuals;
- smiled at less;
- receive less eye contact from the coach;
- called on less to answer questions;
- given less time to answer questions;
- have their answers responded to less frequently;
- praised more often for marginal and inadequate responses;
- praised less frequently for successful responses; and
- interrupted more often.

---

*Players tend to achieve in accordance with
the coaches' expectations.*

Coaches and former athletes will be able to understand how even a few of the above responses could reduce motivation and achievement. It is saddening that many capable children are inappropriately labeled as non-achievers on the basis of delayed maturity, poor prior experience, inadequate body size, body composition, and/or many other factors which mask their true ability. Yet, if expectations are low, achievement is likely to be low.

There are at least two important messages in this guideline:

- Expect that, as the coach, you are going to significantly improve the skills, fitness, knowledge of rules and strategies, and attitude of every one of your players during the course of the season.
- Set realistic goals for your players. Make a commitment to help each player achieve those individual goals, and expect improvement.

2. Structure Instruction

Your players' achievements are strongly linked to clear communication of the intended outcomes of instruction (objectives), why the goals and objectives are important (essential or prerequisite skills), and what to do to achieve outcomes (instructional directions).[2, 3] Effective instruction is based upon the systematic organization of the content to be taught. The critical steps to take are as follows:

1. Select the essential skills, fitness capacities, knowledge of rules and strategies, and personal/social skills from the many options available.

2. Clearly identify the elements of acceptable performance for each objective that you include in your plans.

3. Organize and conduct your practices to maximize the opportunity your players have to acquire the objectives by using the effective teaching practices contained in this chapter.

3. Establish An Orderly Environment

High achievement is related to the following elements:[4]

- an orderly, safe, business-like environment with clear expectations;
- player accountability for effort and achievement; and
- rewards for achievement of expectations.

Where such conditions are missing, achievement is low.

The following coaching actions will lessen behavioral problems that interfere with learning and, at the same time, promote pride and responsibility in team membership.

- Maintain orderly and disciplined practices.
- Maintain clear and reasonable rules that are fairly and consistently enforced.

Caution: strong, over-controlling actions can backfire. Over-control causes frustration and anxiety while under-control leads to lack of achievement. The best of circumstances is a relaxed, enjoyable but business-like environment. The ability to balance these two opposing forces to maximize achievement and enjoyment by keeping both in perspective may be one of your most difficult tasks.

4. Group Your Players

Decisions about the size and composition of groups for various learning tasks are complex, but nonetheless related to achievement.[8] Typically, in groups of mixed ability, the player with average ability suffers a loss in achievement, while the player with low ability does slightly better. The critical condition for grouping to be effective is to have players practicing at the skill levels needed to advance their playing ability. Typically, this involves groups of similar ability being appropriately challenged. Although this can be difficult to achieve, most effective coaches design practices that maximize a type of individualized instruction.

Your team will have individuals at many levels of ability. While this situation presents a seemingly impossible grouping task, there are some good solutions to this problem.

- When a skill, rule, or strategy is being taught that all your athletes need to know, use a single group for instruction.

- As you identify differences in your players' abilities, divide the team and place players of similar ability in small groups when working on these tasks.

- When a skill, rule, or strategy is being practiced where individual athletes are at several levels of ability (initial, intermediate, or later learning levels), establish learning stations that focus on specific outcomes to meet each groups' needs.

The placement of players into smaller learning groups must be independently decided for each skill, rule, or strategy. A player who is placed at a high level group for practicing individual techniques for receiving and controlling the ball should not necessarily be placed in a high level group for practicing shooting or defensive techniques. It is important that the following occur at each learning station:

- order is established and maintained (an assistant may be necessary),

- tasks that are to be mastered at each station must be clearly understood,

- many opportunities must be provided at each station, and

- a means for giving immediate, specific, and positive feedback must be established.

5. Maximize On-Task Time

Research on the amount of time that athletes are active in the learning process, rather than standing in lines or watching others perform, reveals that actual "engaged" learning time in practices is regularly less than 50 percent of the total practice time, and often falls to five to ten percent for individual athletes. There are several actions you can take as a coach to maximize the use of available time.

- Reduce the number of athletes who are waiting in line by using more subgroups in your drills.

- Secure sufficient supplies and equipment so that players do not have lengthy waits for a turn.

- Reduce the transition time between drills by preplanning practices to minimize reformulation of groups and equipment set-up time.

- Use instructional grouping practices that have players practicing skills at their appropriate performance level.

- Clearly outline and/or diagram each portion of practice and communicate as much of that information as possible before going on the field.

- Complete as many pre and post warm-up/cool-down activities as possible outside of the time scheduled on the field.

- Recruit assistants (parents or older players) to help you with instructional stations under your supervision.

Remember: saving 10 minutes a day across 14 weeks of two practices per week equals 280 minutes of instructional time for each player. Time gained by effective organization is available for practicing other skills of the game.

6. Maximize The Success Rate

The relationship among successful experiences, achievement, and motivation to learn is very strong.[4, 5] The basic message in this research is to ask players to attempt new learning that yields 70-90 percent successful experiences. This level of success will motivate them to want to continue to achieve. There are two major implications of the finding:

- reduce each skill, rule, or strategy into achievable sub-skills and focus instruction on those sub-skills; and

- provide feedback to the players such that, on most occasions, something that they did is rewarded, followed by specific instructions about what needs more work, and ending with an encouraging "Try again!"

7. Monitor Progress

If you organize your practice to allow athletes to work at several stations in accordance with their current abilities and needs, it follows that players often will work independently or in small groups. When players are left to work on their own, they often spend less time engaged in the activities for which they are responsible. When coaches are actively moving about, monitoring progress, and providing individual and small group instructional feedback, players make greater gains.[4] Within this context, you can provide much corrective feedback, contingent praise, and emotionally neutral criticism (not personal attacks or sarcasm) for inappropriate behavior. These actions have a positive influence on both achievement and attitude.

8. Ask Questions

Asking questions also relates to player achievement.[1] Questions must, however, promote participation or establish, reinforce, and reveal factual data associated with physical skills, rules, or strategies. Use of this teaching technique seems to work best when there is a pause of three or more seconds before you ask for a response, at which time the players are cued to think about the answer.[6]

9. Promote A Sense Of Control

Your players should feel that they have some control over their own destiny if they are to reach their potential as soccer players. This sense of control can be developed by:

- organizing your instruction to result in many successful experiences (i.e., opportunities to provide positive feedback);

- teaching your players that everyone learns at different rates and to use effort and their own continuous progress as their primary guides (avoid comparing their skill levels to those of other players.); and

- encouraging individual players to put forth their best effort (reward best efforts with positive comments, pats on the back, thumbs up signs, or encouraging signals).

In these ways, players quickly learn that the harder they work and the more they try, the more skillful they will become. At the same time, you will be eliminating the natural feeling of inferiority or inability that grows in the presence of feedback which is limited to pointing out errors. Although some players develop in almost any practice situation, many potentially excellent players will not continue in an environment where they feel there is no possibility of gaining the coach's approval.

Summary

The information in this supplement provides a base from which effective practices can be developed and implemented. No coach can claim that they use all of these guidelines throughout all of their practice sessions. All coaches should, however, seek to use more of these techniques more frequently as they plan and implement their practices.

References

1. Brophy, J.E. & Evertson, C. (1976). *Learning from teaching: A developmental perspective.* Boston, MA: Allyn and Bacon.

2. Bruner, J. (1981, August). *On instructability.* Paper presented at the meeting of the American Psychological Association, Los Angeles, CA.

3. Fisher, C.W., Berliner, D.C., Filby, N.N., Marliave, R.S., Caher, L.S., & Dishaw, M.M. (1980). Teaching behaviors, academic learning time and student achievement: An overview. In C. Denham and A. Lieberman (Eds.) *Time to learn.* Washington, D.C.: U.S. Department of Education, National Institute of Education.

4. Fisher, C.W., Filby, N.N., Marliave, R.S., Cahen, L.S., Dishaw, M.M., Moore, J.E., & Berliner, D.C. (1978). Teaching behaviors, academic learning time and student achievement. Final report of *Phase III-B, Beginning teacher evaluation study, technical report.* San Francisco, CA: Far West Laboratory for Educational Research and Development.

5. Rosenshine, B.V. (1983). Teaching functions in instructional programs. *The Elementary School Journal*, 83, 335-352.

6. Rowe, M.B. (1974). Wait time and rewards as instructional variables: Their influence on language, logic, and fate control. Part one, Wait time. *Journal of Research in Science Teaching*, 11, 81-94.

7. Rutter, M., Maugham, B., Mortmore, P., & Ousten, J. (1979). *Fifteen thousand hours.* Cambridge, MA: Harvard University Press.

8. Webb, N.M. (1980). A process-outcome analysis of learning in group and individual settings. *Educational Psychologist*, 15, 69-83.

SAMPLE PRACTICE PLAN

QUESTIONS TO CONSIDER
- How should coaches determine the amount of detail to be included in their practice plans?
- How is a practice plan related to a season planning calendar?
- What are the features of an effective practice?
- How can practice plans help a coach to achieve objectives previously listed for the team?

Introduction

This supplement contains a sample practice plan and an overview of the organization and content of the plan. This plan is presented as an example of what might be included in a well-organized practice of intermediate level youth players (10 to 13 years of age) conducted by a highly organized coach. This practice plan illustrates the fifth of eight practices before the first game. Its outline is derived from the procedures outline in the season planning calendar presented in Section I, Chapter 2, Planning for the Season.

Organization and Content of the Sample Practice Plan

Note that a considerable amount of detail is included in the sample practice plan. This is provided to make it easier to understand the nature of the activities included in the practice. When you prepare a plan for your own use, the level of detail can be substantially reduced. If you are a seasoned coach, you may only need the names of the drills, key coaching points, and a few diagrams. However, most inexperienced coaches will need more detail.

Note that this sample practice plan contains all of the features of an effective practice which are presented in Table 5-1 of this chapter. These features have also been checked at the bottom of the first page of the sample practice plan.

PRACTICE PLAN

OBJECTIVES: *Review and practice set plays (throw-in, free kicks, penalty kick, and drop ball); practice passing and receiving and controlling with the inside and outside of both feet; practice goalkeeper distribution (bowled ball and sling throw) and saves (standing scoop and various air balls); review offensive and defensive traction in small group games.*

DATE: *April 14*

#: _____5_____

TIME	COACHING ACTIVITIES (name, description, diagram, key points)
4:30	*Overview of practice activities:*
	(1) set plays: throw-in, free kicks, penalty kick, and drop ball
	(2) individual techniques for field players
	(3) individual techniques for goalkeepers
	(Key point: Respond to any questions from the players!)
4:31	*Warm-up: (1) independent dribbling, (2) dancing with the ball, and (3) juggling*
	Stretching: (1) calf stretch (2) seated straddle
	(3) kneeling quad stretch (4) trunk and hip stretch
	(5) shoulder stretch

EQUIPMENT: *All players bring a ball. Bring 16 cones, portable chalkboard, chalk, eraser, and handouts to review set plays.*

NOTE: Features of an effective practice include: ✓ practice overview; ✓ warm-up; ✓ individual skills and drills; ✓ small group skills and drills; ✓ team skills and drills; ✓ cooldown; ✓ team talk. (Check the features included in this practice plan.)

EVALUATION: _____

_____

PRACTICE PLAN CONTINUED

TIME	COACHING ACTIVITIES (name, description, diagram, key points)
4:36	*Review and practice set plays:* *(1) indirect and direct free kicks: (a) chalk talk to review handout on free kicks, (b) practice set plays with passive pressure from the defense, middle, and offensive thirds of the field. (Key points: 10 yards from the ball, quick set up and alignment of defensive wall)*
4:50	*(2) penalty kick: (a) chalk talk to review handout on the penalty kick, (b) practice penalty kicks with goalkeepers, offense, and defense. (Key points: kicker—place ball, select target, kick with confidence; goalkeeper—both feet on the goal line concentrate on the ball, signal when ready)*
5:00	*(3) throw-in: (a) chalk talk to review handout on "who takes the throw-in" from various locations on the field, (b) practice throw-in using checking runs and groups of 3s (thrower, receiver and defender) with passive pressure. (Key points: avoid foul throw-ins, make good lead passes which can be handled by the receiver)*
5:06	*(4) drop ball: (a) chalk talk to review handout on the drop ball, (b) practice drop ball restarts from various locations on the field. (Key points: ball must strike the ground before kicking, player receiving ball directly from a drop ball kick is not off side)*

PRACTICE PLAN CONTINUED

TIME	COACHING ACTIVITIES (name, description, diagram, key points)
	Practice individual field player techniques: passing and receiving and controlling with the inside and outside of the foot (passive pressure on defense). (Keep groups of 3s from previous drills.)
5:11	*(1) Open space—pass—receive* *(Key points: make lead pass which can be controlled when teammate is in open position, quickly gain control of the pass; rotate positions after a few successful passes)*
5:16	*(2) "On"—"time" receiving drill* *"On"* *"Time"* *(Key points: communicate early to player receiving pass if time, use "touch and turn" techniques to turn the ball)*
5:21	*(3) Lead passing drill* *(Key points: make lead pass and sprint to open space, use 2 groups so players are not waiting in lines, gain control of the ball with a dribble before returning a pass, try to keep the ball on the ground, select various individual passing and receiving techniques (inside and outside of the foot, use both feet)*

	PRACTICE PLAN CONTINUED
TIME	**COACHING ACTIVITIES** (name, description, diagram, key points)

Practice individual goalkeeper techniques: distribution—bowled ball and sling throw; saves—standing scoop and various air ball saves (partner drills).

TIME		
5:26	*(1) bowled ball and standing scoop save*	*(Key points: bowler—step toward target, release ball close to the ground, follow through in direction of target; receiver—position body in line with the ball, position hands and arms close together behind the ball, scoop ball to chest by wrapping hands and arms around the ball)*
5:31	*(2) sling throw and various air ball saves (scoops—low and waist-high; overhead—chest, head, and above-head).*	*(Key points: thrower—side toward target, exchange arm positions, release ball over head, impart backspin, follow through by taking step forward after release; receiver—back up ball whenever possible)*
5:36	*(3) crab walk, dive, and catch drill*	*(Key points: catch ball with overhand positioning, absorb force of landing along the side of the body)*

PRACTICE PLAN CONTINUED

TIME	COACHING ACTIVITIES (name, description, diagram, key points)
	Small group games and tactics:
	General rules of play—each team has a goal marked by cones, teams can score from either direction by kicking the ball on the ground through their opponent's goal, and the game does not stop after a goal.
5:40	*(1) 2 v 3* *(Key points: review tactics of play*
	(a) Defense—goal-side marking, pressuring, jockeying, and support
	(b) Offense—checking run and wall pass)
5:47	*(2) 3 v 3*
5:55	*Cool-down (same as warm-up and stretching at beginning of practice) During cool-down activities, remind players to: (1) review handouts on team formation, positional play, and set plays for next practice, and (2) bring a ball and wear shin guards for every practice.*

Objectives

The objectives of the sample practice plan should be taken directly from the objectives previously listed by the coach in a season planning calendar in Section I, Chapter 2. These objectives may need to be modified slightly because of what the coach was able to cover in previous practices and what the coach has learned from assessing the abilities of the players in previous practices.

Overview of Practice Activities

The overview of practice activities should last only a minute or less. The coach only needs to simply state what is planned for the practice. This helps to mentally prepare and organize the players for the practice. The overview gets the players to "think soccer" again. Therefore, a good time to respond to players' questions is immediately after the overview.

Warm-up and Stretching

The soccer specific warm-ups included in this sample practice plan consist of three light aerobic activities. These activities are used to increase the breathing rate, heart rate, and muscle temperature to exercise levels. They also help to reacquaint the athletes to their practice environments and prepare the muscles and joints for stretching activities which follow.

The five stretching activities were selected to maintain flexibility in several muscle groups and joints of the body. On average, approximately 45 seconds can be spent on each of the seven activities included in this phase of the practice. Thus, it is assumed that the players are familiar with each of the seven activities and can quickly change from one to the next. If any of these stretches needs to be taught to the players, more time will be needed for the warm-up session or some activities will need to be excluded.

Review and Practice Set Plays

The coach must be ambitious and highly organized to cover four set plays in the 30 minutes allotted. The only way this could be achieved is for the players to have received handouts on these set plays at a previous practice and to have been encouraged to read and study these set plays before the current practice. Key points of each of the set plays is briefly reviewed on a portable chalkboard before having the players practice them.

Note that practice for the throw-in and drop ball are grouped together at the end of this phase of the sample practice plan. These are organized in this manner because both of them require players to work in groups of threes. This same grouping is used for all practice activities in the next phase of the practice. This organizational arrangement saves the time necessary for players to change from one group size to another.

Practice Individual Field Player Techniques

The drills selected and the manner in which they are conducted should challenge the players to achieve higher levels of performance of individual skills. Selection and conduct should be based upon what the coach has learned from observing the players in previous practices and an understanding of the direction players must proceed to achieve future goals.

In this sample practice plan, 15 minutes is provided for three drills. Players should be required to use the inside and outside of both feet during this phase of their practice. While the players are engaged in the practice of individual techniques, the coach should be active in observing performances, providing individual and immediate feedback to the players, and developing ideas about what to include in future practices to improve their level of performance.

Note that in addition to passing and receiving the ball with the inside and outside of both feet, players should be alerted to other aspects of play that are integral parts of these drills. These aspects include offensive and defensive techniques associated with opening and closing space, making lead passes, and communicating. Also, if the drills run at a brisk pace, the players may concomitantly enhance their fitness level. The potential for simultaneous enhancement of individual techniques, tactical knowledge, and fitness of players within the same practice activities is an example of economical training.

Practice Individual Goalkeeping Techniques

Many of the same comments associated with the practice of individual field player techniques (previous section) pertain to the practice of individual goalkeeper techniques.

It is inappropriate to encourage or permit the labeling of a young player as a "goalkeeper" and not to encourage these players to experience other field positions. Similarly, players who consider themselves to be field players should also be exposed to the individual techniques and tactics associated with the goalkeeper position. In this sample practice plan, all participate in the 14 minutes of drills directed at enhancing individual techniques of distribution (bowled ball and sling throw) and making saves (standing scoop and various air ball saves). For older players who had clearly determined their preference about playing either a field or goalkeeper position, the practice of individual techniques for these two types of positions would be separated. This separation could be handled in the practice through the use of an assistant coach.

Small Group Games

Fifteen minutes has been allotted for two small group games (2 v 3 and 3 v 3) in this practice plan. From the players' perspectives, competitive games are often the highlight of the practice. Alerting your players at the beginning of the practice (Overview of Practice Activities) that you have scheduled some competitive game for the end of practice encourages them to participate in other phases of the practice in an efficient manner. It should be noted, however, that small group games and controlled scrimmages are not just a fun reward for a team that pays attention during the practice. These competitive and dynamic activities are lead-up games to full-sided competition. A knowledgeable coach can use small sided games and controlled scrimmages to teach players offensive and defensive tactics as well as the transition of individual techniques into the skills of play.

The two small sided games selected for this sample practice plan build upon less complicated games (1 v 2 and 2 v 2) included in previous practices and lead up to a controlled scrimmage.

Cool-Down

In this sample practice plan the same activities are used in the cool-down as were planned for the warm-up and stretching for the beginning of the practice. The cool-down activities could differ from the warm-up activities. The important aspect of the cool-down activities, however, is that they involve the body parts exercised during the practice. This will help clear out waste products built up in the muscle, reduce the pooling of blood in the extremities, reduce the potential for soreness in the muscles, and prevent the loss of flexibility that may accompany intense muscular exercise.

Note that, in an attempt to save time, simple information can be given to the players while they are engaged in their cool-down activities.

Equipment

After coaches plan their practice, they should review each activity to determine what equipment will be needed to carry out the practice. A written list, included on the practice plan, is helpful when coaches are in a hurry to get to practice on time.

Evaluation

The evaluation of the practice should be completed after the practice and before planning the next practice. This evaluation should address (a) the appropriateness of the organization and content of the practice, (b) the success of the coaching methods used, and (c) the degree to which planned objectives (physical skills, tactics, personal and social skills, and fitness) were achieved. This type of evaluation is helpful in improving your coaching methods and in directing future practices to meet the needs of your players.

Summary

The sample practice plan and overview of its organization and content are presented in this supplement to provide guidance and insight to coaches for planning their own practice plans. It is not presented to be directly used by coaches because each team is unique in its needs at any point in time during the season. Therefore, coaches should plan each practice session to meet the specific needs of their players.

PRACTICE PLAN

OBJECTIVES:_____

_____

_____

_____

DATE:_____

#: _____

TIME	COACHING ACTIVITIES (name, description, diagram, key points)

EQUIPMENT:_____

_____

NOTE: Features of an effective practice include: _____ practice overview; _____ warm-up; _____ individual skills and drills; _____ small group skills and drills; _____ team skills and drills; _____ cool-down; _____ team talk. (Check the features included in this practice plan.)

EVALUATION: _____

_____

PRACTICE PLAN CONTINUED

TIME	COACHING ACTIVITIES (name, description, diagram, key points)

DRILL NAME: _____ **CLASSIFICATION(S):**_____

OBJECTIVES: _____

EQUIPMENT: _____

SOURCES: _____

DIAGRAM: **DIRECTIONS:**

COMMENTS: _____
_____

MOTIVATING YOUR PLAYERS

Martha Ewing and Deborah Feltz

QUESTIONS TO CONSIDER
- Why do children play soccer?
- What techniques can you use to minimize the number of "dropouts" from your team?
- What are the four elements of "positive" coaching?
- What can you do to help your players set realistic goals for themselves?

INTRODUCTION

The key to understanding your athletes' motivation is to understand each of their needs. As a coach, you play an important role in determining whether an athlete's needs are fulfilled. Previous research indicates that motivation will be high and young athletes will persist in a sport if their needs are met by that sport. But what are those needs and why do children desire to participate in sports?

WHY YOUNG ATHLETES PARTICIPATE IN SOCCER

In order to help your players maintain or improve their motivation in soccer, you must understand why they participate and why some of them stop participating. Based on interviews with young athletes who participated in a variety of sports, the following reasons for playing were identified and are listed in the order of their importance.

1. To have fun

2. To improve skills and learn new ones

3. For thrills and excitement

4. To be with friends or make new friends

5. To succeed or win

While these research findings provide some insight as to why most children play soccer, they are only general guidelines. The best information available to you is to learn from the athletes on your team why they are participating in the soccer program.

To improve your players' motivation, you must know why they participate in soccer.

WHY YOUNG ATHLETES DROP OUT OF SOCCER

Knowing why some youngsters stop playing soccer can help you find ways to encourage them to continue playing. From a survey of 1,773 young athletes[6] who dropped out of soccer and other sports, we learned that the reason for dropping out was because they did not achieve the goals they set when they initially enrolled to play.

This is not surprising if you consider that their reasons for getting involved in sports represent goals that can only be achieved through participation. When these goals are not being met, withdrawal occurs. Some of the reasons most often cited for dropping out of sports are discussed in the following paragraphs.

Other Interests

Children are often very good at assessing their relative ability in various activities. They may "shop around" and participate in several sports and other activities before deciding which ones provide them the greatest chance of being successful.

Dropping soccer to achieve in other activities, such as music, basketball, swimming, dance, and scouting, is acceptable. When children tell you or their parents that they want to pursue other activities, they should be encouraged to do so but welcomed to return to soccer later if they desire.

Work

Many children who would like to participate in soccer discontinue because their help is needed at home or they desire to obtain a job. If it is possible, practices and games should be arranged at times that allow all individuals to stay involved. Attempt to find a creative alternative, so that having a job does not preclude participation in soccer. Although much can be learned from work, the lessons that can be learned in sport are also valuable.

Another compelling reason for sports participation during childhood is that this experience may be a prerequisite for successful performance in later years. However, children who find that they must discontinue their participation should be assured that they may return to soccer at a later time.

No Longer Interested

For many children, playing soccer is a prestigious achievement. However, once they get involved, some may determine that soccer is not as glamorous as it first appeared. Although these children may have enjoyed their sport experience, they may decide that other interests are more important and/or enjoyable.

Children with interests in other activities should not be forced by parents or pressured by coaches and peers to continue participation in a soccer program. Doing so often transforms a normally well-behaved child into one who becomes a discipline problem. Parents and coaches should give children a chance to explore other activities and return to soccer if they so decide.

Not Enough Playing Time

Children sign up for sports because they anticipate the enjoyment and skill development that will result from their involvement. Many young athletes who cited "not playing enough" as a reason for dropping out were telling coaches that they needed more playing time to achieve their goal. These children are not usually asking to be starters or even to play the majority of the time. However, to be told indirectly that they aren't good enough to play during a game can be devastating to a child's feelings of self-worth. Coaches of young athletes need to ensure that a fair and equitable pattern of play occurs both during practices and games.

Skills Were Not Improving

Young athletes want to learn skills and see themselves improving in those skills. Coaches need to recognize that each athlete is different in his/her skill level. Instruction should be designed to help each athlete on the team improve in performance abilities.

It is important to show athletes how they have improved. Too often, young athletes compare their skills to the skills of other athletes rather than their own past performances. This type of comparison is destructive to the self-esteem of unskilled players. Players of all ability levels should be taught to evaluate their performance based on the progress they are making.

Did Not Like the Coach

This reason for dropping out may be another way for athletes to tell coaches that they were not playing enough and their skills were not improving. In a study of youth sport participants, the athletes who did not like the coach said they did not like being yelled at, thought the coaches played only their favorite players, and did not think the coaches were fair.

To be effective, coaches must treat young athletes with the same respect that coaches expect from the athletes. It is not necessary or effective to yell at athletes to communicate with them. Avoid all sarcastic and degrading comments. Use a positive approach to create an enjoyable and motivating environment for players to learn and have fun playing the game.

HOW TO HELP MOTIVATE YOUR PLAYERS

Athletes are most highly motivated when they obtain what they seek from their participation in sport. Therefore, motivational techniques that you select should be based on the reasons athletes have for joining the team. The following strategies may help you improve your players' motivation.

Know Why Your Athletes Are Participating

Young athletes differ in their personalities, needs, interests, and objectives for playing soccer. You must, therefore, get to know your athletes as individuals to determine why they participate. One way to accomplish this is through a team meeting at the start of the season.

Ask your players why they are participating and what their personal objectives are for the season. They may be asked this question before, during, and after practices and special events or whenever you have a chance to talk one-on-one with your players.

Help Your Athletes Improve Skills And Learn New Skills

Skill improvement is a very important reason for joining a soccer team. Therefore, practice sessions should focus on skill development, with regular opportunities for players to measure their progress. In addition, you can help athletes set performance goals that are appropriate for them. For example, as young players first learn to receive and control the ball, they should practice on rolling balls that approach with a slow pace. More advanced players should be encouraged to practice receiving, controlling, and redirecting techniques on half volleys and air balls. As players improve, they can understand and measure their progress both in practice and in game situations.

Make Practices and Games Enjoyable

As indicated by various studies, young athletes want to have fun. This means they want to play; they do not want to sit on the bench or stand in long lines waiting their turn at a drill. One of the best ways to ensure that practices are enjoyable is to use short, snappy drills that result in all players being involved most of the time. You can also keep your players' interest by incorporating new and challenging drills. Your players may even be able to invent useful drills of their own.

Having a chance to display their skills during a game is an excellent motivator of young athletes.

In games, too, all players can be involved, even if they are sitting on the bench. Team members can be watching the individuals who are playing similar positions to learn from their good techniques or their mistakes. They can also watch for strategies used by the other team. Most importantly, however, they should all have a chance to play in every game. The knowledge that they will have a chance to display their skills during the course of the contest is a primary source of motivation before and after the experience. Players who sit on the bench, unable to test their skills in a game, are not likely to have fun.

Allow Players to be with Their Friends And Make New Friends

Many athletes view their soccer participation as a chance to be with their friends while doing something they enjoy. Allowing your players to have fun with their friends does not mean your practices have to be disruptive. You can encourage an esprit de corps within the team. Social activities, such as a midseason pizza party, require more time on your part but may foster rewarding friendships among players and coaches.

Remember, many of your players' friends may be on opposing teams. Encourage athletes to continue their friendships with players on opposing teams and even develop new friendships with opponents.

Help Players Understand the Meaning of Success

Children learn at an early age to equate winning with success and losing with failure. If athletes win a game, they feel good or worthy. If they lose, they feel incompetent or unworthy. This attitude toward winning can be discouraging to players, unless they are always winning. One of your most important roles, therefore, is to help your players keep winning in perspective. One way to accomplish this is to help your players understand that winning a game is not always under their control. For example, after losing a game, you may explain the loss to your team, "We ran the offense well today, but their goalie played very well, so we didn't get as many goals as we expected."

Your players also need to know that, although striving to win is an important objective in soccer, being successful in soccer also means making personal improvements and striving to do one's best. This attitude can be developed by:

- encouraging maximum effort during practices and games,

- rewarding effort, and

- helping players set important but realistic goals that they can attain and thus feel successful when they are achieved.

In helping your players understand the meaning of success, it is also important not to punish them when they fail, particularly if they gave a maximum effort.

Your coaching approach is the factor with the greatest influence on player motivation.

Use the Positive Approach to Coaching

Probably the most important factor that influences your players' motivation is the approach you take in coaching. There are many different styles or approaches used by coaches, but most fall into either of two categories: the negative approach and the positive approach.

● Negative Approach

The negative approach is the most visible model of coaching. The negative approach, demonstrated by some professional, college, and even high school coaches, is often highlighted in the media. This approach is one in which the coach focuses on performance errors and uses fear, hate, and/or anger to motivate players.

The negative approach doesn't work very well with young athletes. Constant criticism, sarcasm, and yelling often frustrate young athletes, deteriorate their self-confidence, and decrease their motivation. Remember that young athletes are just beginning to develop their skills, and they have fragile self-concepts.

Focus on correct aspects of performance and use liberal amounts of praise and encouragement.

● Positive Approach

The positive approach, in contrast, is one where the coach focuses on the correct aspects of performance and uses plenty of encouragement and praise for the tasks that players perform correctly. When errors occur, a coach who uses the positive approach corrects mistakes with constructive criticism.

A positive, supportive approach is essential when coaching young athletes if high levels of motivation are to be maintained. Key principles for implementing a positive approach to coaching are listed and explained in the following paragraphs.

Key Principles for Implementing A Positive Approach to Coaching[5]

- **Be liberal with rewards and encouragement.**

  The most effective way to influence positive behavior and increase motivation is through the frequent use of encouraging statements and rewards. The single most important difference between coaches whom young athletes respect most and those they respect least is the frequency with which coaches reward them for desirable behaviors.

  The most important rewards you can give are free. They include a pat on the back, a smile, applause, verbal praise, or a friendly nod. The greater your use of encouraging statements and rewards, the more your players will be motivated.

- **Give rewards and encouragement sincerely.**

  For rewards to be beneficial, they must be given sincerely. It will mean little to your players to tell them they played well if, in fact, they played poorly. This does not mean that you should not give them positive feedback about their performance when they make mistakes. You can point out their errors and at the same time praise them for the plays they performed well. It is important to be positive but also honest.

- **Reward effort and correct technique, not just results.**

  It is easy to praise a player who just scored a goal, but it is less natural to praise a player who tried hard but missed the shot. Sometimes, too, we forget to reward correct technique when it does not result in scoring goals. It is important, however, to reward players' efforts and the use of correct technique if you want this behavior to continue. An excellent shot on goal that is stopped by a spectacular save from the goalkeeper should be recognized as if it went in the goal. Occasionally, spend a few extra minutes with the lesser skilled players, before or after practice, to help them learn the correct techniques. This extra attention and caring will greatly increase their motivation to keep trying.

- **Have realistic expectations.**

    Base your rewards and encouragement on realistic expectations. Encouraging your soccer players to strive for World Cup standards without the feelings of success associated with achieving the many levels of performance leading to such standards will probably make them feel as though they have failed. It is much easier for you to give honest rewards when you have realistic expectations about your players' abilities.

Help Players Set Goals

Young athletes learn from parents and coaches that success is equated with winning and failure is equated with losing. Adopting this view of success and failure confuses the players. Let's take, for example, the play of Mary and Sue, members of the winning and losing teams, respectively.

Both girls played about half of the game. Mary's unsporting conduct was noticed quickly by the referee. After her second intentional tripping penalty, the referee cautioned her (yellow card). Early in the second half, she pushed an opponent in the penalty area, which resulted in her ejection (red card) and a penalty kick goal for the other team. Sue, on the other hand, masterfully used her practiced skills to set up three scoring opportunities and finally scored her first goal of the season. Because Mary was a member of the winning team, she was able to "laugh off" the penalty kick that she caused and revel in the success of her team. On the other hand, Sue felt that her efforts were worthless and joined her teammates in the disappointment of a 3-2 loss.

As adults, we recognize the inaccuracy of these perceptions. But, our actions at the end of a contest may tell our players that a winning score is what really matters.

Equating success or failure with winning or losing results in mixed messages to the athlete.

Athletes need a way to compare their current performances with their past performances to determine whether they are successful. This can be accomplished through goal setting. You can help each of your athletes establish individual goals. By doing this, each athlete can regain control over personal success or failure. In addition to removing the mixed messages, remind your players that there are some factors that are out of their control that may determine the outcome of a game. For example, the person your athlete is defending may be playing the best game of his/her career. Although your athlete is playing very well, there is just no stopping the opposing player. Or, due to injury or illness, a player is forced to play an unfamiliar position. Or, the grass is much higher than your players are used to playing on and all their passes are slightly off the mark. These examples highlight the need to establish personal improvement goals consistent with the objective of winning, but not entirely dependent on their achievement, to maintain player motivation. There are several guidelines for goal setting that can markedly help performance.

● Guidelines for Goal Setting

● Success should be possible for everyone on the team.

When implementing a goal setting program, each athlete must experience some success. In other words, each athlete should perform at a level that demands a **best effort** for the existing conditions. Help each athlete realize that effort equals success by focusing rewards on such efforts.

● Goals under practice conditions should be increasingly more challenging and goals during competition more realistic.

When you set up drills to work on passing or shooting, help your players set goals for practice that will challenge each of them to exceed a previous effort. For example, when practicing shooting on goals, you may ask your "star" kicker to make seven out of 10 shots in practice, while another player may be challenged with four out of 10. You should not expect the same level of performance in a game because neither you nor the players control all the factors. With this approach, motivation at practice is increased and players have a realistic chance of experiencing self-worth in a game.

● Goals should be flexible.

If goal setting is to be effective, goals must be evaluated frequently and adjusted depending on the athlete's success ratio. If an athlete is achieving the set goal, raise the goal to provide a greater challenge and motivation. If the goal is too difficult and the athlete is feeling frustration or failure, the goal should be lowered rather than have the athlete continue to experience failure. Having to lower the level of a goal may also be frustrating. Therefore, it is important to be as accurate as possible when initially setting goals for individual players.

● Individual goals should be set rather than team goals.

In general, team goals should not be made. This is because team goals are not under anyone's control, and they are often unrealistic. It is too difficult to assess accurately how a team will progress through a season. Will your team improve faster than other teams, at the same pace, or be a latecomer? If you set winning a certain number of games (e.g., eight of 10 games) as a goal and the team loses their first three games, you cannot achieve the goal even by winning the remaining seven games. This will only cause greater discouragement among team members. Work on individual improvement through goal setting and let the team's improvement reflect the individual's improvement.

Goal setting can be very effective in improving a player's performance, confidence, and self-worth. To be effective, however, you must know your players well enough to know when they are setting goals that are challenging, controllable, and realistic. In addition, goals must be adjusted to ensure feelings of self-worth.

DEALING WITH COMPETITIVE STRESS

Some coaches believe the best way to motivate a team for competition is to get them "psyched-up" before the game. With young athletes, however, getting psyched-up is not usually the problem; rather, the problem for them is getting "psyched-out."

Competitive stress in young athletes can originate from many sources—the athlete, the teammates, the coach, and the parents. When young athletes were asked what caused them to worry, among the most frequently given answers were:

1. improving their performance,

2. participating in championship games,

3. performing up to their level of ability, and

4. what their coach and parents would think or say.

Thus, young soccer players are most likely to be worried about performance failure. This worry about failure may increase players' anxieties, which, in turn, may cause poor performance, and eventually may decrease motivation. Figure 6-1 illustrates this cycle.

Figure 6-1. *A cyclic representation of performance failure.*

A good way to help your players avoid the effects of competitive stress is to reduce their fear of failure. This can be achieved by encouraging them to enjoy the game and to do their best. When your players lose or make a mistake, do not express displeasure; rather, correct their mistakes in a positive way by using the following sequence:

1. Start with a compliment. Find some aspect of the performance that was correct.

2. Tell the player what was wrong and how to correct it.

3. Give another positive statement such as, "Everyone makes mistakes. Keep working at it and you will get it."

This approach allows players to keep practicing their skills without the fear of making a mistake. The following guidelines may be helpful in preventing competitive stress.

Guidelines for Preventing Competitive Stress

- Set realistic goals.

- Use the positive approach when correcting mistakes.

- Eliminate the type of "pep talks" that communicate overemphasis on the game and the outcome.

APPROPRIATE USE OF TEAM TROPHIES, MEDALS, AND OTHER AWARDS*

Anyone who has ever attended a post-season soccer team party is aware that presenting trophies and awards is a common practice. Young athletes may receive any number of external awards, ranging from small ribbons to large trophies. However, whether it is appropriate to give children these awards is a controversial issue.

The advocates of awards such as medals, trophies, ribbons, certificates, and jackets indicate that they increase the children's desire and motivation to participate. Critics, in contrast, suggest that giving rewards to young athletes for activities in which they are already interested turns play into work and decreases their desire to participate. What is the answer? Awards or no awards?

While the advocates and critics of this issue would have us view it as a simple one, researchers have found that no simple answer exists. The purpose of this section is to provide you with information on how and in what situations external rewards influence young athletes' self-motivation to participate in sports.

---

* Much of the material presented in this section has been adapted from the work of Gould,[3,] 1980.

Understanding Rewards

An activity is defined as intrinsically motivating if an individual engages in that activity for personal interest and enjoyment, rather than for external reasons such as receiving a trophy, money, or publicity. In essence, young athletes are intrinsically motivated when they play for the sake of playing. Until recently, coaches assumed that if external rewards are given for activities that are already intrinsically motivating, the result will be a further increase in intrinsic motivation.

However, research has shown that this is not always the case. The presentation of extrinsic rewards for an already self-motivated activity may result in reduced intrinsic motivation. The following adapted story[1] illustrates how rewards can undermine intrinsic motivation.

> An old man lived next to an open field that was a perfect location for the neighborhood children's "pick-up" baseball games. Every afternoon the children would come to the field, choose sides, and engage in a noisy game. Finally, the noise became too much for the old man, so he decided to put an end to the games. However, being a wise old man who did not want to stir up trouble in the neighborhood, he changed the children's behavior in a subtle way.

> The old man told the children that he liked to hear them play, but because of his failing hearing, he had trouble doing so. He then told the children that if they would play and create enough noise so he could hear them, he would give each of them a quarter.

> The children gladly obliged. After the game, the old man paid the children and asked if they could return the next day. They agreed, and once again they created a great deal of noise during the game. However, this time the old man said he was running short of money and could only pay them 20 cents each. This still satisfied the children. However, when he told them that he would be able to pay only 5 cents on the third day, the children became angry and indicated that they would not come back. They felt that it was not worth the effort to make so much noise for only 5 cents apiece.

In this example, giving an external reward (money) for an already intrinsically motivating activity (playing baseball and making noise) resulted in decreased intrinsic motivation in the children. Hence, when the rewards were removed, the amount of participation decreased.

An increasing number of individuals have suggested that this phenomenon also occurs in organized youth sports such as soccer. In many programs, young athletes are presented with a substantial number of external awards (trophies, jackets, ribbons, etc.) for participating in an already desirable activity. Critics of external awards feel that giving these rewards decreases the youngsters' intrinsic motivation and when the rewards are no longer available, they no longer participate. Thus, external rewards may be one cause of discontinued participation in soccer.

Effects of Intrinsic Awards

There are two aspects of every reward that can influence a young athlete's intrinsic motivation.[2] These include:

- the controlling aspect of the reward, and
- the informational aspect of the reward.

● Controlling Aspects of Rewards

Extrinsic rewards can decrease intrinsic motivation when they cause players to perceive that their reasons for participating have shifted from their own internal control to factors outside (or external to) themselves. This was illustrated clearly in the story of the old man and the children. The children's reasons for playing shifted from internal factors (fun and self-interest) to external factors (money). Then, when the rewards were diminished, they no longer wanted to play. In essence, the children were no longer participating for the fun of it, but were participating solely for the reward. If young soccer players are made to feel that their primary reason for participating is to receive a trophy or a medal to please their parents, their intrinsic motivation will probably decrease.

● Informational Aspects of Rewards

External rewards can also communicate information to individuals about their competence and self-worth. If the reward provides information that causes an increase in a child's feelings of personal worth and competence, it will increase intrinsic motivation. If it provides no information about self-worth or competence or reduces these feelings about oneself, it will decrease intrinsic motivation.

*Seek to elevate feelings of self-worth
in the awards you give.*

A "Most Improved Player" award is a good example of how material rewards can enhance motivation. This award usually tells the player that he/she has worked hard and learned a lot. This award would probably increase intrinsic motivation. Constant failure and negative feedback, however, would decrease a young player's feelings of competence and self-worth and, in turn, would decrease intrinsic motivation. Consequently, you must help children establish realistic goals. When rewards are given, they should be based upon some known criteria (performance, effort, etc.). This helps to ensure that rewards provide the recipients with information to increase feelings of self-worth and competence.

● Informational Versus Controlling Aspects of Rewards

Because most rewards in children's athletics are based upon performance, thus conveying information about the recipient's self-worth, giving external rewards should never undermine intrinsic motivation. However, this may not always be true. Even though external rewards may convey information about a child's sense of personal competence, the child may perceive the controlling aspect as being more important than the information conveyed.[4] Thus, instead of increasing the young athletes' intrinsic motivation, the extrinsic rewards undermine children's interest in sports by causing them to perceive their involvement as a means to an end. They are pawns being "controlled" by the pursuit of winning the reward.

Practical Implications

Extrinsic rewards have the potential to either increase or decrease intrinsic motivation. Two key factors determine which will occur:

- If children perceive their soccer involvement as being controlled primarily by the reward (e.g., they are participating only to win the trophy or to please Mom or Dad), intrinsic motivation will decrease. In contrast, if children feel they are controlling their involvement (playing because they want to), then intrinsic motivation will increase.

- If the reward provides information that increases the young players' feelings of self-worth and competence, intrinsic motivation will increase. If, however, the reward provides no information at all or decreases a person's feelings of competence or self-worth, then intrinsic motivation will decrease.

These findings have important implications for you as the coach. Be very careful about using extrinsic rewards! These rewards should be relatively inexpensive and not used to "control" or "coerce" children into participation in already desirable activities. Moreover, because you play such a vital role in determining how children perceive rewards, you must keep winning in perspective and stress the non-tangible values of soccer participation (fun and personal improvement) as opposed to participating solely for the victory or the reward.

The frequent use of inexpensive or "free" rewards will increase player motivation.

One way to increase intrinsic motivation is to give your players more responsibility (more internal control) for decision making and for rule making.[4] This could be done by getting input from your athletes about making team rules or letting them help organize practices. Younger players could be selected to lead a drill or favorite warm-up exercise and given some playing time at positions they desire. Older, more experienced players could help conduct practices and make actual game decisions (allowing players to call some plays without interference, for example).

Intrinsic motivation can also be increased by ensuring that when external rewards are given, they provide information that increases your players' feelings of self-worth and competence. The easiest way to accomplish this is to have realistic expectations of the players. Not all children will have a winning season or place first in the tournament. However, some realistic goals can be set with each athlete in terms of improved personal skills, playing time, etc., and the players can be rewarded for achieving their goals. This could be accomplished through the use of "Unsung Hero" and/or "Most Improved Player" awards.

These "official" rewards are not nearly as important, however, as the simple ones that you can give regularly. Remember, some of the most powerful rewards are free (pat on the back, friendly nod, or verbal praise). These rewards should be frequently used to acknowledge each athlete's contribution to the team, personal improvement, or achievement of a personal goal.

Finally, remember that the rewards must be given for a reason that has meaning to your players. Rewards not given sincerely (not based upon some criteria of success) may actually decrease intrinsic motivation. Therefore, coaches must set realistic, attainable goals and reward children when they attain those goals.

SUMMARY

Children play soccer because they want to improve their skills, have fun, be with friends, and be successful. Children who drop out of soccer typically do so because one or more of their goals was not met. You can maximize your players' desire to participate, and help prevent them from dropping out, by getting to know them as individuals.

Learn why they are participating. Focus on skill development in practice sessions and make sure the practices are enjoyable. Allow time for friendships to develop by creating a cordial environment both on and off the field. Help players understand the meaning of success and have them set realistic goals.

Using a positive approach to coaching is the most effective way to improve players' performance. Positive coaching will also make playing and coaching more enjoyable. Be sure to reward effort and correct techniques in addition to the results that meet your expectations.

Having realistic expectations of players' performances will provide more opportunities to give rewards. However, where players make mistakes, use the positive approach to correcting errors. The positive approach involves issuing a compliment, correcting the error, and then finishing with another positive statement. Using a positive approach and helping players reach their goals are effective ways to motivate your players toward maximum performance.

Extrinsic rewards have the potential to either increase or decrease intrinsic motivation. Extrinsic rewards are most effective when they are kept in perspective, are inexpensive, and are used to reflect improvements in personal competence. The non-tangible values of participation in soccer should be stressed, as opposed to participating only for winning or for the reward.

REFERENCES

1. Casady, M. (1974). The tricky business of giving rewards. *Psychology Today* 8(4),52.

2. Deci, E.L. (1975). *Intrinsic motivation.* New York: Plenum.

3. Gould, D. (1980). *Motivating young athletes.* East Lansing, MI: Institute for the Study of Youth Sports.

4. Halliwell, W. (1978). Intrinsic motivation in sport. In W.F. Straub (Ed.), *Sport psychology: An analysis of athlete behavior.* Ithaca, NY: Movement Publications.

5. Smoll, F.L. & Smith, R.E. (1979). *Improving relationship skills in youth sport coaches.* East Lansing, MI: Institute for the Study of Youth Sports.

6. Youth Sports Institute (1977). *Joint legislative study on youth sports program, phase II.* East Lansing, MI: Institute for the Study of Youth Sports.

SUGGESTED READINGS

Orlick, T. (1980). *In pursuit of excellence.* Ottawa, Ontario: Coaching Association of Canada.

Singer, R.N. (1984). *Sustaining motivation in sport.* Tallahassee, FL: Sport Consultants International, Inc.

Smoll, F.L., & Smith, R.E. (1979). *Improving relationship skills in youth sports coaches.* East Lansing, MI: Institute for the Study of Youth Sports.

7

COMMUNICATING WITH YOUR PLAYERS

Martha Ewing and Deborah Feltz

QUESTIONS TO CONSIDER
- How can you send clear messages to your players?
- What is the positive approach to communication?
- What are the characteristics of a good listener?
- How can good communication skills improve your ability to coach?

INTRODUCTION

The most important skill in coaching is the ability to communicate with your players. It is critical to effectively carry out your roles of leader, teacher, motivator, and organizer. Effective communication not only involves skill in sending messages, but skill in interpreting the messages that come from your players and their parents.

SENDING CLEAR MESSAGES

Any means you use to convey your ideas, feelings, instructions, and/or attitudes to others involves communication. Thus, when communicating with your players, your messages may contain verbal as well as nonverbal information. Nonverbal messages can be transmitted through facial expressions such as smiling, or through gestures and body movements.

When you send messages to your players, you may, without thinking, send unintentional nonverbal information as well as your intentional verbal message. If your nonverbal message conflicts with what you say, your message will probably be confusing. For example, when you tell your players that they have done a good job and let your shoulders slump and heave a heavy sigh, don't be surprised if your players are less receptive to your next attempt at praise.

Another example of mixed messages occurs when you tell your players they should never question officials' calls and then you denounce an official's decision. If the need should arise to question an official's call, you should ask the official for clarification in a professional manner.

Using a Positive Approach to Communicate

Communication is more effective when you use the positive approach. The positive approach to communication between you and your athletes involves establishing:

- mutual trust,
- respect,
- confidence, and
- cooperation.

Essential Factors in Sending Clear Messages

● Getting and Keeping Attention

Getting and keeping your athletes' attention can be accomplished by making eye contact with them, avoiding potential distractions, being enthusiastic, and emphasizing the importance of what you have to say. For example, when you want to instruct your players on a new skill, organize them so everything you do is visible to them. Be sure that they are not facing any distractions, such as children playing on a nearby field. It is also helpful to use a story, illustration, or event that will highlight the importance or focus attention on the instruction that is to follow.

● Using Simple and Direct Language

Reduce your comments to contain only the specific information the player needs to know. For example, when a player makes a mistake in a pass-and-shoot drill, make sure your feedback is simple, focuses on one error at a time, and contains only information that the player can use to correct the mistake. Keep information simple and specific.

The positive approach to communication is an essential element of good coaching.

● Checking With Your Athletes

Make certain that your players understand what you are trying to say. Question them so you will know if they understood the key points of your message. For example, let's say you are trying to explain how to run the three-on-two passing-and-shooting drill. After showing them the drill, you can save time and frustration by asking your players before they practice the drill where they should pass the ball, what openings they should look for to decide if they should shoot or pass, and where they should move after passing or shooting the ball. If your athletes cannot answer these questions, they will not be able to run the drill.

- **Being Consistent**

Make sure your actions match your words. When a discrepancy occurs between what you say and what you do, players are affected most by what you do. "Actions speak louder than words." You need to practice what you preach if you wish to effectively communicate with your players and avoid the loss of credibility that comes with inconsistent behaviors.

- **Using Verbal and Nonverbal Communication**

Your athletes are more likely to understand and remember what you have said when they can see it and hear it at the same time. Using the previous example, simultaneously demonstrating the three-on-two drill while explaining the key points will result in clearer instructions.

BEING A GOOD LISTENER

Remember, too, that you must be a good listener to be an effective communicator. Communication is a two-way street. Being receptive to your players' ideas and concerns is important to them and informational to you.

*Part of good coaching involves
listening to your players.*

By listening to what your athletes say and asking them how they feel about a point, you can determine how well they are learning. Their input provides you the opportunity to teach what they do not understand.

Essential Factors in Good Listening Skills

- **Listening Positively**

Players want the chance to be heard and to express themselves. You can encourage this by using affirmative head nods and occasional one- to three-word comments (e.g., "I understand.") while you're listening. The quickest way to cut off communication channels is by giving "no" responses or negative head nods.

- **Listening Objectively**

Avoid prematurely judging the content of a message. Sincerely consider what your players have to say. They may have good ideas! A good listener creates a warm, non-judgmental atmosphere so players will be encouraged to talk and ask questions.

- **Listening With Interest**

Being a good listener means being attentive and truly interested in what your players have to say. Look and listen with concern. Listen to what is being said and how it is being said. Establish good eye contact and make sure your body also reflects your interest in your player's message. Be receptive to comments that are critical of you or your coaching. Criticism is the most difficult communication to accept, but it is often the most helpful in improving behavior.

- **Checking for Clarity**

If you are uncertain of what your athletes are communicating to you, ask them what they mean. This will help to avoid misinterpretation.

Being receptive to your players thoughts and comments is important to them, and it also provides you with essential information.

SUMMARY

The ability to communicate with your players is critical in your role as a coach. It is a skill that involves two major aspects: speaking and listening. Coaches who are effective communicators get and keep the attention of their players, send clear and simple messages, and check to make sure their message is consistent with their actions. They also have good listening skills, which involve listening positively, helpfully, objectively, and with concern.

SUGGESTED READINGS

Martens, R. (1987). *Coaches' guide to sport psychology*. Champaign, IL: Human Kinetics.

8

MAINTAINING DISCIPLINE

Martha Ewing and Deborah Feltz

QUESTIONS TO CONSIDER
- What is the best way to prevent misbehavior?
- Should players be involved in establishing team rules?
- How should team rules be enforced?
- What are the key points of an effective plan for handling misconduct?

INTRODUCTION

Coaches often react to athletes' misbehavior by yelling, lecturing, or using threats. These verbal techniques are used because we often do not know what else to do to regain control. Many discipline problems could be avoided, however, if coaches anticipated misbehavior and developed policies to deal with it.

Harsh comments may prevent misbehavior, but they often create a hostile, negative environment that reduces learning and motivation.

PLAN FOR SOUND DISCIPLINE

Although threats and lectures may prevent misbehavior in the short term, they create a hostile, negative atmosphere. Typically, their effectiveness is short-lived. Hostility between a coach and team members neither promotes a positive environment in which it is fun to learn the game of soccer nor motivates players to accept the coach's instructions.

Sound discipline involves a two-step plan that must be in place before the misbehaviors occur. These steps are: 1) define team rules, and 2) enforce team rules.

Children want clearly defined limits and structure for how they should behave. You can accomplish this without showing anger, lecturing, or threatening. As the coach, it is your responsibility to have a systematic plan for maintaining discipline before your season gets under way. If you have taken the time to establish rules of conduct, you will be in a position to react in a reasonable manner when children misbehave.

Children want clearly defined limits and structure for how they should behave.

● Define Team Rules

The first step in developing a plan to maintain discipline is to identify what you consider to be desirable and undesirable conduct. This list can then be used to establish relevant team rules. A list of potential behaviors to consider when identifying team rules is included in Table 8-1.

Your players (especially if you are coaching children who are 10 years of age or older) should be involved in establishing the rules for the team. Research has shown that players are more willing to live by rules when they have had a voice in formulating them.[1] This can be done at a team meeting, early in the season. The following introduction has been suggested[2] to establish rules with players:

> *"I think rules and regulations are an important part of the game because the game happens to be governed by rules and regulations. Our team rules ought to be something we can agree upon. I have a set of rules that I feel are important. But we all have to follow them, so you ought to think about what you want. They should be your rules, too."*

Table 8-1. *Examples of desirable and undesirable behavior to consider when making team rules.*

Desirable Behavior	Undesirable Behavior
Making every effort to attend all practices and games except when excused for justifiable reasons	Missing practices and games without legitimate reasons
Being on time for practices and games	Being late or absent from practices and games
Attending to instructions	Talking while the coach is giving instructions
Concentrating on drills	Not attending to demonstrations during drills
Treating opponents and teammates with respect	Pushing, fighting, and/or using abusive language with opponents and teammates
Giving positive encouragement to teammates	Making negative comments about teammates
Avoiding penalties	Intentionally fouling during the game
Bringing required equipment or uniform to practices and games	Forgetting to bring required equipment or uniform to games and practices
Reporting injuries promptly	Waiting till after the team roster is set to report an injury
Helping to pick up equipment after practices	Leaving equipment out for others to pick up

Rules of conduct must be defined in clear and specific terms. For instance, a team rule that players must "show good sportsmanship" in their games is not a very clear and specific rule. What, exactly, is showing good sportsmanship? Does it mean obeying *all* the rules, calling one's own fouls, or respecting officials' decisions? The Youth Sports Institute has adopted a code of sportsmanship which defines sportsmanship in more specific terms.[1] This code has been reprinted in Table 8-2. You may wish to use some of the items listed as you formulate your team rules.

Players are more willing to live by rules when they have had a voice in formulating them.

Remember, you are a part of the team and you should live by the same rules. You should demonstrate the proper behaviors so the children will have a standard to copy. As a coach, you must also emphasize that behaviors of coaches as seen on television (such as screaming, throwing chairs, and belittling and embarrassing players) are also examples of undesirable conduct!

Table 8-2. *Youth sportsmanship code.*

Areas of Concern	Sportsmanlike Behavior	Unsportsmanlike Behavior
Behavior toward officials	• no misconduct penalties • when questioning officials, do so in the appropriate manner, (e.g., lodge an official protest, have only designated individuals such as a captain address officials) • treat officials with respect and dignity at all times • thank officials after game	• arguing with officials • swearing at officials • misconduct penalties
Behavior toward opponents	• treat all opponents with respect and dignity at all times • talk to opponents after the game	• arguing with opponents • making sarcastic remarks about opponents • making aggressive actions toward opponents
Behavior toward teammates	• give only constructive criticism and positive encouragement	• making negative comments or sarcastic remarks • swearing at or arguing with teammates
Behavior toward spectators	• no talking	• arguing with spectators • making negative remarks/swearing at spectators
Behavior toward coach	• share likes and dislikes with coach as soon as possible	
Rule acceptance and infraction	• obey all league rules	• intentionally violating league rules • taking advantage of loopholes in rules (e.g., every child must play, so coach tells unskilled players to be ill on important game days)

• Enforce Team Rules

Not only are rules needed to maintain discipline, but these rules must be enforced so reoccurrences are less likely. Rules are enforced through rewards and penalties. Players should be rewarded when they abide by the rules and penalized when they break the rules. The next step, therefore, in developing a plan to maintain discipline, is to determine the rewards and penalties for each rule. Your players should be asked for suggestions at this point because they will receive the benefits or consequences of the decisions. When determining rewards and penalties for the behaviors, the most effective approach is to use rewards that are meaningful to your players and appropriate to the situation. Withdrawal of rewards should be used for misconduct. A list of potential rewards and penalties that can be used in soccer is given in Table 8-3.

The best way to motivate players to behave in an acceptable manner is to reward them for good behavior. When appropriate behavior is demonstrated, comment accordingly or be ready to use nonverbal interactions such as smiling or applauding. Some examples are:

- "We only had three fouls in that game, that's the fewest we ever had. Way to be!"

- "I know you are all very disappointed in losing this game. I was real proud of the way you congratulated and praised the other team after the game."

- "Do you realize that for our first five practices everyone was dressed and ready to play at 3 o'clock, our starting time? That helped make the practice go better. Keep it up! Let's see if we can make it a tradition!"

Penalties are only effective when they are meaningful to the players. Examples of ineffective penalties include showing anger, giving a player an embarrassing lecture, shouting at the player, or assigning a physical activity (e.g., running laps or doing push-ups). These penalties are ineffective because they leave no room for positive interactions between you

Table 8-3. *Examples of rewards and penalties that can be used in soccer.*

Rewards	Penalties
Being a starter	Being taken out of a game
Playing a desired position	Not being allowed to start
Leading an exercise or part of it	Sitting out during practice
Praise from you	• until responding properly
• in team meeting	• a specific number of minutes
• to media	• rest of practice or sent home early
• to parents	Dismissed from drills
• to individual	• for half of practice
Decals	• next practice
Medals	• next week
Certificates	• rest of season
	Informing parents about misbehavior

and your players. Avoid using physical activity as a form of punishment; the benefits of soccer, such as learning skills and improving cardiovascular fitness, are gained through activity. Children should not associate these types of beneficial activities with punishment.

> *Rewards and penalties that are meaningful to players and appropriate to the situation are most effective.*

One approach for enforcing rules is to use a yellow and red card. You can use the yellow card to warn and inform players that their behavior is unacceptable. This educates each player and the team about what is acceptable and provides an opportunity to correct behavior without punishment. Subsequent misbehavior should result in a red card and an appropriate penalty.

Sometimes it is more effective to ignore inappropriate behavior if the infractions are relatively minor. Continually scolding players for minor pranks or "horseplay" can become counterproductive. If team deportment is a constant problem, the coach must ask, "Why?" Misbehavior may be the players' way of telling the coach that they need attention or that they do not have enough to do. Coaches should check to see if the players are spending a lot of time standing in lines while waiting a turn to practice. Try to keep your players productively involved so they don't have time for inappropriate behavior. This is accomplished through well-designed practice plans. A lack of meaningful soccer activity in your practices could lead to counterproductive or disruptive behavior.

> *Misbehavior may be the players' way of telling the coach they need attention or do not have enough to do.*

When the rules for proper conduct have been outlined and the rewards and penalties have been determined, they must then be stated clearly so the players will understand them. Your players must understand the consequences for breaking the rules and the rewards for abiding by the rules. Violators should explain their actions to the coach and apologize to their teammates. You must also follow through, consistently and impartially, with your application of rewards for desirable conduct and penalties for misconduct.

Nothing destroys a plan for discipline more quickly than its inconsistent application. Rules must apply to all players equally and in all situations. Thus, if your team is in a championship game and your star player violates a rule that requires that he or she not be allowed to start, the rule must still be enforced. If not, you are communicating to your players that the rules are not to be taken seriously, especially when the game is at stake.

It is impossible to predetermine all rules that may ultimately be important during the season. However, by initiating several rules early in the season, a standard of expected behavior will be established. Positive and negative behaviors that are not covered by the rules can still be judged relative to these established standards and appropriate rewards or punishment can be given.

Key Points to An Effective Discipline Plan

- Specify desirable and undesirable conduct clearly in terms of rules.

- Involve players in establishing the team rules.

- Determine rewards and penalties for rules that are meaningful to players and allow for positive interaction between you and your players.

- Apply rewards and penalties consistently and impartially.

SUMMARY

Although threats, lectures, or yelling may deter misbehavior in the short term, the negative atmosphere that results reduces long-term coaching effectiveness. A more positive approach to handling misbehavior is to prevent it by establishing, with player input, clear team rules and enforcement policies. Use fair and consistent enforcement of the rules, primarily through rewarding correct behaviors rather than penalizing wrong behaviors.

REFERENCES

1. Seefeldt, V., Smoll, F., Smith, R.E., & Gould, D. (1981). *A winning philosophy for youth sports programs.* East Lansing, MI: Institute for the Study of Youth Sports.

2. Smoll, F., & Smith, R.E. (1979). *Improving relationship skills in youth sport coaches.* East Lansing, MI: Institute for the Study of Youth Sports.

9

DEVELOPING GOOD PERSONAL AND SOCIAL SKILLS

Annelies Knoppers

QUESTIONS TO CONSIDER
- Which personal and social skills should youth soccer coaches attempt to foster?
- Why are personal and social skills important?
- How can a coach bolster the self-esteem of athletes?
- How important is fun in youth sports?
- What can a coach do to ensure that sport participation is a fun experience for athletes?
- What strategies can be used to help youngsters develop positive interpersonal skills?
- What is sportsmanship and how can it be taught?

INTRODUCTION

Youth sport experiences can play, and often do play, a crucial role in the development of personal and social skills of youngsters. The learning of these skills is different from that of physical skills in the following ways:

- Athletes will learn something about these skills whether or not we plan for such learning. If we do not plan for this learning, however, it is possible that the sport experience will be a negative one for some of the athletes. If we do plan, then it is more likely that the sports experience will be a positive one. Obviously then, this is different than the learning of physical skills. If you don't teach your players to do a specific sport skill, they will not learn anything about these skills. In contrast, at every practice and game, players are learning something about the personal and social skills regardless of planning.

- You as the coach continually model these skills. You may never have to model certain physical skills, but you will always show personal and social skills.

- The learning of these skills is also different from learning physical skills in that you cannot design many drills for the personal and social skills. These skills are a part of every drill and experience.

Coaches, therefore, can have an influence on children that goes well beyond the sport setting. The extent of this influence is increased when:

- the coach and athletes work together over a long period of time,

- the athletes are participating in sport because they want to, and

- the coach is respected and liked by the athletes.

Research has also shown that many parents want their children to participate in sports so their daughters and sons can develop personal and social skills through their sport experiences.[1] Thus, coaches can and should work on the development of these skills in athletes.

The basic skills on which a beginning coach should focus are: self-esteem, fun in sport, interpersonal skills, and sportsmanship. Although self-esteem and interpersonal skills are not solely developed through sport, sport experiences can play a crucial role in the enhancement of these skills. In contrast, having fun in sport and showing sportsmanlike behavior are elements specific to the sport setting. Therefore, the coach is often held responsible for their development.

Regardless of the type of personal and social skills emphasized, the more coaches are liked and respected by the athletes and the more they work to create a positive atmosphere, the more likely it is they will influence the development of those skills in their players. The development of these skills is also likely to be enhanced when there is respect for teammates, opponents, officials, the spirit and letter of the rules, and the sport. Consequently, coaches who are very critical when athletes practice and compete, who are angry after a game or after errors, or who will do anything for a win, should change their ways or get out of coaching. Coaches who are unhappy or angry with athletes who make mistakes or lose contests retard the development of personal and social skills.

PERSONAL AND SOCIAL SKILLS

Self-Esteem

Self-esteem is the extent to which an individual is satisfied with oneself, both generally and in specific situations. The level of your athletes' self-esteem will affect their performance, relationship with others, behavior, enjoyment, and motivation. Thus, self-esteem plays a large part in the lives of your athletes as well as in your own life.

All of the players on your team will have feelings about themselves and their ability to do the things you ask of them. Those feelings were developed through experience. They will tend to behave in a way that reflects how they feel about themselves, making that behavior a self-fulfilling prophecy.

> *The level of self-esteem in young athletes*
> *influences their performance level.*

Examples

If Sam feels clumsy when playing the goalkeeper position, he is likely to fumble the ball frequently, which reinforces for him that he is clumsy.

If adults or kids always laugh at Susan's dribbling technique, then she may be very self-conscious about dribbling and always pass the ball.

A combination of a sense of failure and the derisive or negative comments from others can, therefore, lower self-esteem. Luckily, the level of self-esteem is not something that is fixed forever. It can be changed, not overnight nor with a few comments, but over a period of time with a great deal of encouragement. Consequently, enhancing levels of self-esteem requires consistent and daily planning by a coach. Positive changes in the self-esteem of players come about through the implementation of a coaching philosophy that places a priority on this change. Mere participation in sport will not automatically enhance Susan's self-esteem; her coach must plan for experiences and develop strategies that promote self-esteem.

● Show Acceptance of Each Athlete

Showing acceptance of each athlete means you must take a personal interest in each of your players regardless of their ability, size, shape, or personality. You need to be sensitive to individual differences and respect those differences. Coaches have to accept their athletes as they are. This does not mean that you have to accept or condone all their behaviors and actions. It means you should still show an interest in Tom even though he seems to whine a lot. You can talk with him about his whining, but you still should give him the same amount of attention as the other players, praise him for good behavior, encourage his effort, chat with him about his non-sport life, and compliment him when he does not whine.

You also can show your acceptance of each player by demonstrating an interest in them as people, not just as athletes. Show an interest in their school life and their family as well as in the things they like and dislike. Take the time to make each athlete feel special as both a player and a person. All athletes should know that without them the team would not be such a great place to be.

● React Positively to Mistakes

In practice, be patient. Don't get upset with errors. Instead, focus on the part of the skill that was correctly performed and on the effort made by the player. Give positive suggestions for error correction. Helpful hints on how to do so are given in Chapter 5, Planning Effective Instruction. Often in games, it is best to let mistakes go by without comment; simply praise the effort and the part of the skill that was performed correctly.

Kids usually know when they make mistakes and do not need an adult to point them out publicly. A coach who constantly corrects errors publicly not only embarrasses the players, but may also be giving them too much information. Ask them privately if they know why the error occurred. If they know, then no correction needs to be given. Encourage them also to ask for help when they need it: "Coach, why did I miss that ball?" This type of questioning encourages self-responsibility and ensures that an athlete is ready to respond to your helpful suggestions.

● Encourage Athletes

Encouragement plays a vital role in building self-esteem. Coaches can never encourage their athletes enough. Athletes benefit most from coaches who are encouraging. Also, athletes who have supportive coaches tend to like sports more and are more likely to develop a positive self-image in sports. Encouragement is especially crucial for athletes who have low self-esteem, who have difficulty mastering a skill, who make crucial errors in a game, who are not highly skilled, and who are "loners." Encouragement conveys to the athlete that the coach is on their side, especially if that encouragement is individualized.

Appropriate Times for Encouragement

- when a skill performance is partially correct
- when things aren't going well; the more discouraging the situation, the more encouragement is needed
- right after a mistake; focus on the effort, not the error
- when any effort is made to do a difficult task
- after each game and practice; do not let players leave feeling upset or worthless

How to Give Encouragement

In general, give encouragement by publicly naming the athlete so that recognition is directly received for the effort. If an athlete is struggling with something personal, then encourage the athlete privately.

- Publicly acknowledge each athlete's effort and skill as they occur.
- Recognize each athlete as they come off the field in either a verbal way: "Good hustle in going for that ball, Joan!" or in a nonverbal way: a smile, pat on the back, or wink.
- Praise players who encourage each other.
- Monitor your behavior or have someone else observe a practice or game.
- Be sincere; make the encouragement both meaningful and specific.

Examples

> After the goalkeeper dropped a ball, instead of saying "Nice try, John!" say "Way to charge that ball, John! Good hustle!"

> After a player fell, instead of saying "I'm sorry you fell, Sue!" say "Way to get back up on your feet so quickly, Sue! I like your determination!"

> Before a game, instead of saying "Play well in this game, OK?" say "I want all of you to try to do a little better than you did in the last game. I know you can do it!"

- **Additional Tips for Enhancing Self-Esteem**

  - Credit every player with the win.

  - Applaud physical skills (or parts of them) that were performed correctly.

  - Praise the use of appropriate social skills and effort.

  - Be more concerned that each player gets a substantial amount of playing time than whether or not the team wins.

  - Give special and more attention in practices and games to nonstarters.

  - Give athletes responsibilities; ask for help in setting up team rules and in creating new drills.

  - Never call athletes by degrading names; poke fun at their physiques, abilities, or gender; or use ethnic, racial, or gender stereotypes or slurs.

Examples

> Instead of saying (in a derogatory manner) "John runs like a girl!" say "John needs to improve his running."

> Instead of saying (in a derogatory manner) "You played like a bunch of sissies!" say "We're going to have to work on being a bit quicker and more assertive!"

> Instead of saying "Paul really looks funny the way he runs after the ball!" say "Of all the kids on this team, Paul seems to show the most determination in going after the ball. Good for him!"

Fun in Sport

One of the main reasons why youngsters participate in sport is to have fun. Conversely, if they do not enjoy being on the team, players are more likely to drop out. Fun, therefore, is a crucial element in participation. Even though fun occurs spontaneously in sport, each coach should plan carefully to ensure that each youngster is enjoying the sport experience. The following ideas, when put into practice, increase the likelihood that the athletes and you will enjoy the team experience.

A primary reason young athletes participate in sports is to have fun.

- Conduct well-organized practices. Plan so all the players have the maximum amount of physical activity that is feasible in conjunction with your objectives for a practice. Try to eliminate standing in line and waiting for turns as much as possible. If you have a large group, use the station method to keep all the players busy (See Chapter 5, Planning Effective Instruction).

- Select drills that are suitable for the skill level of the players.

- Create fun ways of learning skills; use innovative drills and games for practicing fundamental skills; and ask the players for suggestions and innovations.

- Watch the players' faces; if you see smiles and hear laughter, your players are enjoying practice!

- Project fun yourself; tolerate some silliness; avoid sarcasm; and be enthusiastic!

- Use games or drills that end when each person has won or has performed a skill correctly a specific number of times.

- Give positive reinforcement.

- Encourage athletes to praise, compliment, and encourage each other; do not allow them to criticize each other nor use degrading nicknames.

- Make sure athletes regularly change partners in drills.

- Allow each child to learn and play at least two positions, if possible, and to play a lot in every game.

- Keep the atmosphere light; don't be afraid to laugh and to gently joke .

- Smile; show that you enjoy being at practice or at the games. Say, "I really enjoyed this practice!" or "This is fun!"

- Take time to make each athlete feel very special. "The team could not function as well as it does without YOU!"

Interpersonal Skills

Since sport involves teammates, opponents, officials, and coaches, it can be a great place to develop good interpersonal, or people, skills. Sport, however, can also be a place where youngsters learn poor interpersonal skills. The type of skills that the athletes learn depends on the coach. If you, for example, praise Deb because she encouraged Donna, then you are reinforcing a positive interpersonal skill and creating a cooperative environment. If you say nothing when you hear Mike call one of the Hispanics on the team Chico, then you are reinforcing a racial slur and an inequitable climate. Just as youngsters need to be taught the most efficient way to receive and control the ball, they also need to be taught how to relate to others in a way that bolsters self-esteem and sensitivity.

● The Coach as Model

If you want your athletes to develop good people skills, you must consistently model the skills you wish them to develop. If you explain to them that they are not to yell and scream at each other and yet you yell and scream at them, you are giving a conflicting message: "Do as I say, not as I do." Similarly, if you state that your athletes may never criticize each other because it shows lack of respect and yet you criticize officials, you are sending a mixed message.

The greater the inconsistencies in your messages (that is, between what you say and what you do), the less likely that the players will develop good people skills. When you send mixed messages, players are likely to ignore what you say and imitate your behavior. Thus they will yell, scream, and criticize if you yell, scream, and criticize. As part of practice and game plans, therefore, you should give serious thought to the type of behaviors you wish your athletes to show to each other, opponents, officials, and coaches.

> *The overriding principle that should guide your planning and behavior is to show respect and sensitivity to all others without exception.*

What does respectful behavior look like? According to Griffin and Placek[3], a player who shows respect for others:

- follows rules;
- accepts officials' calls without arguing;
- compliments good play of others including that of opponents;
- congratulates the winner;
- plays safely;
- says "my fault" if it was;
- accepts instruction;
- will hold back rather than physically hurt someone; and
- questions coach and officials respectfully.

Players show sensitivity to the feelings of others when they:

- pair up with different teammates each time;
- cheer teammates on, especially those who are struggling;
- help and encourage less skilled teammates;

- stand up for those who are belittled or mocked by others;

- are willing to sit out sometimes so others can play;

- feel OK about changing some rules so others can play or to make the competition more even; and

- refrain from using abusive names and stereotypic slurs, and from mocking others.

The above behaviors are those you must model, teach, discuss, and encourage to enhance the people skills of your players. When you "catch" your players using these skills, praise them! Praise as frequently, if not more, the use of these skills as you would praise correct physical performance.

However, modeling, teaching, discussing, and encouraging these behaviors is not enough. You must also intervene when players use poor interpersonal skills. If you see such actions and ignore them, you are giving consent and approval.

When should you intervene? Griffin and Placek[3] suggest that you should act when a player:

- criticizes teammates' play;

- yells at officials;

- pushes, shoves, or trips teammates or opponents;

- hogs the ball;

- gloats and rubs it in when the team wins;

- baits opponents, e.g., "you're no good";

- bosses other players;

- will hurt someone just to win;

- makes fun of teammates because of their shape, skill, gender, race, or ethnic origin;

- calls others names, like "wimp," "stupid," "klutz," etc.;

- blames mistakes on others;

- complains to officials;

- shares a position unwillingly;

- ignores less skilled players;

- complains about less skilled players;

- gets into verbal or physical fights; and

- uses racial, ethnic, or gender slurs.

Obviously, the lists of desirable and undesirable behaviors could be much longer. Their overall theme suggests that everyone should show respect and sensitivity to all people. This includes coaches, officials, teammates, and opponents. Coaches should be firmly committed to this people principle and should try to express it in their coaching.

Tips for Enhancing People Skills

- Explain the people principle and establish a few basic rules as examples of the principle (e.g., praise and encourage each other).

- Discuss how you feel when you are encouraged and when you are hassled. Ask them how they feel.

- Praise behavior that exemplifies the people principle.

- Work to eliminate stereotypic grouping of players for drills; don't let players group themselves by race, gender, or skill level. They should rotate so all will have a chance to work with everyone else.

- Call the entire team's attention to an undesirable behavior the first time it occurs and explain or ask why that behavior does not fit the people principle.

- Talk to the team about the use of racial jokes and slurs such as calling a Native American "Chief," an Asian American "Kung Foo," and a Hispanic "Taco," and the derogatory use of gender stereotypes such as "sissies," "playing/throwing like a girl," and "wimp." Explain how these behaviors convey disrespect and insensitivity and cannot be tolerated. Remember, too, that often these verbalizations by players echo those they have heard used by adults.

- Assign drill partners on irrelevant characteristics such as birthday month, color of shirt, number of siblings, etc.

- Stress the "one for all and all for one" concept.

- Monitor your own behavior.

Sportsmanship

Sportsmanship is a familiar term that is difficult to define precisely. When we talk about sportsmanship, we usually are referring to the behavior of coaches, athletes, and spectators in the competitive game setting, especially in stressful situations. Thus, it is easier to give examples of sportsmanlike and unsportsmanlike behaviors than to define sportsmanship. For some examples, see Table 8-2, Youth Sportsmanship Code, in Chapter 8, Maintaining Discipline.

Displaying Sportsmanship

Treatment of Opponents

Sportsmanlike behaviors

- At the end of the game, athletes shake hands sincerely with their opponents and talk with them for a while.

- An opponent falls and Joan helps him back on his feet.

- John forgets his shin guards and the opposing team lends him a pair.

- A team brings orange slices and shares them with their opponents.

- After the game, a coach praises the play of both teams.

Unsportsmanlike behaviors

- Joan stomps away in disgust after her team loses.

- An athlete verbally hassles an opponent, saying "You dummy! We're going to run right over you!"

- A goalie swears after the opponents score.

- After a player on the Cosmos is tripped by an opposing player, the Cosmos players decide they have to "get physical," too.

Treatment of Officials

Sportsmanlike behaviors

- The Cosmos coach saw an Alliance player touch the ball last before it went out of bounds. When the ball is awarded to the Alliance, because the official thought the ball was touched last by a player on the Cosmos, the Cosmos coach says nothing.

- The only Cosmos player who asks the official to explain a call is the captain. When other Cosmos players have a question, they ask the captain to speak for them.

- When the captain or coach speaks to an official, they do so in a respectful and courteous manner.

Unsportsmanlike behaviors

- The coach of the Cosmos throws the clipboard to the ground after an official misses a call.

- When an official makes two calls in a row against the Alliance, the coach yells "Homer!"

Reaction to Rules

Sportsmanlike behaviors

- Since league rules permit only one practice per week, the coach of the Tigers holds only one practice and schedules no "secret" practices.

- One league requires that all its players play an equal amount of time. Although some coaches ask lesser skilled players to "be sick" on important game days, the coach of the Panthers continually stresses that all players are expected and needed for every game.

Unsportsmanlike behaviors

- The players on the Eagles are taught by their coach how they can break the rules without being detected.

- In order to get play stopped, the coach of the Falcons tells an athlete to fake an injury.

- Sue elbows Joan whenever the official is not looking in their direction.

Creating a Positive Climate

Since one of the goals of youth sports is to teach sportsmanship, a coach should know in which situations unsportsmanlike actions are most likely to occur. Often these situations are under the control of the coach and by changing them, the likelihood of unsportsmanlike behavior occurring decreases.[2]

Situations when unsportsmanlike behavior is most likely to occur are those in which coaches, parents, and athletes view:

- competition as war rather than as a cooperative, competitive game;

- opponents as enemies rather than as children playing a game;

- abusive language towards opponents and officials as "part of the game" rather than as disrespectful and intolerant behavior;

- errors by officials as proof that they favor the other team rather than as evidence that officials make mistakes, too;

- winning as the only important part of the game rather than as being only a part of the game; and

- every game as serious business rather than as a playful, fun-filled, and skillful endeavor.

Obviously then, a coach can decrease the likelihood of the occurrence of unsportsmanlike behavior by viewing youth sport as a playful, competitive, cooperative activity in which athletes strive to be skillful and to win and yet know that neither winning nor perfect performance are required. This type of attitude creates a positive climate and tends to enhance sportsmanship.

Teaching Sportsmanship

Stress-filled situations are the second type of condition under which unsportsmanlike behaviors tend to occur. These situations are created by the game rather than by the coach. As a coach, therefore, you must teach the athletes how they should behave in these situations. Sportsmanship can be taught.

Role Modeling

Often the behavior of athletes in a stress-filled situation reflects that of their coach. If you stay calm, cool, and collected when the score is tied in the championship game, so will your players. To do so, however, you need to keep the game in perspective which you can do by answering "no" to the following questions:

- Will the outcome of the game matter a month from now?

- Will it shake up the world if our team wins or loses today?

- Is winning more important than playing well and having fun?

Once you begin to answer "yes" to these questions, the game has become so important to you that you will be more likely to snap at the players and argue with the officials. Perhaps then you should ask yourself whether you should stay in youth sports.

On the other hand, if you can answer "no" to the above questions, you are probably approaching the game from a healthy perspective and are more likely to stay calm, cool, and collected and exhibit good sportsmanlike behavior.

Using the "People Principle"

If children are to behave in a sportsmanlike manner, they must be told specifically what is expected of them and must be praised for doing so. The "people principle," which was described in an earlier section, requires all to show respect and sensitivity to others.

The people principle is the basic guideline for sportsmanlike behavior.

Use Praise

When athletes follow the people principle, they should be praised.

Examples

Sally helps her opponent back up to his feet. Coach immediately says "Way to be, Sally!"

You know Johnny thinks the official made a mistake, but Johnny says nothing. You immediately say "Way to stay cool, Johnny!"

Eliminate Unsportsmanlike Behaviors

Ideally, when an athlete behaves in an unsportsmanlike way, you should say something immediately, and if possible, pull the child aside. Firmly indicate:

- that the behavior was inappropriate,
- how it violates the "people principle,"
- that you expect everyone to follow this principle,
- that the athlete will be in trouble if the behavior is repeated, and
- that you know the athlete will try hard not to do it again.

If the behavior is repeated, remind the athlete of the previous discussion and give an appropriate penalty. For examples of penalties see Chapter 8, Maintaining Discipline.

If athletes are to develop sportsmanship, you must not tolerate any unsportsmanlike actions. Sometimes it is easy to ignore a youngster's outburst because you feel the same frustration. By ignoring it, however, you are sending the message that at times such behavior is acceptable. Consequently, athletes will not acquire a clear sense of sportsmanship.

Discuss Sportsmanship

Young athletes need to have time to discuss sportsmanship because it is so difficult to define precisely. Team meetings before or after a practice provide a good opportunity for discussion. The following tips should help you facilitate such a discussion:

- Ask opening questions such as "Who can give an example of sportsmanlike behavior? Unsportsmanlike behavior? Why is one wrong and not the other?"

- Read the examples from this section of both types of behaviors and ask the athletes to label them as sportsmanlike or unsportsmanlike. Ask them to explain their reasoning.

- Encourage role playing. "What would it be like to be an official who is trying to do what's best and to have a coach or players yelling at you?"

- Discuss the relationship between the importance attached to winning and sportsmanship.

- Point out examples from college and professional sports. Ask the players to classify the behaviors and to give a rationale.

During these discussions, refrain from lecturing. Think of yourself as a facilitator who attempts to encourage discussion and an exploration of the people principle.

The extent to which your athletes display or react to sportsmanlike or unsportsmanlike behavior will determine the frequency with which you should hold such discussions at practice. To reinforce these discussions, you should point out examples of both types of behaviors at the brief team meeting after some game. Publicly praise each player who acted in a sportsmanlike manner and remind those who acted otherwise of your expectations. Remember also to continually examine your own behaviors to ensure that you are demonstrating the type of actions in which you want your players to engage.

SUMMARY

The extent to which athletes develop personal and social skills through the sport experience depends a great deal on you. Just as physical skills cannot be mastered without planned and directed practice, neither can personal and social skills be developed without specific strategies and guidelines. If a coach does not plan such strategies nor set guidelines for the development of these skills, then the sports experience may be a negative one for the athletes. They may lose self-esteem, develop a dislike for sport participation, and drop out. Conversely, those athletes who feel good about themselves, their teammates, and the sports experience are more likely to stay in sport. Thus a coach has a responsibility to develop these skills.

REFERENCES

1. Berlage, G. (1982). Are children's competitive team sports socializing agents for corporate America? In A. Dunleavy, A. Miracle, & O.R. Rees (Eds.), *Studies in the sociology of sport.* Fort Worth, TX: Texas Christian University Press.

2. Coakley, J. (1986). *Sport in society* (3rd ed.). St. Louis, MO: Times/Mirror Mosby.

3. Griffin, P., & Placek, J. (1983). *Fair play in the gym: Race and sex equity in physical education.* Amherst, MA: University of Massachusetts.

SUGGESTED READINGS

Martens, R. (Ed.). (1978). *Joy and sadness in children's sports.* Champaign, IL: Human Kinetics.

National Coaching Certification Program (NCCP I) (1979). *Coaching theory, level one.* Ottawa, Ontario: Coaching Association of Canada.

National Coaching Certification Program (NCCP II) (1979). *Coaching theory, level two.* Ottawa, Ontario: Coaching Association of Canada.

Orlick, T., & Botterill, C. (1975). *Every kid can win.* Chicago: Nelson Hall.

Tutko, T., & Burns, W. (1976). *Winning is everything and other American myths.* New York: Macmillan, Inc.

Yablonsky, L., & Brower, J.J. (1979). *The little league game.* New York: Times Books.

10

EVALUATING COACHING EFFECTIVENESS

Paul Vogel

QUESTIONS TO CONSIDER
- Why evaluate coaching effectiveness?
- What should be evaluated?
- Who should evaluate coaching effectiveness?
- What steps can be used to conduct an evaluation?

INTRODUCTION

No individual can coach with 100 percent effectiveness. While beginning coaches who have had no formal coaching education programs, sport-specific clinics, or prior coaching experience are particularly susceptible to using ineffective techniques, experienced professionals have their weaknesses as well. To determine where both strengths and weaknesses exist, beginning as well as experienced coaches should conduct systematic evaluations of their effectiveness.

> *All coaches can significantly improve their coaching effectiveness by completing an evaluation and then acting on the results.*

At least two evaluation questions should be asked.

1. Was the coaching effective in achieving its purpose(s)?

2. What changes can be made to improve the quality of coaching?

The evaluation described herein provides a relatively simple procedure for estimating the effects of your coaching efforts. It will also help you identify ways to improve your techniques.

WHAT SHOULD BE EVALUATED?

Evaluation should be based on more than whether or not you're a good person, worked the team hard, or even had a winning season. The important issue is whether or not you met the objectives identified for your players at the beginning of the season (see Chapter 2), including technique, knowledge, tactics, fitness, and personal-social skills. The worksheet in Supplement 10-1 at the end of this chapter can be reproduced and used to help you evaluate player outcomes.

Coaching effectiveness should be judged by the degree to which players meet their objectives.

For a discussion on how to use Supplement 10-1, see "Step 2: Collect the Evaluation Data" later in this chapter.

WHO SHOULD EVALUATE?

Initially, you should evaluate your own effectiveness. To ensure a broader and more objective evaluation, however, you should have others participate in the evaluation. For example, by using the worksheet in Supplement 10-1, you may rate the majority of your players as achieving one or more objectives in the areas of individual techniques, knowledge, tactics, fitness, and personal-social skills. Other persons, however, may feel that what you thought was appropriate was in fact an inappropriate technique, incorrect rule or tactic, contraindicated exercise, or improper attitude. Obtaining such information requires courage on your part, but it often yields important information to help you improve your coaching effectiveness.

Self-evaluation is a valuable means for improving your coaching effectiveness.

To obtain the most useful second party information, use individuals who meet the following three criteria:

1. They are familiar with your coaching actions.

2. They know the progress of your players.

3. They are individuals whose judgment you respect.

A person fulfilling these criteria could be an assistant coach, parent, official, league supervisor, other coach, local expert, or even one or more of your players.

The evaluation form illustrated in Supplement 10-2 provides another way to obtain information relative to coaching effectiveness as perceived by others. This form can be used for individual players (one form per player) or for the team as a whole (one form for the entire team). The purpose of the form is to obtain information that will reveal areas of low ratings. Follow-up can be completed in a debriefing session with the rater to determine the reasons for low ratings and to identify what can be done to strengthen the ratings. Debriefing sessions with this type of focus have proven to be highly effective in identifying ways to improve programs and procedures.

WHAT STEPS CAN BE USED TO CONDUCT AN EVALUATION?

Four steps can be used to complete an evaluation of your coaching effectiveness. These are:

1. identify the objectives,

2. collect evaluation data,

3. analyze the evaluation data to identify reasons why some coaching actions were ineffective, and

4. implement the needed changes.

Step 1: Identify the Objectives

The form in Supplement 10-1 can be used to identify the objectives you have for your players. Simply list the specific individual techniques, knowledges, tactics, fitness abilities, and personal-social skills you intend to develop in your players. Completion of this step clearly identifies what you believe is most important for your players to master. It also provides a basis for later evaluation.

A prerequisite to conducting an evaluation of coaching effectiveness is to clearly identify the objectives that you want your players to achieve.

Once the objectives are identified, the remaining evaluation steps can be completed. This step also provides a good opportunity for you to obtain information from others regarding the appropriateness of your season objectives for the age and experience level of your players.

Let your players know what the objectives are. Research shows that when players know what they need to learn, they experience improved achievement.

Step 2: Collect the Evaluation Data

The primary source of evaluative data should be your self-evaluation of the results of all or various parts of the season. However, assessments by others, combined with self-assessment, are more valuable than self-evaluation alone. Both approaches are recommended.

- ● **Completing the Coach's Assessment of Player Performance**

After you have identified your intended objectives and entered them in the first column of the "Coach's Evaluation of Player Outcomes" form, enter the names of your players in the spaces on the top of the form. Next, respond either Y (Yes) or N (No) to the question, "Did significant improvements occur?" as it relates to each of the season objectives for each player.

Your decision to enter a Y or N in each space requires you to define one or more standards. For example, all of your players may have improved on a particular season objective but you may feel that several did not achieve enough to receive a Y. However, an N may also seem inappropriate. To resolve this difficulty, clarify the amount of player achievement for each objective that you are willing to accept as evidence of a significant positive improvement. There is no exact method of determining how much gain is enough; therefore, you need to rely on your own estimates of these standards. The procedures suggested on the following pages of this chapter allow for correction of erroneous judgments. It is also possible to use a scale to further divide the response options: 0 = none, 1 = very little, 2 = little, 3 = some, 4 = large, and 5 = very large. Given ratings of this type you may establish 4 and/or 5 ratings as large enough to be categorized as a Y and ratings of 3 or less as an N.

It is important to remember that players who begin the season at low levels of performance on various objectives have the potential for more improvement than players who are near mastery. Players who begin the season at high levels of performance often deserve Y rather than N responses for relatively small gains.

Injury, loss of fitness, or development of inappropriate individual techniques, knowledge, tactics, or personal-social skills are detrimental effects that can occur and should be identified. In this situation the appropriate entry is an N circled to distinguish it from small or slight gains.

You must decide if your players achieved significant gains on the outcomes you intended to teach.

Completion of the coach's evaluation form will reveal your perception of the degree to which your players achieved important objectives. By looking at one objective across all players as well as one player across all objectives, patterns of your coaching effectiveness will emerge. (This is explained in more detail in Step 3.)

● Obtaining Information from Selected Other Persons

To obtain information from others about your coaching effectiveness, use the form in Supplement 10-2. Remember, the form can be used for individual players or for the entire team. Note that the estimates of performance are relative to other players of similar age and gender participating in the same league. When using the form to rate individual players, ask the evaluator to simply place a check in the appropriate column (top 25 percent, mid 50 percent, or bottom 25 percent) for each performance area. When using the form to rate the entire team, estimate the number of players judged to be in each column.

Ratings of player performance at the end of the season (or other evaluation period) are not very useful without knowing player performance levels at the beginning of the season. Changes in performance levels are the best indicators of your coaching effectiveness. To determine change in player performance, it is necessary to estimate performance before and after coaching occurred. Pre and post ratings may be difficult to obtain, however, because of the time it requires of your raters.

A good alternative is to have the evaluators record pre and post ratings at the end of the evaluation period. For example, if three of your players were perceived to be in the top 25 percent of their peers at the beginning of the season and seven players were perceived to be in that performance category at the end of the season, the net gain in performance would be four. Your desire may be to have all of your players move into the top 25 percent category during the course of the season. Such a desire is, however, probably unrealistic. Having 50 percent of your players move from one performance level to the next would be an excellent achievement.

It would be nice to look at your evaluations of player performance and the evaluations of their performance by others and see only Y responses or ratings in the top 25 percent. Such a set of responses, however, would not be helpful for improving your coaching effectiveness. An excessive number of high ratings typically signals the use of a relaxed set of standards.

All coaches vary in their ability to change behavior across stated outcome areas and across various individual players on a team. The incidences where individual players do not attain high ratings on various objectives are most useful to reveal principles of coaching effectiveness that are being violated. Accordingly, use standards for your self-ratings (or for the ratings by others) that result in no more than 80 percent of the responses being Y on the "Coach's Evaluation of Player Outcomes" or moving from one category of performance to another when rated by others. As you will see in Step 3, ratings that are more evenly distributed among the response options are the most helpful for determining how your effectiveness may be improved.

Use of the form "Evaluation of Player/Team Performance Relative to Others" (Supplement 10-2) provides you with an estimate of changes in player performance as viewed by other persons whose judgment you respect. The relatively broad performance areas upon which the evaluation is based does not, however, provide enough detailed information to fully interpret the data obtained. Simply stated, more information is needed. Additional information needed can be obtained by using the technique of debriefing.

A debriefing session, based upon the information included in the completed evaluation form, provides a good agenda for discussing potential changes in your coaching procedures with the person who completed the evaluation. The debriefing should include these elements:

- Thank the individual for completing the evaluation form and agreeing to discuss its implications.

- Indicate that the purpose of the debriefing session is to identify both strengths and weaknesses, but that emphasis should be focused on weaknesses, and how they may be improved.

- Proceed through the outcome areas and their corresponding ratings, seeking to understand why each area resulted in large or small gains. For example, if a disproportionate number of players were rated low relative to their peers on offensive skills, and there were very small gains from the beginning to the end of the evaluation period, you need more information. Attempt to determine what offensive skills were weak and what might be changed to strengthen them in the coming season.

- In your discussion, probe for the things you can do (or avoid doing) that may produce better results. Make a special attempt to identify the reasons why a suggested alternative may produce better results.

- Take careful notes during the discussion. Record the alternative ideas that have good supporting rationales and how they might be implemented.

The information collected in this way is invaluable for helping to identify good ideas for increasing your ability to help players achieve future season objectives.

Coaching strengths are pleasing to hear,
but identified weaknesses are more
helpful for improving effectiveness.

Step 3: Analyze the Data

The first step necessary to analyze the information collected is to total the number of Y responses entered for each player across all season objectives.

From a coaching improvement viewpoint, it is necessary to have a mixture of Y and N responses across both the objectives and players. It is important that no more than 80 percent of your ratings be Y responses on the coaches' self-evaluation form. Tell other raters that no more than 80 percent of the players can be listed as showing improvement from one performance level to another in their pre/post estimates. It may be necessary to "force" the appropriate number of Y and N responses to meet this requirement.

When you have met the criteria of no more than 80 percent positive answers, divide the number of Y responses by the total number of objectives and enter the percent of Y responses in the row labeled "Total" for each player. Similarly, sum the number of Y responses across players for each objective and enter the percent of Y responses in the column labeled "Total" for each season objective.

The pattern of Y and N responses that emerges from "forced ratings" can be very helpful in identifying the season objectives and/or the kinds of players for which your coaching is most or least effective. By looking at the characteristics of the players who obtained the highest ratings versus those who achieved the lowest ratings, you may obtain good insight into things you can change to be more effective with certain kinds of players. This same type of comparison provides similar insight into how to be more effective in teaching certain objectives.

The real benefits of this kind of analysis come with evaluating the reasons why no or few players received Y responses. Answers to these "Why?" questions reveal changes you can make to improve your coaching effectiveness.

To help you determine why you were (or were not) successful with your coaching in certain player performance areas, a "Checklist of Effective Coaching Actions" was developed (Supplement 10-3). It provides a number of items you can rate that may help you identify ways to increase your coaching effectiveness. For example, if five of your players made insufficient progress in the individual defensive technique of pivot tackle, you could review the checklist to help determine coaching actions you used (or did not use) that may be related to helping players of similar skill level, fitness, or character qualities. As you identify coaching actions that may have detracted from player improvement, note these and then alter your subsequent coaching actions accordingly.

● Interpreting Unmet Expectations

The above suggestions provide a systematic method for you to identify ways to improve your coaching ability. There are, however, other ways to interpret lack of achievement. The first and foremost (and nearly always incorrect) is to blame lack of performance on lack of talent or player interest.

Be sure to consider all possibilities for self-improvement before accepting other reasons for unmet expectations.

Effective coaches can improve the capabilities of their players, even those with only average abilities. The most helpful approach you can use to improve your coaching effectiveness is to assume that when the performances of your players do not meet your expectations, the solutions to the problems will be found in your coaching actions. This assumption may prove to be wrong, but you must be absolutely sure that you have considered all possibilities for self-improvement before accepting other reasons for unmet expectations.

If you determine that insufficient player achievement is not likely to be due to ineffective coaching, it is possible that the expectations you hold for your players are unrealistic. Remember, motivation is enhanced when players perceive that they are improving. Expectations that are too high can have a negative effect on motivation and improvement. Reasonable expectations divided into achievable and sequential steps will result in appropriate standards of performance.

Allotment of insufficient time for teaching and learning the objectives selected for the season can also result in poor player achievement, even when performance expectations and other coaching actions are appropriate. Players must have sufficient time to attempt a task, make errors, obtain feedback, refine their attempts, and habituate the intended actions before it is reasonable to expect them to demonstrate those actions in competition. Attempting to cover too many objectives within limited practice time is a major cause of insufficient achievement.

If the changes identified to improve coaching effectiveness are not implemented, evaluation is a waste of time.

Step 4: Act on the Needed Changes

The primary reason for conducting an evaluation of your coaching effectiveness is to learn what can be done to improve the achievement levels of your players. Identifying the changes that will lead to improvements, however, is a waste of time if those changes are not implemented. Improvements can occur in planning, instruction, motivation, communication, knowledge of the game, and evaluation. Regardless of your level of expertise, by systematically evaluating your coaching actions, you can find ways to become more effective and more efficient.

SUMMARY

By systematically evaluating player performance on the intended outcomes of the season, you can estimate the effectiveness of your coaching actions. Limited achievement of players in some performance areas can signal a need to change some coaching actions. Use of the forms and procedures outlined in this chapter will reveal changes you can make to improve your coaching effectiveness. By taking action on the changes that are identified, you can make significant steps toward becoming a more effective and efficient coach.

COACH'S EVALUATION OF PLAYERS OUTCOMES

Coach_____ Season _____Date _____

EVALUATION QUESTION:	Did significant results occur on the objectives included in the performance areas listed below?																
CATEGORIES	**SEASON OBJECTIVES**	ROSTER														**TOTAL %YES**	**OTHER NOTES**
TOTAL (% YES)																	
EVALUATIVE RESPONSES:	Record your assessment of player outcomes for each objective by answering the evaluative questions with a Y (YES) or N (NO) response.																

EVALUATION OF PLAYER/TEAM PERFORMANCE RELATIVE TO OTHERS

Evaluator:_____ Player/Team _____Season _____

EVALUATION QUESTION:	In comparison with other players in the league, how does the player (or team) listed above perform in the areas listed below?						
PERFORMANCE AREAS	**PLAYER OR TEAM PERFORMANCE LEVELS**						**COMMENTS**
	SEASON START			**SEASON END**			
	TOP 25%	MID 50%	BOTTOM 25%	TOP 25%	MID 50%	BOTTOM 25%	

INDIVIDUAL EVALUATION:

For each performance area indicate, by placing a check in the top, mid, or bottom column, the start and end performance level of the player.

TEAM EVALUATION:

For each performance area estimate the number of players (% or actual numbers) in the top, mid, or bottom performance levels at the start and end of the season.

CHECKLIST OF EFFECTIVE COACHING ACTIONS[1]

INTRODUCTION

This checklist can be used to identify coaching actions that may be related to player achievement (or lack of achievement) of desired outcomes. It, therefore, serves as an aid to identify the reason(s) why a player(s) did not achieve one or more of your expected outcomes.

To use the checklist in this way, read the items in each content category (i.e., coaching role, organization, effective instruction) and ask yourself, "Could the coaching actions (or inactions) implied by this item have contributed to the unmet expectation?" Answer the question by responding with a Y or N. If you wish to rate the degree to which your actions (inactions) were consistent with the guidelines implied by the items, use the five-point rating scale described below. Items that result in N (No) or low ratings suggest that you are not following effective coaching practices. The process of seeking answers to specific concerns identified by your reaction to checklist items is an excellent way to obtain information most likely to help you become more effective as a coach.

Directions

Rate the degree to which you incorporate each of the following items into your coaching activities. Check Y or N or use the following five-point scale where: 1 = Strongly Disagree, 2 = Disagree, 3 = Neutral, 4 = Agree, and 5 = Strongly Agree.

---

1. Modified from Vogel, P.G. (1987). Post season evaluation: What did we accomplish? In V.D. Seefeldt (Ed.) *Handbook for youth sport coaches*. Reston, VA: American Alliance for Health, Physical Education, Recreation and Dance.

Item	Rating
	Disagree Agree

Coaching Role

1. My primary purpose for coaching was to maximize the benefits of participation for all of the players. (N) 1 2 3 4 5 (Y)

2. The beneficial (individual techniques, knowledge, tactics, fitness, attitudes) and detrimental (time, money, injury, etc.) effects of participation were constantly in mind during planning and coaching times. (N) 1 2 3 4 5 (Y)

3. I communicated through actions and words that I expected each player to succeed in improving his/her level of play. (N) 1 2 3 4 5 (Y)

Organization

4. I completed a plan for the season to guide the conduct of my practices. (N) 1 2 3 4 5 (Y)

5. Performance expectations set for the players were realistic and attainable. (N) 1 2 3 4 5 (Y)

6. I conscientiously decided which objectives must be emphasized in the pre, early, mid, and late season. (N) 1 2 3 4 5 (Y)

7. Objectives for developing my practices were drawn from those identified and sequenced from pre, to late season. (N) 1 2 3 4 5 (Y)

8. The amount of total practice time allocated to each season objective was sufficient. (N) 1 2 3 4 5 (Y)

9. My practices would be characterized by others as orderly, safe, businesslike, and enjoyable. (N) 1 2 3 4 5 (Y)

10. Objectives were broken down as necessary to allow players to achieve them in several small steps. (N) 1 2 3 4 5 (Y)

Knowledge of the Sport

11. I am familiar with the rationale for each season objective selected and clearly communicated to my players its purpose and described how it is to be executed. (N) 1 2 3 4 5 (Y)

12. I was able to identify the key elements of performance necessary for achievement of each season objective. (N) 1 2 3 4 5 (Y)

Effective Instruction

13. I clearly communicated (by word and/or example) the key elements to be learned for each objective included in a practice. (N) 1 2 3 4 5 (Y)

14. Practice on an objective was initiated with a rationale for why the objective is important. (N) 1 2 3 4 5 (Y)

15. Instruction did not continue without player attention. (N) 1 2 3 4 5 (Y)

16. Practice on an objective provided each player with many practice trials and with specific and positive feedback. (N) 1 2 3 4 5 (Y)

17. During practice, I regularly grouped the players in accordance with their different practice needs on the season's objectives. (N) 1 2 3 4 5 (Y)

18. I used questions to determine if the players understood the objectives and instruction. (N) 1 2 3 4 5 (Y)

19. The players sensed a feeling of control over their own learning, which resulted from my emphasis of clearly identifying what they needed to learn and then encouraging maximum effort. (N) 1 2 3 4 5 (Y)

20. My practices were planned and clearly associated the use of learning activities, drills, and games with the season objectives. (N) 1 2 3 4 5 (Y)

21. I evaluated my practices and incorporated appropriate changes for subsequent practices.   (N) 1 2 3 4 5 (Y)

Motivation

22. My practices and games resulted in the players achieving many of their goals for participation.   (N) 1 2 3 4 5 (Y)

23. I taught the players how to realistically define success in terms of effort and self-improvement.   (N) 1 2 3 4 5 (Y)

24. An expert would agree, upon observing my practices, that I use a positive, rather than a negative, coaching approach.   (N) 1 2 3 4 5 (Y)

Communication

25. There was no conflict between the verbal and non-verbal messages I communicated to my players.   (N) 1 2 3 4 5 (Y)

26. I facilitated communication with the players by being a good listener.   (N) 1 2 3 4 5 (Y)

27. Accepted behaviors (and consequences of misbehavior) were communicated to players at the beginning of the season.   (N) 1 2 3 4 5 (Y)

28. Players were involved in developing or confirming team rules.   (N) 1 2 3 4 5 (Y)

29. Enforcement of team rules was consistent for all players throughout the season.   (N) 1 2 3 4 5 (Y)

Involvement with Parents

30. Parents of the players were a positive, rather than negative, influence on players' achievement of the season objectives.   (N) 1 2 3 4 5 (Y)

31. I communicated to the parents my responsibilities and the responsibilities of parents and players to the team.   (N) 1 2 3 4 5 (Y)

Conditioning

32. The intensity, duration, and frequency of physical conditioning I used was appropriate for the age of the players.   (N) 1 2 3 4 5 (Y)

33. I routinely used a systematic warm-up and cool down before and after practices and games.   (N) 1 2 3 4 5 (Y)

34. The physical conditioning aspects of my practices appropriately simulated the requirements of the sport.   (N) 1 2 3 4 5 (Y)

Injury Prevention

35. I followed all recommended safety procedures for the use of equipment and facilities.   (N) 1 2 3 4 5 (Y)

36. I did not use any contraindicated exercises in my practices.   (N) 1 2 3 4 5 (Y)

Care of Common Injuries

37. I established and followed appropriate emergency procedures and simple first aid as needed.   (N) 1 2 3 4 5 (Y)

38. I had a well-stocked first aid kit at each practice and game, including players' medical history information and medical release forms.   (N) 1 2 3 4 5 (Y)

Rehabilitation of Injuries

39. None of the players experienced a recurrence of an injury that could be attributed to inappropriate rehabilitation.   (N) 1 2 3 4 5 (Y)

Evaluation

40. I completed an evaluation of player improvement on the season objectives.   (N) 1 2 3 4 5 (Y)

41. I identified the coaching actions (or inactions) that appeared most closely related to unmet player expectations.   (N) 1 2 3 4 5 (Y)

42. I made the changes in coaching action needed to improve my coaching effectiveness.   (N) 1 2 3 4 5 (Y)

Section III

YOUTH SOCCER RULES OF PLAY

11

SOCCER RULES OF PLAY
(With Suggested Modifications for the Youth Game)

Eugene W. Brown

QUESTIONS TO CONSIDER
- What are the 17 laws of the game of soccer and how are they interpreted?
- What modifications could be made to the laws of the game of soccer to meet the developmental needs of youth players?
- How should the laws of the game of soccer be applied in order to promote safety, enjoyment, and fairness?

INTRODUCTION

The laws of the game are the official regulations established by the Federation Internationale De Football Association (FIFA).[1] They govern play according to a uniform set of international standards. From time to time, these laws are changed to conform with developments in the game. FIFA recognizes the importance of changing these laws to meet the specific needs of youth play. FIFA has noted that, as long as the principles of the laws are maintained, they may be modified in their application. According to FIFA, the types of modifications permissible for players of school age, however, are limited to five specific areas. They include (a) the size of the field; (b) the size, weight, and material of the ball; (c) the width between the goal posts and the height of the cross bar from the ground; (d) the duration of the game; and (e) the number of substitutions that can be used in a game. This chapter contains statements and interpretations of the laws of play as well as suggested modifications for youth play. The contents of this chapter are systematically organized to help those associated with youth soccer (players, parents, coaches, and referees) gain a practical understanding of the laws of the game.

Practical Considerations

Throughout this chapter, practical considerations for the applications of the laws of the game will be suggested. These practical considerations are ways to apply the laws of the game in order to promote safety, enjoyment, and fairness in accord with the spirit of the laws.

Modifications for Youth Play

Throughout this chapter, modifications in the laws for youth play will be suggested. These modifications are presented with the intent of maintaining the principles and spirit of the laws of the game while meeting the educational and developmental needs of youth players. Modifications are not stated with the intent of ultimately changing the laws of the game, but are presented as a progression to:

- assist coaches in developing a systematic approach to teaching the game of soccer to their athletes, and

- assist youth players in developing their understanding and skills of soccer in order to ultimately play under the official laws of the game.

LAWS OF PLAY

Law I—The Field of Play

The soccer field must be rectangular. Each line, mark, or fixture designating the soccer field has a specific purpose (see Figure 11-1). These purposes include:

- determining if a goal is scored,

- determining if the ball is in or out of play,

- identifying important areas of the field, and

- aiding in the start and restart of play.

Practical Considerations

- The field must be safe for play. In other words, the field should be free of hazardous objects such as rocks, glass, and projecting structures (e.g., pipes and sewer covers).

- Goal nets and corner flags should be used.

Modifications for Youth Play

- Field sizes for younger players (ages 6-11) should be smaller than the regulation field (see Table 11-1).

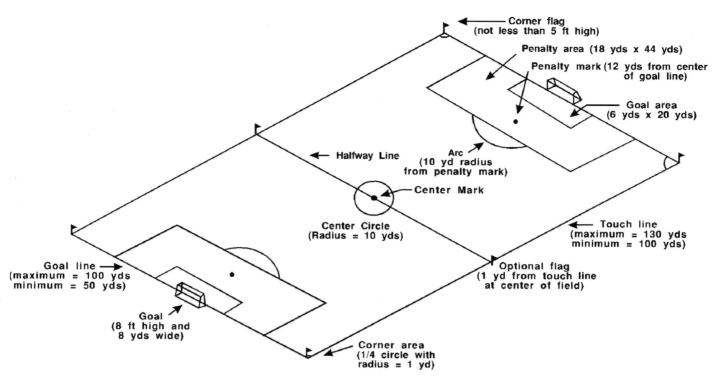

Figure 11-1. *Regulation field of play.*

AGE GROUP	DIMENSIONS	
(Years)	**Width (Yards)**	**Length (Yards)**
below 8	50	60 - 80
8 - 11	50 - 60	80 - 110
12 and above	60 - 75	110 - 120

* Note that 11 per side games are not recommended for youth players below the age of 11 years (see Table 11-3). However, if a league tradition of full-sided games is difficult to alter, the above dimensions are recommended.

Table 11-1. *Recommended field for 11 players per side.*

Law II—The Ball

A spherical ball made of leather or approved synthetic materials, with a 27- to 28-inch circumference and a weight of 14 to 16 ounces, is to be used for play. This is a standard size 5 ball.

● Practical Consideration

- Balls must be safe for play. Safety encompasses such common-sense observations as proper inflation and panels that are not projecting from the ball.

- Modifications for Youth Play

Use of smaller and lighter weight balls permits younger players to kick, punt, and throw them greater distances. However, smaller balls are more difficult to maneuver and accurately pass and shoot. A light weight (10- to 12-ounce) ball with a 27- to 28-inch circumference may be more appropriate for youth play. Balls with these characteristics, however, are not presently being manufactured. Ball sizes commonly used for different age groups, with their corresponding dimensions, are presented in Table 11-2.

- Balls used for youth play should be compatible with the physical characteristics of young athletes.

- Balls that are too large (or small), heavy, or hard may discourage or hurt younger players.

Table 11-2. Ball sizes commonly used for play.

AGE GROUP (Years)	BALL SIZE	CIRCUMFERENCE (inches)	WEIGHT (ounces)
below 8	3	23 - 25	10 - 12
8 - 11	4	25 - 27	12 - 14
12 and above	5	27 - 28	14 - 16

Law III—Number of Players

Full-sided games are played by two teams of 11 players. Games can be started as long as each team has at least seven players present. One player for each team must be identified as a goalkeeper. Substitutions may be made in accordance with the rules of competition under which the game is being played. In youth games, substitution is commonly permitted, for either team, at the start of any period (e.g., halftime, overtime), after a goal is scored, before a goal kick, and before a throw-in, but only for the team taking the throw.

- Practical Considerations

- A substitute may not enter the field of play until permitted by the referee.

- A substitute may not enter the field of play until the player being replaced has left the field.

- A substitution may be made only during certain stoppages of play in accordance with the rules of competition under which the game is being played.

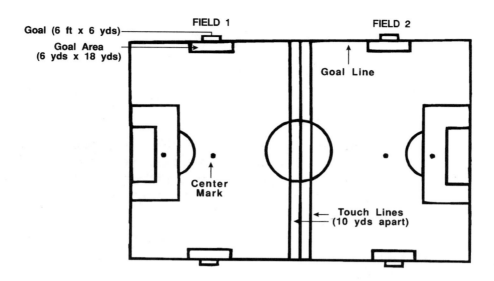

Figure 11-2. *Two fields for small-sided games on a full-size soccer field.*

AGE GROUP	NUMBER OF PLAYERS	DIMENSIONS	
(Years)	PER SIDE	Width (Yards)	Length (Yards)
below 8	7	40 - 50	60 - 70 *
8 - 10	7 - 9	50 - 60	70 - 80 *
11 and above	11	65 - 80	110 - 120

* Note that two small-sided cross field games could be played on a full-size (regulation) soccer field (see Figure 11-2).

Table 11-3. *Recommended number of players per side and field dimensions.*

- Dividing the youth games into quarters provides an additional stoppage of play to assist coaches in making substitutions.

Modifications for Youth Play

Small-sided games are recommended for players below the age of 11 years (see Table 11-3). Figure 11-2 shows a field layout for small-sided games.

- Small-sided games provide a greater opportunity for involvement by each player.

- Small-sided games are not as complicated as full-sided games.

- It is easier to coach a team with a smaller number of players.

Law IV—Players' Equipment

Players on one team must wear similarly colored shirts that distinguish them from the opposing team members. A goalkeeper, in order to be identifiable, must wear a shirt of a different color from either team, opposing goalkeeper, and referee.

Shin guards are required equipment. They must be covered entirely by the stockings. They must be worn by all players. Coaches can play an important role in getting youth players "into the habit" of wearing shin guards by insisting that they are worn during practices as well as during games.

Court shoes or studded soccer shoes that conform to the rules of safety are permissible.

Molded Cleats

If molded cleats are worn,

- the studs shall be made of rubber, plastic, polyurethene, or similar material;
- each shoe shall have no fewer than 10 studs;
- the studs shall project no more than ¾ inch; and
- the studs shall have a diameter of ⅜ inch or more.

Shoes with Replaceable Studs

If shoes with replaceable studs are worn,

- the studs shall be made of leather, rubber, aluminum, plastic, or similar material;
- the studs shall project no more than ¾ inch; and
- the studs shall have a diameter of ½ inch or more.

Any player who does not meet the equipment requirements before the game is not permitted to play until these requirements are met. A player in the match who does not meet the requirements will be sent off and not allowed to re-enter until a complete uniform is worn.

- ● **Practical Considerations**
  - Players must not wear anything that is dangerous to another player or to themselves.

Law V—Referees

One referee has full responsibility for the match. This person starts and stops play, keeps time, keeps score, and punishes teams for unfair play by giving the ball to the team that has been fouled. For serious infractions, the referee can disallow a player from continuing to play, resulting in the

Figure 11-3. *Penalty Kick—The referee points to the penalty kick mark to signal a penalty kick.*

Figure 11-4. *Goal Kick—The referee points to the half of the goal from which the goal kick is to be taken.*

Figure 11-5. *Play on / Advantage—This signifies that the referee has seen a foul, but chose not to call it because by doing so it would take away the advantage from the team fouled.*

Figure 11-6. *Corner Kick—The referee raises an arm and hand in the direction of the corner from which the kick is to be taken.*

Figure 11-7. *Substitution.*

Figure 11-8. *Indirect Free Kick—This signal should be held until the kick has been taken and the ball is played by another player or goes out of play.*

Figure 11-9. *Caution or Ejection— When the referee raises a yellow card, a player or coach is being cautioned. If the card raised is red, that player or coach is being ejected from the game.*

team playing one or more players short for the rest of the match. The referee's decisions are final. Common referee signals are illustrated in Figures 11-3 through 11-9.

- ● Practical Considerations

  - The referee must be neutral.

  - The referee must be concerned for the safety of the players.

  - Fair play must be promoted so players, coaches, and spectators enjoy the game as much as possible.

  - Communication with the referee during play should be politely carried out by the team captain.

- ● Modifications for Youth Play

In youth play, the referee should avoid stopping play by repeatedly calling trivial fouls. Referees who work youth games must be aware of the fact that a judgment of intent must be made before whistling a foul. Accidental or incidental contact is extremely common among the youngest players. Malicious behavior and the intent to injure rarely occur. Allowing the youth game to flow unimpeded as much as possible is important to the players' enjoyment of and commitment to the game. On the other hand, referees must also be aware that injuries at the youth level are almost never feigned. When young players appear to be hurt or injured, it is advisable for the referee to stop the game immediately and allow qualified individuals to attend to them.

Whenever possible, the referee should inform youth players about the nature of the calls that are made. This is extremely helpful in teaching the players the laws of the game.

  - Referees of youth games must know the laws of the game in order to project this knowledge to young or inexperienced soccer players.

Law VI—Linespersons

Two linespersons assist the referee by indicating when the ball is out of play and which team puts it back into play by signaling for a throw-in, goal kick, corner kick, goal, or offside. However, the final decision on anything having to do with the match belongs to the referee. FIFA does note that it is the duty of the referee to act upon the information of neutral linespersons with regard to incidents that were not personally noted by the referee. Linespersons assist with the match in any other way that the referee deems important. Common linespersons' signals are shown in Figures 11-10 through 11-17. The two linespersons and one referee compose what is commonly called a three-person officiating system. Communication among these three individuals is a critical component of game control.

Figure 11-10. *Throw-in—The team that attacks the goal in the direction that the flag is pointed receives the throw-in.*

Figure 11-11. *An offside has occurred.*

Figure 11-12. *Offside—After calling offside, the signal indicates that the offside occurred on the far side of the field.*

Figure 11-13. *After calling offside, this signal indicates that the offside occurred near the middle of the field.*

Figure 11-14. *After calling offside, this signals that the offside occurred near the side of the field.*

Figure 11-15. *Substitution.*

Figure 11-16. *Goal Kick.*

Figure 11-17. *Corner Kick.*

- **Practical Considerations**

  - Linespersons must be neutral.

  - Spectators must provide sufficient space along the sideline for the linespersons to carry out their responsibilities.

  - Coaches and team officials should assist in assuring that spectators do not interfere with any aspect of the game.

- **Modifications for Youth Play**

  In some youth leagues, each team provides a linesperson (club linesperson). Under these circumstances, the linespersons only signal when the ball goes out of play. Also, some leagues use two referees, who have equal responsibility for making decisions. Under this two-person officiating system, no linespersons are used.

  - Club linespersons should be neutral.

  - Club linespersons should not be allowed to flag for a foul or offside.

Law VII—Duration of the Game

A game is divided into equal halves. Adult matches last 90 minutes. A halftime interval of five minutes shall be provided. Time shall be extended in either half for the taking of a penalty kick when the call was made before regulation time expired. Generally, ties will stand, since overtimes are only played in tournament or championship games.

- **Practical Considerations**

  - Ties are not a disgrace and should be viewed by coaches, players, and spectators as a match played by two equal teams on that given day.

  - The referee is the official time keeper for the match.

  - The referee may extend the time of play for time lost due to an injury, wasting of time by a team, or other conditions that interfere with either team playing a full match.

- Modifications for Youth Play

  - The time period for a game should be modified for youth play (see Table 11-4).

  - Dividing youth games into equal quarters permits additional opportunity for coaches to make substitutions and provide instructions to players.

Table 11-4. Recommended duration of a game.

AGE GROUP (Years)	DURATION (Minutes)
below 8	40
8 - 10	50
11 - 12	60 - 70
13 - 14	70 - 80
above 14	80 - 90

Law VIII—The Start of Play

This law describes the methods and rules for starting play with a place kick and a drop ball. (see Table 11-5).

Place Kick

Which team takes the place kick (kickoff) at the beginning of the game and at the beginning of overtime, if required, is determined by a coin toss. The winner of the toss has a choice of either kicking off or selecting which goal to defend. Teams reverse sides to start the second half. A place kick is also used to restart play after a goal has been scored. It is taken by the team scored upon.

Table 11-5. Conditional applications of the place kick rules.

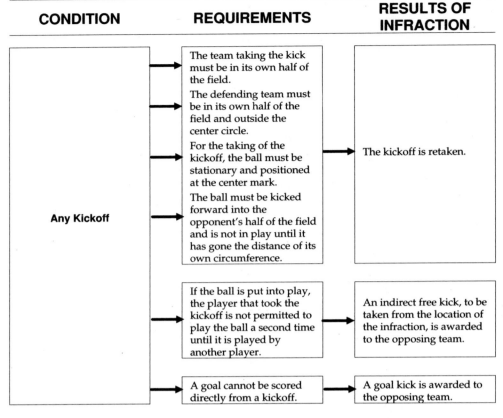

CONDITION	REQUIREMENTS	RESULTS OF INFRACTION
Any Kickoff	The team taking the kick must be in its own half of the field.	The kickoff is retaken.
	The defending team must be in its own half of the field and outside the center circle.	
	For the taking of the kickoff, the ball must be stationary and positioned at the center mark.	
	The ball must be kicked forward into the opponent's half of the field and is not in play until it has gone the distance of its own circumference.	
	If the ball is put into play, the player that took the kickoff is not permitted to play the ball a second time until it is played by another player.	An indirect free kick, to be taken from the location of the infraction, is awarded to the opposing team.
	A goal cannot be scored directly from a kickoff.	A goal kick is awarded to the opposing team.

Drop Ball

If the referee must stop play for a reason not stated in the Laws of the Game and the ball has not passed over one of the touch lines or goal lines immediately before stopping play, the game must be restarted by a drop ball at the place where the ball was when play was stopped (see Table 11-6).

Table 11-6. Conditional applications of the drop ball rules.

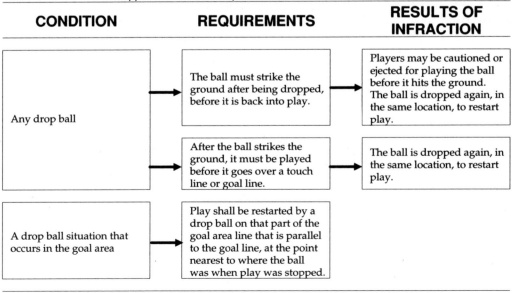

CONDITION	REQUIREMENTS	RESULTS OF INFRACTION
Any drop ball	The ball must strike the ground after being dropped, before it is back into play.	Players may be cautioned or ejected for playing the ball before it hits the ground. The ball is dropped again, in the same location, to restart play.
	After the ball strikes the ground, it must be played before it goes over a touch line or goal line.	The ball is dropped again, in the same location, to restart play.
A drop ball situation that occurs in the goal area	Play shall be restarted by a drop ball on that part of the goal area line that is parallel to the goal line, at the point nearest to where the ball was when play was stopped.	

Practical Considerations

- The referee does not need to wait for players from both teams to gather around in order to drop the ball back into play. However, common sense dictates that the ball be dropped between two opposing players.

- Players should be advised by the referee to not play the ball before it strikes the ground.

- If the referee is uncertain which team played the ball last before it went over a touch line or goal line, play shall be restarted with a drop ball near where it went out of bounds.

LAW IX—Ball In and Out of Play

The ball is out of play when it entirely crosses the goal line or touch line (see Figure 11-18), or the referee stops the game. The ball is in play if it rebounds from a goal post, cross bar, or corner flag and stays within the field of play. It is in play if it rebounds from a referee or linesperson when they are on the field and the ball stays within the field of play.

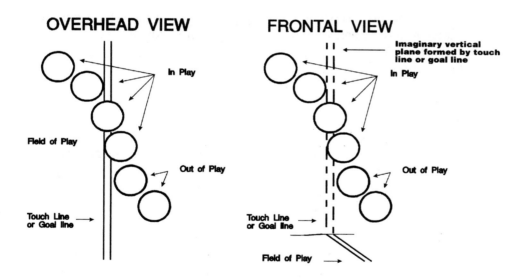

Figure 11-18. *Ball in or out of play.*

Practical Consideration

- Players should be coached to keep playing until the ball is completely over the goal line or touch line and the referee whistles to stop play.

Law X—Method of Scoring

The ball must go all the way over the goal line, under the cross bar, and between the goal posts for a goal to be scored (see Figure 11-19).

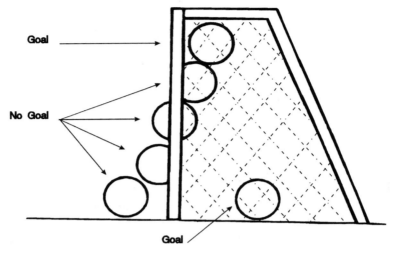

Figure 11-19. *Goal or no goal.*

● **Practical Consideration**

- Players should be coached to keep playing until the referee signals that a goal has been scored. This is especially true of defensive players, whose actions may be interpreted by the referee as a goal having been scored.

Law XI—Offside

The most complex rule in soccer is the offside rule. Its complexity is derived from the contingencies and judgments associated with the application of the rule.

Offside Position

First, a player must be in an **offside position** (see Figure 11-20) at the time the ball is played by a teammate before being considered to be offside. All of the following conditions must occur in order for a player to be in an **offside position:**

- offensive player in opponent's half of the field

- offensive player nearer to opponent's goal line than at least two opponents (Note that an offensive player who is *even* with the second to last opponent or with the two last opponents is not in an offside position.)

- offensive player not in possession of the ball and closer to the opponent's goal line than the ball

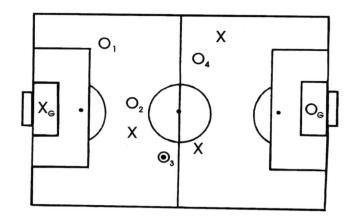

Offensive Player	Offside Position?	Reason(s)
O$_1$	Yes	Offensive player in opponent's half of the field
		Fewer than 2 defenders between offensive player and opponent's goal line
		Offensive player not in possession of the ball and closer to the opponent's goal line than the ball
O$_2$	No	Even with second to last defender (not closer to opponent's goal line than at least two defenders)
O$_3$	No	Offensive player is in possession of the ball
O$_4$	No	Offensive player in own half of the field

Figure 11-20. *Offside position or not?*

Seeking to Gain an Advantage

In addition to being in an offside position, a player must be seeking to gain an advantage from the position by attempting to either play the ball or hinder or distract opposing players. However, if a player receives a ball directly from a throw-in, corner kick, goal kick, or drop ball, the player is not offside.

If a player is declared offside, an indirect free kick is taken by the opposing team from the position of the offside player.

- ● Practical Consideration

  - Goals should be the result of skillful play and hard work and not the result of players standing in an offside position, in front of the opponent's goal, waiting to score.

Law XII—Fouls and Misconduct

There are four major sections of this law. Each section describes what is (or is not) permitted and the result of an infraction to a rule.

Legal Charge

The term "charge" describes allowed intentional contact between players. This allowed contact:

- *must be shoulder to shoulder with arms (especially elbows) close to the body;*

- *is permitted only while the ball is near enough to play;*

- *must be intended to gain possession of the ball and not to knock down or injure an opponent, or otherwise violent in nature; and*

- *is permitted when at least one foot of each player is in contact with the ground.*

● Section I—The Nine Penal Fouls

The nine penal fouls are the most serious fouls in soccer. Four are committed by the arms, three are committed by the legs, and two are committed by the body. Table 11-7 details the nine penal fouls and their results.

Figure 11-21 may help you remember the nine penal fouls. Note, four are committed by the arms, three are committed by the legs, and two are committed by the body.

● Section II—The Five Non-Penal Fouls

The second section of Law XII deals with less serious types of fouls. These are the five non-penal fouls described in Table 11-8.

● Section III—Cautionable Offenses

The third section of Law XII involves conduct or behavior that is considered unacceptable (see Table 11-9). A referee designates a cautionable offense by holding up a yellow card to the player who committed the misconduct. A player who commits a second cautionable offense (i.e., already has been issued a yellow card) must be ejected from the contest.

● Section IV—Ejectionable Offenses

The fourth section of Law XII involves more serious misconduct (see Table 11-10). A referee designates an ejectionable offense by holding up a red card to the player who committed the act of serious foul play or violent conduct. This also includes the use of foul or abusive language directed at a referee, linesperson, team official, or player.

Table 11-7. The nine penal fouls.

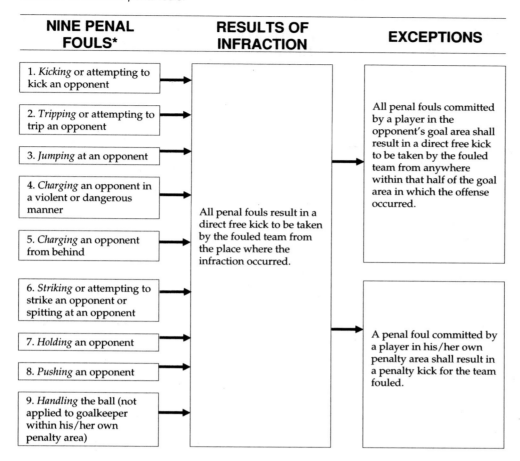

NINE PENAL FOULS*	RESULTS OF INFRACTION	EXCEPTIONS
1. *Kicking* or attempting to kick an opponent		
2. *Tripping* or attempting to trip an opponent		All penal fouls committed by a player in the opponent's goal area shall result in a direct free kick to be taken by the fouled team from anywhere within that half of the goal area in which the offense occurred.
3. *Jumping* at an opponent		
4. *Charging* an opponent in a violent or dangerous manner	All penal fouls result in a direct free kick to be taken by the fouled team from the place where the infraction occurred.	
5. *Charging* an opponent from behind		
6. *Striking* or attempting to strike an opponent or spitting at an opponent		
7. *Holding* an opponent		A penal foul committed by a player in his/her own penalty area shall result in a penalty kick for the team fouled.
8. *Pushing* an opponent		
9. *Handling* the ball (not applied to goalkeeper within his/her own penalty area)		

* All penalty fouls, except handling, are fouls that are intentionally committed against an opponent.

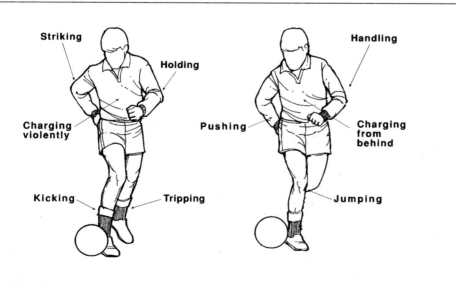

Figure 11-21. Remembering the nine penal fouls.

Table 11-8. *The five non-penal fouls.*

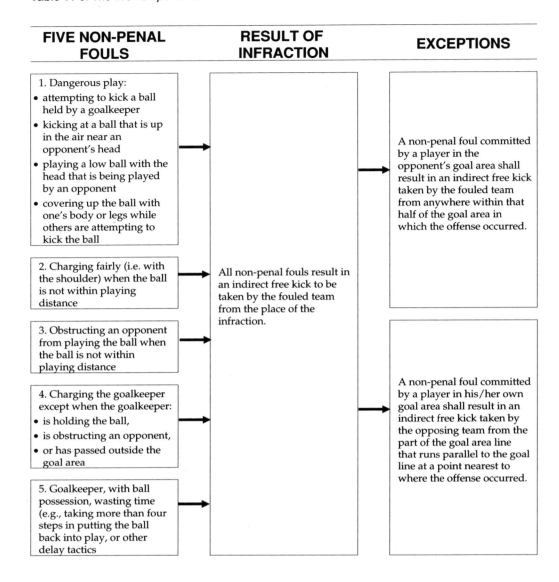

FIVE NON-PENAL FOULS	RESULT OF INFRACTION	EXCEPTIONS
1. Dangerous play: • attempting to kick a ball held by a goalkeeper • kicking at a ball that is up in the air near an opponent's head • playing a low ball with the head that is being played by an opponent • covering up the ball with one's body or legs while others are attempting to kick the ball	All non-penal fouls result in an indirect free kick to be taken by the fouled team from the place of the infraction.	A non-penal foul committed by a player in the opponent's goal area shall result in an indirect free kick taken by the fouled team from anywhere within that half of the goal area in which the offense occurred.
2. Charging fairly (i.e. with the shoulder) when the ball is not within playing distance		
3. Obstructing an opponent from playing the ball when the ball is not within playing distance		A non-penal foul committed by a player in his/her own goal area shall result in an indirect free kick taken by the opposing team from the part of the goal area line that runs parallel to the goal line at a point nearest to where the offense occurred.
4. Charging the goalkeeper except when the goalkeeper: • is holding the ball, • is obstructing an opponent, • or has passed outside the goal area		
5. Goalkeeper, with ball possession, wasting time (e.g., taking more than four steps in putting the ball back into play, or other delay tactics		

- Practical Considerations

  - Soccer is a game that should be won through the use of skill. Law XII provides a framework for penalizing unacceptable actions and behaviors that detract from the skill of playing the game.

  - For more serious fouls, there should be more severe penalties.

- Modifications for Youth Play

  - Penal and non-penal fouls, committed by young players, are often the result of them not knowing the rules of play or carelessness.

Table 11-9. Cautionable offenses.

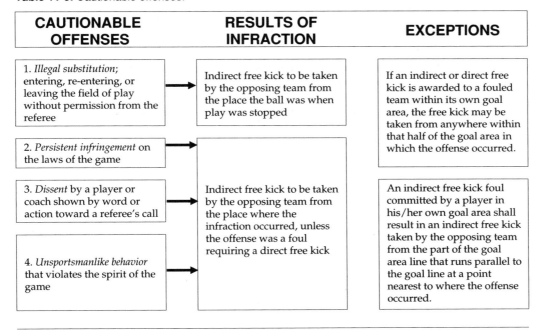

CAUTIONABLE OFFENSES	RESULTS OF INFRACTION	EXCEPTIONS
1. *Illegal substitution;* entering, re-entering, or leaving the field of play without permission from the referee	Indirect free kick to be taken by the opposing team from the place the ball was when play was stopped	If an indirect or direct free kick is awarded to a fouled team within its own goal area, the free kick may be taken from anywhere within that half of the goal area in which the offense occurred.
2. *Persistent infringement* on the laws of the game	Indirect free kick to be taken by the opposing team from the place where the infraction occurred, unless the offense was a foul requiring a direct free kick	An indirect free kick foul committed by a player in his/her own goal area shall result in an indirect free kick taken by the opposing team from the part of the goal area line that runs parallel to the goal line at a point nearest to where the offense occurred.
3. *Dissent* by a player or coach shown by word or action toward a referee's call		
4. *Unsportsmanlike behavior* that violates the spirit of the game		

- Referees must use careful judgment and tact in cautioning and ejecting young players because this action can emotionally devastate them. The issuing of either yellow or red cards must never be done in an accusatory or harsh fashion.

Table 11-10. Ejectionable offenses.

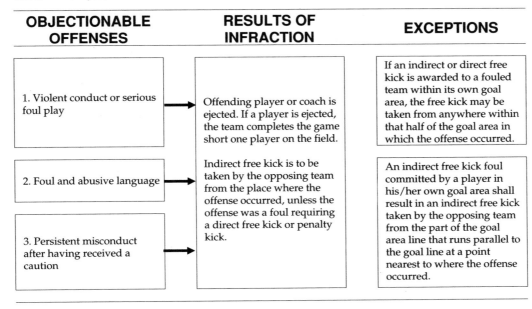

OBJECTIONABLE OFFENSES	RESULTS OF INFRACTION	EXCEPTIONS
1. Violent conduct or serious foul play	Offending player or coach is ejected. If a player is ejected, the team completes the game short one player on the field.	If an indirect or direct free kick is awarded to a fouled team within its own goal area, the free kick may be taken from anywhere within that half of the goal area in which the offense occurred.
2. Foul and abusive language	Indirect free kick is to be taken by the opposing team from the place where the offense occurred, unless the offense was a foul requiring a direct free kick or penalty kick.	An indirect free kick foul committed by a player in his/her own goal area shall result in an indirect free kick taken by the opposing team from the part of the goal area line that runs parallel to the goal line at a point nearest to where the offense occurred.
3. Persistent misconduct after having received a caution		

Law XIII—Free Kick

If a foul or misconduct occurs while the ball is in play, a free kick is awarded to the fouled team. Law XII (Fouls and Misconducts) refers to two types of free kicks—**Direct Free Kick** and **Indirect Free Kick** (see Table 11-11). All free kicks are taken from where the foul occurred, unless the foul is committed in either team's goal area.

Definitions

Direct Free Kick: A goal can be scored by kicking the ball directly into the opponent's goal without being touched or played by another player.

Indirect Free Kick: A goal can be scored only if the ball is touched or played by another player after it is kicked into play.

● **Practical Considerations**

- A player taking any free kick may choose to take the kick when opponents are closer than the rules permit in order to take advantage of quickly returning the ball into play.

- A player taking any free kick may request that the referee ensures that the defenders are at least 10 yards from the point where the kick will be taken.

- Coaches should stress to their players that encroachment on free kicks (i.e., not backing up 10 yards right away) is a cautionable offense and may result in a yellow card being issued.

- The spirit of fair play dictates that opponents not interfere with the other team's ability to put the ball into play from a free kick.

Table 11-11. *Conditional applications of free kick rules.*

CONDITIONS	REQUIREMENTS	RESULTS OF INFRACTION
Any free kick	The ball must be stationary before being kicked into play.	The free kick is retaken.
	When the ball is put into play, it cannot be touched or played a second time by the player taking the free kick until another player has touched or played the ball.	An indirect free kick, to be taken from the location of the infraction, is awarded to the opposing team.
	A player cannot put the ball into play and score directly on his/her own goal.	The goal does not count and a corner kick is awarded to the opposing team.
Any free kick taken from inside own penalty area	The ball is in play when it has moved a distance equal to its circumference and is inside the field beyond the penalty area.	The free kick is retaken.
	The goalkeeper may not receive the free kick directly into his/her hands in the penalty area.	
	* Opposing players must be 10 yards from the ball at the time of the kick and must remain outside the penalty area until the ball has passed out of the penalty area.	Opposing players may be cautioned for unsporting conduct. If cautioned, the free kick is retaken.
Any free kick taken from outside own goal area	The ball is in play when it has moved a distance equal to its circumference.	The free kick is retaken.
	*Opposing players must be 10 yards from the ball until it is played, unless they are standing on their own goal line between the goal posts.	Opposing players may be cautioned for unsporting conduct. If cautioned, the free kick is retaken.
Any free kick taken from inside own goal area	The free kick may be taken from anywhere within that half of the goal area in which the offense occurred.	The free kick is retaken from within the appropriate half of the goal area.
Any indirect free kick taken inside own goal area	The indirect free kick cannot be used to score directly on an opponent's goal.	A goal kick is awarded to the opposing team.
	The indirect free kick cannot be used to score directly on player's own goal.	A corner kick is awarded to the opposing team.
Any indirect free kick awarded taken within opponents' goal area	The indirect free kick must be taken from the part of the goal area line that runs parallel to the goal line at a point nearest to where the offense occurred.	The indirect free kick is retaken.

*See following Practical Considerations.

Law XIV—Penalty Kick

A penalty kick is awarded to the offended team when one of the nine penal fouls (see Law XII—Fouls and Misconduct) is intentionally committed by a player in his/her own penalty area. It should be noted that the location of the penal foul, not the location of the ball, determines whether a penalty kick is awarded. For a penalty kick, the ball is placed on the penalty mark and a goal can be scored directly from the kick. It should be noted that, if a penalty kick is awarded just before halftime or full time, that period is extended for the taking of the penalty kick. For any penalty kick, if the kicked ball is deflected into the goal from the goal posts, cross bar, or goalkeeper, the goal is counted. However, during an extension of time for the taking of a penalty kick, no time is permitted for the kicker or any other person to follow up on a rebounding ball. See Table 11-12 for details.

- ● **Practical Considerations**

  - Because a penalty kick is an excellent scoring opportunity, overt distracting motions by either the kicker or goalkeeper must not be allowed.

  - Spectators and coaches should remain in designated areas (e.g., outside the field and between the two penalty areas) throughout the game. They should not be allowed behind the goal, especially when a penalty kick is being taken.

Table 11-12. *Conditional applications of penalty kick rules.*

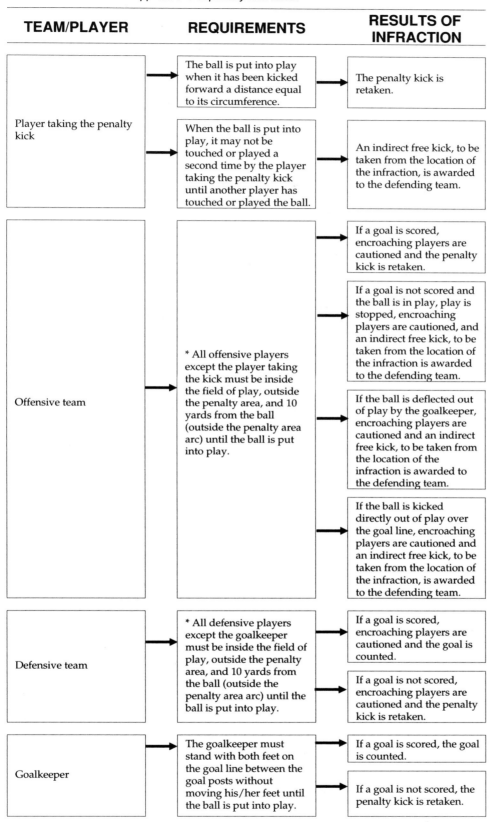

TEAM/PLAYER	REQUIREMENTS	RESULTS OF INFRACTION
Player taking the penalty kick	The ball is put into play when it has been kicked forward a distance equal to its circumference.	The penalty kick is retaken.
	When the ball is put into play, it may not be touched or played a second time by the player taking the penalty kick until another player has touched or played the ball.	An indirect free kick, to be taken from the location of the infraction, is awarded to the defending team.
Offensive team	* All offensive players except the player taking the kick must be inside the field of play, outside the penalty area, and 10 yards from the ball (outside the penalty area arc) until the ball is put into play.	If a goal is scored, encroaching players are cautioned and the penalty kick is retaken.
		If a goal is not scored and the ball is in play, play is stopped, encroaching players are cautioned, and an indirect free kick, to be taken from the location of the infraction is awarded to the defending team.
		If the ball is deflected out of play by the goalkeeper, encroaching players are cautioned and an indirect free kick, to be taken from the location of the infraction is awarded to the defending team.
		If the ball is kicked directly out of play over the goal line, encroaching players are cautioned and an indirect free kick, to be taken from the location of the infraction, is awarded to the defending team.
Defensive team	* All defensive players except the goalkeeper must be inside the field of play, outside the penalty area, and 10 yards from the ball (outside the penalty area arc) until the ball is put into play.	If a goal is scored, encroaching players are cautioned and the goal is counted.
		If a goal is not scored, encroaching players are cautioned and the penalty kick is retaken.
Goalkeeper	The goalkeeper must stand with both feet on the goal line between the goal posts without moving his/her feet until the ball is put into play.	If a goal is scored, the goal is counted.
		If a goal is not scored, the penalty kick is retaken.

* NOTE: If both offensive and defensive players encroach on the taking of a penalty kick, encroaching players are cautioned and the penalty kick is retaken irrespective of the outcome of the kick.

Law XV—Throw-in

A throw-in is awarded when the entire ball passes over the touch line (ball in touch) on the ground or in the air (see Law IX, Ball In and Out of Play). The throw-in is awarded to the team that did not touch the ball last before going into touch. The ball is back in play when it enters the field from a proper throw-in. See Table 11-13 for details.

Table 11-13. Conditional applications of throw-in rules.

TEAM/PLAYER	REQUIREMENTS	RESULTS OF INFRACTION
Player taking the throw-in	At the moment the ball is delivered, the thrower must: • face the field of play, • have part of each foot either on the touch line or on the ground outside the field of play (see Figure 1-11), • use both hands with approximately equal force to deliver the ball, and • deliver the ball from behind and over the head.	A throw-in, to be taken from where the ball initially went out of play, is awarded to the opposing team.
	The thrown ball must enter the field of play.	The throw-in is retaken.
	The throw-in must not bounce before entering the field of play.	The throw-in is retaken.
	The throw-in must be taken from the point where the ball went out of play.	A throw-in, to be taken from where the ball originally went out of play, is awarded to the defending team.
	A ball thrown back into play cannot be touched or played a second time by the thrower until another player has touched or played the ball.	If the ball is handled by the thrower, a direct free kick, to be taken from the location of the foul, is awarded to the defending team.
		If the ball is not handled, but played by the thrower, an indirect free kick, to be taken from the location of the infraction, is awarded to the defending team.
Defensive team	Defensive players cannot interfere with the taking of the throw-in.	After offending players are cautioned, the throw-in is retaken.

- **Practical Consideration**

  - The purpose of the throw-in is to quickly restart play. It should not be used as a method to delay the game or to gain an unfair advantage.

Law XVI—Goal Kick

A non-scoring ball, which was played or touched last by a player on the attacking team over his/her opponent's goal line, is put back into play by the defending team taking a goal kick. Note that the entire ball must pass beyond the goal line, either on the ground or in the air, in order for a goal kick to be awarded (see Law IX—Ball In and Out of Play). The

Table 11-14. *Conditional applications of goal kick rules.*

TEAM/PLAYER	REQUIREMENTS	RESULTS OF INFRACTION
Player/team taking the goal kick	The ball must be stationary before being kicked back into play.	The goal kick is retaken.
	The ball must be kicked inside the field or play beyond the penalty area in order to be in play.	The goal kick is retaken.
	When the ball is put into play, it cannot be touched or played a second time by the player taking the goal kick until another player has touched or played the ball.	If the ball is handled, a direct free kick, to be taken from the location of the foul, is awarded to the opposing team.
		If the ball is not handled, but is played or touched by the kicker, an indirect free kick, to be taken from the location of the infraction, is awarded to the opposing team.
	A goal cannot be scored directly on either goal from a goal kick.	If the ball is kicked into the opponent's goal, a goal kick is awarded to the opposing team.
		If the ball is kicked into the kicker's own goal, the goal kick is retaken because the ball was not put back into play.
Defensive team	*Opposing players must be outside the penalty area until the ball is kicked beyond the penalty area.	Encroaching players may be cautioned for unsporting conduct. If cautioned, the goal kick is retaken.

* See Practical Considerations.

ball is put back into play from a point anywhere within that half of the goal area nearest to where it went out of play. Table 11-14 details infractions and results.

● **Practical Considerations**

- The player taking a goal kick may choose to take the kick when opponents are inside the penalty area in order to take advantage of quickly returning the ball into play.

- The player taking a goal kick may request that the referee ensures proper positioning of defenders.

Law XVII—Corner Kick

A non-scoring ball, which was played or touched last by a player on the defending team over his/her own goal line, is returned to play from a corner kick by the attacking team. Note that the entire ball must pass beyond the goal line, either on the ground or in the air, in order for a corner kick to be awarded (see Law IX—Ball In and Out of Play). *The whole of the ball must be placed entirely within the quarter-circle* nearest the point where the ball went out of play. The corner flag must not be displaced in order to facilitate the taking of a corner kick. A goal may be scored directly from a corner kick. See Table 11-15 for details.

● **Practical Considerations**

- The player taking a corner kick may choose to take the kick when opponents are closer than the rules permit in order to take advantage of quickly returning the ball into play.

- The player taking the corner kick may request that the referee ensures proper positioning of defenders.

Table 11-15. Conditional applications of corner kick rules.

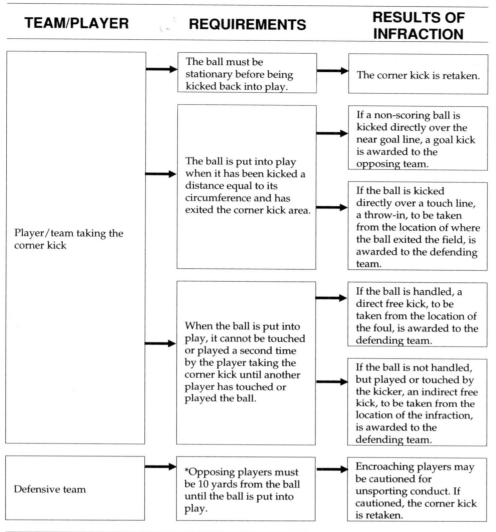

TEAM/PLAYER	REQUIREMENTS	RESULTS OF INFRACTION
Player/team taking the corner kick	The ball must be stationary before being kicked back into play.	The corner kick is retaken.
	The ball is put into play when it has been kicked a distance equal to its circumference and has exited the corner kick area.	If a non-scoring ball is kicked directly over the near goal line, a goal kick is awarded to the opposing team.
		If the ball is kicked directly over a touch line, a throw-in, to be taken from the location of where the ball exited the field, is awarded to the defending team.
	When the ball is put into play, it cannot be touched or played a second time by the player taking the corner kick until another player has touched or played the ball.	If the ball is handled, a direct free kick, to be taken from the location of the foul, is awarded to the defending team.
		If the ball is not handled, but played or touched by the kicker, an indirect free kick, to be taken from the location of the infraction, is awarded to the defending team.
Defensive team	*Opposing players must be 10 yards from the ball until the ball is put into play.	Encroaching players may be cautioned for unsporting conduct. If cautioned, the corner kick is retaken.

* See Practical Considerations.

SUMMARY

This chapter contains a summary presentation of the 17 laws of the game of soccer. They are systematically organized to help those associated with youth soccer (players, parents, coaches, and referees) learn the laws. Several of the laws are presented in a flow chart format, which not only facilitates learning, but also provides quick and easy referencing.

REFERENCES

1. Federation Internationale De Football Association (1990). *Laws of the game and universal guide for referees—USSF supplement.* United States Soccer Federation.

SUGGESTED READINGS

Harris, P., & Harris, L. (1985). *Fair or foul—The complete guide to soccer officiating.* (5th ed.) Manhattan Beach, CA: Soccer For Americans.

Lover, S. (1985). *Soccer laws illustrated.* London: Pelham Books Ltd.

Lover, S. (1986). *Soccer match control.* London: Pelham Books Ltd.

Maisner, L., & Mason, B. (1987). *The rules of soccer: Simplified.* (8th ed.) Los Angeles, CA: MFB Enterprises, Inc.

12

GLOSSARY OF SOCCER TERMS

Eugene W. Brown and Gary Williamson

QUESTIONS TO CONSIDER
- What is the "advantage clause?"
- What is a "banana kick?"
- What is meant by the term "bending the ball?"
- What is a "dead ball?"

INTRODUCTION

This glossary contains an alphabetical listing and definitions of terms common to the sport of soccer. It is presented for the purpose of familiarizing coaches, parents, and players with terms that will be helpful to them when communicating with others about soccer.

A

Advantage (Advantage Clause)*

Refers to part of Law V (Referees) of the Laws of the Game. It gives the referee the right to refrain from penalizing in cases where calling a penalty would give an advantage to the offending team (e.g., A defender attempting to trip an attacking player, who is dribbling the ball into position to take a shot on goal, should not be called for the foul unless the attacker has been prevented from advancing the ball.). [V]+

Air Ball

Any ball that is not in contact with the ground.

---

* Words in parentheses, following the main entry, are common variations of the term being defined.

+ A roman numeral included in brackets indicates that additional detail may be obtained about the term being defined by reviewing this numbered law in Chapter 11 of this section (e.g., [IV] suggests that additional information can be obtained by reviewing Law IV - Players' Equipment).

Arc

(see **Penalty Arc**)

Attack (Attacking Team)

The team in possession of the ball.

Attacker

A player on the team in possession of the ball can be called an attacker. However, "attacker" usually refers to players in scoring positions.

B

Back

A general name given to a fullback and other field players whose roles are primarily defensive.

Back Door

This term has two separate meanings. It is a term applied to playing the ball through the legs, from in front to behind the body (e.g., playing the ball out the back door). It also refers to the opening to the goal behind the goalkeeper.

Back-Heel

A pass in which the heel is used to kick a ball backward.

Ball-Side

Pertains to the side of the field (in a lengthwise division of the field) where the ball is located (e.g., A ball-side back is a fullback located on the same side of field as the ball.).

Banana (Banana Kick)

A ball kicked into the air that curves laterally (see **Bending the Ball**).

Beat

The act of getting to the ball before an opponent, or when in possession of the ball, out-maneuvering an opponent to get past him/her.

Bending the Ball

Refers to the technique of kicking the ball into the air with an off-center (right or left) and oblique strike by the foot, so that the ball has lateral spin, resulting in a curved path (see **Banana**).

Bending Run

A curved run made by an offensive player to get into position to receive a pass or to possibly draw defenders.

Bicycle Kick

A kick that is made with the body off the ground and leaning backwards. Initially, the non-kicking leg is swung forward and upward and the kicking leg lags behind. The legs then rapidly switch positions (see **Scissors Kick**) and the kicking foot contacts the ball to drive it back and over the head of the kicker.

Blind-Side Run

A run made by an offensive player in an area of the field away from the visual concentration of opponents (i.e., opposite to the ball-side of the field).

Block Tackle

The block tackle refers to the use of the inside of the foot to "block" the movement of the ball at the same time as the opponent attempts to kick or dribble it forward.

Boots

Another name for soccer shoes or cleats.

Breakaway

This situation occurs when the player with the ball is beyond all the defending field players and has an unchallenged path, except for possibly the goalkeeper, to the goal.

Bunch (Bunching)

A close gathering of two or more players from the same team (offense or defense).

C

Carry (Carrying)

A player who maintains the dribble carries the ball. Coaches will often call "carry" if they want their player to continue to dribble the ball.

Catenaccio

The Italian word for "bolt." Catenaccio described the man-to-man defensive system of marking used by the Italians in the 1950s. In this system, one player (the Libero or free back) played behind the other field players to provide defensive support.

Caution

An official action taken by the referee against any player who (a) enters or leaves the field of play without permission, (b) persistently infringes upon the Laws of the Game, (c) shows by word or action dissent toward any decision given by the referee, or (d) is guilty of unsportsmanlike behavior. The referee signifies a caution by holding up a yellow card to the player. [XII]

Center (Centering Pass)

A long pass that is made from the side of the field to the area in front of the goal (see **Cross**).

Center Back

Refers to the center fullback.

Center Circle

A circle at the center of the field drawn with a 10-yard radius from the center mark. The center circle is used for kickoffs to start either half of play and to restart play after a goal is scored. [I, VIII]

Center Forward

This player is a principal attacker who is positioned at the center of the forward line.

Center Line

(see **Halfway Line**)

Center Mark

This mark is at the center of the halfway line. It is used for kickoffs. [I, VIII]

Change of Field (Change Fields)

Refers to a pass from one side of the field to the other (see **Cross**).

Charge (Charging)

The term "charge" describes allowed intentional contact between players. This allowed contact (a) must be shoulder to shoulder with arms (especially elbows) close to the body, (b) is permitted only while the ball is near enough to play, (c) must be intended to gain possession of the ball and not to knock down or injure an opponent, and (d) is permitted when at least one foot of each player is in contact with the ground. If the charge is not performed in this manner, it may result in a foul. [XII]

Checking Run

An offensive maneuver consisting of a run in one direction followed by a quick change of direction. A checking run is used to free an offensive player from a tightly marking defender.

Chip

The act of lofting a ball from the ground into the air by kicking it below its center. This technique can be used to pass (Chip Pass) or shoot (Chip Shot) the ball.

Clear (Clearance)

This occurs when defending players project the ball far away from their own goal to decrease their opponent's immediate chances of scoring. Clears can be made by field players and goalkeepers.

Close Space

Describes a condition in which one or more defenders are positioned between a player with the ball and another player on attack. This defensive arrangement is desirable because an attempted pass between these two attackers is likely to be intercepted.

Club Linesman (Club Linesperson)

A person appointed by the referee whose only role is to indicate when a ball has gone out of play. [VI]

Corner Area

A quarter of a circle, at each of the four corners of the field. The corner area is marked on the field with a one-yard radius from the corner flag. [I, XVII]

Corner Flag

A flag on the non-pointed top of a post, not less than five feet in height. Corner flags are used to designate each of the four corners of the field of play. [I]

Contain

Refers to any defensive technique or tactic that is used to restrict an opponent to a certain area of the field.

Counter (Counterattack)

An attack that is begun immediately after gaining possession of the ball.

Cover

The term cover is used in three different ways in soccer. The term is generally used to describe close marking or guarding of an offensive player who does not have possession of the ball. It is also used to describe the action of a free defender who is ready to take over for a teammate guarding the player with the ball. Finally, it also refers to close marking of offensive players in advance of the ball.

Cross (Crossing Ball)

A pass, usually in the air, that is kicked from one side of the field to the other (see **Change of Field**) or from one side of the field to the area in front of the goal (see **Center**).

Cross Bar

The part of the goal that is parallel to the ground and directly over the goal line. It provides for a 24-foot-wide opening to the goal. [I]

Cross-Over Run (Take-Over Run)

When a dribbler and teammate run toward each other and they pass by side-by-side, they have completed a cross-over run. At the point their paths cross, possession of the ball may be exchanged.

Curving the Ball

(see **Bending the Ball**)

Cushioning the Ball

Refers to the action of a relaxed body part that a player uses to absorb and yield to the impact force of a soccer ball to decrease its pace when attempting to receive and control the ball.

Cutting Down the Angle

(see **Narrowing the Angle**)

D

Danger Area (Danger Zone)

Generally refers to the space in front of the goal where an offensive player in possession of the ball is a threat to score.

Dangerous Play

Any activity that may result in an injury to an opponent, teammate, or player performing the action may be interpreted by the referee as dangerous play. Dangerous play is a non-penal foul, which results in an indirect free kick. [XII]

Dead Ball

A ball that is not in play. A dead ball occurs when a ball passes out of the field of play, during a temporary suspension of play caused by an infraction, or when the game is otherwise stopped by the referee. [IX]

Decreasing the Angle

(see **Narrowing the Angle**)

Defender

Any player on the team that is not in possession of the ball may be called a defender.

Defense

Refers to all techniques and tactics that are used to regain possession of the ball and to prevent the opposing team from scoring.

Deflecting

This term describes the action taken by a goalkeeper in which one or two open hands are used to redirect a shot away from the goal.

Delay

A fundamental principle of defense in which players attempt to impede the progress of the offensive team to gain time to incorporate more players in defense and to employ other defensive tactics.

Depth

The positioning of players on the field from goal line to goal line, to provide mutual tactical assistance in either offensive or defensive play is called depth.

Diagonal Run

A run on offense that begins near one touch line and progesses simultaneously toward the opponent's goal line and opposite touch line.

Diagonal System

(see **Three-Man System**)

Direct Free Kick

A place kick that is awarded to a team as a result of a penal foul being committed against them. The kick is taken from the point of the infraction and a goal may be scored directly from the kick. [XIII]

Distribution

Refers to the various individual techniques used by a player to pass the ball to teammates. It is more frequently used to describe this activity when performed by a goalkeeper.

Down Field

Away from where the ball is located and toward the opposite goal.

Down the Line

Describes a ball passed near a touch line and toward the opponent's goal.

Dribble (Dribbling)

The act of maneuvering the ball on the ground while maintaining control of it by a series of touches with different parts of the feet.

Drive (Drive the Ball)

A powerful kick, usually associated with a ball projected low to the ground, is called a drive.

Drop Ball

The method used by a referee to start play after it has been stopped for an injury, a foreign object on the field, or other circumstances when no laws of the game have been violated. The ball is dropped by the referee. The ball is back into play after it strikes the ground.[VIII]

Drop Kick

A distribution technique used by the goalkeeper. It is performed by dropping the ball from the hands to the ground and then immediately kicking it as a half volley.

Dual System

(see **Two-Man System**)

Dummy Run

An offensive run intended to draw one or more defenders away from a particular area of the field.

E

Echelon Formation

A grouping of players on offense from which they run to assigned locations during the taking of a corner kick or free kick. This is designed to make defensive marking more difficult.

Ejection

An official action taken by the referee against any player who (a) is guilty of violent conduct or serious foul play, (b) uses foul or abusive language, and (c) persists in misconduct after having received a caution. The referee signifies an ejection by holding up a red card to the player. The team whose player is ejected completes the game short one player on the field. [XII]

F

Far Post

The goal post farthest away from the player with the ball.

Feint

Action taken by a player that is intended to deceive an opponent. This action may involve movements of body parts and/or movements of the ball.

Field Player

Any soccer player other than a goalkeeper. [III]

FIFA

An acronym for Federation Internationale de Football Association, which is the international governing body of soccer.

Finish (Finishing)

Refers to a shot on goal to complete an attack.

First Defender

Player marking the attacker with the ball.

First Time

Describes the method of kicking an approaching ball that involves passing or shooting it without first attempting to receive and control the ball. It is also used to describe a half volley trap made on the first bounce of an air ball.

Flank

Refers to the area of the field within approximately 15 feet of either touch line.

Football

Term used internationally for the game North Americans call soccer.

Foot Plant

(see **Planted Foot**)

Formation

The general organization of players to prescribed positions on the field. It is noted by a numerical grouping of the ten field players proceeding from those closest to the goalkeeper to those closest to the opponent's goal (e.g., A 4-3-3 is a formation that uses 4 fullbacks, 3 halfbacks, and 3 forwards, as well as a goalkeeper.).

Forward

Refers to any of the players on the front line of the team's formation.

Foul

There are two types of fouls—the five non-penal fouls and the nine penal fouls (see **Non-Penal Foul** and **Penal Foul**). [XII]

Free Back

A defender positioned behind the fullbacks, who is free to support and cover for whichever fullback needs help (see **Catenaccio, Libero,** and **Sweeper**).

Free Kick

A place kick that is awarded to a team that has been fouled. There are two types of free kicks — direct and indirect (see **Direct Free Kick** and **Indirect Free Kick**). [XIII]

Fullback

A player in the team's last line of defense located immediately in front of the goalkeeper.

Funnel (Funneling)

Refers to the defensive retreat of players toward their own goal, upon losing possession of the ball, from positions on the flanks to central positions. Funneling results in a concentration of defenders in front of their own goal. Funneling limits the attacking space available to opponents in the danger area.

G

Give and Go

(see **Wall Pass**)

Goal

Refers to the target at each end of the field of play (eight feet high by eight yards wide), also a score that is made by projecting the ball into this target. [I, X]

Goal Area

A rectangular area (six yards by 20 yards) that is marked on each end of the field of play. One of the 20 yard sides of each of the rectangles is centered on each of the goal lines. The goal area is primarily used to designate the location to take goal kicks. [I, XVI]

Goalkeeper (Goalie, Keeper)

This player is usually the last line of defense. With few exceptions, the goalkeeper is controlled by the same rules as the field players. The primary difference is that the goalkeepers are permitted to use their hands on the ball in their own penalty area. [III]

Goal Kick

A free kick taken from the goal area. It is a kick that is awarded to the defending team when the ball is played over their goal line by the attacking team. The ball is not back into play from a goal kick until it passes out of the penalty area and onto the field. [XVI]

Goal Line

The two goal lines are the boundary lines located at the ends of the field. They extend from touch line to touch line and pass directly beneath the cross bars of each goal. [I]

Goal Mouth

The area immediately in front of the goal.

Goal Post

The vertical or upright posts that are perpendicular to the goal line. They support the horizontal cross bar at a height of eight feet above the ground. [I]

Goal-Side

Refers to a position between the ball and the goal being defended (e.g., goal-side marking).

Grid

A series of square or rectangular spaces that are marked on the field. Drills and small-sided games are organized by coaches in these restricted spaces to teach their players techniques and tactics.

Ground Ball

Any ball that is rolling or bouncing on the field.

H

Halfback

(see **Midfielder**)

Halftime

The period between the two halves of the game. The rules governing the game designate its length. [VII]

Half Volley

An air ball that is kicked or received immediately after it strikes the ground.

Half Way Line

This line divides the field into two equal halves. It runs widthwise and connects the two touch lines. [I, VIII]

Hand Ball (Hands)

A penal foul that occurs when field players intentionally play the ball with their hands or arms. Goalkeepers are bound by this rule except when playing a ball within their own penalty area. Note that in some leagues females are permitted to use their arms when making a chest trap. [XII]

Head (Heading, Header)

Refers to any of several individual techniques in which the head is used to pass, shoot, or receive a ball. Contact is usually made with the forehead.

Heel Pass

(see **Back-Heel**)

Hitch Kick

(see **Bicycle Kick** and **Scissors Kick**)

Hold (Holding)

A penal foul that occurs when a player grasps an opponent with any part of a hand or arm. [XII]

I

Improvise (Improvisation)

Refers to the ability of an attacking player to be creative and adapt to situations as they occur.

Indirect Free Kick

A place kick that is awarded to a team as a result of an infraction committed against them. A goal cannot be scored directly from an indirect free kick; after the kick, the ball must make contact with another player before a goal may be scored. An indirect free kick is taken from the point of the infraction, unless it is committed in an opponent's goal area. In that circumstance, the kick may be taken from any point within the half of the goal area (right or left) in which the infraction occurred. [XIII]

Inside Forward

Refers to a player on the forward line who is neither a wing nor a center forward.

Instep

Refers to the lace portion of the shoes. It is used in various individual techniques to kick and receive a ball.

Inswinger

A cross that curves toward the goal. This term is most often associated with long corner kicks.

J

Jockey (Jockeying)

Refers to a delay tactic used by a defensive player. In jockeying, a defender may repeatedly feint making a tackle and giving ground to disrupt advances of the dribbler and provide teammates with time to recover.

Juggle (Juggling)

An individual training technique that is used to develop control of the ball. Juggling consists of keeping the ball in the air by repeatedly hitting it with various parts of the body except the hands and arms.

K

Kickoff

An indirect free kick, taken from the center of the field, that is used to start play at the beginning of each half and after each goal. [VIII]

L

Laws of the Game

These are the 17 rules, according to FIFA, that govern the play of the game of soccer.

Lead Pass

A pass that is kicked to a point in front of a teammate. It is usually intended to permit the teammate to continue to run and receive the ball without altering stride.

Legal Charge

(see **Charge**)

Libero

The Italian word for free back (see **Catenaccio, Free Back,** and **Sweeper**).

Linesmen (Linespersons)

These are two officials whose duties are to indicate (a) when the ball is out of play; (b) which side is entitled to a corner kick, goal kick, or throw-in; and (c) when a substitution is desired. In general they are responsible for assisting the referee. [VI]

Linkman

(see **Midfielder**)

Lob

A ball that is kicked high into the air over the heads of opponents.

Lofted Ball

A ball that is kicked high into the air by using either a chip, a half volley, or an air ball kick.

Long Corner (Long Corner Kick)

A corner kick in which a centering pass is made to put the ball back into play.

Looking Off the Ball

(see **Off the Ball**)

M

"Man On"

A call made by a coach or player to warn a team member in possession of the ball or about to receive the ball that a defender will be marking.

Man-to-Man (Person-to-Person)

A style of defense in which one or more players are assigned to guard specific attackers.

Mark

Another term for guard.

Match

A synonym for an official soccer game.

Midfield

A widthwise portion of the field that encompasses about the middle third of the field.

Midfielder (Midfield Player)

A player who has primary offensive and defensive responsibilities in the middle third of the field. Midfielders are also called linkmen and halfbacks because they serve as a connection between the forwards and fullbacks.

Mobility

A basic offensive concept associated with movement of attackers, who are not in possession of the ball, to use existing space and create new space into which passes and other runs can be made.

N

Narrowing the Angle

Refers to the action taken by a goalkeeper who quickly advances, under control, along an imaginary line connecting the center of the goal line and the ball. (This action reduces the open angle that an attacker has to shoot on goal.)

Near Post

The goal post closest to the player with the ball.

Neutral Linesman (Neutral Linesperson)

(see **Club Linesman**)

Non-Penal Foul

Fouls that are less serious than penal fouls. They result in an indirect free kick to be taken by the fouled team from the point of the infraction. [XII]

Nutmeg

A slang term used to describe a situation in which an attacker advances the ball by passing it between the defender's legs.

O

Obstruction

A deliberate movement by a player intended to impede an opponent. Obstruction is penalized by awarding the obstructed player's team an indirect free kick. Note that if the obstruction occurs within playing distance of the ball, a foul is not committed. [XII]

Off the Ball

Refers to a location on the field that is not in the vicinity of the ball. (e.g., An attacking player may make a run off the ball. A dribbler may look off the ball.)

Offside

An illegal offensive position of players in advance of the ball. It is the most complex law within the game. Consult Law XI of the Laws of the Game for the details of this infraction. [XI]

Offside Position

A player must be illegally positioned in advance of the ball (offside position) in order to be offside. However, an offside infraction should not be called unless a player is seeking to gain an advantage from this positioning. [XI]

Offside Trap

A defensive maneuver designed to put attacking players offside. This usually involves fullbacks quickly moving away from their own goal to create a situation in which attackers are positioned illegally in advance of the ball.

"On"

An abbreviation for "man on" (see **"Man On"**).

One Time

(See **One Touch**)

One Touch

Describes the method of passing or shooting an approaching ball without first attempting to receive and control it; in other words, the ball is kicked on the first touch.

Open Space

Describes a condition in which no defenders are positioned between the player with the ball and a teammate. This offensive arrangement is desirable because a pass can freely be made without the likelihood of an interception.

Outside Forward

Refers to a player on either end of the forward line who is positioned nearest the touch line (see **Outside Left, Outside Right,** and **Wing**).

Outside Fullback

Refers to a player on either end of the fullback line who is positioned nearest the touch line.

Outside Left

The player on the left end of the forward line. This player is also called the left wing.

Outside Right

The player on the right end of the forward line. This player is also called the right wing.

Outswinger

A cross that curves away from the goal. This term is most often associated with corner kicks.

Overlap (Overlapping Run)

Occurs when an offensive player runs from a position behind a teammate in possession of the ball to a position in advance of the ball. An overlapping run decreases pressure at the point of attack by either drawing the defender away from the player with the ball or providing an opportunity for the player with the ball to make a pass to the teammate running into open space.

Own Goal

A score resulting from a ball that is inadvertently played by a defender into his/her own goal.

P

Passive Pressure

Inactive opposition to a player in possession of the ball. Passive pressure can be used as a lead-up technique in teaching various individual offensive techniques or it can be used in the game as a delay tactic to slow the advance of an attacking team.

Penal Fouls

These are serious fouls. They result in a direct free kick to be taken by the fouled team from the point of the infraction. Note that if a penal foul is committed by a player in his/her own penalty area, a penalty kick is awarded to the fouled team. [XII]

Penalty Arc

The portion of the circumference of a circle, with a 10-yard radius and center at the penalty kick mark, that extends outside the penalty area. It is used as a restraining line for players during the taking of a penalty kick. [I, XIV]

Penalty Area

A rectangular area (18 yards by 44 yards) that is marked on each end of the field of play. One of the 44 yard sides of each of the rectangles is centered on each of the goal lines. The area is used to (a) determine if a penalty kick should be awarded to a team sustaining a penal foul, (b) restrict players during the taking of a penalty kick, and (c) limit the area in which goalkeepers can use their hands. [I, XIV]

Penalty Kick

A direct free kick taken from the penalty kick mark. It is awarded as the result of a penal foul committed by a team in their own penalty area. At the time the penalty kick is taken, the goalkeeper must be standing with both feet stationary on the goal line. All other players except for the kicker must be outside the penalty area and at least 10 yards from the ball (outside the penalty arc). [XIV]

Penalty Kick Mark (Penalty Kick Spot, Penalty Kick Line)

A mark on the field, 12 yards from the center of the goal line, that is used as a location from which penalty kicks are taken. [I, XIV]

Penetrating Pass

(see **Through Pass**)

Penetration

Refers to the action of an attacking team that quickly advances the ball through the defense and creates scoring opportunities.

Pitch

A British name for a soccer field.

Place Kick

Refers to any free kick (direct free kick, indirect free kick, corner kick, goal kick, kick off, or penalty kick) in which a player is permitted to kick a ball placed in a stationary position on the ground. [VIII, XIII, XIV, XVI, XVII]

Planted Foot

Usually refers to the support foot (non-kicking foot) that is set firmly on the ground when making a kick. The term also refers to a foot that provides support to the body when a player performs other movements such as pivots, jumps, and tackles.

Point of Attack

The location of the ball when it is in the possession of a player.

Position (Positioning)

A player's assigned location and/or responsibility within a team's general organization on the field (e.g., goalkeeper, center halfback, right wing) (see **Formation**).

Preferred Foot

The dominant or favorite foot of a player.

Pressure (Pressuring, Pressurize)

A delay tactic associated with goal-side marking of the player with the ball and also close marking of other attackers to restrict offensive opportunities.

Professional Foul

A foul that is intentionally committed to take away an opponent's advantage.

Punch (Punching)

Describes the action taken by a goalkeeper in which one or both fists are used to knock a shot away from the goal.

Punt

An individual distribution technique that is used by goalkeepers to clear the ball away from their goal. In punting, the ball is released from the hands and then kicked with the instep.

Push (Pushing)

A penal foul that is committed when players use their hands to move an opponent or when they rest their hands on an opponent. [XII]

Push Pass

Another term for an inside of the foot kick in which the ball is passed on the ground over a short distance.

Q

Quick Kick

The rapid taking of any free kick without waiting for defenders to be positioned 10 or more yards from the ball.

R

Read (Reading the Game, Reading the Play)

Refers to the ability of a player to analyze and interpret a game situation, anticipate the outcome, and quickly and appropriately respond.

Recovery Run (Recovering Run)

A defensive run to get to a goal side marking position.

Referee

> The appointed official in charge of the game. The referee is empowered by the Laws of the Game. [V]

Restart

> Describes all methods used to recommence play after it has been stopped. The following is a listing of all restarts: drop ball, throw-in, goal kick, direct free kick, indirect free kick, kick off, corner kick, and penalty kick.

Running Off the Ball

> (see **Off the Ball**)

S

Save

> Refers to the various individual techniques associated with catching, punching, and deflecting a ball that are used by the goalkeeper to prevent a goal.

Scissors Kick

> Refers to any kick performed by a player while off the ground in which the non-kicking foot is swung forward and then back, exchanging positions with the kicking foot. Contact with the ball is made on the forward swing of the kicking foot (see **Bicycle Kick**).

Score

> Refers to a goal (point) awarded when the entire ball passes over the goal line, between the goal posts, and under the cross bar. [X]

Screen

> Refers to a player or group of players positioning themselves so their bodies obstruct their opponent's view of the ball. This term is sometimes synonymously used for shielding (see **Shield**).

Second Defender

> Any defensive player engaged in cornering, supporting, or switching tactics (tactics associated with depth) to assist a teammate working the player with the ball.

Set Play (Set Piece)

> Refers to a predetermined tactic that is usually employed in restart situations.

Shepherd (Shepherding)

> A defensive tactic that involves marking and jockeying of opponents so they move or pass the ball into locations on the field that are not as likely to result in scoring opportunities.

Shield (Shielding)

Refers to the positioning of a player in possession of the ball, between an opponent and the ball. Players shield the ball with their bodies to prevent opponents from gaining possession of the ball. Shielding may or may not be legal, depending on whether or not an opponent is being obstructed (see **Obstruction**).

Short Corner (Short Corner Kick)

A corner kick in which a short pass is used to put the ball back into play.

Shot

A kick, head, or any intended deflection of the ball toward a goal by a player attempting to score a goal.

Shoulder Charge

(see **Charge**)

Side Line

(see **Touch Line**)

Side Volley

A variation of an instep volley in which an air ball, located to the side of the body, is kicked. When making a side volley, the player's trunk leans away from the ball and approaches a horizontal orientation.

Skills

Individual techniques such as receiving and controlling the ball with the chest, kicking the ball with the outside of the foot, and marking an opponent in possession of the ball become skills when they are used under game conditions.

Slide Tackle (Sliding Tackle)

Refers to any attempt to dispossess an opponent of the ball in which the defensive player slides to the ground in making the tackle (see **Tackle**).

Small-Sided Games

Refers to play during practices or modified match competition in which fewer than 11 players per team are employed.

Space

(see **Close Space** and **Open Space**)

Square Pass

Refers to (a) a pass that is laterally made with respect to the field, or (b) a pass by a player to his/her side.

Stopper

A defender who is centrally located in front of the fullbacks.

Strategy

(see **Tactics**)

Striker

Generally refers to any player in a forward position who has relatively frequent opportunities to shoot on goal. This term, however, is more frequently used to describe an inside or center forward.

Strong Foot

The preferred or dominant foot of a player.

Style of Play

Refers to the nature of play demonstrated by an individual or a team. The following terms are some examples of descriptors of style: short passing, long passing, deliberate play, aggressive play, finesse, counterattacking, defensive, and offensive.

Substitute (Substitution)

This is a player who replaces a teammate on the field. Substitutions must be made in accordance with the rules of competition under which the game is being played. In most youth games, an unlimited number of substitutions may be made. These usually occur at the start of any period (e.g., halftime, overtime); after a goal is scored; before a goal kick; and before a throw-in, but only for the team taking the throw. [III]

Support

Refers to offensive or defensive assistance provided by a teammate. Offensively, a player may provide support to a marked teammate with the ball by taking a position in an open space behind the play to receive a support pass. Defensively, a player may provide support to a teammate who is marking an attacker with the ball by taking a ready position behind the teammate.

Support Foot

(see **Planted Foot**)

Support Pass

(see **Support**)

Sweeper

This player is a free back behind the last line of defenders (see **Libero**). The primary responsibilities of the sweeper are to provide support for the defender at the point of the attack and to intercept passes that penetrate the defense.

Swerved Ball

(see **Banana** and **Bending the Ball**)

Switch

A switch occurs when two players change assignments and/or positions.

System (System of Play)

Amalgamation of style of play and team formation (see **Style of Play** and **Formation**). Note that two teams, using the same team formation, may demonstrate a drastically different system of play because of the differences in their styles of play. Similarly, the overall systems of play of two teams using different formations may be relatively alike.

T

Tackle (Tackling)

Refers to the various individual defensive techniques in which the feet are used to dispossess an opponent of the ball or to interfere with the intended play.

Tactics

Offensive and defensive skills, whether performed by one player, in combination with a few teammates, or by an entire team, become tactics when they are used with the intent to create a strategic advantage in play.

Take a Dive (Taking a Dive)

Refers to the acting displayed by a player pretending to be fouled by an opponent. It usually involves falling or diving to the ground in response to contact by an opponent. A player who is judged by the referee as taking a dive can be given a caution for unsportsmanlike behavior.

Take-Over Run

(see **Cross-Over Run**)

Techniques

The basic individual movements used both offensively and defensively in soccer (e.g., inside of the foot kick, block tackle, and dribbling the ball with the outside of the foot).

Ten Yards (10 Yards)

Refers to the minimum distance from the ball that defenders are permitted during the taking of any free kick, with the exception of an indirect free kick that is located less than 10 yards from the defending team's goal line. [XIII]

Three-Man System

A standard officiating system in which one referee and two linespersons are used.

Through Pass

A lead pass that penetrates the fullback line.

Throw-In

Refers to the method of restarting play after the ball has gone out of bounds over the touch line. A goal cannot be scored directly from a throw-in. [XV]

"Time"

This is a call used to inform a teammate with the ball or about to receive the ball that defenders will not be immediately marking.

Toe Ball

A kick in which contact with the ball is made only with the toe of a shoe.

Toe Poke

An individual technique for tackling the ball away from an opponent in which the foot is extended to reach the ball and poke it away with the toe of the shoe.

Total Football (Total Soccer)

A system employed by the Dutch National Team in the 1974 World Cup. This system requires all players to possess a high level of both offensive and defensive skills because they freely change positions and responsibilities during a match.

Touch

This term is used in three different ways. (a) To describe a fine sense of control some players have in maneuvering the ball. (b) The area beyond the side lines of the field. A ball that is "into touch" can be touched with the hands to throw it back into play. (c) The term "touch" is combined with a number to describe how many contacts a player has with the ball during a possession. For example, a player that "two touches" the ball receives the ball and then kicks it on the next touch (see **First Time**).

Touch Line

A side boundary (side line) of the field that extends from one goal line to another. [I, IX, XV]

Trap (Trapping)

A term generally used to define the process of receiving a soccer ball. The term "trap" is commonly combined with a body part to identify the body segment used to gain control of the ball (e.g., thigh trap, chest trap, sole of the foot trap).

Trip (Tripping)

A penal foul that occurs when players use their feet and legs to unbalance or attempt to unbalance an opponent. [XII]

Two-Man System

A modified system of officiating in which two referees on the field have legal authority in controlling play.

U

Up Field

(see **Down Field**)

V

Volley

A kick made on an air ball (e.g., side volley, instep volley).

W

Wall (Defensive Wall, Human Wall)

A barrier formed by two or more defenders standing side-by-side to assist their goalkeeper in defending against a free kick.

Wall Pass

A one touch return of a pass to a player who sprints into open space to receive the ball back. The player making the return pass is used as a wall to rebound (pass) the ball back.

Warning

An admonishment given to a player who has infringed in some way upon the rules. Referees will sometimes use a warning before giving a caution (showing a yellow card) to a player.

Weak Foot

The non-dominant foot of a player.

Weak Side

Refers to the side of the field opposite to where the ball is located.

Width

An offensive principle of play in which attacking players take up positions spread across the field from one touch line to another. This type of positioning spreads the defense and creates more open space.

Wing (Winger)

A player on either end of the halfback or forward line may be called a winger (see **Outside Forward, Outside Left,** and **Outside Right**).

World Cup

The official world championship of soccer. It is sanctioned by FIFA and held once every four years.

Wrong Side of the Ball

Refers to the positioning of defenders between their opponent's goal and the ball. This positioning is opposite to goal-side positioning.

Z

Zone

> A system of defense in which players are assigned to protect specific areas of the field.

Section IV

INDIVIDUAL TECHNIQUES
FOR SOCCER FIELD PLAYERS

13

KICKING

Eugene W. Brown and Gary Williamson

QUESTIONS TO CONSIDER
- What are the four components of a kick?
- What are the techniques used in kicking?
- What are the key elements of various kicking techniques?
- What are common errors young soccer players make when executing kicking techniques?
- What are the coaching techniques that are effective in teaching youth players how to kick?

INTRODUCTION

In the sport of soccer, kicking is used to pass or shoot a ball. Kicking for distance, accuracy, and speed are three elements of kicking. Their importance in passing and shooting varies with the conditions of play at the time the ball is kicked.

There are several individual techniques for kicking a soccer ball. Specific information about each individual technique is presented in this chapter. However, four components of kicking, which are relevant to most kicking techniques, should be understood before attempting to learn about the specifics.

Four Components of Kicking

1. Approach

The movement of a player toward the ball before kicking is the approach. The manner in which this is performed is important because it may affect the outcome of the kick. A full-speed run to the ball is not usually desirable because a player will not likely be able to control the kick that follows. There are two types of approaches:

Straight Approach

In a straight approach, the path a player takes to the ball is in alignment with the direction of the intended path of the kicked ball (See Figure 13-1A). One exception to this is seen in the outside of the foot kick.

Angled Approach

In an angled approach, the path a player takes to the ball is not in alignment with the direction of the intended path of the kicked ball. An angled approach to the ball may vary from a straight line to a curved path (see Figure 13-1B).

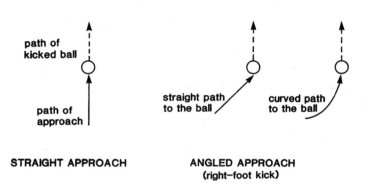

path of
kicked ball

path of
approach

straight path
to the ball

curved path
to the ball

STRAIGHT APPROACH

ANGLED APPROACH
(right–foot kick)

Figure 13-1. *Paths of the straight approach (A) and the angled approach (B).*

The last step of an approach, whether straight or angled, should be a leap. A leap provides time for and aids in the backswing of the kicking leg (see Figure 13-2C-F). During a leap, the knee of the kicking leg should be flexing and the hip of the kicking leg should be extending. The degree to which either of these actions occur should be related to the desired ball

A.   B.   C.   D.   E.   F.

Figure 13-2. *Side view of approach.*

velocity. For maximum ball velocity, the hip of the kicking leg should be fully extended before swinging the leg forward.

2. Pre-Impact

Pre-impact follows an approach. It begins with the placement of the supporting foot on the ground, at the end of the leap (see Figure 13-3A), and ends immediately before the kicking foot impacts the ball. As a player contacts the ground, the support leg acts like a strut: to block the forward movement of its hip, to start the forward rotation of the other hip, and to initiate forward swing of the thigh of the kicking leg. The knee of the kicking leg, however, continues to flex. Just before impact, the speed of the thigh's forward rotation should rapidly decrease. This is associated with a rapid extension of the knee of the kicking leg (see Figure 13-3C-E).

It should be noted that the arms are used to counterbalance the forceful forward swing of the kicking leg. The arms are generally held out to the sides of the body. As the kicking leg is swung forward, the arm on the same side of the body is swung back and the arm on the opposite side is swung forward (see Figure 13-3A-F). The function of the arms to counterbalance the action of the kicking leg continues through impact and follow through.

There are two factors in an angled approach that provide it with a greater potential to maximize ball velocity in a kick. These factors are an "open hip position" and the "use of a longer lever."

Figure 13-3. *Pre-impact.*

Hip Position

An angled approach has a more open hip position at the start of the pre-impact when compared with a straight approach. This is to say that in the angled approach the hip of the kicking leg is drawn farther back (see Figure 13-4A and B). Because of the increased range to swing the hip of the kicking leg forward from this opened position, greater forward velocity can be achieved in the kicking leg.

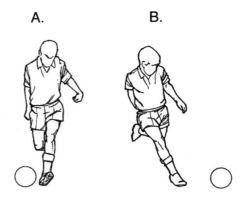

Figure 13-4. *Position of the hip of the kicking leg at the start of pre-impact. A. Closed hip position in straight approach. B. Opened hip position in angled approach.*

Lever Length

In an angled approach, the support foot is placed farther from the side of the ball than in a straight approach (see Figure 13-5A and B). In the angled approach, the trunk leans away from the ball, allowing the player to fully extend the kicking leg (lever) when impacting the ball (see Figure 13-5B). On the other hand, in the straight approach, the knee of the kicking leg must be bent for the foot to clear the ground (see Figure 13-5A). The longer lever achieved in the angled approach provides for potentially greater ball velocity in the kick.

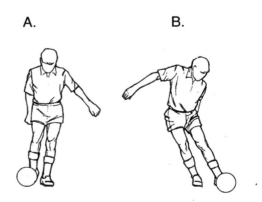

Figure 13-5. *Lever length at impact in a straight (A) and an angled approach (B).*

3. Impact

The part of the foot that contacts the ball varies with the kicking technique used. Before teaching the different kicking techniques, beginning players should be taught the names and corresponding parts of the foot (see Figure 13-6).

Regardless of which kicking technique is to be used, there are five factors that influence how the ball will be projected from the foot.

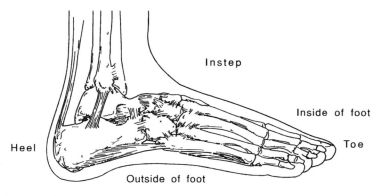

Figure 13-6. *Parts of the foot.*

Placement of the Support Foot

If the support foot is to the side and front of the ball, the kicking foot will likely make contact with the ball on the downswing and compress the ball against the ground. If the support foot is alongside the ball, contact will be made at the bottom of the arc of the kicking foot, resulting in a low drive. Support foot placement to the side and behind the ball will result in the ball being struck on the upswing of the kicking foot, lifting the ball into the air.

Trunk Lean

The lean of the trunk is usually associated with support foot placement. The farther behind the ball the support foot is placed, the farther back the trunk tends to lean in order to assist the kicking foot to reach the ball. As the support foot is positioned farther forward, the greater the tendency for the trunk to be upright.

Point of Impact

Figure 13-7 represents the effect of the point of impact on the subsequent projection of the ball.

It should be noted that the spin and resulting curve imparted to the ball can be increased by an oblique kick of the ball. This is known as "bending the ball" or "swerving the ball." It is a useful technique in projecting a ball around a defender who has "closed space" and in kicking a ball around a defensive wall when taking a free kick.

Firmness of Impact

If the ankle and foot of the kicking leg are held firm on impact, the ball will attain a greater velocity when compared with a kick taken with a loosely held foot.

Location and Result

1—low drive, curve to right

2—low drive

3—low drive, curve to left

4—ball kicked into ground

5—lofted ball, back spin

Figure 13-7. *Location of impact and resulting projection of the ball.*

Area of Foot Contact

As the area of foot contact with the ball increases, there is a similar increase in ball control. Thus, players can more easily control the direction of an instep kick than they can control the direction of a toe kick.

4. Follow-Through

The movement of the body that occurs immediately after the completion of impact is the follow-through. During the follow-through, the speed of the kicking leg is decreased and controlled. It is during this time that the player should gain control of the movements of the body in order to proceed to subsequent activity.

The follow-through does not have any effect on the ball because the foot and ball are no longer in contact. However, the follow-through is the result of the approach, pre-impact, and impact. Thus, from a coaching perspective, it is important for you to observe and analyze how the body parts move during the follow-through. These movements may provide you with an understanding of the previous movements in the kick.

INDIVIDUAL TECHNIQUES

There are many ways to kick a soccer ball. Variations in technique depend upon: the part of the foot that impacts the ball, the location of the foot's impact on the ball, the direction of movement of the foot during impact, and the location of the ball (ground, half volley, or air). The remainder of this section will be a presentation of various techniques of kicking based upon parts of the foot impacting the ball.

Inside of the Foot Kicks

The inside of the foot is used to kick the ball relatively short distances. It is, however, the most accurate type of kick because of the large surface area of the foot used to contact the ball. This kick can be used to accurately shoot the ball on goal from short distances and to make short, controlled passes to teammates.

● Kicking a Ground Ball

Low Drive

When maintaining the ball on the ground with this kick, it is referred to as a "push pass." The push pass is used to kick the ball accurately over short distances. This kick consists of the four components of kicking previously described. For the inside of the foot kick, a straight approach is made under a controlled speed and is followed by a leap onto a support foot, which is pointed in the direction of the intended target. During the leap, the backswing is shortened and the kicking leg is rotated outward (see Figure 13-8A-C) to orient the kicking foot so that the inside of the foot is squared to the back of the ball. On impact, the support foot should be alongside the ball. The trunk and head should be over the ball. The kicking foot should contact the ball at the bottom of the leg swing with the ankle fully flexed to provide a firm impact (see Figure 13-8C). The orientation of the kicking foot should be maintained into follow-through and continue its motion in the direction of the intended target.

Figure 13-8. Inside of the foot kick on a ground ball ("push pass").

Key Elements

- Approach the ball in line with the intended direction of the kick (straight approach).
- Place the support foot to the side of the ball.
- Point the support foot in line with the intended target.
- Shorten the backswing.
- Turn the kicking leg outward.
- Impact the ball with the kicking ankle fully flexed and firm.
- Follow through with the swing of the kicking leg in the direction of the target.

Common Errors

- Kicking without an approach, resulting in an inefficient leg swing
- Placing the support foot too far from the ball
- Kicking the ball off center
- Not contacting the ball with the inside of the foot

● Kicking a Half Volley

Half volleys that are played with the inside of the foot can be directed toward the ground or lofted into the air. The variation in the path of the ball depends upon the direction the foot is moving and the location of foot contact at the moment the inside of the foot contacts the ball.

Low Drive

If the intent is to drive the ball low from a half volley, the support foot should be to the side and slightly to the rear of where the ball contacts the ground, the trunk should be upright or leaning slightly forward, and the foot should make contact slightly above the center of the ball (see Figure 13-9A to F).

Key Elements

- Position the support foot to the side and slightly to the rear of the ball.
- Time the swing of the kicking foot to make contact with the ball momentarily after the ball contacts the ground.
- Flex the hip and knee to elevate the foot in order to contact the ball slightly above the center of the ball.

Common Errors

- Improper positioning of the support foot
- Leaning the trunk back away from the ball
- Contacting the ball on the upswing of the kicking leg

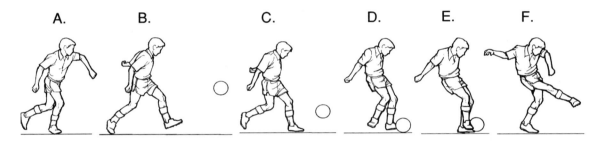

Figure 13-9. *Driving a ball low from a half volley with the inside of the foot kick.*

Lofted Ball

If the intent is to loft the ball into the air with the inside of the foot kick, the support foot should be to the side and rear of where the ball strikes the ground, the trunk should be leaning away from the ball, and the foot should make contact slightly below the center of the ball on the upswing of the kicking leg. This kick is used to project the ball over the heads of defending players.

Key Elements

- Position the support foot to the side and rear of the ball.
- Time the swing of the kicking foot to make contact with the ball after the ball has bounced a short distance from the ground.
- Lean the trunk back, away from the ball.

Common Errors

- Improper timing of the leg swing
- Not contacting the ball with the inside of the foot

Swerved Ball

A third variation that can be performed on a half volley results in a swerved (curved) path of the projected ball. Swerving the ball is caused by an angled approach and resulting oblique impact of the inside of the instep and inside of the foot to the ball. In this technique, knee extension occurs simultaneously with a forward swing of the kicking leg (see Figure 13-10A to E). This type of kick is used to curve a ball around a defender.

Key Elements

- Make an oblique impact of the foot to the ball.
- Kick the ball with a medium arc so the spin can cause the ball to take a curved path.

Common Error

- Using too much of the instep to kick the ball

A.   B.   C.   D.   E.

Figure 13-10. *Swerving a ball from a half volley with the inside of the instep and inside of the foot kick.*

● Kicking an Air Ball

The same variations in kicking technique that can be achieved by using the inside of the foot on a half volley can be achieved with the inside of the foot on an air ball. The movement patterns, purposes, key elements, and common errors in using the inside of the foot to kick an air ball are very similar to those described for the inside of the foot kick on a half volley.

Instep Kicks

The instep kick is the most powerful kick in soccer. It is used to kick the ball long distances or to kick it with considerable pace. This type of kick can be used to make powerful kicks on goal from short or long distances and to make long passes to teammates. The four components of kicking, previously described, completely apply to the movement pattern used in making an instep kick.

● Progression for Teaching the Instep Kick to Beginning Players

Beginning players often have difficulty learning the instep kick because:

- it requires coordination of rapidly moving body parts;

- it requires accurate foot placement and body positioning;

- they perceive previously learned "toe" kicking as initially more successful and are, therefore, reluctant to use the instep kick; and

- they are anxious about the possibility of an injury from kicking the ground.

Because of the difficulties encountered by many beginning players in performing the instep kick, it is important that coaches understand these problems and have a teaching progression to facilitate the learning of this technique. The following description is a five-step approach that can be used to teach beginning soccer players the instep kick.

Step 1—Manual Guidance

A key factor in the success of any kick in soccer is the placement of the supporting foot (the non-kicking, planted foot). If the support foot is improperly positioned relative to the ball, the resultant kick will likely be errant. Manual guidance of the kicking leg (See Figure 13-11) helps to reduce this problem because the ball is placed by the coach directly to the side of the support foot after the support foot has been positioned. The player maintains balance on the support foot by holding the shoulders of the coach. This supported position properly aligns the head and trunk of the player over the ball. In this position, the athlete must flex the hip of the kicking leg just enough for the extended foot to clear the ground during leg swing. The coach holds the ball with one hand from behind so as not to be struck on the fingers and guides the player's kicking leg back and forth, flexing and extending the athlete's knee. The extended instep

Figure 13-11. *Coach and player positioning during manual guidance.*

should contour to the ball and be guided in making firm contact. This guided action provides the athlete with a "feel" for proper instep contact, proper body positioning over the ball, proper support foot positioning, and a reduction in anxiety toward subsequent attempts at the instep kick.

Step 2—Supported Kick

The next phase in this progression is the supported kick (see Figure 13-12). This can be attempted after only a few minutes of practice with manual guidance. It differs from the manual guidance technique in that the player controls the kicking motion of the leg and foot contact. Support is still maintained by placing the hands on the shoulders of the coach. The ball is now held by the coach with two hands from behind and positioned, as before, directly to the side of the support foot. The player must be instructed to control the force of the kick. The intent of this phase is not to teach forceful kicking, but to instruct in leg control, proper foot contact (contour with the ball), and proper body alignment.

Figure 13-12. Coach and player positioning during supported kicking.

Step 3—Leap Kick

Once the player demonstrates control of the kicking leg in the supported kicking phase, the athlete should be instructed to add a step onto the support foot before kicking. This step should become exaggerated into a short leap (see Figure 13-13). Again, the force of the kick must be controlled by the athlete. The coach holds the ball with both hands, as in

Figure 13-13. Coach and player positioning during leap kick.

the previous phase. Feedback should be continually given about the leap, support foot positioning, leg swing, body positioning, and instep contact with the ball.

Step 4—Independent Kicking, Straight Approach

After the player masters the leap kick with the instep, the coach can move to the side and observe several independent instep kicks. As control of the leap and kicking action progresses, the player should be encouraged to precede the leap by a few approach steps from directly behind the ball.

Step 5—Independent Kicking, Angled Approach

The final phase in this progression is to teach an angled approach to the ball. When kicking with the right foot, the approach should be from behind and to the left of the ball; the approach is made from behind and to the right of the ball when kicking with the left foot. Two basic differences exist between the straight and angled approach. First, the support foot is planted farther from the ball in the angled approach (see Figure 13-14), but it is still positioned directly to the side of it. Second, the hip and knee of the kicking leg do not need to be flexed for the extended foot to clear the ground. This is because the body leans away from the ball, providing a sufficient distance for the kicking leg to fully extend into impact. After players learn how to make an angled approach and instep kick on a placed ball, they should be encouraged to dribble the ball before kicking.

Figure 13-14. *Instep kick following an angled approach.*

● Kicking a Ground Ball

The same three results can be achieved with an instep kick on a stationary ball and a ball rolling on the ground. These results are a low drive, lofted ball, and swerved ball.

Low Drive

An angled or straight approach to the ball can be used to drive the ball low. The primary factor in achieving a low drive is the position of the support foot. When kicking a low drive from the straight approach, the support foot should be placed directly to the side of the ball. From this position, the knee of the kicking leg will be over the ball and contact will be made by the kicking foot at the bottom of its arc (see Figure 13-15). When kicking a low drive from an angled approach, the support foot is placed to the side of the ball, but several inches from it. This results in positioning the knee of the kicking leg over the ball and to its side. From this position, contact will be made by the kicking foot at the bottom of its arc.

Figure 13-15. Placement of the support foot and path of the kicking foot in a low drive with the instep kick from a straight approach.

Lofted Ball

To kick the ball into the air with either the straight or angled approach, the support foot must be farther to the rear of the ball than with the low drive. With the support foot farther back, impact with the ball is made on the upswing of the arc of the kicking foot.

Note that it is easier to kick the ball into the air with the angled approach. By lowering the angle of the foot across the back of the ball, the instep can contact the ball below its center, resulting in a lofted ball with backspin. This type of kick is referred to as a "chip" (see Figure 13-16).

Figure 13-16. Foot position when chipping the ball with the instep.

Swerved Ball

By combining the movement pattern for lofting the ball with an off center impact on the inside of the instep with the ball, a curved projection can be achieved.

● Kicking a Half Volley

A low drive, lofted ball, and swerved ball from either a straight or angled approach can be achieved on a half volley with an instep kick (see Figure 13-17). The movement patterns in these kicks are similar to that used in kicking a ground ball with the instep. Kicking a half volley, however, is more difficult because of the speed of the approaching ball and the precision required in striking the ball after it rebounds momentarily from the ground.

Figure 13-17. Use of the instep kick to drive the ball low from a half volley.

• Kicking an Air Ball

A low drive, lofted ball, and swerved ball from either a straight or angled approach can be achieved on an air ball with an instep kick. The movement patterns in these kicks are similar to those used in kicking a half volley with the instep. However, making accurate instep kicks on air balls are difficult because it is hard to precisely contact the ball.

Key Elements (Instep Kicks in General)

- Take a controlled approach run to the ball.

- When attempting to achieve maximum ball velocity, fully extend the hip and flex the knee of the kicking leg during the leap to the support foot.

- Properly position the support foot based upon the type of approach and variation of instep kick intended.

- Point the support foot in the direction of the target.

- Keep the ankle of the kicking foot fully extended through impact and follow-through (see Figure 13-18).

Figure 13-18. *Proper kicking foot position during follow-through in the instep kick. The ankle is fully extended.*

Common Errors (Instep Kicks in General)

- Not contacting the ball with the instep

- Not making contact in the proper location on the ball

Side Volley

A fourth variation of an air ball kick with the instep is the side volley. This kick can be used to play a ball directly out of the air or after it has bounced. Generally, the side volley instep kick is initiated by rotating the support leg and foot outward during the leap (see Figure 13-19A to C). This results in an opened hip position with the support foot pointing outward and the hip of the kicking leg trailing the hip of the support leg (see Figure 13-19C and D). The body should lean away from the ball with the trunk approaching a horizontal position (see Figure 13-19C and D). From the opened hip position, the thigh of the kicking leg is swung forward and followed by a whipping action of the lower leg into contact with the ball (See Figure 13-19C to E). The kicking leg is swung through an oblique plane while the arms are held out away from the body and rotated in the opposite direction to counterbalance the action of the kicking leg (see Figure 13-19C to F).

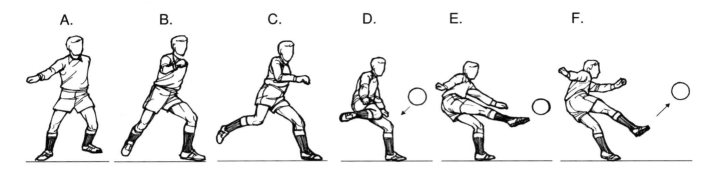

Figure 13-19. Side volley with the instep.

Key Elements

- Open the hips.
- Lean the trunk away from the ball.
- Counterbalance the leg swing by rotating the arms opposite to the direction of the kicking leg.

Common Errors

- Positioning the support foot so the body is too close to the ball and contact with the ball cannot be made with a fully extended kicking leg
- Improperly striking the ball

Scissors Kick

This is another variation of the instep kick that is named for the action of the legs before kicking the ball. These kicks are performed with the body off the ground. Therefore, the pre-impact leap and foot plant is absent. In the scissors kicks, to create an effect similar to the leap, the non-kicking leg is swung forward first in order to aid in extension of the hip and flexion of the knee of the kicking leg. The legs then exchange positions by swinging the non-kicking leg back and the kicking leg forward.

Basically, there are three types of scissors kicks.

Front Scissors Kick

This kick is used on an air ball or on a ball that has bounced into the air. It is very difficult to accurately strike a fast-moving air ball. Therefore, the front scissors kick is used more often on a ball whose pace has been slowed by bouncing. Before the kick, the player leaps into the air to elevate the kicking leg to the height of the ball so the ball can be kicked low (see Figure 13-20). It should be noted that contact with the ball in the front

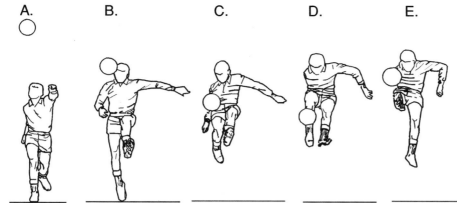

Figure 13-20. Front scissors kick with the instep.

scissors kick can be made with the outside or inside of the foot, as well as with the instep, by changing the position of the kicking leg and foot on the forward swing.

Overhead Scissors Kick (Bicycle Kick)

To perform an overhead scissors kick, the player jumps into the air by swinging the non-kicking foot upward and leaning the trunk backward (see Figure 13-21A to D). The legs then exchange positions by "scissoring" the kicking leg upward and the non-kicking leg downward (see Figure 13-21D-F). As the kicking leg swings upward to contact the ball, the chin is brought to the chest and the arms are swung down to a position where they can help absorb the force of landing.

Bicycle kicks are difficult to perform and can result in an injury to the arms and back if the force of landing is not properly absorbed. These kicks should not be taught to players until they are at least 14 years of age and have developed their skills in the other individual kicking techniques.

This kick can be used on a ball that approaches with a steep arc, to volley it in a direction opposite to which a player is facing. The overhead scissors kick can be used by fullbacks to clear a ball away from their goal when they are facing their goal and being challenged. Care must be taken

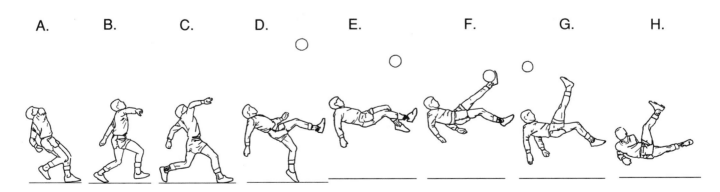

Figure 13-21. Overhead scissors kick as a defensive clear.

in this circumstance to avoid an indirect free kick from dangerous play associated with high kicking.

The overhead scissors kick can also be used by an attacking player to shoot on goal. In attempting to shoot on goal, the ball should be struck when the kicking leg is swinging back toward the goal. To aid in a lower trajectory of the ball, the player should put top spin on the ball by flexing the ankle on contact.

Over the Shoulder Scissors Kick

This is performed in a similar manner to the overhead scissors kick (see Figure 13-21). It differs in that the body is turned to the side and the kicking leg is swung obliquely across the body toward the opposite shoulder. This kick may also permit the player to get a view of the goal by looking over the opposite shoulder before the kick. With this kick, the force of landing is absorbed primarily with the side of the body and the arm opposite the kicking leg.

Outside of the Foot Kicks

It is relatively difficult to control a kick with the outside of the foot because ball contact with the foot involves a glancing strike of the ball with the small area comprising the outside of the foot. This type of impact imparts spin to the ball and projects it laterally to the line of the leg swing (see Figure 13-22). Because the direction of leg swing and ball projection are not the same, the outside of the foot kick can be used to deceive opponents.

Figure 13-22. *Ball spin and projection resulting from an outside of the foot kick with the right foot.*

● Kicking a Ground Ball

Low Drive

The four components of kicking apply to the outside of the foot kick, with the exception that an angled approach is not used in this technique. In order for the outside of the foot to properly contact the ball, a straight approach is needed. At the end of the approach, a leap is taken onto the support foot, which should be planted along side the ball. As the kicking leg swings forward, it should be turned slightly inward (see Figure 13-23C and D). At contact, the kicking foot should be pointed down and inward across the back of the ball (see Figure 13-23D). It should be noted that the leg swing in this kick is similar to that taken in a straight approach instep kick. Contact is made with the outside of the foot by properly positioning the kicking leg and foot and not by turning the body sideways and swinging the leg laterally.

A.   B.   C.   D.   E.   F.

Figure 13-23. *Outside of the foot kick.*

● Kicking A Half Volley

A low drive, lofted ball, and swerved ball can be achieved on a half volley with the outside of the foot kick. The movement patterns in these kicks are similar to that used in kicking a ground ball with the outside of the foot. Difference in elevation of ball projection is directly related to support foot position, kicking leg angle at foot contact, and body lean.

To drive the ball low:

- the support foot should be close to where the half volley strikes the ground,
- the knee of the kicking leg should be ahead of the ankle when the foot strikes the ball, and
- the body should be leaning forward on foot contact with the ball.

To project the ball into the air:

- the support foot should be a short distance back from where the half volley strikes the ground,
- the kicking leg should be swinging upward with its knee behind its ankle, and
- the body should be leaning backward on foot contact with the ball.

Note that the only difference between kicking a lofted ball (with minimal spin) and a swerved ball is in the orientation of the kicking leg and foot. To reduce the lateral spin imparted to the ball, the kicking leg and foot must be inwardly rotated more than in kicking a swerved ball (see

Figure 13-24). By increasing the inward rotation of the kicking leg, the orientation of the surface of the outside of the foot becomes more perpendicular to the ball.

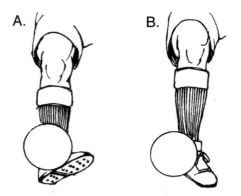

Figure 13-24. *Orientation of the kicking leg and foot when lofting or swerving a ball with the outside of the foot on a half volley. A. Lofted kick. B. Swerved kick.*

● Kicking an Air Ball

A low drive, lofted ball, and swerved ball can be achieved with an outside of the foot kick on an air ball. The movement patterns in these kicks are similar to those used in kicking a half volley with the outside of the foot.

Key Elements (Outside of the Foot Kicks in General)

- Properly position the support foot based upon variation of kick intended.

- Rotate the kicking leg inward.

- Contact the ball with the ankle of the kicking leg fully extended and the foot pointed down and across the back of the ball.

Common Error (Outside of the Foot Kicks in General)

- Turning the kicking leg side of the body toward the ball and attempting to swing the leg laterally to contact the ball (see Figure 13-25).

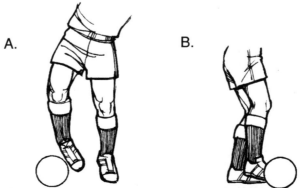

Figure 13-25. *A. Proper body orientation and leg swing for the outside of the foot kick. B. Improper body orientation and leg swing.*

(Note this improper pattern of movement is regularly seen when players are initially attempting to learn the outside of the foot kick.)

Heel Pass (Back-Heel)

In this pass, the heel is used to kick a ground ball backward to a teammate who is trailing the ball. By stepping over the ball with the kicking foot, defenders may be deceived into thinking that the ball is going to be passed forward. The back-heel can be performed on a stationary ball or a rolling ball. Basically, the player steps over the ball with the kicking foot and then flexes the knee in order to strike the ball with the heel (see Figure 13-26).

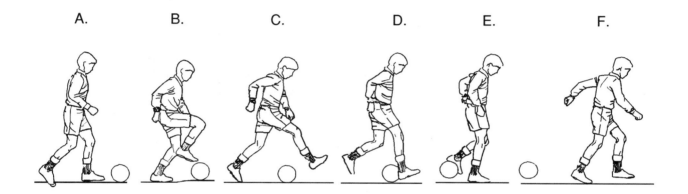

A.   **B.**   **C.**   **D.**   **E.**   **F.**

Figure 13-26. Back-heel on a rolling ball.

Toe Kick (Toe Poke)

Many beginning players will use the toe of their shoe to kick the ball. This is because they have not learned other individual kicking techniques. The toe kick or toe poke has limited use in soccer. The primary situation in which it is useful occurs when a ground ball is away from a player, but near his/her opponent. In this circumstance, the leg and ankle may be extended to poke the ball away from the opponent.

PROGRESSION FOR TEACHING KICKING

When teaching your players individual kicking techniques, a progression from relatively easy kicks to relatively difficult kicks should be followed. Supplement 13-1 contains a listing of the individual kicking techniques, and these are rated by level of difficulty. This supplement, therefore, can be used as a general guide in determining a sequence in which various kicks should be taught (beginning, intermediate, and advanced).

In addition to using Supplement 13-1 to guide you in sequencing your teaching of the individual kicking techniques, factors that influence the level of difficulty in kicking the ball are summarized in Table 13-1. When teaching your players individual kicking techniques, you can adjust the difficulty they experience by varying the combination of factors selected for practicing these techniques. For example, using the instep to swerve a ball that is placed on the ground is not as difficult as swerving a fast-moving half volley with the instep when pressured by an opponent. By being aware of these factors, you will be able to select kicking tasks that are challenging to your players but not overwhelming. Supplement 13-2 contains some examples of kicking drills and games that should help you to provide practice experiences to teach your players individual kicking techniques.

Table 13-1. Factors influencing the level of difficulty in kicking the ball.

	Factors					
Level of Difficulty	**Type of Ball to be Played**	**Pace of Ball**	**Positioning**	**Technicque Selection**	**Pressure**	**Target**
Relatively easy	Stationary or rolling	Still too slow	Little movement required to position the body to kick the ball	Preselected by coach or player based upon predetermined ball path and pace	No defensive pressure	Stationary
Moderate	Rolling	Intermediate	Some movement to position the body with ample time provided		Passive defensive pressure	
Relatively difficult	Half volley or air ball	Intermediate to fast	Player must move quickly to get into position to play the ball	Selection made by player based upon conditions of play immediately preceding the kick	Full defensive pressure	Moving

YOUTH SOCCER TECHNIQUES— KICKING
Difficulty Rating Form

Level of Player* Approximate Age*	Suggested Emphasis		
	Beginning 6-9 yrs.	Intermediate 10-13 yrs.	Advanced 14 yrs. & up
Individual Techniques			
Inside of the foot kicks			
ground ball			
low drive	X	X	X
half volley			
low drive		X	X
lofted ball		X	X
swerved ball		X	X
air ball			
low drive	X	X	X
lofted ball	X	X	X
"chip"		X	X
swerved ball		X	X
half volley			
low drive		X	X
lofted ball		X	X
swerved ball			X
air ball			
low drive	X	X	X
lofted ball	X	X	X
swerved ball			X
side volley			X
front scissors			X
overhead scissors			X
over-the-shoulder scissors			X
Outside of the foot kicks			
ground ball			
low drive	X	X	X
half volley			
low drive			X
lofted ball			X
swerved ball			X
air ball			
low drive			X
lofted ball			X
swerved ball			X
Heel pass (back-heel)		X	X
Toe kick		X	X

*Note that "Beginning," "Intermediate," and "Advanced" does not always correspond with the age range given beneath it. Coaches should use this classification system as an approximation, adjusting the techniques to suit their players' ability levels.

PASSING AND SHOOTING DRILLS AND GAMES

NAME	DIAGRAM	DESCRIPTION	KEY POINTS	VARIATIONS
Between the Legs	10 yds	Two players position themselves about 10 yards apart. One player stands with his/her feet spread apart. Using an inside of the foot kick, the other player tries to kick the ball on the ground through the partner's legs. After each kick, the players reverse roles. One point is awarded to a player each time he/she kicks the ball through the partner's legs. The player scoring the most points wins. (6 years and older)*	This game is used to encourage accurate kicking. Note that both players should alternate feet in kicking to develop accurate passing with both feet.	1. Use the outside of the foot or instep to kick the ball. (7 years or older) 2. Increase the distance between the partners. (7 years or older) 3. Dribble the ball to the appropriate distance before kicking it. (7 years and older)
Target Ball	20 yds / 20 yds	Two opposing teams of about four players each line up approximately 20 to 30 yards apart. To start the game, two balls are given to each team. The object of the game is to kick a ball into the target ball, placed in the middle of the target zone, to knock it across the opponent's restraining line marked by two cones. If the target ball goes over the side line, it is returned to the center of the target zone at a point perpendicular to where it went over the side line. Balls must be received and kicked from behind the restraining line. Balls that stop in the target zone or beyond the side line can be retrieved by the team closest to the ball. (6 years and older)	This game is used to encourage players to kick accurately with speed under the pressure of a game.	1. Use two or more balls for targets. (7 years and older) 2. Increase the distance between the restraining line. (8 years and older) 3. Increase the number of players per team. (7 years and older) 4. Use cones in the middle instead of a ball. One point is given for each cone knocked over. (7 years and older)

*Suggested age for practicing the drill is included in parentheses.

PASSING AND SHOOTING DRILLS AND GAMES

NAME	DIAGRAM	DESCRIPTION	KEY POINTS	VARIATIONS
Continuous Line Passing	REP	A ball is passed back and forth between lines of two or more players. After making a pass, the player runs to the end of the opposite line. (6 years and older)	Various individual passing and receiving techniques can be selected by the coach for practice.	1. Use two- or one-touch passing. (10 years and older) 2. Use chip or swerve passing. (10 years and older) 3. Use two or more balls in the drill. (8 years and older) 4. Use three lines in a triangle or four lines in a square formation. Passes are made to the first person in the next line, followed by a run to the end of that line. One- or two-touch passing, as well as additional balls, can be introduced into these drills. (10 years and older)

PASSING AND SHOOTING DRILLS AND GAMES

NAME	DIAGRAM	DESCRIPTION	KEY POINTS	VARIATIONS
Rapid Fire		Four or more balls are positioned in an arc around the outside of the penalty area. A field player successively shoots each ball on goal, attempting to score on the goalkeeper. After each shot, the field player must run around the flag before attempting another shot on goal. The instep of the right foot must be used on balls approached from the left and left instep used on balls approached from the right. Score can be kept on the number of shots on goal and number of goals. (7 years and older)	This drill provides practice for both shooting and goalkeeping.	
Independent Passing		In a confined space, partners pass, receive and control, dribble, and return pass. All pairs are moving throughout the space simultaneously. (7 years and older)	Players should be encouraged to make right- and left-footed passes on the ground with the inside and outside of the foot and with the instep. Passes should not strike another ball or person. This drill requires players to look up and make passes to a moving target.	1. Increase the space and have players lofting the ball to their partner. (10 years and older)
Name Call		Position the players in a formation you usually use for your team. Give five of the players a ball. They are to call the name of a player who doesn't have a ball and make a pass to that player. (7 years and older)	Encourage long and short accurate passes. This drill also involves receiving and controlling skills. This drill can also help players to learn the names of teammates on a newly formed team.	1. Select specific type of kicks to be used. (7 years and older)

PASSING AND SHOOTING DRILLS AND GAMES

NAME	DIAGRAM	DESCRIPTION	KEY POINTS	VARIATIONS
Cross and Shoot	REP	Two lines are formed near midfield along the touch line. In one line, each of the players has a ball. The first player in line with a ball dribbles near the touch line toward the cone near the corner. Simultaneously, the first player in the other line makes a diagonal and looping run toward the goal. Once past the cone, an instep kick is made to pass the ball toward the player making the run. The player receiving the pass attempts a shot on goal. Players change lines after each turn. (7 years and older)	The object of this drill is to teach players how to make good crossing passes, time their runs toward the goal, and shoot on goal. This drill also provides practice for goalkeepers. The drill should be performed from each side so that players practice crosses from the left as well as from the right.	1. Use a defender to assist the goalkeeper. (10 years and older) 2. Have two players make runs against one defender and goalkeeper. (12 years and older)
Straight On Shooting		Each player in line near midfield has a ball. The first player in line dribbles toward the goal and takes a shot when reaching the edge of the penalty area. The drill is repeated by the next player in line. Players retrieve their own ball and get back in line. A line for each goal should be used. (7 years and older)	Inside and outside of the foot and instep kicks can be used to shoot on goal. Restrict the shooter to taking the shot before entering the penalty area. This forces the shooter to be in control of the dribble and also protects the goalkeeper.	1. Use a defender in addition to the goalkeeper. (7 years and older) 2. Toss the ball so that the player must run onto the ball and kick it before it enters the penalty area. (7 years and older)

PASSING AND SHOOTING DRILLS AND GAMES

NAME	DIAGRAM	DESCRIPTION	KEY POINTS	VARIATIONS
Three-Person Weave (Lead Pass and Run Behind)		Three lines with an equal number of players in each are formed at one end of the field. All players in the center line have a ball at their feet. The drill is started with a lead pass to the lead player in one of the two outside lines. The player who makes the pass runs behind the player receiving it. The next lead pass is made to the opposite side followed by a run behind the receiving player. The group of three players proceed down the field followed by other groups engaged in three-person weaves. (7 years and older)	Various individual techniques can be used to pass, receive, and advance the ball. Movements of each of the players must also be coordinated with the others.	1. Use two- or one-touch passing. (10 years and older) 2. Pass and Run in Front is a variation of the Three-Person Weave. Instead of running behind the player receiving the lead pass, the person makes a square pass to the side and then runs in front of the player receiving the ball. (9 years and older)
Wall Pass and Shoot		Several players, each with a ball, form a line at midfield. A line of retrievers is at each side of the goal. The first person in line with a ball makes a pass to the first player in one of the retrieving lines. The pass is received and returned (wall pass). The ball is then shot on goal. The passer and retriever go to the end of the opposite line. The next wall pass is made to the player in front of the other retrieving line. While players are in the retrieving lines they should attempt to return balls to the center circle. (8 years and older)	Accurate passes and shots and timed runs are practiced during this drill. The type of pass and shot can be established by the coach.	1. Add the option for the retriever to turn and shoot if "turn" is called by the coach prior to receiving the initial pass. (9 years and older) 2. Add a goalkeeper to drill. (8 years and older)

PASSING AND SHOOTING DRILLS AND GAMES

NAME	DIAGRAM	DESCRIPTION	KEY POINTS	VARIATIONS
Pass and Change Positions	10 yds	This drill is performed in groups of three. In a triangle, the ball is passed back and forth along one side. The players not receiving the ball exchange positions. (8 years and older)	In this drill, passes must be timed so that the receiving player gets to the proper position to receive the pass. Players must also make runs off the ball. By extending the length of time the drill is performed, the development of fitness becomes a component.	1. Use one-touch passing. (10 years and older)
First Time Wall Ball	REP	Two or more players line up behind a player with the ball. The player with the ball starts the game by kicking the ball so that it rebounds from the wall (wall area restricted to 8' x 24'). The second player runs to get into position to one-touch kick the ball back to the wall before the ball has stopped moving. While this occurs, the player who previously kicked the ball runs to the back of the line. The object of the game is to have the lowest score. A point is given to a player for a) not kicking the ball before it stops moving, b) not hitting the wall with a kicked ball, and c) kicking the ball so that it hits the wall outside the restricted target. Players maintain the same order throughout the game. A player who scores a point begins the next round. (9 years and older)	This game forces players to make various first-time kicks on rolling balls, half volleys and air balls. It also encourages accuracy of shot placement and control of kicking force. If three to five players are used, this game becomes a good game for physical conditioning.	1. If availability of wall space is a problem, the game could use 4' x 8' x 3/4" plywood sheets for targets. (10 years and older) 2. Have all players use their non-dominant foot for all kicks. (12 years and older)

PASSING AND SHOOTING DRILLS AND GAMES

NAME	DIAGRAM	DESCRIPTION	KEY POINTS	VARIATIONS
Soccer Baseball		One team is up to bat and the other is out on the field. The first person up kicks the ball from the corner kick area onto the field and attempts to run around the three cones and back home before the fielders control the ball, pass it to all fielders, and shoot it in the goal. A run is scored if the kicker returns home before the ball enters the goal. An out is made if the person up kicks the ball over the near goal line or touch line, intentionally interferes with the ball after initially kicking it, or does not return to the corner kick area before opposing team kicks the ball in goal. After all players on the batting team get up, teams switch responsibilities. A set number of innings are played and the team with the most runs wins. Note, as soon as a shot is taken on goal, the next batter may rapidly kick a ball into play. (10 years and older)	Receiving, controlling, dribbling, passing, covering open space, quickly organizing the defense, and kicking are important parts of this game.	1. Add a goalkeeper from the batting team to try to stop the shots on goal. (12 years and older) 2. Add one or more defenders from the batting team to try to tackle the passes away. (12 years and older)

PASSING AND SHOOTING DRILLS AND GAMES

NAME	DIAGRAM	DESCRIPTION	KEY POINTS	VARIATIONS
Narrow and Wide Continuous Lead Passing	 7 yds	Two lines with an equal number of players in each are formed behind two cones placed about seven yards apart. All players in one line have a ball at their feet. The first two players make lead passes back and forth while moving down the field and attempting to maintain a seven-yard spacing between them. After the first pair has gone about 15 yards down field, the next pair follows by making passes in a similar manner. This continues until all pairs are making lead passes and moving down the field. Cones positioned seven yards apart can be positioned along the way to help the players maintain their spacing. When the first group reaches the other end of the field, they turn to the outside, proceed to make lead passes back and forth between the other players without hitting them or their balls, and return to the end of the field where they started. This process can then be repeated. (10 years and older)	This drill provides practice in controlling short and long lead passes and passing into open spaces. The coach can also select which individual passing and receiving techniques are to be used.	1. Use one-touch passing. (14 years and older) 2. Use chip passes from the outside position. (14 years and older)

PASSING AND SHOOTING DRILLS AND GAMES

NAME	DIAGRAM	DESCRIPTION	KEY POINTS	VARIATIONS
Over the Top		In a group of three players, a ball is passed with the inside of the foot to the center person. It is then returned with the same kick. After receiving the return pass, the player attempts to chip the ball over the middle person's head. The player on the opposite side receives the ball while the middle person turns to face the receiver. The drill is then repeated. (12 years and older)	Both inside of the foot kicks and chip passes are practiced in this drill. Players should be encouraged to practice these passes with both feet. This drill also provides practice for receiving and controlling ground balls, half volleys, and air balls.	1. Use a swerved pass to kick the ball around the middle person. (12 years and older)
Throw In Over the Goal and Shoot		Two lines of players are formed. Each of the players in line behind the goal has a ball. The second line is formed outside the arc. A throw-in is made to project the ball over the goal to the center of the penalty area line. The first player in line attempts to kick a half volley or air ball into the goal past the goalkeeper. Shots missing the goal are to be retrieved by the player who took the kick. After a throw or kick, the player goes to the other line. (12 years and older)	Kicking, throw-in, and goalkeeping techniques can be practiced with this drill. Both goals can be used to accommodate an entire team.	1. Instead of using a throw-in to feed the ball to the shooters, the goalkeeper rolls or bounces a ball to the kicker. (7 years and older)

PASSING AND SHOOTING DRILLS AND GAMES

NAME	DIAGRAM	DESCRIPTION	KEY POINTS	VARIATIONS
Five Pass Keep Away		Divide the players into two teams. Mark off a field space appropriate in size for the number and skill of the players competing. A free pass is made from out of bounds by a player on one team to a teammate. As soon as the teammate receives the ball, the opposing team attempts to gain possession of it. If five successive passes are made without an opposing team touching the ball, a point is scored. If the ball is played out of bounds by a team, the game is started again by a free kick in bounds from the other team. (12 years and older)	Encourage players to offensively move to create space, communicate with their teammates, and make passes that can be controlled. Defensively, players should be encouraged to close space and mark.	1. Use a goalkeeper on each team who is permitted to handle the ball. (12 years and older) 2. Permit only three-, two-, or one-touch passing. (14 years and older) 3. Only count balls that are passed on the ground. (14 years and older)

14

RECEIVING AND CONTROLLING

Eugene W. Brown

QUESTIONS TO CONSIDER

- What are the four fundamentals of receiving a soccer ball?
- What are the three categories of individual techniques for receiving a soccer ball?
- What are the key elements, common errors, and variations of each of the individual techniques for receiving and controlling a soccer ball?
- What progression is recommended for teaching youth players how to receive and control a soccer ball?
- What factors influence the level of difficulty players experience when receiving and controlling a soccer ball?

INTRODUCTION

Terminology

There are several terms that, to varying degrees, define the process of receiving a soccer ball. These terms include trapping, controlling, collecting, and redirecting. The term "trap" (or trapping) is commonly combined with a body part to identify the body segment used to gain control of the ball (e.g., thigh trap, chest trap, or sole of the foot trap). However, many coaches are technically opposed to the use of the word "trap" because it implies a final stationary position of the ball held in place.

Soccer is a dynamic game, and static positioning of the ball is rarely desired. Therefore, combined terms such as receiving and controlling or collecting and redirecting the ball are technically more acceptable because they don't imply that the ball is stopped before initiating subsequent ball movement.

Purpose of Receiving the Ball

A ball is received either as a result of an intended pass, an errant pass, a deflection, or an interception. In any case, the purpose of receiving the ball is to gain control of it so it can be subsequently passed, dribbled, or shot.

Fundamentals of Receiving the Ball

There are many different ways to receive a soccer ball. Regardless of how the ball is received, *the fundamental principles are the key elements in all techniques used to receive a ball.*

● Positioning

Players should be coached to quickly move to position to receive the ball. If they are in position quickly, they will have more time to receive the ball and make situational adjustments. Moving to position, when opponents are near, usually requires movement toward the ball.

● Selecting

There are different techniques that could be used to receive a soccer ball. While moving to position, a player must decide which technique to use.

Selecting the reception technique should be determined by the:

- path of the ball (steep to shallow arc),
- direction of the ball (toward or away from the body or across the midline of the body),
- level of the ball (rolling, half volley, or air ball),
- position and movement of opponents,
- intended activity after receiving the ball, and
- ability of the player.

● Receiving

When receiving a ball, it is usually desirable to decrease the speed of the ball so it can be controlled in subsequent play. Cushioning and wedging are the two methods of decreasing the speed of a ball.

Cushioning

Cushioning occurs when a relaxed body part absorbs and yields to the impact of the ball. Decreasing the speed of the ball by cushioning it may be performed by several different body parts.

Wedging

Wedging usually involves the formation of an angle between a surface of the foot and the ground to absorb the impact of the ball by lodging it between these surfaces.

● Redirecting

The goals of redirecting the ball are to move it into open space in order to provide additional time to gain control, pass, dribble, shoot, or move it into positions that will threaten the defense. The direction of movement of the ball, after contacting a body part, depends upon several factors at the moment of contact.

Factors That Influence Redirection of the Ball:

- point of contact with the ball

- orientation and direction of movement of the body part

- direction of movement of the ball

Subtle changes in how the body makes contact with the ball may result in different outcomes. Players should not be encouraged to explore ways to redirect the ball until they have achieved a moderate level of success in decreasing the speed of the ball when receiving it.

Fundamental Errors in Receiving the Ball

Errors occur when players fail at one or more of the fundamentals of receiving the ball. These errors may occur in the use of any technique to receive and control the ball. Therefore, you should observe all individual techniques for possible occurrence of these fundamental errors.

INDIVIDUAL TECHNIQUES

Receiving a Rolling Ball

All techniques for receiving a rolling ball involve the use of the feet. Rolling balls are relatively easy to receive and control because they may be played anywhere along their path. Therefore, ample opportunity is usually available for a player to judge the movement of the ball and to get into position to receive and control it. All techniques for receiving a rolling ball should be taught to beginning players. In teaching these techniques, you should be aware that factors such as ball speed, irregularity of the surface of the field, and defensive pressure can increase or decrease the difficulty a player experiences in receiving and controlling a rolling ball.

When teaching players how to receive a rolling ball, they should be instructed to lift the receiving foot as the ball arrives. If the receiving foot is lifted too early in preparation to receive a ball, a static balance must be maintained on the support foot. From this position, adjustments to movements of the ball and opponents cannot be made. This is a common error that occurs in youth players during the early stages of learning to receive rolling balls, half volleys, and some air balls. At the moment a ball is received, the foot and ankle should be relaxed and moving in the same direction as the ball. If the foot strikes into the ball, the ball will tend to rebound from the foot and make control more difficult.

Common Errors in Receiving Rolling Balls

Errors that often occur in any of the techniques used to receive and control a rolling ball include the following:

- lifting the receiving foot too early

- striking at the ball

Sole of the Foot

This method of receiving is used on balls approaching a player from the front. As the ball approaches, the player should move toward the ball (see Figure 14-1A). At the last moment, the receiving foot is lifted upward to wedge the ball between the ball of the foot and ground (see Figure 14-1B).

It is nearly impossible to wedge the ball between the sole of the foot and ground if the sole is held horizontally. An angle should be formed by the sole of the foot and ground to increase the margin for error in receiving the ball. The knees of the support and receiving legs should be slightly bent at the time contact is made with the sole of the foot (see Figure 14-1C). The action of the receiving foot is to swing upward over the ball. Many beginning players, however, will attempt to stop the ball by stepping down on it. This tends to add speed to the ball, and if the step is not properly timed, the ball may be completely missed. If a player attempts to forcefully step on the ball, off-center contact with the ball may result in a twisted ankle.

The arms should be elevated to the sides of the body to aid in balance and to shield the ball from defenders who may approach from the side or rear (see Figure 14-1C). Some coaches do not teach this method of receiving because it usually results in stopping the ball. However, if the ball is wedged between the receiving foot and ground, it is in a good position to be maneuvered with the sole of the foot .

Key Elements

- Move to meet the ball.

- Swing the receiving foot upward over the ball at the last moment.

- Form an angle between the sole of the receiving foot and the ground.

- Control the ball with the ball of the foot.

- Use the arms for balance and to shield defenders from the ball.

Figure 14-1. *Receiving a rolling ball with the sole of the foot.*

Common Errors

- Lifting the receiving foot too early
- Stepping down on the ball
- Orienting the sole of the receiving foot horizontally

● Inside of the Foot

In receiving the ball with the inside of the foot, positioning should result in the ball rolling across the midline of the body. The receiving leg should be rotated outward at the hip in order to lift and position the receiving foot perpendicular to the path of the ball (see Figure 14-2A). The ankle is flexed, and contact with the ball should be made with the broad area of the inside of the foot as the receiving leg begins its backward swing. If the ball is played below its center by the inside of the toes, it may rebound over the foot and roll away. Playing the ball with the broad region of the inside of the foot, near the ankle, provides more control because of the larger surface area in contact with the ball. It also decreases the possibility of the ball rebounding over the foot.

The support leg is slightly bent at the knee and acts as the point of counterbalance for movement of the trunk and receiving leg. As the receiving leg swings back to cushion and wedge the ball, the trunk simultaneously counterbalances the leg swing by leaning forward.

The ball is finally controlled in back of the support leg. At this point, the ball is wedged between the inside of the receiving foot and ground (see Figure 14-2C). This is a good position from which to shield the ball from defenders because the arms are raised to the sides of the body, one shoulder is forward, and the ball is behind the support foot.

Key Elements

- Position the receiving foot perpendicular to the path of the ball.
- Flex the ankle of the receiving leg.
- Contact the ball with the broad region of the inside of the foot near the ankle.
- Swing the receiving foot back to cushion the ball.

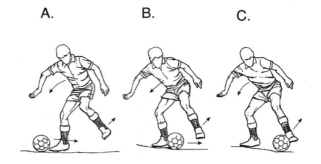

A.   **B.**   **C.**

Figure 14-2. *Receiving a rolling ball with the inside of the foot.*

- Counterbalance the movements of the receiving leg with movements of the trunk.

Common Errors

- Striking at the ball

- Receiving the ball with the inside of the foot near the toes

- Attempting to control the ball in front of the support foot

Variations

- Redirecting the ball forward—By being somewhat rigid with the joints of the receiving leg and ankle, the ball can be redirected forward. The ball should be received in stride, slightly in front of the support foot. The body should be leaning forward and off balance in the forward direction so it can quickly move to play the rebound.

- "Touch and turn"—Rotating the receiving leg outward so that the line of the receiving foot is beyond perpendicular to the path of the ball will result in the ball being deflected to the side and rear of the body. In order to maintain control by moving with the ball, the player must pivot on the support foot and lean in the direction of the rebound. It should be noted that the amount of turn can vary from 0 degrees to 180 degrees.

- Redirecting the ball "out the back door"—Rotating the receiving leg outward so the line of the receiving foot is less than perpendicular to the path of the ball will result in the ball being deflected to the back of the body (see Figure 14-3). Sight and shielding of the ball are momentarily interrupted as the player pivots about the support foot toward the rebounding ball.

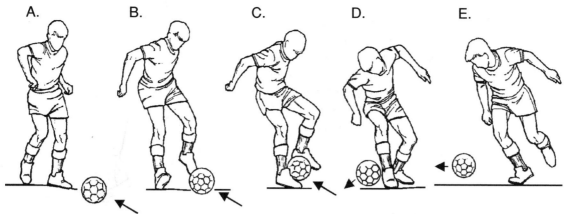

Figure 14-3. *Receiving a rolling ball with the inside of the foot and redirecting it between the legs ("out the back door").*

● Outside of the Foot

In receiving the ball with the outside of the foot, positioning should result in the ball rolling across the midline of the body. Balls that cross to the left of the midline are received with the right foot and those crossing to the right of the midline are received with the left foot.

Contact with the ball is made with the outside of the receiving foot, which is positioned in front of and lateral to the support foot (see Figure 14-4C). At the time contact is made, the supporting leg is flexed at the knee, the arms are elevated to the sides of the body to aid in balance, and the trunk is leaning back and to the side to counterbalance the receiving leg (see Figure 14-4C).

The speed of the ball is reduced in contacting the outside of the foot. However, the receiving foot primarily functions to redirect the ball back across the front of the body. This is accomplished by swinging the receiving foot back across the midline of the body and turning the leg outward while the ball is in contact with the foot (see Figure 14-4D and E).

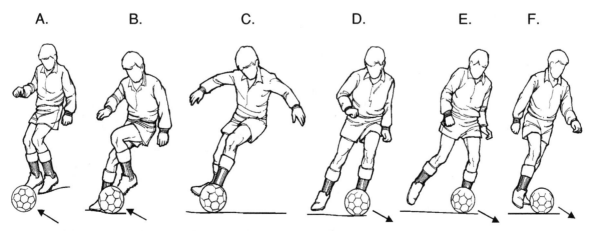

Figure 14-4. *Receiving a rolling ball with the outside of the foot.*

As the ball rebounds from the foot, the body pivots about the support foot and a step should be taken onto the receiving foot in the direction of the rebound (see Figure 14-4E and F). It is important for the body to be leaning in the direction of the rebound so the ball can be quickly followed. Youth players often hesitate between redirection and pursuit of the ball. This may result in an interception by a defender.

Beginning players should be encouraged to determine the method of receiving the ball by the conditions of play at the time they receive the ball. Once beginning players learn to receive the ball with the outside of the foot, they will often inappropriately use the outside of the dominant foot instead of the inside of the non-dominant foot. If a defender is running after the ball and approaching from the dominant side of the body of the receiving player, the ball can be shielded better with a reception by the inside of the non-dominant foot.

Key Elements

- Use the trunk to counterbalance the movements of the receiving leg.

- Take some of the speed off the ball and redirect the ball into open space.

- Lean the trunk in the direction the ball is to be redirected.

Common Errors

- Selecting to receive the ball with the outside of the dominant foot when the inside of the non-dominant foot should be used

- Not moving quickly toward the redirected ball

Progress for Teaching Rolling Ball Reception Techniques

The following sequential approach can be used to teach the various techniques used to receive, control, and redirect rolling balls. Teach your players to:

1. perform the proper movement pattern of a designated technique on a ball that is not moving;

2. move to position and use a designated technique to receive and control a slowly passed ball;

3. move to position and use a designated technique to receive and control a ball passed with considerable speed;

4. move to position and use a designated technique to receive, control, and redirect a ball passed with considerable speed;

5. move to position and select and perform an appropriate receiving, controlling, and redirecting technique on balls passed in various directions; and

6. move to position and select and perform an appropriate receiving, controlling, and redirecting technique when pressured by a defender.

Receiving a Half Volley

A ball that is in the air and then played immediately after striking the ground is referred to as a half volley. All techniques for receiving a half volley involve the use of the feet. As a group, techniques for receiving half volleys are moderately difficult because the ball is usually moving relatively fast and reception is limited to the short period of time immediately after the ball strikes the ground.

Common Errors in Receiving Half Volleys

Errors that often occur in any of the techniques used to receive a half volley include the following:

- Lifting the receiving foot too early

- Striking at the ball

- Failing to "first time" the ball—When receiving, it is often important to play a ball the first time it strikes the ground. If a ball is allowed to bounce additional times before it is received with a half volley technique, it may be intercepted by an opponent. Even though a ball is moving relatively fast on its initial contact with the ground, players should be encouraged to "first time" the ball.

- Improper positioning—Beginning players will have difficulty judging where to position themselves in order to receive a ball with a half volley technique. The tendency of beginning players is to move to a position too far from where the ball will strike the ground. From this position, they will either overextend their leg to reach the ball or allow the ball to bounce too high toward them before receiving it. When practicing half volley techniques, balls should be projected high enough into the air to allow a receiving player sufficient time to judge where the ball will strike the ground and to move to position.

● Sole of the Foot

Even though techniques of receiving half volleys are moderately difficult to learn and perform, beginning players should be taught to receive a half volley with the sole of the foot. It is the easiest half volley technique to perform, and it provides a means of gaining control of balls that are frequently kicked into the air in youth games. Body movements in receiving a half volley with the sole of the foot are similar to those used in receiving a rolling ball with the sole of the foot. (See Receiving a Rolling Ball, Individual Technique, Sole of the Foot.) The primary differences are the path of the ball and the time for the reception.

In this half volley technique, the ball is wedged between the sole of the foot and the ground, immediately after the ball strikes the ground. If the ball rebounds a short distance from the ground before contacting the ball of the foot, the angle of the sole of the foot should cause back spin on the ball. This will tend to keep the ball close to the receiver. Back spin can be exaggerated by drawing the sole of the foot back across the top of the ball.

Common Errors

See Common Errors in Receiving Half Volleys.

- **Inside of the Foot**

Initial leg movements in receiving a half volley with the inside of the foot are different than those in receiving a rolling ball with the inside of the foot. Contact with the rolling ball is made first in front of the body as the receiving leg swings back to finally wedge the ball between the ground and inside of the foot. (See Receiving a Rolling Ball, Inside of the Foot.) In the half volley, initial contact is made in the wedging position immediately after the ball strikes the ground beyond the front foot. This is a good position to shield the ball from opponents and is similar to the final positioning in receiving a rolling ball with the inside of the foot. To assume this position, an exaggerated step (leap) should be taken onto the support foot simultaneously with a lifting of the receiving leg and a leaning forward of the trunk. By lifting the receiving foot, the ball may be cushioned and wedged by the inside of the foot.

Receiving a ball beyond the support foot provides: a proper orientation of the foot to wedge the ball with the ground, a good body position to shield the ball from opponents, and a margin of error for balls that bounce forward from the inside of the receiving foot. This technique should be used on balls with shallow to medium arcs. It is very difficult to wedge a half volley with the inside of the foot on a ball that has a nearly vertical projection.

Key Elements

- Take an exaggerated step (leap) onto the support foot.
- Lower the trunk and elevate the receiving leg.
- Receive the ball with the broad area of the inside of the foot.
- Receive the ball beyond the support foot.

Common Errors

- Not aligning the receiving foot perpendicular to the path of the ball
- Receiving with the inside of the toes
- Receiving the ball forward of the support foot

Variations

Variations in technique for receiving and controlling a half volley with the inside of the foot are based upon how the ball is redirected. They are the same as those for receiving a rolling ball with the inside of the foot. (See Receiving a Rolling Ball, Inside of the Foot, Variations.)

- ## Outside of the Foot

Body movements in receiving a half volley with the outside of the foot are similar to those used in receiving a rolling ball with the outside of the foot. (See Receiving a Rolling Ball, Individual Techniques, Outside of the Foot.) The primary differences are the path of the ball and the time for reception.

Progressions for Teaching Half Volley Reception Techniques

The following sequential approach can be used to teach the various techniques used to receive, control, and redirect half volleys. Teach your players to:

1. use designated half volley techniques to receive and control balls that are tossed short distances;

2. use designated half volley techniques to receive, control, and redirect balls that are tossed short distances;

3. move to position and use designated half volley techniques to receive, control, and redirect balls that are tossed short distances;

4. move to position and use designated half volley techniques to receive, control, and redirect balls that are tossed or kicked long distances;

5. move to position and select and perform appropriate receiving, controlling, and redirecting techniques on balls that are passed or kicked in various directions; and

6. move to position and select and perform appropriate receiving, controlling, and redirecting techniques when pressured by a defender.

Receiving a Ball in the Air

A ball in the air is difficult to receive because: it is usually moving relatively fast, there is only a short time period to intercept its path, and additional reception techniques must be used when it rebounds to the ground.

- ## Inside of the Foot

This technique is used on "air balls" with shallow to medium arcs that cross the midline of the body. Body positioning and movement is similar to that used in receiving a rolling ball with the inside of the foot. (See Receiving a Rolling Ball, Individual Techniques, Inside of the Foot.) In receiving an air ball, the receiving foot must be lifted to the height of the approaching ball and swung back to cushion the ball (see Figure 14-5A and B). However, the ball is not wedged to the ground, as in receiving a half volley with the inside of the foot. It rebounds from the foot to the

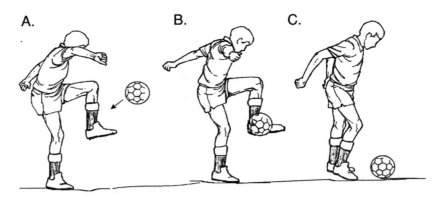

Figure 14-5. *Receiving a ball in the air with the inside of the foot.*

ground for subsequent play (see Figure 14-5C). Players who are flexible at their hip joints will be able to make inside-of-the-foot contact with balls above their waist and possibly bring them under control.

Key Elements

- Position the receiving foot perpendicular to the path of the ball.
- Contact the ball with the broad region of the inside of the foot near the ankle.
- Relax the foot and ankle and swing the receiving leg back to cushion the ball.
- Control the ball beyond the support foot.

Common Errors

- Striking at the ball
- Receiving the ball with the inside of the foot near the toes
- Attempting to control the ball in front of the support foot

Variations

All variations described under Receiving a Rolling Ball, Individual Techniques, Inside of the Foot, can be performed on an air ball. However, it should be noted that these are advanced techniques.

● Outside of the Foot

This technique is used on balls with shallow to medium arcs that cross the midline of the body. Note that an air ball with this type of trajectory could be received with either the outside of one foot or the inside of the opposite foot. Body movements in receiving an air ball with the outside of the foot are similar to those used in receiving either a rolling ball or half volley with the outside of the foot. (See Receiving a Rolling Ball, Individual Techniques, Outside of the Foot.)

In receiving an air ball, the receiving foot must be lifted to the height of the approaching ball. The foot is initially swung in the same direction as the ball to cushion it (see Figure 14-6A-C). The trunk should counterbalance the leg swing and lean toward the path of the intended redirection of the ball (see Figure 14-6C).

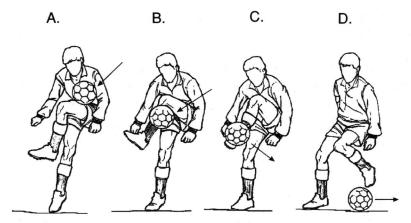

Figure 14-6. Receiving a ball in the air with the outside of the foot.

Key Elements

- It should be noted that the key elements and common errors for receiving an air ball with the outside of the foot are the same as those for receiving a rolling ball with the outside of the foot. (See Receiving a Rolling Ball, Individual Techniques, Outside of the Foot.)

● Instep

An air ball that approaches from directly in front of a player may be received with the instep. The receiving leg is swung upward and extended to meet the ball (see Figure 14-7A). This movement will raise the body up onto the toes of the support foot or even lift the body off the ground. The arms are raised to the sides to aid in lateral balance. Just before ball contact with the instep, the foot should drop rapidly back toward the ground (see Figure 14-7B and C). The ball contacts the foot during this backswing.

Contact should be made in line with the path of the ball through its center. The speed of the backswing decreases as the foot approaches the ground. The range and speed of the leg swing should be adjusted to the

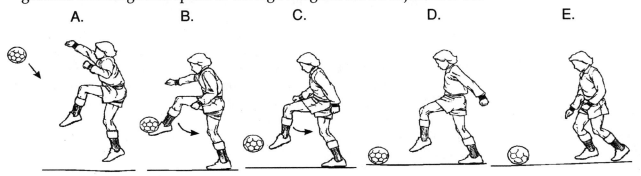

Figure 14-7. Receiving a ball in the air with the instep.

speed of the approaching ball. The receiving foot should be lifted above the height of the knee of the support leg and rapidly swung back in receiving a fast ball. However, for slower balls, the foot should not be lifted as high or swung back as quickly. If the movement of the foot is properly coordinated with the movement of the ball, the speed of the ball can be reduced so it returns slowly to the ground from the receiving foot.

Key Elements

- Extend the instep to meet the ball.
- Swing the foot back before ball contact.
- Elevate the arms for balance.
- Adjust the speed of the backswing to the speed of the approaching ball.

Common Errors

- Contacting the ball off center
- Improper timing and speed of backswing

Variations

Variations in techniques for receiving and controlling an air ball with the instep are based upon the location of contact between the foot and path of the ball. Foot contact directly under the center of the ball can redirect the ball forward. By contacting the ball off center, the ball can be intentionally redirected to one side or the other.

● Inside of the Thigh

This technique for receiving a ball in the air is limited by the range of movement of the thigh. It is used to quickly react and receive a ball with a shallow arc that approaches from the front of the body near the midline at a knee to hip height. However, if there is sufficient time to react to the ball, players will usually move to receive a low arcing ball with a foot.

In preparation to receive the ball with the inside of the thigh, the receiving leg is lifted just prior to ball contact by flexing its knee and hip (see Figure 14-8A and B). The arms are raised to the sides of the body to aid in balance and to possibly shield the ball from opponents (see Figure 14-8B). Ball contact is made with the broad region of the inside of the thigh near the crotch as the leg is rotated outward and swung back (see Figure 14-8C). The foot of the receiving leg is returned to the ground perpendicular to the line of the support foot (see Figure 14-8D). If the ball is properly cushioned, it will return to the ground between the feet for subsequent play.

Key Elements

- Contact the ball with the broad, fleshy region of the inside of the thigh.
- Make contact when the thigh is perpendicular to the path of the ball.
- Swing the thigh back to cushion the ball.

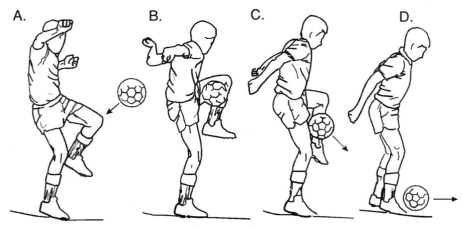

Figure 14-8. *Receiving a ball in the air with the inside of the thigh.*

Common Errors

- Receiving the ball on the inside of the thigh near the knee
- Improperly timing the leg swing

Variations

- "Touch and turn"—In this technique, the ball is not completely stopped by the receiving leg, but slowed by the inside of the thigh. The amount of deflection of the ball rebounding from the thigh can vary from 0 degrees to 180 degrees. The trunk rotates toward the rear and the foot of the receiving leg steps in the direction of the rebound.

● Top of the Thigh

The top of the thigh can be used to receive balls with low or high arcs that approach the front of the body at or near hip height. Basically, just before impact, the leg is raised by flexing the hip and knee in order to position the thigh slightly beyond perpendicular to the path of the

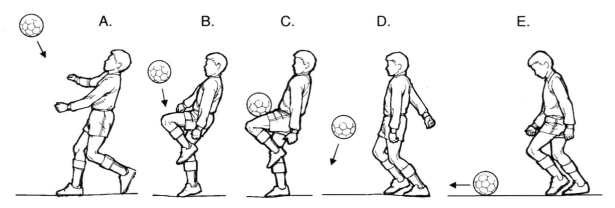

Figure 14-9. *Receiving a ball in the air with the top of the thigh.*

approaching ball (see Figure 14-9A and B). The thigh is quickly lowered (see Figure 14-9C and D). Ball contact with the thigh should be made on the broader, fleshy part of the thigh and not near the knee (see Figure 14-9C). When contact is made, the line of the thigh and the path of the ball should be perpendicular to each other. During contact, the thigh continues its rearward swing and the foot of the receiving leg is returned to the ground behind the body (see Figure 14-9D and E). The ball should return to the ground slightly in front of the receiving foot where it can be easily played.

Note that when receiving a ball with a low trajectory the trunk must lean forward more than when receiving a ball with a high trajectory (see Figure 14-10). This aids in the positioning of the top of the thigh perpendicular to the path of the approaching ball.

Key Elements

- Contact the ball with the broad, fleshy region of the top of the thigh near the trunk.

- Make contact when the top of the thigh is perpendicular to the path of the ball.

- Contact the ball through its center and in line with its path.

- Swing the thigh back to cushion the ball.

Common Errors

- Balancing too long on the support foot

- Lifting the receiving leg too early

- Receiving the ball near the knee

- Improperly timing the leg swing

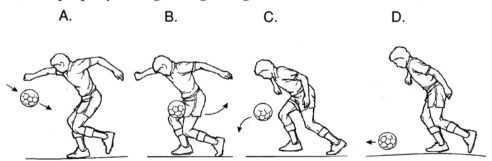

Figure 14-10. *Receiving a ball with a low trajectory with the top of the thigh.*

Variations

Variations in technique for receiving and controlling an air ball with the top of the thigh are based upon the location of contact through the center of the ball. Thigh contact through the center of the ball can be used to redirect the ball forward. By contacting the ball off center, the ball can be intentionally redirected to one side or the other.

- ## Chest

Balls that approach the midline of the body at or near chest height can be received with the chest. To receive the ball, the trunk should be arched with the hips forward and the arms elevated to the sides (see Figure 14-11A and B). The feet should be straddled in a forward-backward direction to aid in balancing the body. If the feet are straddled to the sides of the body, the impact of the ball may cause the player to fall backward. In assuming a proper arch, a player will experience muscle tension in the backleg (across the hip joint and in the front of the thigh of the back leg).

Initially, the body weight is mostly supported by the front foot (see Figure 14-11A). Just before and during contact, the arch of the trunk should increase, and the body weight shifts toward the back foot to cushion the impact of the ball (see Figure 14-11B and C). Contact is made high on the chest (see Figure 14-11D). At ball contact, elevating the arms to the front and sides of the body will depress the chest slightly and form a cup with the chest to aid in absorbing and controlling the ball.

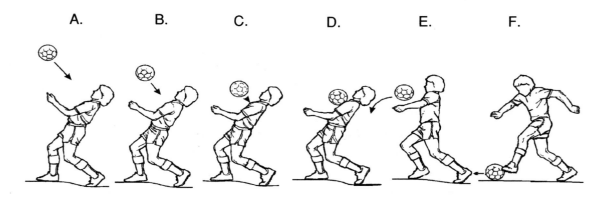

Figure 14-11. *Receiving a ball in the air with the chest.*

Orientation of the trunk in receiving a ball depends upon the path of the ball. A ball with a shallow arc may be received with the trunk nearly perpendicular to the ground, whereas the trunk should be inclined backward when receiving a ball with a steep arc. After contact, the ball will rebound forward. The straddle positioning of the feet will permit the player to push off from the back foot and move forward to play the ball.

It should be noted that in many leagues girls are permitted to cross their arms in front of their chest for protection (see Figure 14-12). However, if proper contact is made high on the chest, girls should be able to receive the ball without this precaution.

Key Elements

- Straddle the feet in a forward-backward direction.

- Orient the trunk perpendicular to the path of the ball.

- Elevate the arms to the front and sides of the body.

Figure 14-12. Arm position permitted for girls when receiving the ball with the chest.

- Contact the ball high on the chest.
- Arch the trunk backward to cushion the ball.

Common Errors

- Straddling the feet to the sides of the body
- Contacting the ball with the arms because they are in front of the body and too close together
- Contacting the ball low on the chest or in the region of the stomach
- Leaning forward with the trunk

Variations

- Redirecting the ball forward—By not completely absorbing the force of the ball, it can be made to rebound forward off the chest into space.
- "Touch and turn"—In this technique, the ball is not completely stopped by the chest. The ball is received slightly off center of the chest. As the player arches back to cushion the ball, the trunk is turned in the direction of the path of the ball by raising one arm and lowering the other closest to the ball. The foot on the same side of

A.   B.   C.   D.   E.   F.

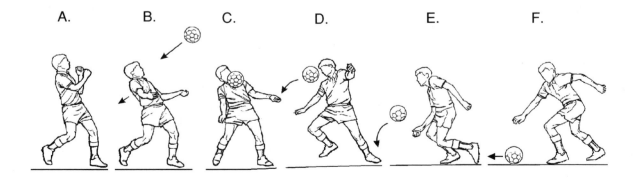

Figure 14-13. Receiving a ball in the air with the chest and redirecting it backward ("touch and turn").

the body as the lowered arm should be straddled back. The body pivots on the feet and then moves in the direction of the rebound (see Figure 14-13).

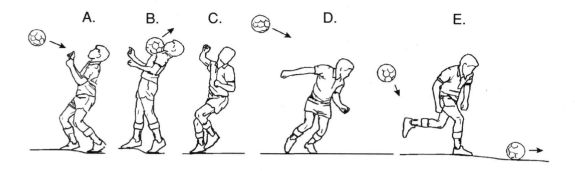

Figure 14-14. *Receiving a ball with the chest and redirecting it backward ("over the top").*

- "Over the top"—By orienting the chest beyond perpendicular to the path of a ball with a low trajectory, the ball can be made to rebound off the chest and continue in its same direction (see Figure 14-14). The foot work is the same as in "touch and turn" with the chest.

● **Head**

To decrease the velocity of the ball with the head is a difficult task, because the forehead is very hard and the range of movement of the head in cushioning the ball is relatively small. In receiving the ball with the head, the feet should be in a forward-backward straddle with the weight mostly on the front foot (see Figure 14-15A). The trunk should be leaning forward and the hips and knees flexed. Just before and during contact, the weight of the body should be shifted to the back foot by extending the front leg, taking a step backward onto the back foot, and lowering the body (see Figure 14-15B-D). If properly timed and cushioned, the ball should rebound to the ground in front of the player. Forward body move-

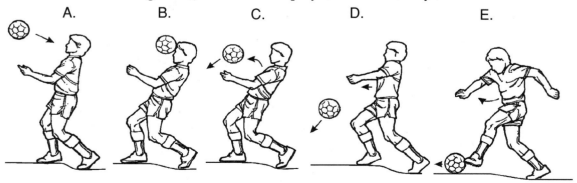

Figure 14-15. *Receiving a ball in the air with the head.*

ment to play the rebound can be initiated by pushing off the back foot (see Figure 14-15E).

Key Elements

- Straddle the feet in a forward-backward direction.
- Contact the ball with the forehead.
- Shift the body weight from the front to the back foot.

Common Errors

- Straddling the feet to the sides of the body
- Improperly timing the backward movement of the head

Variations

Variations in this technique are based upon the redirection of the ball. This can be accomplished by either deflecting the ball from the surface of the forehead or by turning the head to the side while the ball is still in contact. (See this section, Chapter 16, Heading.) The variations that can be performed include: redirecting the ball forward into space, "touch and turn," and "over the top."

Progressions for Teaching Air Ball Reception Techniques

By substituting air balls for half volleys, the progression for coaching players to receive, control, and redirect a half volley can be followed in teaching the air ball techniques.

PROGRESSIONS FOR TEACHING RECEPTION AND CONTROL

A sound method for teaching soccer techniques to your players is to begin with techniques that are relatively easy for them to learn and perform. After being successful, they will be eager to try more difficult techniques.

Factors that influence the level of difficulty in receiving and controlling the ball are summarized in Table 14-1. When teaching your players to receive and control the ball, you can vary the difficulty by varying the combination of factors selected for the practice of these techniques. By being aware of these factors, you will be able to select receiving and controlling tasks that are challenging to your players but not overwhelming. This understanding should also provide you with insight into how to meet the individual needs of your players.

Table 14-1. *Factors influencing the level of difficulty in receiving and controlling the ball.*

Factors								
Level of Difficulty	**Level of the Ball**	**Conditions of Play**	**Pace of the Ball**	**Field Conditions**	**Positioning**	**Technique Selection**	**Pressure**	**Control and Redirection**
Relatively easy	Rolling	Practice-like	Slow	Flat, soft, level, dry, calm	No movement to reposition body; ball is received in place	Preselected by coach or player based upon pre-determined ball path and pace	No defensive pressure	Receiving without concern for redirection
Moderate	Half volley		Intermediate		Some movement to reposition body with ample time provided		Passive defensive pressure	
Relatively difficult	Air ball	Game-like	Fast	Bumpy, wet, windy		Selection made by player based upon conditions of play immediately preceding reception	Full defensive pressure	Receive control, and redirect for subsequent play

By altering some factors in receiving and controlling tasks, you can make techniques easier for the less skilled players or more difficult for the skilled players. For example, to receive and control a tossed ball, in place, with the sole of the foot on a half volley is not as difficult as running to place to receive a kicked ball with the sole of the foot on a half volley when pressured by a defender.

Practicing Receiving and Controlling Techniques

In order to practice receiving and controlling techniques, a ball must be passed to a player. Therefore, the opportunity for players to practice techniques depends upon the passes they are given. If passes are inappropriate, receiving and controlling techniques cannot be practiced.

In practice sessions, passes can be either a thrown or kicked ball. As a coach, you must decide on the type of pass your players will use. The basis for this decision is: (a) the level of control the players have in making selected passes, and (b) the required path of the ball.

● Rolling Balls

All techniques for receiving and controlling rolling balls should be learned by beginning level players. When teaching your players these techniques, you can usually rely upon them to be able to make an accurate pass to a partner with the inside of the foot. With 6- and 7-year-old players, however, you may need to make the passes yourself or have players roll the ball from their hands to a partner. As your players' kicking skills become more accurate, you may request them to use the inside of the foot or the instep to pass the ball to a teammate. Remember that practice on receiving and controlling techniques should not result in practice on chasing the ball.

● Half Volleys and Air Balls

Most youth players find it is difficult to accurately kick a ball to a partner so an individual half volley or air ball reception can be practiced. Therefore, when players are beginning to learn how to receive and control half volleys and air balls, it is recommended that they practice on passes that are thrown to them. As kicking skills improve, practice should include more half volley and air ball receptions on kicked balls.

There are two underhand tosses that should be used: (a) one hand and (b) two hand. They are not part of the game of soccer but can be consistently and accurately performed by players in aiding their teammates to learn to receive and control half volleys and air balls. Table 14-2 presents recommended tosses for practicing various half volley and air ball receiving and controlling techniques.

The one-hand toss is employed for practicing techniques used to receive balls with shallow to medium arcs. It simulates a ball traveling in a shallow to medium arc. The air ball reception techniques to practice with this toss are inside of the foot, outside of the foot, and inside of the thigh. The two-hand toss is employed for practicing techniques used to receive balls with medium to steep arcs. The half volley reception techniques to practice with this toss are sole of the foot, inside of the foot, and outside of the foot.

Table 14-2. Recommended tosses in practicing half volley and air ball reception and control.

Recommended Underhand Toss to be Used	Path of the Ball	Reception Technique	
		Half Volley	Air Ball
One hand	Shallow to medium arc		Inside of the foot, outside of the foot, and inside of the thigh
Two hands	Medium to steep arc	Sole of foot, inside of the foot, and outside of the foot	

YOUTH SOCCER TECHNIQUES— RECEIVING AND CONTROLLING
Difficulty Rating Form

Level of Player* Approximate Age*	Suggested Emphasis		
	Beginning 6-9 yrs.	Intermediate 10-13 yrs.	Advanced 14 yrs. & up
Individual Techniques			
Rolling Ball			
sole of the foot	X	X	
inside of the foot	X	X	
redirecting forward	X	X	
"touch and turn"	X	X	X
"out the back door"		X	X
outside of the foot	X	X	
Half volley			
sole of the foot	X	X	X
inside of the foot		X	X
redirecting forward		X	X
"touch and turn"			X
"out the back door"			X
outside of the foot		X	X
Air ball			
inside of the foot		X	X
redirecting forward		X	X
"touch and turn"			X
"out the back door"			X
outside of foot		X	X
instep		X	X
inside of the thigh		X	X
"touch and turn"			X
top of the thigh		X	X
chest		X	X
"touch and turn"			X
"over the top"			X
head		X	X
redirecting forward			X
"touch and turn"			X
"over the top"			X

*Note that "Beginning," "Intermediate," and "Advanced" does not always correspond with the age range given beneath it. Coaches should use this classification system as an approximation, adjusting the techniques to suit their players' ability levels.

RECEIVING AND CONTROLLING DRILLS AND GAMES

NAME	DIAGRAM	DESCRIPTION	KEY POINTS	VARIATIONS
Windshield Wiper (Passing and Receiving)		One player makes arching runs back and forth. At the end of each run, a rolling ball is received with the inside of the foot, controlled, and returned. The other player turns in place in order to get into position to receive and redirect the ball with the inside of the foot ("touch and turn") and make a return pass. After several passes, players should switch roles. (7 years and older)*	This drill is used to teach players lead passing and running into space as well as receiving and redirecting techniques. Note that both players should alternate feet in receiving the ball.	1. Use the outside of the foot to receive and re-direct the ball. (8 years and older)
Kick and Receive (Half Volley, Sole of the foot)		One ball per player is needed. Players punt the ball into the air and then run to make a "first time" reception. (8 years and older)	You should encourage your players to appropriately challenge themselves by the height and distance they punt the ball. If the challenge is too difficult or too easy, the drill will not be very useful.	1. After kicking the ball, players must kneel down, sit down, or do a forward roll before running to receive the ball. (9 years and older) 2. Change the receiving technique. 　a. Half Volley—inside of the foot or outside of the foot. (10 years or older) 　b. Air Ball—instep or top of the thigh. (10 years and older) 3. Allow players to choose the reception technique. (10 years or older)

*Suggested age for practicing the drill or game is included in parentheses.

RECEIVING AND CONTROLLING DRILLS AND GAMES

NAME	DIAGRAM	DESCRIPTION	KEY POINTS	VARIATIONS
Kick and Receive Under Pressure		One ball is required for every two players. Partners stand side by side to start. The player with the ball kicks it into the air. Both players run to receive and control the ball. The player who gains control kicks the ball into the air and the drill is started again. This drill can be made into a game by awarding one point each time a player controls the ball. (10 years and older)	Players should be encouraged to: (a) quickly run to position, (b) select the appropriate reception technique, (c) properly perform the reception selected, (d) shield their opponent from the ball, and (e) redirect the ball into the open space away from their opponent.	1. After kicking the ball, players must kneel down, sit down, or do a forward roll before running to receive the ball. (10 years and older)
"On"—"Time" Receiving		A. A ball is passed on the ground to the teammate in the middle. The player passing the ball shouts "On" immediately after the pass. The ball is received with the inside of the foot, controlled, and returned with an inside of the foot kick. The ball is received with the inside of the foot. B. A ball is passed on the ground to the teammate in the middle. The player passing the ball shouts "Time" immediately after the pass. The ball is received with the inside of the foot, redirected ("touch and turn"), and passed with the inside of the foot to the third player, who receives it with the inside of the foot. After the drill is performed several times, change the positions of the players. (10 years and older)	This drill teaches communication between players as well as receiving and redirecting. "On" is used to signify that the player receiving the ball is being guarded by an opponent. "Time" means that sufficient time is available to control the ball before dribbling, passing, or shooting.	1. This drill can be altered by changing the passes and reception techniques, which will influence the level of difficulty of this drill. (10 years and older) 2. Use a one-touch return pass when "On" is called. (10 years and older)

RECEIVING AND CONTROLLING DRILLS AND GAMES

NAME	DIAGRAM	DESCRIPTION	KEY POINTS	VARIATIONS
Bow Tie		Four cones are arranged in a square. One player passes the ball on the ground from the inside of one cone to the outside of the diagonal cone. The other player makes the line passes. Both players run back and forth along their side of the square. The player receiving the diagonal pass uses the inside of the foot and the square pass is received and redirected with the outside of the foot. After several passes are made, have the players switch passes. (11 years and older)	This drill is used to teach players lead passing and running into space as well as receiving and redirecting techniques. Note that both players should alternate feet in receiving the ball.	1. Use different reception techniques. (11 years and older)
Intercepter		Cones form the boundaries of three consecutive squares. An offensive player is in each of the outside squares and a defensive player is in the middle. Players are restricted in passing and receiving to their own square. The object for the offensive players is to pass the ball from one outside square, across the middle square, and receive and control it within the boundaries of the other outside square. The object for the defensive player is to intercept and control the ball within the center square. One point is awarded to each of the offensive players for a pass that is received and controlled within the space of an outside square. If the defensive player is able to intercept and control a passed ball within the center square, he/she takes the place of the player who made the pass. (9 years and older) Note that the size of the squares will need to be modified to be compatible with the ability of the players.	This drill encourages players to move to open space and make quick passes that can be controlled by their teammate. It also motivates players to concentrate on receiving and controlling a ball within a confined space. Making the squares relatively long and narrow will encourage chip passes and, therefore, reception of half volley and air balls.	1. Use of two or more offensive and defensive players in each of the squares. (9 years and older)

15

DRIBBLING AND MAINTAINING CONTROL

Eugene W. Brown and Gary Williamson

QUESTIONS TO CONSIDER
- What are the purposes of dribbling?
- What are the three fundamentals of all individual dribbling techniques?
- What are the key elements and common errors of the individual dribbling techniques?
- What progressions should be used to teach individual dribbling techniques?
- What are the individual techniques that can be used to maintain control of the dribble?
- What progressions should be used to teach techniques for maintaining control of the dribble?

INTRODUCTION

Purpose of Dribbling

The skill of dribbling involves maneuvering the ball on the ground with different parts of the feet. There are several purposes for dribbling. These include:

- advancing the ball into scoring position,

- maneuvering the ball past an opponent in order to maintain possession,

- maneuvering the ball into open space where sufficient time is available to pass or shoot,

- maintaining possession to provide time for teammates to get into open space to receive a pass, and

- creating a numerical advantage in other areas of the field after beating a player or drawing defenders.

Dribbling is a skill that should be used mainly in the middle and attacking third of the field. It is very risky for a player to dribble out of the defensive third of the field because a successful tackle by an opponent may result in an opportunity for the opponents to score a goal. It should also be noted that advancing the ball by dribbling is not as quick as advancing the ball by passing, provided that teammates are in open positions to receive a pass. Therefore, a pass should be used instead of a dribble, whenever these methods for advancing the ball achieve the same purpose, because the pass reduces time for opponents to take up good defending positions.

Fundamentals of Dribbling

There are three individual dribbling techniques that can be used to maneuver the ball on the ground. Irrespective of which technique is used, all dribbling involves the fundamentals of control, vision, and rhythm.

● Control

The relative ease with which a player maintains possession of the ball when dribbling is a measure of control. When opponents are closely marking a player dribbling the ball, the ball must be maintained close to the feet (close control) so that the ball can be quickly maneuvered away from the marking players. When defenders are not marking closely, the ball can be dribbled farther away from the feet in maintaining control. With all individual dribbling techniques, it is more difficult to maintain close control when tightly marked by opponents than it is to maintain control of the dribble when opponents are loosely marking.

● Vision

Beginning players tend to primarily focus their vision on the ball when dribbling. Good vision, however, involves viewing the ball and peripherally viewing the setting around the ball momentarily before each touch of the ball. Between touches of the ball, good vision involves focusing the eyes on the setting away from the ball ("looking off the ball") and possibly seeing the ball peripherally. Beginning players tend to have their heads tilted forward to maintain vision of the ball and are susceptible to unexpected tackles. On the other hand, skilled dribblers tend to maintain a more elevated posture of the head and neck when dribbling. When defenders see a dribbler look off the ball, they become hesitant in their attempts to tackle. When the player with the ball looks up, defenders realize that the dribbler may be viewing teammates who are open to receive a pass. Thus, additional space and time may be provided for the dribbler because the defender may prepare to respond to a pass. Skilled dribblers use this technique of looking off the ball to reduce defensive pressure even when they know their teammates are not open to receive a pass.

- **Rhythm**

Rhythm, associated with all individual dribbling techniques, refers to the ability of a player to naturally move with the ball without substantially interrupting the running pattern. It involves a compatibility between the pace and position of the rolling ball and the speed of the run.

INDIVIDUAL DRIBBLING TECHNIQUES

Dribbling with the Inside of the Foot

This is the easiest dribbling technique to learn because one foot acts as a partner to the other foot in touching the ball back and forth between the feet. Before contact is made with the ball, the player turns the dribbling foot outward by rotating the leg outward as it moves forward into contact (see Figure 15-1B-D). A leap should not be taken onto the support foot. Placement of the support foot on the ground should be part of a natural running pattern. Contact with the ball is made with the broad region of the inside of the foot and inside of instep. Because of the large area of contact, control is relatively easy to maintain in this type of dribble. In dribbling with the inside of the foot, the ankle should not be as flexed and firm as is suggested for an inside of the foot kick. When contacting the ball, the trunk should be inclined slightly forward, arms should be in natural cycle with the running pattern, and the support foot should be behind and to the side of the ball (see Figure 15-1C). During the follow-through, the foot and leg used for the dribble should rotate back into a natural running stride position (see Figure 15-1B and C). The inside of the foot dribble is the slowest of the three individual dribbling techniques because of the interruption of the run associated with the outward rotation of the leg to orient the foot for ball contact.

A.　　B.　　C.　　D.　　E.

Figure 15-1. Dribbling with the inside of the foot.

DRIBBLING AND MAINTAINING CONTROL

Dribbling with the Outside of the Foot

Dribbling with the outside of the foot usually involves contact of the ball with the outside of the foot and outside of the instep. The player should attempt to maintain a rhythmical running pattern with only slight breaks in form associated with inward rotation of the striking foot and leg (see Figure 15-2). Foot contact with the ball is made with the ankle fully extended and the foot positioned diagonally across the back of the ball.

When using the outside of the foot and outside of the instep to dribble, the ball tends to move forward and laterally to the foot contacting the ball. Thus, successive touches of the ball with the same foot tends to move the ball along a curved path to the side of the body, unless the foot and leg used for the dribble are rotated markedly inward on contact (see Figure 15-2B).

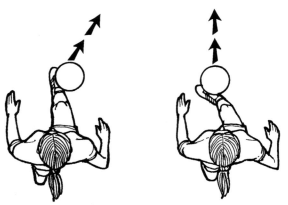

Figure 15-2. Dribbling with the outside of the foot—leg position and direction of ball.

Dribbling with the Instep

Use of the full instep to dribble requires the knee of the kicking leg to be flexed slightly more on contact than in dribbling with either the outside or inside of the foot. This is because, in the full instep dribble, the foot is pointed directly downward and needs additional space for its toe to clear the ground (see Figure 15-3). The leg, however, should not be rotated outward or inward. On contact, the knee of the dribbling leg should be positioned directly over the ball. Slight breaks in a rhythmical running pattern are associated with the additional hip and knee flexion required for foot clearance. It should be noted that dribbling with the instep is the most deceptive individual dribbling technique because slight inward or outward rotations of the contacting foot result in a dribble with the inside or outside of the instep, respectively, causing the direction of the dribble to change.

Figure 15-3. Dribbling with the instep.

Key Elements (Dribbling in General)

- Keep control of the ball as close as necessary to maintain possession.
- During each touch, focus on the ball and peripherally view the setting around the ball.
- Between touches, focus on the setting away from the ball and peripherally view the ball.
- Perform the dribble without substantial interruptions in the running pattern.

Common Errors (Dribbling in General)

- Dribbling when passing would achieve the same objective
- Dribbling with the head down and always focusing on the ball

PROGRESSIONS FOR TEACHING INDIVIDUAL DRIBBLING TECHNIQUES

Each of the three individual dribbling techniques should be taught to beginning players. The following, however, are guidelines that are helpful in sequencing your approach to teaching these techniques.

- Have your players practice the three individual dribbling techniques with both of their feet.
- Select drills that encourage your players to progress from practicing dribbling techniques at a slow pace to practicing these techniques at a fast pace.
- Encourage your players to progress from dribbling the ball moderate distances away from their feet to dribbling under close control.
- Challenge your players by having them initially practice dribbling in unlimited space, then gradually restrict their practice space.

INDIVIDUAL TECHNIQUES TO MAINTAIN CONTROL OF THE DRIBBLE

Dribbling, in its simplest form, involves the use of a combination of the three individual dribbling techniques to move the ball along the ground in a straight path toward an opponent's goal. This approach, however, is not likely to be successful in a game situation in which defenders are marking the dribbler and attempting to tackle the ball away. Thus, the application of dribbling to game conditions must be more creative and include additional techniques to aid players in maintaining control of the ball. The following is a description of these controlling techniques.

Change of Pace

Defenders attempting to tackle the ball away will run along with the dribbler. This can be exploited by the dribbler through a quick change of pace. If the dribbler is running fast, quickly slowing the pace of the dribble will create a space between the dribbler and the defender who is slow to react to this change. Similarly, a quick increase in the pace of a slow dribble may unbalance the defender and create space so the ball is out of tackling range.

● Slowing the Pace

Quickly slowing the pace of the dribble can be accomplished in three ways (see Figure 15-4A-C). Hooking the ball with the inside of the instep and hooking the ball with the outside of the instep to slow the roll of the ball involve contacting the front of the ball with these parts of the foot. Adjusting the pressure applied by the sole of the foot to the top of the ball can also be used to slow the movement of the ball or completely stop its roll.

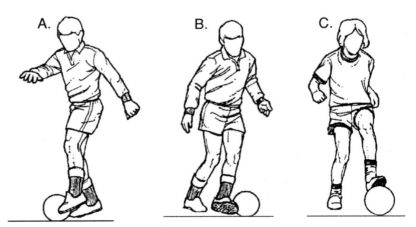

Figure 15-4. *Slowing the pace of a rolling ball by hooking the ball with the inside of the instep (A); by hooking the ball with the outside of the instep (B); and by applying pressure with the sole of the foot (C).*

Increasing the Pace

Basically, the pace of the dribble can be increased with any of the three individual dribbling techniques. This can be accomplished by running more quickly and striking the ball so it moves farther from the body on each dribble. It should be noted that the outside of the foot and instep dribbles are faster dribbling techniques than the inside of the foot dribble. Therefore, the inside of the foot dribble should not be used when attempting to accelerate the pace of the dribble.

Change of Direction

A quick change in direction of the motion of the ball can be used to create space between the dribbler and defender. Three techniques to change the direction of the roll of the ball are turning the ball with inside of the foot, outside of the foot, and sole of the foot.

Turning the Ball with the Inside of the Foot

To perform this technique, a short leap is taken to the side of the ball onto a support foot, which should be turned outward (see Figures 15-5A-C). The body should turn and lean in the direction of the leap. As the leap and support foot placement occurs, the inside of the opposite foot is positioned so it can contact the ball and change the direction of roll toward the support foot (see Figures 15-5B-F). This technique is very useful when a defending player approaches from behind and to the side of the dribbler. A quick turn with the inside of the foot behind the defender

Figure 15-5. *Turning the ball with the inside of the foot.*

decreases the defensive pressure and creates space for the dribbler (see Figure 15-5). This technique also can be effective in beating a defender who approaches from the front of the dribbler. At the last moment, when the defender attempts to tackle the ball away, a sharp turn is made (see Figure 15-6).

Figure 15-6. Turning the ball with the inside of the foot in front of a defender.

- ## Turning the Ball with the Outside of the Foot

To turn the ball with this technique, the support foot is placed to the rear and side of the ball (see Figure 15-7A and B). The body leans to the side opposite the support foot, and contact is made with the outside of the foot to move the ball in the direction of the body's lean (see Figure 15-7C and D).

A.   B.   C.   D.

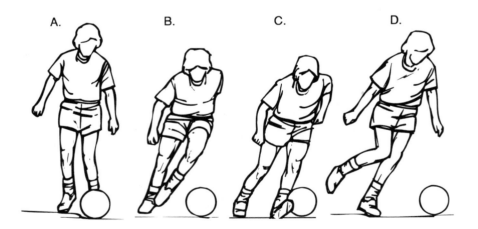

Figure 15-7. Turning the ball with the outside of the foot.

- ## Turning the Ball
  ## with the Sole of the Foot

The ball of the foot, when in contact with the top of the ball, can be used to change the direction of the dribble. The new direction will depend upon the direction of swing of the contacting foot. To turn the ball across the front of the body toward the left or right requires an appropriate leg and foot swing and body lean (see Figure 15-8). To draw the ball back in a direction opposite to its original path, the contacting foot must swing back, the body must pivot on the support foot, and the body must lean backward so it can easily move with the ball.

Figure 15-8. Using the sole of the right foot to turn the ball across the front of the body toward the left.

Shielding

Positioning the body between the defensive player and the ball is called shielding the ball. The purpose of shielding is to protect the ball from a defender. When dribbling, the ball should be played with the foot opposite the side of the defensive pressure. Dribblers should also lower their body by bending their knees, carrying their arms away from and to the sides of their bodies, and leaning toward the defender to be ready to absorb a defensive charge (see Figure 15-9A and B).

Figure 15-9. Shielding the ball while dribbling with the outside of the foot (A) and while dribbling with the inside of the foot (B).

Feinting

A feint is action taken by a player that is intended to deceive an opponent. This action may involve movements of body parts and/or movements of the ball. Feints are used by players in possession of the ball as well as players not in possession of the ball.

There are many individual feints that can be made by a dribbler. The feint that is selected should be based upon the situation that confronts the dribbler and ease of performance. When making a feint, a dribbler can be facing a defender, facing in the same direction as a defender, or shielding the ball from a defender. Regardless of which situation the dribbler is confronted with, feints with the body are easier to perform than feints that involve deceiving an opponent through movements of the ball.

Two factors that are important to the performance of a feint are the location and timing of the action. If the player in possession of the ball performs a feint too far away from the defender, the defender will have time to recover. If the feint is performed too close to the defender, the dribbler may have the ball tackled away. A good feint involves convincing deception performed at an appropriate distance from the defender, followed by rapid acceleration to beat the unbalanced opponent.

The following are examples of individual feinting techniques that use movements of body parts and/or movements of the ball to deceive an opponent in various situations. Note that each of these feints can be performed in either direction. However, they are shown in only one direction.

- **Body Feint and Inside of the Foot Dribble**

This is a body feint that is used when a defender approaches the dribbler from the front. Basically, an exaggerated step and trunk movement are taken toward the side as if to accelerate the pace of the dribble past the defender. As the defender leans in response to the feint, the ball is pushed with the inside of the foot in the opposite direction (see Figure 15-10).

A.   B.   C.   D.   E.   F.

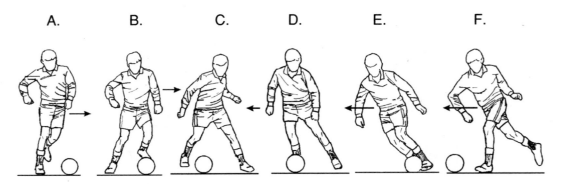

Figure 15-10. Body feint and inside of the foot dribble.

- **Body Feint and**
  Outside of the Foot Dribble

This is performed in a similar manner to the body feint and inside of the foot dribble (see Figure 15-11).

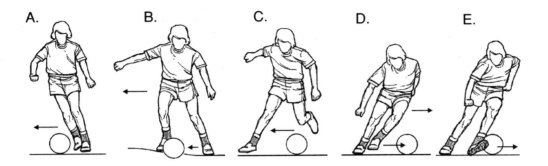

Figure 15-11. Body feint and outside of the foot dribble.

- **Feint the Kick and Go**

As the defender approaches from the front, the dribbler makes a leap and swings a leg back as if to make a kick. If this action halts the approach of the defender, the dribbler uses the kicking foot to quickly push the ball past the defender.

- **Inside-Out Feint and**
  Outside of the Foot Dribble

This is a body feint that is used when a defender approaches the dribbler from the front. One foot is swung toward the midline of the body, around the front of the ball, and then planted to the side of the ball (inside-out). As the foot is planted, the body should lean in the direction of

Figure 15-12. Inside-out feint and outside of the foot dribble.

the planted foot as if to continue the dribble in that direction. The outside of the opposite foot is used to push the ball beyond the defender in a direction opposite to the initial body lean (see Figure 15-12).

- ### Outside-In Feint and Inside of the Foot Dribble

This is similar to the previous feint except that one foot is swung around the outside and then to the front of the ball before being planted across the midline of the body (outside-in). The other leg then crosses in front of the planted foot to play the ball with the inside of its foot (see Figure 15-13).

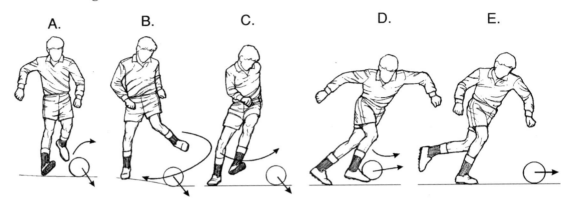

Figure 15-13. *Outside-in feint and inside of the foot dribble.*

- ### Step Over and Inside of the Foot Turn

This body feint is used on a rolling ball when a defender approaches the dribbler from behind and the dribbler wants to advance the ball back up field. A feint is made by an outside-in swing of one leg as if to begin turning the ball back up field. The ball continues to roll between the dribbler's legs and a quick turn is made in the opposite direction by pivoting

Figure 15-14. *Step-over and inside of the foot turn.*

on the support foot and then playing the ball with the inside of the opposite foot (see Figure 15-14).

This feint is an excellent turn for fullbacks who are running down a ball toward their own goal while being marked from behind. The feint should be made toward the middle of the field and the inside of the foot turn should be made toward the nearest touch line.

● Sole of the Foot Draw Back and Out the Back Door

This is a feint with the ball. It is performed when a defender makes a controlled approach from the front. The dribbler exposes the ball to the defender. When the defender extends a leg to tackle the ball away, the ball is drawn back with the sole of the foot, which is then positioned behind the body. The ball rolls toward the foot positioned beyond the body and rebounds or is played forward through the opening between the legs (back door). The dribbler then quickly moves to advance the ball past the defender.

● Sole of the Foot Stop and Turn

This feint is performed when a defender and dribbler are running side by side and at full speed. Using the sole of the foot away from the defender, the dribbler stops the ball, pushes it back in the opposite direc-

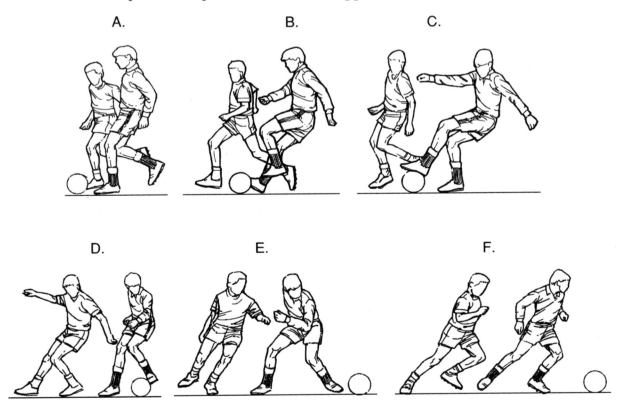

Figure 15-15. Sole of the foot stop and turn.

DRIBBLING AND MAINTAINING CONTROL

tion, and turns to play the ball. If performed quickly, the defender will continue to move forward for a short distance while the dribbler is turning and creating space (see Figure 15-15).

- **Sole of the Foot Stop and Go**

This feint is similar to the previous feint and is appropriately used after once beating the defender with the sole of the foot stop and turn. In this feint, the dribbler slows the pace of the dribble, then places the sole of a foot on top of the ball as if to stop it. As the defender stops to be in tackling range, the dribbler quickly pushes the ball forward again with the sole of the foot (see Figure 15-16).

Figure 15-16. Sole of the foot stop and go.

- **Feint the Stop and Go**

This feint is similar to the sole of the foot stop and go. In this feint, the dribbler fakes the use of the sole of the foot to stop the ball by placing the foot over the ball, but not in contact. The foot is then pulled back behind the ball where the foot is then used to quickly dribble the ball forward. The change of pace in the dribbler's run is used in this feint to unsettle the defender.

PROGRESSIONS FOR TEACHING TECHNIQUES TO MAINTAIN CONTROL OF THE DRIBBLE

Once your players are able to maintain close control of the ball with either foot in performing each of the three individual dribbling techniques at full pace, they are ready to begin practicing other techniques that will be helpful in maintaining control of the dribble. The following guidelines will be helpful to you in sequencing your approach to teaching these techniques.

- Each technique that is introduced should be practiced from both the right and left sides of the body.

- Progress from practicing these techniques at a slow pace to a fast pace.

- Select drills that encourage your players to progress from dribbling at a uniform pace to dribbling with frequent changes in pace.

- Initially introduce into your practices dribbling drills that do not include defensive pressure and then progress to include in practices dribbling drills with full defensive pressure.

- When teaching feints, progress from body feints to ball feints.

SUMMARY

Individual techniques for dribbling and maintaining control of the dribble are an important and integral part of the game of soccer. Virtually all practices designed for youth players should include drills and games that expose all members of the team to dribbling experiences. However, it should be noted that the limited time available for structured practices is not sufficient for youth players to master the vast variety of dribbling and controlling techniques and to determine which of these techniques they can successfully apply to game situations. Therefore, coaches should encourage their players to creatively explore dribbling outside scheduled practices.

SUGGESTED READING

Coerver, W. (1986). *Soccer fundamentals for players and coaches*. Englewood Cliffs, NJ: Prentice-Hall.

SUGGESTED VIDEOTAPE

van Doorn, J. (Producer), & Budie, H. (Director). (1986). *Soccer fundamentals with Wiel Coerver (Part 1)*. Amsterdam, The Netherlands: B.V. Uitgeversmaatschappij Elsevier.

YOUTH SOCCER TECHNIQUES— DRIBBLING
AND MAINTAINING CONTROL
Difficulty Rating Form

Level of Player *	Suggested Emphasis		
	Beginning	Intermediate	Advanced
Approximate Age *	6-9 yrs.	10-13 yrs.	14 yrs. & up
Individual Techniques			
Dribbling			
inside of the foot	X	X	X
outside of the foot	X	X	X
instep	X	X	X
Maintaining Control			
slowing the pace			
hooking the ball with the inside of the instep	X	X	X
hooking the ball with the outside of the instep	X	X	X
applying pressure to the top of the ball with the sole of the foot	X	X	X
increasing the pace			
inside of the foot	X	X	X
outside of the foot	X	X	X
instep	X	X	X
changing direction (turning the ball)			
inside of the foot	X	X	X
outside of the foot	X	X	X
sole of the foot	X	X	X
shielding			
inside of the foot	X	X	X
outside of the foot	X	X	X
Feinting			
body feints		X	X
ball feints			X
body and ball feints			X

* Note that Beginning, Intermediate, and Advanced does not always correspond with the age range given beneath it. Coaches should use this classification system as an approximation, adjusting the techniques to suit their players' ability levels.

DRILLS AND GAMES FOR DRIBBLING AND MAINTAINING CONTROL

NAME	DIAGRAM	DESCRIPTION	KEY POINTS	VARIATIONS
Independent Dribbling		In a designated space (e.g., penalty area) all members of the team dribble their own ball. Players are not to make contact with their teammates or their teammates' balls. (6 years and older)	By decreasing the space, increasing the number of players, and encouraging the players to dribble at a faster pace, the drill can be made more challenging.	1. Run among the players and occasionally hold up a certain number of fingers. The players attempt to be the first to shout out the correct number. This encourages the players to look up from the ball they are dribbling. (6 years and older) 2. While the players are dribbling, shout out selected commands for them to make specific feints, turns, changes of pace, and changes in direction. After they respond to the command, they continue dribbling. (6 years and older) 3. While the players are dribbling, shout out body parts for them to stop the ball with (e.g., foot, knee, chest, forehead, etc.). After they respond to the command, they are then told to dribble again. (6 years and older) 4. Variations 1-4 can be combined. (6 years and older)

*Suggested age for practicing the drill or game is included in parentheses.

DRILLS AND GAMES FOR DRIBBLING AND MAINTAINING CONTROL

NAME	DIAGRAM	DESCRIPTION	KEY POINTS	VARIATIONS
Follow the Leader		All players in a single file with a ball at their feet follow a leader (coach or player). The leader should challenge the players in line by changing direction and pace. (6 years and older)	Players should be encouraged to stay close to the person in front of them and to make sharp turns and changes of direction where and how the leader makes these movements.	1. Overtake—On command, the last person in line sprints to the front of the line while dribbling and takes over the leader's role. (6 years and older) 2. Leave Behind—On command, all players stop their ball and move forward to dribble the ball in front of them. The first player in line sprints to the end of the line to dribble the last ball and the second player in line becomes the leader. (6 years and older)
Obstacle Dribble		Place several cones or flags irregularly spaced apart in a curved line. Each player attempts to dribble a zig-zag path between these markers, as fast as possible, without losing control. (6 years and older)	Spacing and the location of each cone can be used to regulate the pace and directional changes in the dribble. The farther cones are apart, the faster players can dribble. Sharp turns can be implemented by placing cones off-line. Specific individual dribbling techniques, turns, and feints can also be imposed by the coach.	1. Relay races can be run by using parallel obstacle courses. (7 years and older) 2. Instead of dribbling a zig-zag path, have your players approach a marker, make an inside of the foot push pass around one side of the marker, run around the opposite side of the marker, then gain control of the dribble. (8 years and older)

DRILLS AND GAMES FOR DRIBBLING AND MAINTAINING CONTROL

NAME	DIAGRAM	DESCRIPTION	KEY POINTS	VARIATIONS
Zig-Zag Line Dribble		All players line up on one goal line with a ball at their feet. They dribble a zig-zag path across the field to the opposite goal line. After each change of direction they should switch to play the ball with the opposite foot. Make sure sufficient spacing is available between players so they don't dribble into each other. (6 years and older)	This drill is helpful to beginning level players who need practice at maintaining close control of the ball, using both feet on the dribble, and changing directions.	1. Zig-Zag Line Dribble with Passive Pressure—Use a defender in front of each dribbler. The defender applies passive pressure by loosely marking and not attempting to tackle the ball away. (7 years and older) 2. Zig-Zag Line Dribble with Full Pressure—This is the same as variation number one except the defender attempts to tackle the ball away. (8 years and older)
1 Versus 1 Keep Away		Four cones mark a 10-yard by 10-yard square for each pair of players. One member in each pair has a ball. On a signal to start, this player attempts to maintain possession of the ball while the other player attempts to tackle it away. If a foul is committed or a ball is played out of bounds, the opposing player receives possession to restart a game. Whoever has possession of the ball when play is signaled to stop receives one point. The player who began play in possession of the ball begins the next game on defense. After several games, the player with the greatest number of points in each pair wins. (7 years and older)	During the game, players practice individual dribbling, shielding, and feinting techniques on offense and marking and tackling techniques on defense. The size of the square can be adjusted to emphasize different functions. Decreasing the size of the square makes dribbling and maintaining control more difficult and marking and tackling easier. Increasing the size of the square makes dribbling and maintaining control easier and marking and tackling more difficult.	1. Place an additional cone inside the square. Award a point each time the player in possession of the ball is able to hit the cone with the ball. (8 years and older) 2. Use two cones instead of one as described in variation number one. (8 years and older)

DRILLS AND GAMES FOR DRIBBLING AND MAINTAINING CONTROL

NAME	DIAGRAM	DESCRIPTION	KEY POINTS	VARIATIONS
Human Goal	 10 yds	Four players are in each group. Two of these players stand approximately 10 yards apart with their legs spread to form goals. The remaining two players compete against each other. The object of the game for the competing players is to defend their goal and score through either side of their opponent's goal. Goals count only if the ball rolls between the legs of a player forming a goal. The game does not stop after a goal is scored. Therefore, it is possible for a player to score more than one goal in succession. When a set period of time ends the game, the player in each group with the highest number of goals wins. At the end of each game, the players in each group switch roles. (7 years and older)	During this game, players practice individual dribbling, shielding, feinting, and shooting techniques on offense and marking and tackling techniques on defense. If the time period for competition is relatively long, the aerobic and anaerobic energy production systems of the players may be challenged.	1. Other small-sided teams can be used in this game (e.g., 2 v 1, 2 v 2, 3 v 2, and 3 v 3). (8 years and older)

DRILLS AND GAMES FOR DRIBBLING AND MAINTAINING CONTROL

NAME	DIAGRAM	DESCRIPTION	KEY POINTS	VARIATIONS
Crisscross Dribbling	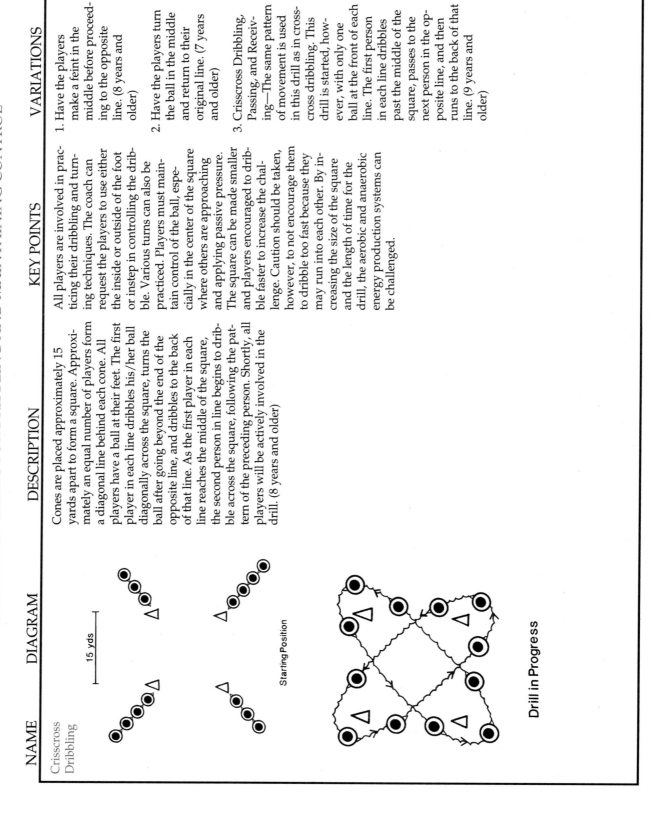	Cones are placed approximately 15 yards apart to form a square. Approximately an equal number of players form a diagonal line behind each cone. All players have a ball at their feet. The first player in each line dribbles his/her ball diagonally across the square, turns the ball after going beyond the end of the opposite line, and dribbles to the back of that line. As the first player in each line reaches the middle of the square, the second person in line begins to dribble across the square, following the pattern of the preceding person. Shortly, all players will be actively involved in the drill. (8 years and older)	All players are involved in practicing their dribbling and turning techniques. The coach can request the players to use either the inside or outside of the foot or instep in controlling the dribble. Various turns can also be practiced. Players must maintain control of the ball, especially in the center of the square where others are approaching and applying passive pressure. The square can be made smaller and players encouraged to dribble faster to increase the challenge. Caution should be taken, however, to not encourage them to dribble too fast because they may run into each other. By increasing the size of the square and the length of time for the drill, the aerobic and anaerobic energy production systems can be challenged.	1. Have the players make a feint in the middle before proceeding to the opposite line. (8 years and older) 2. Have the players turn the ball in the middle and return to their original line. (7 years and older) 3. Crisscross Dribbling, Passing, and Receiving—The same pattern of movement is used in this drill as in crisscross dribbling. This drill is started, however, with only one ball at the front of each line. The first person in each line dribbles past the middle of the square, passes to the next person in the opposite line, and then runs to the back of that line. (9 years and older)

Starting Position

Drill in Progress

DRILLS AND GAMES FOR DRIBBLING AND MAINTAINING CONTROL

NAME	DIAGRAM	DESCRIPTION	KEY POINTS	VARIATIONS
Left Boomerang	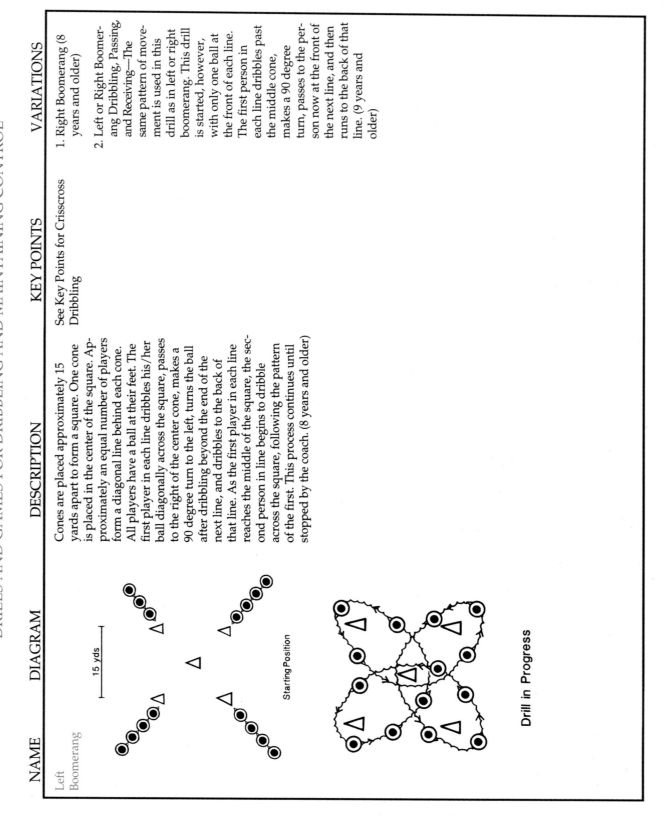	Cones are placed approximately 15 yards apart to form a square. One cone is placed in the center of the square. Approximately an equal number of players form a diagonal line behind each cone. All players have a ball at their feet. The first player in each line dribbles his/her ball diagonally across the square, passes to the right of the center cone, makes a 90 degree turn to the left, turns the ball after dribbling beyond the end of the next line, and dribbles to the back of that line. As the first player in each line reaches the middle of the square, the second person in line begins to dribble across the square, following the pattern of the first. This process continues until stopped by the coach. (8 years and older)	See Key Points for Crisscross Dribbling	1. Right Boomerang (8 years and older) 2. Left or Right Boomerang Dribbling, Passing, and Receiving—The same pattern of movement is used in this drill as in left or right boomerang. This drill is started, however, with only one ball at the front of each line. The first person in each line dribbles past the middle cone, makes a 90 degree turn, passes to the person now at the front of the next line, and then runs to the back of that line. (9 years and older)

15 yds

Starting Position

Drill in Progress

DRILLS AND GAMES FOR DRIBBLING AND MAINTAINING CONTROL

NAME	DIAGRAM	DESCRIPTION	KEY POINTS	VARIATIONS
Dribble Tag	(10 yds)	Four cones mark each 10-yard by 10-yard square. Two players, each with a ball, are located in each square. One player in each square who is "it" attempts to dribble or kick his/her ball into the opponent's ball. If the opponent's ball is hit or played out of the square, the players switch roles. (8 years and older)	This drill forces players to look up from their ball in controlling their dribble. By increasing the size of the square, it becomes more difficult to tag the opponent's ball.	1. In each square, two or more players can attempt to protect their balls from the player who is "it." (8 years and older) 2. In each square, two or more players can attempt to protect their balls from two or more players who are "it." (10 years and older) [Note that in both variation number one and two, the square must be made larger to accommodate the number of players and their ability.]

DRILLS AND GAMES FOR DRIBBLING AND MAINTAINING CONTROL

NAME	DIAGRAM	DESCRIPTION	KEY POINTS	VARIATIONS
Burglar	burglar → (triangle diagram with back door)	Three players form a triangle by holding hands. One of these players is designated as "the back door." On the ground within the triangle is a ball. A fourth player ("the burglar") stands outside the triangle. The object of the drill is for the burglar to run around the triangle and make quick changes of direction to tag the back door. The players forming the triangle must quickly rotate in response to movements of the burglar while maintaining the ball within the triangle and shielding the back door from the burglar. The burglar is not permitted to reach over the top of the shielding players. After a designated period of time or after the burglar touches the back door, the players change roles. (9 years and older)	This drill helps players develop shielding techniques. It can be used, also, to develop fitness.	

DRILLS AND GAMES FOR DRIBBLING AND MAINTAINING CONTROL

NAME	DIAGRAM	DESCRIPTION	KEY POINTS	VARIATIONS
Ladder Dribble	10 yds / 40 yds / Starting Position	Four 10-yard by 10-yard squares are designated by 10 cones as shown in the diagram. One defender is assigned to each square. One attacker, with a ball, starts the game outside one of the two end squares. The object of the game for each player is to gain and maintain possession of the ball and score points by dribbling it back and forth from one end line to the other, through as many squares as possible, without losing possession. One point is awarded to an attacking player for every square dribbled through under control. Defending players must stand in the middle of their square until the ball enters their square. If the ball is tackled away once within a square, or is played over the side lines, the defender in that square switches roles with the attacker. If the ball is played forward, without control, into the next square, a point is not awarded to the attacking player and the attacking player switches roles with the player in the square in which the ball entered. The first player to score a set number of points wins the game. (12 years and older)	All individual techniques for dribbling and maintaining control, as well as individual defensive techniques, are practiced in this game.	1. The ladder can be made longer (five squares) or shorter (three or two squares) to accommodate all players on a team. (12 years and older) 2. By using two defenders in each square and two attackers the game can be made into a passing game. (12 years and older)

DRILLS AND GAMES FOR DRIBBLING AND MAINTAINING CONTROL

NAME	DIAGRAM	DESCRIPTION	KEY POINTS	VARIATIONS
Target Dribbling		All players start inside a goal area with a ball. They kick their ball into play outside the penalty area. When signaled, all players attempt to get a ball, dribble it to within shooting range, and shoot it into the goal from outside the penalty area. The last player to shoot a ball into the goal or any player kicking a ball out of bounds scores a point. A player who kicks a ball out of bounds must immediately stop competing. The object of the game is not to score points. Players who choose to pursue the same ball may compete for control of a ball. (10 years and older)		

16

HEADING

Eugene W. Brown

QUESTIONS TO CONSIDER
- What are the individual techniques used to head a ball?
- What are the key elements and common errors of each of the individual heading techniques?
- What are the four factors that should be considered before encouraging young athletes to engage in heading activities?
- What developmental progression should be used in teaching heading?

INTRODUCTION

Purpose of Heading

The technique of heading involves the use of the head to pass, shoot, or receive a soccer ball. Specifically, the head may be used to clear a high cross, advance the ball to a teammate, receive a high pass, or deflect a lofted ball into the goal.

The importance of heading in the game of soccer varies with the nature of play engaged in by competing teams and the age (or ability) of the players. Heading skills are important in games involving intermediate and advanced youth players who can purposefully make accurate air ball passes.

Because of miskicks and unjustified vocal encouragement by spectators to always kick balls long distances, balls are often played into the air by beginning players. However, because of their lack of accuracy in making air ball passes and their general lack of ability to purposefully head the ball, beginning players should be encouraged to try to control the ball on the ground.

Fundamentals of Heading

- ## Body Position and Movement

Prior to heading a ball, the trunk should be arched back (see Figure 16-1B). This movement will result in a noticeable tension in the stomach muscles and will aid in the subsequent vigorous forward bending movement of the trunk that follows (see Figures 16-1C-D).

- ## Arm Position and Movement

During the preparatory phase of heading, the arms are held forward and to the side of the body and bent slightly at the elbows (see Figure 16-1A). This will assist in lateral balance. As the forward bending movement of the trunk occurs, the arms may be forcefully drawn back (see Figure 16-1C-D). This movement of the arms assists the trunk's forward movement and resultant impact velocity of the head to the ball.

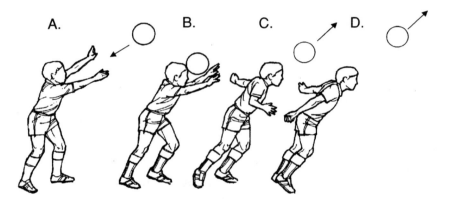

Figure 16-1. Sequence of movement in heading.

- ## Method of Contact

Contact with the ball should be made with the forehead (see Figure 16-2). This generally flat region of the head permits good ball control. The frontal bone of the skull, which encompasses the forehead, is also relatively thick and strong. The eyes should be kept open and focused on the ball throughout the performance of the skill to insure that contact is made with the forehead.

Heading the ball in regions other than the forehead may be painful and injurious and should be avoided. Additional forward speed of the head is obtained by simultaneously flexing the neck as the forehead is extended into the ball. When contact occurs, the jaw should be held firmly in place with the mouth open and the tongue retracted. The muscles of the neck should be tightened to prevent the head from recoiling.

Figure 16-2. *Forehead contact with the ball.*

INDIVIDUAL TECHNIQUES

There are important variations in heading techniques associated with the path and speed of the approaching ball, movement and position of the player before initiating an attempt at heading, and desired direction and speed of the pass or shot. Basically, the variations can be grouped into two categories: heading while on the ground (standing) and heading while in the air (jumping).

Heading While on the Ground

● Forward Heading

When heading while on the ground, the feet should be spread in a comfortable forward-backward alignment. This positioning provides the proper balance so the body weight can be shifted backward, then forward in the direction of the intended flight of the ball. Which foot is selected for the forward or back position should be based upon the player's personal preference. The back foot is turned out to provide lateral stability and to act as a base for the back leg to drive the body forward. When moving forward into the ball, a stride may be taken onto the front foot in the intended direction of the path of the ball.

This technique is the basic method of heading. It is composed of the fundamentals of heading (body position and movement, arm position and movement, and method of contact) and the foot position and movement described in the preceding paragraph. The sequencing of these elements can be seen in Figure 16-1.

- Shift the body weight to the back foot by arching the trunk, then drive off the back foot into the ball.

- Elevate the arms forward and to the side of the body and then draw them back as the trunk bends forward.

- Contact the ball with the forehead.

- Keep the eyes open.

- Tighten the muscles of the neck to prevent the head from recoiling on contact with the ball.

Common Errors

- Straddling the feet to the sides of the body

- Permitting the ball to strike the head and not actively striking at the ball

- Tucking the chin to the chest and contacting the ball on the top of the head

- Closing the eyes

● Sideward Heading

In sideward heading, one side of the body is positioned toward the direction of the approaching ball. During the preparatory phase, the trunk is laterally flexed, the body weight shifted to the back foot, and the forward arm elevated (see Figure 16-3B). This positioning is followed by an extension of the back leg, a lowering of the forward arm simultaneously

Figure 16-3. *Sequence of movement in sideward heading.*

with a raising of the rearward arm, and a rapid movement of the trunk into lateral flexion toward the ball (see Figure 16-3C-E). Note the use of the side of the forehead.

Sideward heading may be used to impart additional velocity to a slowly approaching ball or to change the direction of the rebound by turning the head and using the side of the forehead. This technique can be performed from a position with the feet on the ground or in the air after a jump (see Heading While in the Air).

Key Elements

- Laterally flex the trunk away from the ball, then toward the ball.
- Lower the forward arm and raise the rearward arm as the head moves to contact the ball.
- Push off the back foot to move the body and head forward to contact the ball.

Common Errors

- Not contacting the ball with the forehead
- Improperly timing the body and head movement

● Backward Heading

Heading the ball backward can be accomplished from either a position on the ground or in the air. The result of deflecting the ball backward depends upon the direction of the approaching ball and the angle of the forehead at impact (see Figure 16-4). When performing this skill from a standing position, additional velocity and height of projection can be ob-

Figure 16-4. *Orientation of forehead and path of the ball.*

tained by flexing the hips, knees, and ankles followed by rapid extension of these joints into impact (see Figure 16-5). This results in an arching of the trunk.

Key Elements

- Properly orient the head to achieve desired deflection of the ball.
- Contact the ball with the forehead.

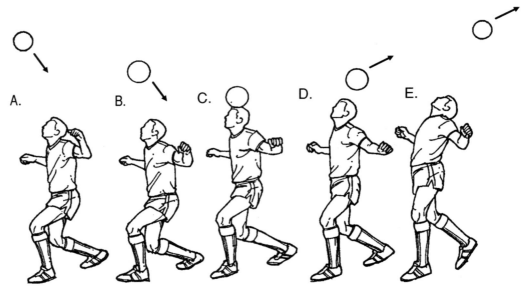

Figure 16-5. *Sequence of movement in heading backward.*

Common Errors

- Improperly timing the extension of the body.

Heading While in the Air

Heading the ball while in the air can be initiated from either a jump or a dive. There are several reasons for jumping into the air to play the ball. These include:

- playing a ball that is too high to be played from the ground,

- beating opponents who are attempting to head the ball,

- surprising the defense, and

- forcefully shooting a goal.

Jump Heading

There are two styles of jumping to head the ball: 1) from a two-foot takeoff (see Figure 16-6) and 2) from a one-foot takeoff following a running approach. After the takeoff, the techniques of heading in either style are similar. To head the ball forward, the body is arched backward followed by rapid flexion in which the trunk and legs jackknife forward. The arms, which are swung upward to aid in the jumping movement, are swung backward to help move the trunk and head forward into impact.

In addition to the takeoff, the basic difference between these styles of heading is that, in the two-foot jump, takeoff and landing occur in virtually the same spot. The run and one foot takeoff results in considerable forward movement of the body from takeoff to landing.

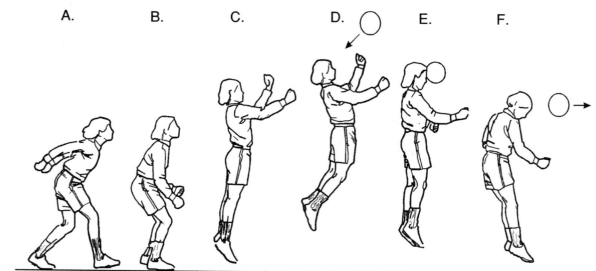

Figure 16-6. Sequence of movement in jumping to head the ball forward from a two-foot takeoff.

Key Elements

- Jump forcefully upward under control.

- Arch the body backward, then jackknife it forward.

- Properly time the jump and body movements with the approach of the ball.

- Whenever possible, land on both feet, under control.

Common Errors

- Not jumping high enough, resulting in insufficient time to arch and jackknife the body before landing

- Jumping and landing off-balance

Jumping to head the ball can also be used to orient the body for sideward heading or to head the ball backward. In both cases the head and body movement are similar to performing these techniques while on the ground.

Progressions for Coaching

Before teaching youth players how to jump to head the ball, they should be moderately skilled in each of the individual heading techniques from a standing position. The following sequence can be used to teach your players how to apply each of the individual heading techniques when jumping to head the ball.

Teach your players to:

1. jump from both a one-foot and two-foot takeoff;

2. jump and head a ball held up high;

3. jump and head a tossed ball;

4. run, jump, and head a tossed ball;

5. run, jump, and head a kicked ball; and

6. run, jump, and head a kicked or tossed ball while pressured by opponents.

● Diving Head

This is a potentially dangerous technique and generally should not be taught to players under 14 years of age. Players below this age can learn and properly perform this skill, but their judgment, as to whether they are endangering themselves, may be faulty. This skill results in the head being lowered to a height where other players may be kicking at the ball.

Even the rules of soccer discourage the use of this skill when others are attempting to kick the ball. Under these conditions, an indirect free kick will be awarded to the team whose player was attempting to play a low ball with the feet. The player attempting to head the ball will be penalized for dangerous play.

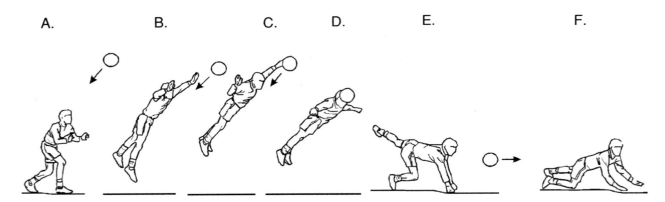

Figure 16-7. *Sequence of movement in diving to head the ball.*

The technique of executing a "diving header" is usually initiated by a run to meet the ball. During the last few steps the body is lowered and the trunk is inclined forward (see Figure 16-7A). Takeoff is usually from one foot (see Figure 16-7B). The arms are lifted about shoulder height on the takeoff, then lowered into impact (see Figure 16-7D). The arms should continue their swing so the hands are positioned to aid the legs in making initial contact with the ground to absorb the ground impact force on the body (see Figure 16-7E and F).

The purpose of this skill is to drive the ball toward the goal in shooting. Note that the same result could be accomplished by using the foot. Therefore, teaching this potentially dangerous skill to youth players under 14 years of age should be discouraged.

Key Elements

- Lower the body and incline the trunk forward on the approach run.
- Cautiously determine when to use a diving header.
- Initially absorb the impact of landing with the hands and legs.

Common Errors

- Creating a dangerous play
- Initially impacting the ground with the trunk

Progressions for Coaching

Only short periods of training should be dedicated in any practice session to teaching players how to dive to head the ball. Because of the potential discomfort experienced when landing, you should instruct your players to wear extra clothing and padding to those sessions in which you plan to have them practice diving headers. This technique should be practiced where the ground is soft and the grass is thick. If gymnastic mats are available, they can be used to initially teach your players how to dive and land softly.

The following sequential approach can be used to teach diving headers. Teach your players to :

1. dive and land correctly from a short, slow approach without attempting to head the ball;
2. dive and land correctly from a running approach without attempting to head the ball;
3. run slowly, dive, and head a tossed ball; and
4. perform the diving header on a tossed or kicked ball at game pace.

DEVELOPMENTAL CONCERNS

There are four factors that should be considered before encouraging young athletes to strike the ball with their head.

1. Ball Impact Force

The impact force in heading is determined from the weight of the ball and the speed at which it approaches the head. The impact force can be very large because of high ball speeds that result from kicking.

2. Neck Muscle Strength

The muscles of the neck, which are important in heading, are relatively weak in athletes under 12 years of age. Observation of the heading techniques employed by such players reveals this lack of neck strength. Because youth players have weak neck muscles, they will often align their head, neck, and trunk with the path of the approaching ball in order to absorb the impact force in line with the body, and to prevent possible injury. By comparison, the adult player will properly receive this force more perpendicular to the line of the head, neck, and trunk.

3. Control of Head Movements

Relatively weak muscles of the neck and incomplete motor development in young athletes may result in improper forehead contact with the ball. Contacting the ball with regions of the head other than the forehead may increase chances of injury.

4. Development of the Spine

The bones (vertebrae) that compose the spine do not fully develop until 25 to 30 years of age. Potential impact forces from heading may be injurious to the neck (cervical) vertebrae of young soccer players. Therefore, any form of heading should not be practiced by players under 8 years of age.

RECOMMENDED PROGRESSIONS FOR TEACHING HEADING

Should young athletes be taught to head a soccer ball? The answer to this question is, "Yes, if coaches select teaching methods and practice techniques that are commensurate with the physical development of their young athletes." Supplement 16-1 contains a suggested progression for teaching heading skills. Each coach, however, must assume the responsibility of determining, in all cases, whether or not individual players can safely perform each step in the progression.

SUMMARY

Coaches can reduce the discomfort and potential for injury associated with young athletes who engage in heading soccer balls. This can be accomplished through instruction on the proper ways to perform the techniques and by selection of an appropriate progression that is compatible with the physical development of the athlete.

SUGGESTED READINGS

Smodlaka, V.N. (1984). Medical aspects of heading the ball in soccer. *The Physician and Sportsmedicine*, 12(2), 127-128, 131.

Progression for Teaching Heading

Age (Years)	Focus of Activity and Instruction	Comments and Concerns
Under 8	Not Recommended	Heading is not recommended because of relatively weak neck musculature and lack of control of movement of the head.
8-9	1. Teach proper body positioning and movement. 2. Instruct players to hold a ball against their own forehead while they assume the proper feet and body position with eyes open. 3. Allow players to lightly bounce a ball off their own forehead.	Allowing the player to control light bounces off their own forehead permits self-regulation and reduces fear. At most, 20 minutes of practice time in a 10-week session should be allotted for heading practice. Emphasis on other skills such as dribbling, kicking, and receiving is more important at this age.
10-11	1. Instruct players to toss, head, and catch a ball themselves. Vary the drill by either having them receive and control the headed ball or head the ball to a teammate positioned three to five yards away. 2. Teach your players to juggle the ball with their head. 3. Initiate heading drills in which underhand tosses, using two hands, are made to a partner. 4. Use heading drills which challenge your players by requiring them to: move to head the ball, head to a moving target, or head the ball in different directions.	Continue using drills in which players have self-control over heading impact forces. However, a transition should be made to heading balls tossed by a partner standing up to five yards away. The coach must continually monitor tosses for excessive height, distance, and spin on the ball. Approximately five minutes of every other practice is appropriate for work on heading skills with this age group.

Progression for Teaching Heading

Age (Years)	Focus of Activity and Instruction	Comments and Concerns
12-13	1. Allow players to toss a ball 10 to 20 feet to a partner who returns the ball with a head pass. 2. Players should be taught how to jump and head. 3. Players should be taught how to trap a ball with the head.	Heading becomes a more important part of the game at this age. Most players have sufficient neck strength and control of head movements to head tossed balls. Additional heading skills, such as jumping to head the ball and trapping, should be taught. As much as 5 minutes per practice session could be spent in practicing heading skills through the use of a variety of drills.
14 and above	1. Permit players to practice heading balls which are thrown or kicked 20-40 feet. 2. All heading techniques should be taught.	Most players will be mature enough to head balls which are kicked to them. They should be able to execute variations of heading skills from a standing and airborne position.

YOUTH SOCCER TECHNIQUES—HEADING
Difficulty Rating Form

Level of Player* Approximate Age**	Suggested Emphasis		
	Beginning 6-9 yrs.	Intermediate 10-13 yrs.	Advanced 14 yrs. & up
Individual Techniques			
Heading while on the ground			
Forward heading	X	X	X
Sideward heading		X	X
Backward heading		X	X
Heading while in the air			
Jump heading forward		X	X
Jump heading sideward			X
Jump heading backward			X
Dive heading			X

*Note that Beginning, Intermediate, and Advanced does not always correspond with the age range given beneath it. Coaches should use this classification system as an approximation, adjusting the techniques to suit their players' ability levels.

**Heading is not recommended for players under 8 years of age, irrespective of the ability of the player.

HEADING DRILLS AND GAMES

NAME	DIAGRAM	DESCRIPTION	KEY POINTS	VARIATIONS
Sit-Up and Head		One player lies on the ground in a sit-up position with knees bent and arms over head. A partner, with extended arms, holds a ball to be headed by the player performing the sit-up. (8 years and older)*	This drill simultaneously develops abdominal strength and heading skills. As the header sits up, the arms should be positioned to the side of the body so that they can be forcefully drawn back to aid in forward movement of the head into contact.	1. After a sit-up is initiated, the ball is tossed to the player performing the sit-up. The ball is headed back to the tosser. (10 years and older)
Heading from the Knees	≈3 yds	One player tosses a ball to a partner who is kneeling on the ground and arching the trunk backward. The header flexes the trunk and heads the ball back to the tosser. The header will often fall off balance forward onto the hands where a push-up can be performed from the knees to get back into position for the next toss. (11 years and older)	This is a good drill to practice the movement pattern of the trunk and arms used in jump heading. It also can be used to exercise the abdominal muscles, which are important in heading.	
Heading on the Move	≈3 yds	Two lines are formed with one ball for each pair of players. An underhand toss is made to a partner, then headed back to be caught. This is repeated as both players move across the field. Partners switch roles, after moving a predetermined distance, and return to the starting point by repeating the drill. (10 years and older)	The player heading the ball should move on the balls of the feet. Just prior to heading, proper feet and body position must be assumed in order to correctly perform the technique.	1. Move backward and head forward. (10 years and older) 2. Head the ball twice before returning it to the tosser. (10 years and older) 3. Start the drill with the toss but continue heading back and forth without catching the ball. (10 years and older) 4. Use jump heading from one or two feet takeoffs. (12 years and older)

*Suggested age for practicing the drill or game is included in parentheses.

HEADING DRILLS AND GAMES

NAME	DIAGRAM	DESCRIPTION	KEY POINTS	VARIATIONS
Windshield Wiper (Heading)		The player with the ball makes an underhand toss to a partner, then makes an arching run. The player receiving the toss heads the ball sideward, back to the tosser at the new position. The header faces the tosser again. A toss is made, followed by a sideward head to the tosser who is running back to the original position. (11 years and older)	Header should jog in place prior to the toss. If the tosser runs to the header's left, the left foot should be straddled forward in performing the sideward head. The right foot is straddled forward in sideward heads to the right.	1. Have the tosser vary the direction of the run and make the direction unpredictable to the header. (11 years and older) 2. Combine skills by having the tosser perform a designated trap on the return pass. (11 years and older) 3. Use jump heading from one-foot or two-feet takeoff. (12 years and older)
Quick Reaction Heading		Two of the three players have a ball in their hand. Thi middle player receives a tossed ball, and heads it back to the tosser. As soon as the head contacts the ball, the other player tosses the ball toward the middle player who is quickly turning in order to react and head the second toss back. (11 years and older)	The header should be on the balls of the feet in order to quickly adjust body position and perform the head. An attempt should be made to position the feet in a diagonal straddle during the performance of this technique.	1. Start drill with a toss but continue heading back and forth without catching the ball. (11 years and older) 2. Use jump heading from one- or two-feet takeoff. (12 years and older)
Heading Shots on Goal		A ball is tossed to a player running toward the goal who tries to score. The goalkeeper tries to prevent the score. The tosser goes to the end of the line for heading. The header retrieves a ball and goes to the end of the line for tossing. (12 years and older)	A ball headed down toward the goal line and away from the goalkeeper is difficult for the goalkeeper to stop. Therefore, players should be encouraged to head the ball low and to the sides of the goalkeeper.	1. Alter the position of the heading line to encourage sideward heading. (12 years and older) 2. Vary the type of heading by having players jump or dive head the ball. (14 years and older)

HEADING DRILLS AND GAMES

NAME	DIAGRAM	DESCRIPTION	KEY POINTS	VARIATIONS
Flick On Heading	(diagram: ≃5 yds, ≃5 yds)	A ball is tossed underhand to the header in the middle. The ball is headed backward to the third player who catches it. The header quickly turns and faces the player holding the ball. The ball is tossed back to the header who again heads the ball backward to the player who made the first toss. (11 years and older)	Emphasize the proper techniques described in section on Backward Heading.	1. Head the ball straight up, then head it backward on the second attempt. (11 years and older) 2. Tosser calls either "return" or "back" to signal the header to return the ball to the tosser or head the ball backward. (11 years and older) 3. Use jump heading from a one-foot or two-feet takeoff. (12 years and older)
Pressure Heading	(diagram: ≃5 yds)	A ball is tossed over a defender to a teammate who jumps to head the ball back to the tosser. The defender provides passive pressure. (12 years and older)	Jump heading should be initiated from a two-foot takeoff. When closely marked, a one-foot takeoff may cause the header to jump into and foul the defender. Emphasis should be placed on achieving maximum vertical height in the jump and heading the ball at this point.	1. Increased pressure from the defender ranging from passive to trying to win the ball. (12 years and older) 2. Instead of returning the ball, the header could head the ball to another open space to be trapped. (12 years and older) 3. Perform this drill similar to the Windshield Wiper drill with the tosser moving to an open space to receive a return pass. (12 years and older)

HEADING DRILLS AND GAMES

NAME	DIAGRAM	DESCRIPTION	KEY POINTS	VARIATIONS
"On" "Time" Heading		A. A ball is tossed to a teammate. A defensive player, who was marking the tosser, turns and runs to mark the receiver. The tosser immediately shouts, "On," meaning that a player is marking the receiver. The ball is headed back to the tosser. Heading can be performed with feet in contact with the ground or from a jump. This will depend on the pressure imposed by the defender. B. From the same formation as in A., the ball is tossed to a teammate. If the defender does not turn to mark the player receiving the ball, the tosser shouts "Time" and the ball is trapped and controlled by the receiver. (12 years and older)	In game situations, the player receiving a high pass needs to focus attention on the ball. Teammates can assist by letting the receiver know whether or not an opponent is marking. This drill teaches communication between players as well as heading under pressure. The defender should be encouraged to be unpredictable in marking the receiver.	1. Same as Variation 2 in Pressure Heading Drill. (12 years and older) 2. If the defender turns to mark the header, the tosser breaks to one side or another as in the Windshield Wiper drill and shouts, "On." A sideward head is made back to the tosser. The sound of the tosser's voice aids the receiver in determining direction to head the ball. (12 years and older)
Clearing Headers		Two lines of players are formed; one at the corner of the goal area and another between the intersection of the penalty kick area and corner of the penalty area. A ball is tossed high into the air by the first player in the line outside the penalty area. The tosser runs up field, away from the goal and toward the nearest side line, to receive a long clearing head pass, which should be trapped and controlled. Both players return to the end of their respective lines. Eventually, the headers and tossers should switch roles. Note two drills can be set up at each goal to accommodate 20 or more players. (13 years and older)	In a clearing pass, the distance and direction of the pass is very important. The ball should be cleared so it lands far outside the penalty area and toward the touch line. This will make it difficult for the opponent to score a goal directly from intercepting the clearing pass.	1. Use another player to pressure the header. (13 years and older) 2. Substitute chipping kicks for the toss. (14 years and older) 3. Use a goalkeeper to occasionally call for the tossed or kicked ball instead of using a clearing header. The goalkeeper can then punt or throw the ball to the kicker or tosser. (14 years and older)

HEADING DRILLS AND GAMES

NAME	DIAGRAM	DESCRIPTION	KEY POINTS	VARIATIONS
Toss-Head-Catch		This is a small-sided game. Two games could be run cross field simultaneously with six or more players per side. Cones can be used as goals. The game is started with a throw from the middle of the field. The team in possession of the ball must pass the ball using a toss-head-catch pattern. Possession of the ball will be lost if: 1. the ball hits the ground, 2. a pass is intercepted by the opposing team, 3. the toss-head-catch pattern is not followed, 4. a player in possession of the ball takes more than three steps or five seconds before tossing it, 5. one player plays the ball twice in succession, or 6. the ball is played out of bounds. Goals can only be scored by heading. (13 years and older)	Offensively, this game teaches runs into open spaces to receive a tossed ball to be headed. It also reaches players to run to support the header. Defensively, it teaches close marking and anticipation of passes.	
Soccer Volleyball		This game is played on either an indoor or outdoor volleyball court with a regulation net. A volleyball may be substituted for a soccer ball. The game is played and scored in the same manner as regulation volleyball with the following exceptions: 1. all passes of the ball are performed by heading the ball, and 2. the serve is performed by tossing the ball into the air and heading it over the net from behind the base line. (14 years and older)	This game emphasizes fine control of height and direction in heading.	1. Allow other parts of the body to be used to pass the ball. (14 years and older) 2. Allow one bounce between passes. (14 years and older)

17

THROW-IN

Eugene W. Brown

QUESTIONS TO CONSIDER
- What are the rules of play that govern the throw-in?
- What are the fundamental components of a throw-in?
- What are the individual throw-in techniques and their advantages?
- What are the key elements and common errors in performing the throw-in?
- What progression can be used to teach the throw-in to youth players?
- During play, what factors should determine who takes the throw-in?
- How may various throw-in errors be corrected?
- What are set plays used for the throw-in?

INTRODUCTION

Purpose of the Throw-In

The throw-in is an essential part of the game of soccer. It is the method by which the ball is put back into play after it goes out of bounds over the touch line (side line). Therefore, youth soccer players must not be put into game competition without knowing this important skill.

The team in possession of the ball for the throw-in has the advantage if they are able to quickly and accurately put the ball into play. A properly thrown ball is as effective as a well-executed pass.

Rules of Play Governing the Throw-In

The rules of play restrict the variability in technique used for the throw-in. They define the location and method for the throw-in.

● **Location**

1. The throw-in must occur at the point where the ball went out of bounds.

2. The throw-in must be taken with both feet on the ground, either on the touch line or outside the touch line. An illegal throw-in would have one or both of the feet completely over the touch line in the field of play. If one foot is off the ground, this is also an illegal throw-in. (See Figure 17-1.)

Figure 17-1. *Legal (A and B) and illegal foot placement (C through E) during the throw-in.*

● **Method**

1. The thrower must face the field of play.

2. Both feet must be in contact with the ground when the ball leaves the hands.

3. The throw-in is made with a two-handed throw, in which each hand must apply approximately equal force to the ball.

4. The throw-in must consist of one continuous movement in which the ball is taken from behind the head and released over the head.

Even with these restricting rules, considerable variability in technique is possible in this important skill.

Fundamentals of the Throw-In

● **Foot Position**

The stationary throw-in is executed without an approach run. In this type of throw-in, the feet are positioned in either a side straddle, about shoulder width apart (see Figure 17-2), or in a forward-backward straddle (see Figure 17-3). In both cases, the feet should be pointed in the direction of the intended throw.

Balance is an important factor in the throw-in. If a player falls off balance in performing the skill, an illegal throw-in may result. It should be noted that the side straddle provides the thrower with more lateral stability; whereas, the forward-backward straddle provides greater stability in the direction of the intended throw. In the forward-backward straddle, foot position can be maintained throughout the throw-in or a step forward can be taken as the arms swing over the head to release the ball. Determining which foot to straddle forward should be left to each player's preference. Generally, they will position the foot opposite their preferred throwing arm forward. Both methods of straddling the feet are acceptable, but the forward-backward straddle is recommended because body movement and instability in the throw-in are primarily in a forward-backward direction.

Figure 17-2. *Side straddle.*

Figure 17-3. *Forward-backward straddle.*

● Hand Position

The fingers should be spread out comfortably across the back and sides of the ball. The thumbs are positioned close together at the back of the ball (see Figure 17-4). In general, the hands form a cup that conforms to the shape of the ball.

Figure 17-4. *Hand position.*

● Sequential Motion

From an upright position (see Figure 17-5A), the ball is raised over and behind the head and the trunk is arched backward (see Figure 17-5B). This motion shifts the weight of the body toward the back foot and results in a flexion of the knees. Forward movement of the ball results from a rapid sequence involving back leg extension, forward movement of the head and flexion of the trunk (see Figures 17-5C-E). These actions shift the body weight to the front foot (see Figure 17-5E). This sequencing movement is followed by a rapid forward movement of the arms and extension of the lead leg (see Figure 17-5E-F), which blocks the forward movement of its hip and aids in trunk flexion. The forward movement of the trunk is then reduced, which helps to speed the rotation of the arms. Finally, the wrists should snap forward into the release of the ball (see Figure 17-5F). The entire movement in the throw-in is similar to the action of a whip.

Figure 17-5. Sequential movement in the stationary throw-in.

INDIVIDUAL TECHNIQUES

Stationary Throw-in

Basically, the stationary throw-in is entirely composed of the fundamentals of the throw-in (feet position, hand position, and sequential motion described in the previous paragraphs and in Figure 17-5).

Key Elements

- Straddle the feet for balance.
- Spread the fingers across the back and sides of the ball.
- Throw the ball by using a whip-like motion of the trunk and arms.

Common Errors

- Failing to bring the ball behind the head before throwing it forward
- Bringing the ball forward over the side of the head
- Throwing the ball primarily with one hand, resulting in a lateral spin on the ball
- Stepping over the touch line before releasing the ball
- Lifting the feet from the ground after the release of the ball but before the ball is back in play
- Falling off balance

Approach Run and Throw-in

This technique of putting the ball back into play combines an approach run, hop, step, and throw. The approach run and throw-in has a greater potential for maximum ball velocity and distance than the stationary throw-in. If the purpose of the throw-in is to get the ball into play quickly and catch the opponents unprepared, then the stationary throw-in should be used. However, if maximum distance is desired, an approach run should precede the throw-in.

● Approach Run

The intent of the approach run is not to achieve maximum running speed, but to attain a moderate speed that can be controlled during the performance of the throw-in. This can be achieved with an approach of six or fewer steps. During the approach run, the ball is held in front of the body (see Figure 17-6A), with the fingers properly positioned to perform the throw-in.

● Hop, Step, and Throw

A hop and step follows the approach run. The hop occurs simultaneously with the elevation of the ball over and behind the head and the backward arching of the trunk (see Figure 17-6B and C). As in the stationary throw-in, forward movement of the ball results from rapid sequencing of back leg extension, forward movement of the head and flexion of the trunk (see Figure 17-6D-F). This forward movement results in a step being taken so the feet are positioned in a forward-backward straddle (see Figure 17-6D). Note that the distance between the feet in the straddle position should be greater in the throw-in following the approach run than in the stationary throw-in. A greater forward-backward spacing is needed to control the momentum developed during the approach. The spacing between the feet is reduced during and after release of the ball by sliding the back foot forward and finally dragging the top of the toes across the ground (see Figure 17-6E-G). This movement helps to control the momentum developed during the approach.

The action of the trunk, head, and arms are similar in both the stationary throw-in and the throw-in following an approach run (see Figures 17-5 and 17-6). The approach run and throw-in, however, results in a greater range of movement and velocity of the trunk, head, and arms before the ball is released.

Key Elements

- Maintain a controlled approach run.
- Integrate the approach run, hop, step, and throw into one continuous movement pattern.

Figure 17-6. Sequence of movement in the approach run and throw-in.

Common Errors

- Running too fast at the approach
- Misjudging the distance needed to complete the approach run and throw-in

PROGRESSION FOR TEACHING THE THROW-IN

The stationary throw-in should be taught before teaching the approach run and throw-in. The movement pattern of the trunk, head, and arms is similar in both of these throw-ins. Once the stationary throw-in is learned, youth soccer players quickly progress in combining this skill with an approach run. Both variations can be properly performed by most children by the time they are 9 years old. Subsequent improvements in performance are the result of skill refinement and increased strength. (See Supplement 17-1 for appropriate times to teach throw-in skills.)

Stationary Throw-In

The following is an ordered progression for teaching beginning players the stationary throw-in:

1. **Hand position**—Demonstrate, then have players assume proper hand positioning on the ball (see Figure 17-4). Note that it may be better to use one of the players to demonstrate proper hand positioning because the use of a small ball by an adult presents an unrealistic perspective for youth players.

2. **Foot position**—Demonstrate, then have players assume proper positioning of the feet. A side straddle is acceptable, but a diagonal (forward-backward) straddle is preferred.

3. "Arch-touch-bow"—These three words provide a set of teaching cues to assist beginning players to learn the sequential movement in the throw-in (see Figure 17-5). Demonstrate the elevation of the ball and arch of the trunk ("arch"), flexion of the elbows and contact of the back of the neck with the ball ("touch"), and forward movement of the ball and flexion of the trunk ("bow").

Note that the rules of play do not require the ball to contact the back of the neck for the throw-in. However, the "touch" insures that beginning players develop a pattern of bringing the ball behind the head. This required position is often forgotten by youth players in the excitement of competition. Also, note that the bow should not be a deep forward bending of the trunk, but a forceful forward movement of the trunk that is abruptly halted to whip the arms forward.

Demonstrate the "arch-touch-bow" using proper hand and feet positioning. Then, have all players practice this sequence without releasing the ball. While the players are practicing, provide them with individual feedback on positioning of the hands and feet, sequencing of the movement pattern, and whether their feet maintain contact with the ground.

4. Throw-in to stationary target—Add a throw-in during the "bow" phase of movement. Demonstrate the "arch-touch-bow and throw." Divide the team into groups of twos with one ball for each pair of players. Have them practice this sequence with a throw-in to their partner, who is to catch the ball and return it by performing the same sequence. Continually monitor their performances and provide individual feedback. As skill increases, the distance between the partners can be increased. Selected techniques for reception and control can also be substituted for the catch. However, with beginning players, a large proportion of the practice time allocated to the throw-in may be consumed by attempts at receiving and controlling the ball.

5. Throw-in to a moving target—This is practiced in the same manner as No. 4. above, with the exception that a lead pass is thrown to a partner running to catch or receive and control the ball. Note that the direction, distance, and velocity of the ball is important for a teammate to receive and control it.

6. Throw-in to a moving target with pressure—In groups of three's, this drill is performed in a manner similar to No. 5., with the exception that a defender is attempting to intercept the throw-in. The intended receiver of the throw-in must quickly change directions of his/her run in order to get into an open position to receive the ball. While the receiver is altering positions on the field, the teammate making the throw-in must anticipate these changes and alter feet position so the body is properly aligned when the throw-in is finally performed. By rotating positions after a set number of throw-ins, all three members of each group will have the chance to practice throw-ins, receiving, and defending.

Approach Run and Throw-In

1. **"Hop-step"**—Coordinating the "hop-step" with the other body movements in the approach run and throw-in is a difficult task for some youth players. Therefore, you should first demonstrate the entire approach run and throw-in so your players can see the entire skill. But, initially teach them the "hop-step." With the ball properly positioned in their hands, players should repeatedly practice the "hop-step" movement. The arms should be swung upward to initiate the hop (see Figure 17-6B and C). This results in the ball being carried to a position above and slightly behind the head with the trunk arched back. The step will initiate trunk flexion and forward movement of the ball (see Figure 17-6C-E).

2. **Approach run, hop, and step**—Integrate the approach run with the hop and step. Demonstrate this sequence to your players, then give them several trials. Continually monitor whether each player is able to maintain balance and foot contact with the ground after the step.

3. **Approach run and throw-in to stationary target**—Integrating all of the components of this skill will be a difficult task for some of your players. They may need to repeat previous phases of this progression. However, others will quickly catch on to the pattern of movement necessary to perform this skill. By observing performances of each player throwing to a partner, those players having difficulty integrating the components of the skill will be apparent.

4. **Approach run and throw-in to a moving target**—This is performed similar to No. 5. (Progression-Stationary Throw-in), except that an approach run is added.

5. **Approach run and throw-in to a moving target with pressure**—This is performed similar to No. 6. (Progression-Stationary Throw-in).

COMMON ERRORS IN TECHNIQUE AND THEIR CORRECTIONS

Rule violations in the throw-in are often the result of errors in performance. A listing of individual throw-in errors and probable corrections is given in Table 17-1.

Table 17-1. Technique errors in taking the throw-in.

Throw-in Error	Discussion and Probable Correction
Unequal force applied to the ball by the hands during the throw.	• This is evident in a top-like spin imparted to the ball and is usually caused by the player throwing the ball from the dominant hand side of the head. It can be corrected by having your players concentrate in bringing the ball forward directly over the middle of the head and attempting to throw with a little lateral spin.
Lifting the back foot in the forward-backward (diagonal) straddle during the throw.	• If a stationary throw-in is being used, this can be corrected by having the players position the body weight more toward the back foot. If a running approach is used, take a longer straddle step following the hop to keep the body position in back of the front foot.
Falling off balance when using a side straddle.	• Little forward-backward stability is provided by a side straddle. Have the player switch to a diagonal straddle.
Stepping beyond the touch line	• Player should practice throw-ins with a restraining line so they will understand how to confine their approach run.
Failure to bring the ball behind the head.	• Remind the players to "touch" the back of the neck with the ball.
Failure to perform the throw-in with one continuous motion.	• Reinforce the "arch-touch-bow" cues as being one continuous and integrated movement.

YOUTH SOCCER TECHNIQUES—THROW-IN
Difficulty Rating Form

	Suggested Emphasis		
Level of Player* **Approximate Age***	**Beginning** **6-9 yrs.**	**Intermediate** **10-13 yrs.**	**Advanced** **14 yrs. & up**
Individual Techniques			
Stationary throw-in			
side straddle	X		
forward-backward straddle	X	X	
Approach run and throw-in	X	X	X

*Note that Beginning, Intermediate, and Advanced does not always correspond with the age range given beneath it.Coaches should use this classification system as an approximation, adjusting the techniques to suit their players' ability levels.

Set Plays for the Throw-In

When play is restarted by a throw-in, the strategy for putting the ball into play may be spontaneous or it may be preplanned (set play). Selection of an appropriate set play should be based on the ability level of the players and the location of the throw-in. The examples of set plays for various age and ability levels are given in Chapter 20 (Tactics of Play).

18

DEFENSIVE TECHNIQUES

Eugene W. Brown and Gary Williamson

QUESTIONS TO CONSIDER
- For what purposes are individual defensive techniques used?
- What principle is fundamental to all individual defensive techniques?
- What are the individual defensive techniques?
- What progressions are recommended for teaching various individual defensive techniques?
- When should slide tackles be taught to youth soccer players?

INTRODUCTION

Purpose of Defensive Techniques

Basically, individual defensive techniques are used to:

- regain possession of the ball,

- decrease the potential for the offensive team to maintain possession of the ball, and

- decrease the potential for the offensive team to score a goal.

Fundamental Defensive Principle

Marking and tackling are the individual defensive techniques. They can be used in both zone and player-to-player defenses. Application of these basic techniques to team defense (defensive tactics and strategy) is included in Section VI. All players must be taught how to mark and tackle. However, in order for these individual techniques to be effectively used, the fundamental defensive principle that *all players defend immediately upon loss of possession* must be applied.

Marking

Marking involves the defender being positioned near and on the defensive goal side of an opponent. There are two types of marking: marking a player in possession of the ball and marking a player who does not have possession of the ball.

● Marking a Player in Possession of the Ball

When guarding a player in possession of the ball, the defender should be in a slightly crouched position with the weight of the body supported on the balls of the feet (see Figure 18-1). The eyes of the defender should be focused on the area of the hips of the attacker and peripherally viewing the ball and immediate surroundings. This position is typical of good guarding positions in basketball. From this position, quick movements of the feet can be made in response to the opponent's dribble.

The distance from which a defender marks an opponent depends upon the skill and quickness of both players and location of the ball on the field. If the defensive player is more skilled and quicker than the attacker,

Figure 18-1. Body position and focus when marking a player in possession of the ball.

a position of about two yards from the attacker is appropriate. If the opposite is true, additional distance may be needed for the defender to respond to offensive maneuvering. Also, marking in the defensive third of the field must be closer than marking in the offensive third of the field. Closer marking should occur in front of one's own goal to reduce the space attacking players have to maneuver and pass the ball.

● Marking a Player Who Does Not Have Possession of the Ball

A similar defensive posture to that shown in Figure 18-1 should be assumed, even though the offensive player does not individually have possession of the ball. The defensive player should, however, mark from a greater distance and focus more on what is occurring off the ball, to be ready to respond to movements of the ball and other players (see Figure 18-2). Positioning may also be slightly off the line from the ball to the goal in anticipation of offensive play.

Figure 18-2. Body position and focus when marking a player who does not have possession of the ball.

Key Elements

- Position the weight of the body on the balls of the feet.
- Make quick, short steps with the feet.
- Keep visual contact with the offensive player, ball, and surroundings.
- Take a goal side positioning between the offensive player and the goal.

Common Errors

- Not positioning goal side of the ball
- Focusing only on the ball
- Positioning too far or too close to an opponent

Progression for Coaching

The following sequence can be used to teach your players how to mark. Teach your athletes to:

1. assume correct body position and vision,
2. mark player-to-player without the use of a ball (1 versus 1)
3. mark player-to-player when using a ball and two small goals (1 versus 1 with goals), and
4. mark player-to-player in small-sided games.

Tackling

Tackling is the technique of taking a ball directly from an opponent. There are several techniques that can be used to dispossess an opponent of the ball. The type of tackle to be performed depends upon the relative position and direction of movement of the offensive and defensive players. Individual tackling techniques and the conditions under which they should be performed are described in the following paragraphs.

● Front Block Tackle

When approaching an offensive player who has close control of the ball, a front block tackle is appropriate to use. The block tackle refers to the use of the inside of the foot to "block" the movement of the ball at the same time as the opponent kicks or dribbles it forward.

The front block tackle is performed similar to the inside of the foot kick. When close to the attacking player, a leap is taken onto the support foot, which is pointed straight ahead (see Figure 18-3A-C). During this time, the blocking foot is swung back and its forward swing is initiated. The blocking foot continues to swing forward into contact with the ball (see Figure 18-3D-F). In response to the upcoming tackle, the offensive player may also perform a similar movement to block the tackle and continue to move the ball forward. At the moment of simultaneous impact with the ball, the muscles of the blocking leg should be tense, the blocking foot should be forcefully swinging forward, and the body weight should be forward of the support foot to drive the ball forward. The player who performs these components more timely and forcefully usually wins the ball. However, the ball may be kicked unpredictably or wedged between the blocking feet of the two players. If the ball is wedged between the blocking feet, possession of it can be won by scooping it over the attacker's foot (see Figure 18-4), pushing it between the attacker's legs (see Figure 18-5), or drawing it back (see Figure 18-6).

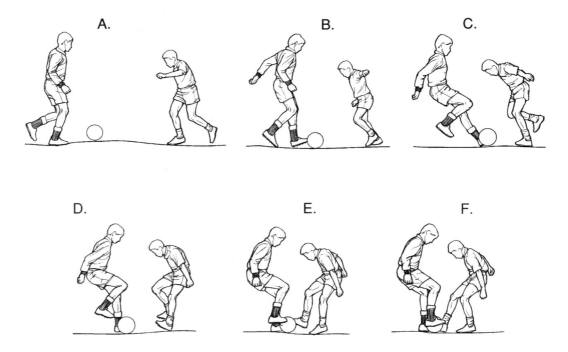

Figure 18-3. Front block tackle.

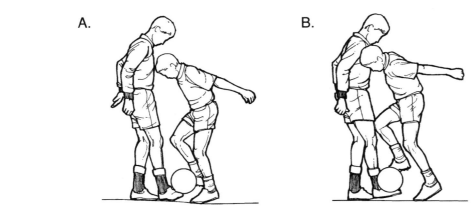

Figure 18-4. *Front block tackle and scoop.*

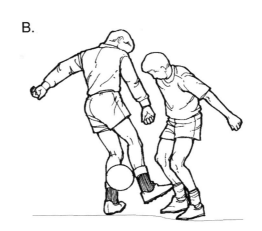

Figure 18-5. *Front block tackle and push between the legs.*

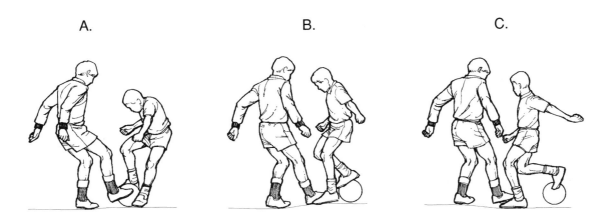

Figure 18-6. *Front block tackle and draw back.*

Key Elements

- Make contact with the center of the ball and drive it forward.
- Place the support foot to the side of the ball.
- Bend the knee of the support leg to lower the body for good balance.
- Tackle as the opponent attempts to play the ball.

Common Errors

- Tackling with a straight blocking leg
- Leaning back from the tackle
- Tackling with a relaxed blocking leg

Progression for Coaching

The following sequence can be used to teach your players how to perform block tackles. In each step of the sequence, both right and left foot block tackles should be practiced.

1. Standing in pairs with a ball between them, have your players attempt to block tackle the ball on your signal.

2. Dancing with the ball (rapid and alternate touches with the sole of the right and left foot) in pairs, have your players attempt to block tackle the ball on your signal.

3. Have one player attempt to block tackle the ball away from an attacking player who approaches with a slow dribble.

4. Have your players engage in drills and games in which full-paced block tackles are likely to occur.

- **Pivot Tackle**

The pivot tackle is used when overtaking an attacking player from behind or intercepting the path of the attacking player from the side. This tackle is performed in a similar manner to the front block tackle. It differs from the front block tackle in the preparation to get the body in position to make the tackle. As the defending player overtakes the attacking player, a leap is taken onto the support foot, which is rotated outward and positioned in advance and to the side of the dribbler (see Figure 18-7A-C). During the leap and foot plant, the trunk of the defensive player should rotate to face the dribbler (see Figures 18-7A-D). This orients the defensive player into a front block tackle position from which the pivot tackle is completed (see Figure 18-7D-F).

Key Elements

- During the leap, rotate the support foot outward and place it in front and to the side of the ball.
- Pivot the trunk 180 degrees to face the attacking player.
- Complete the pivot tackle by performing a front block tackle.

Figure 18-7. Pivot tackle.

Common Errors

- Tackling from a position behind the ball
- Tackling the ball when it is on the foot opposite to the side of the tackle

Progression for Coaching

After mastering the front block tackle, the following progression for practicing the pivot tackle is appropriate. Teach your players to:

1. pivot and tackle a player who is standing with the ball at his/her feet,

2. pivot and tackle a player who is jogging with the ball, and

3. pivot and tackle a player who is dribbling the ball at full speed.

● Side Tackle

The side tackle is used when overtaking an attacking player from behind or intercepting the path of an attacking player from the side. When the defensive player is alongside the attacking player, a legal shoulder-to-shoulder charge should be used. At this point, the foot nearest the dribbler can be used to poke the ball away with the toe from the attacking player (see Figure 18-8). If the defensive player can get his/her shoulder in front of the shoulder of the dribbler, the dribble can be taken over by the tackler.

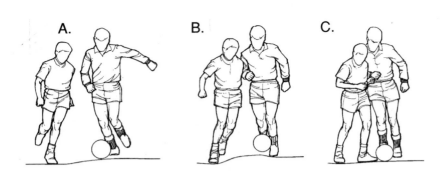

Figure 18-8. Side tackle and toe poke.

Key Elements
- Use a legal shoulder-to-shoulder charge to get close to the ball.
- Tackle the ball with the foot closest to the opponent.
- Tackle the ball between dribbles by the opponent.

Common Errors
- Charging from behind
- Tripping the attacking player

Progression for Coaching

The following sequence can be used to teach your players how to perform the side tackle. Teach your players to:

1. assume a legal shoulder-to-shoulder charge position with a partner while standing still and use a toe poke to kick the ball away,

2. walk with a partner in a legal shoulder-to-shoulder charge position and toe poke the ball away,

3. jog with a partner in a legal shoulder-to-shoulder charge position and toe poke the ball away,

4. run with a partner in a legal shoulder-to-shoulder charge position and toe poke the ball away,

5. jog with a partner in a legal shoulder-to-shoulder charge position and take over the dribble by slipping the charging shoulder in front of the opponent's chest, and

6. run with a partner and attempt to take over the dribble.

- **Slide Tackle**

A slide tackle is a difficult technique for children to learn, and it is potentially dangerous for them to perform. Some youth recreation soccer leagues have prohibited slide tackles by awarding a direct free kick to the team it is used against. This approach uses sound judgment because slide tackles are "last resort" tackles that can be injurious to either the dribbler or the tackler, and the team whose player is on the ground is outnumbered in defense.

Slide tackles should not be taught until your players are able to correctly and consistently perform all of the previously described individual defensive techniques. When you decide to teach your players how to slide tackle, they should be requested to wear sweat pants or other clothing and padding that will protect their legs, hips, and buttocks from scrapes and bruises. Slide tackles should be practiced on grassy areas that have been inspected and determined to be free of exposed stones, glass, or other hazards. If the ground is wet, this will allow the players to slide more easily and soften the blow of landing.

There are two slide tackle techniques—the bent leg slide tackle and the hook slide tackle. Usually they are used when an attacking player is beyond a defender and there is no other way of dispossessing the dribbler of the ball. Either of these variations can be used to (a) kick the ball out of play, (b) prevent a pass or shot, and (c) pass the ball to a teammate.

Bent Leg Slide Tackle

To perform the bent leg slide tackle, the defender should be slightly behind and to the side of the attacking player. As the tackler approaches the ball, the body is lowered and rotated toward the dribbler (see Figure 18-9B and C). Contact with the ground is made by the outside of the non-tackling leg, which is bent at the knee (see Figure 18-9C). The force of contacting the ground can be additionally absorbed by the side of the body and arm closest to the dribbler (see Figure 18-9C and D). The hip rotation of the body toward the dribbler aids the swing of the tackling leg. The ball should be tackled away by the instep (see Figure 18-9C).

Figure 18-9. Bent leg slide tackle.

Hook Slide Tackle

The approach to the ball in the hook slide tackle (see Figure 18-10A and B) is similar to the approach used in the bent leg slide tackle. In the hook slide tackle the trunk should also rotate toward the dribbler. The hook slide tackle, however, differs from the bent leg slide tackle in the usage of the legs. In the hook slide tackle, the leg farthest from the dribbler is used to lower the tackler's body to the ground and rotate it toward the attacker (see Figure 18-10A-C). The leg nearest the dribbler is swung forward to tackle the ball away and absorb the force of landing (see Figure 18-10C and D). Additional force can be absorbed by the hip, trunk, and extended arm (see Figure 18-10D). The instep, toe, or sole of the foot can be used in the hook slide tackle to knock the ball away from the dribbler. This tackle can be used to reach balls farther away from the tackler than can be reached with the bent leg slide tackle. However, the hook slide tackle has a greater potential to result in a foul because in this tackle the opponent is more likely to be contacted before the ball.

Key Elements (Slide Tackling in General)

- Move in close to the opponent.
- Absorb the force of landing with the side of the leg, hip, trunk, and extended arm.
- Tackle the ball between dribbles by the opponent.
- Immediately return to the feet after the tackle.

Figure 18-10. Hook slide tackle.

Common Errors (Slide Tackling in General)

- Improperly timing the tackle, resulting in the dribbler escaping with the ball and a numerical advantage for the attacking team

- Using a slide tackle when other individual defensive techniques could have been performed from a standing position

- Fouling the dribbler

Progression for Coaching

The following sequence can be used to teach your players both the bent leg and hook slide tackles. Teach your players to:

1. assume the proper slide tackle position while lying on the ground,

2. lower themselves from a jog into a proper slide tackle position on the ground,

3. lower themselves from a jog and slide tackle away a ball placed on the ground,

4. slide tackle the ball away from a partner who was instructed to dribble the ball relatively far from the body at a jogging pace,

5. slide tackle the ball away from a partner who was instructed to dribble with close control at a jogging pace, and

6. slide tackle the ball away from a partner who attempts to maintain close control at full pace.

SUMMARY

The teaching of individual defensive techniques are sometimes approached in a manner similar to that used by many coaches to teach goalkeeping techniques. It appears that coaches often feel that their youth soccer players will learn these techniques on their own, just by being involved with the sport. This is not true. Knowledgeable coaches, on the other hand, understand that defensive techniques are an important and integral part of the game. They plan their coaching sessions to include time for instruction, demonstration, and practice of the progressions in order to teach their players how to correctly perform each of these techniques.

YOUTH SOCCER TECHNIQUES— DEFENSIVE
Difficulty Rating Form

Level of Player * Approximate Age*	Suggested Emphasis		
	Beginning 6-9 yrs.	Intermediate 10-13 yrs.	Advanced 14 yrs. & up
Individual Techniques ·			
Marking			
player in possession of the ball	X	X	X
player not in possession of the ball	X	X	X
Tackling			
front block tackle	X	X	X
pivot tackle		X	X
side tackle	X	X	X
slide tackle			
bent leg			X
hook			X

*Note that Beginning, Intermediate, and Advanced does not always correspond with the age range given beneath it. Coaches should use this classification system as an approximation, adjusting the techniques to suit their players' ability levels.

DRILLS AND GAMES FOR DEFENSIVE TECHNIQUES

NAME	DIAGRAM	DESCRIPTION	KEY POINTS	VARIATIONS
Side by Side		Form two lines about 20 yards from the corner of the penalty area. Offensive players are in the line closest to the near touch line and defensive players are in the other line. Each of the pairs of offensive and defensive players has one ball. The first pair gives their ball to the coach, and stands side by side with their backs to the goal. As the coach throws or kicks the ball toward the goal, both players turn, run after the ball, and attempt to gain possession of it. If the offensive player is first to possess the ball, this player attempts to score by getting a shot on goal. If not in possession of the ball, the defensive player attempts to close space, mark, and tackle the ball away. If the defender gains possession of the ball, this player should attempt to clear the ball back over the midfield line. After a goal, clear, or ball played out of bounds, the partners retrieve their ball and return to the end of the opposite line. (6 years and older)*	The coach can give an advantage to the offensive or defensive player by the distance and direction of the toss or kick. The toss or kick can also be used to increase the chance that tackles occur from the front or side of the offensive player. Note that two drills can be run simultaneously on a half field and four drills on a full field.	1. Include a goalkeeper to assist the defensive player and to practice goalkeeping techniques. (6 years and older)
				2. Upon gaining possession of the ball, have the defender attempt to pass the ball through two flags positioned 10 feet apart on the center line. The original offensive player attempts to give immediate chase, close space, mark, and tackle the ball away to prevent the ball from being passed through the flags. (6 years and older)
				3. Use groups of four (two offensive and two defensive players) in this drill. (6 years and older)

*Suggested age for practicing the drill is included in parentheses.

DRILLS AND GAMES FOR DEFENSIVE TECHNIQUES

NAME	DIAGRAM	DESCRIPTION	KEY POINTS	VARIATIONS
Two Versus Two Keep Away		Two teams of two players each compete against each other for approximately 30 seconds in a 10-yard by 10-yard space. The object of the game is for a team to have possession of the ball when the game is stopped. One point is awarded for possession at the end of each game. The team with the most points at the end of several games is the winner. (6 years and older)	This game promotes the defensive techniques of marking players with or without the ball, as well as various tackling techniques. Dribbling, passing, shielding, and movement of the ball are also practiced in this game. Note that by increasing the space, tackling becomes more challenging and by decreasing the space, maintaining possession becomes more difficult.	1. Other combinations of offensive and defensive players and space to play can be used. (6 years and older)
Pursue and Tackle		Pairs of players form two lines along one touch line. One partner is outside the touch line and the other is just inside the touch line with a ball. When given a signal to start, the player with the ball attempts to dribble to the opposite touch line while the opposing player attempts to tackle it away. At the opposite touch line the players reverse roles and the drill is repeated. (6 years and older)	Shielding, dribbling, and tackling techniques are practiced in this drill. Spread the pairs apart along the touch line so they do not interfere with each other.	

DRILLS AND GAMES FOR DEFENSIVE TECHNIQUES

NAME	DIAGRAM	DESCRIPTION	KEY POINTS	VARIATIONS
Tag Along		Pairs of players spread out over the field. One member of each pair has a ball. A whistle or other signal is used to start play. The object of the game is for the defensive player to closely mark the player with the ball, without tackling it away, in order to be able to touch him/her immediately after a signal is given to stop play and before a second signal is given. The offensive player attempts to dribble the ball far away from the defender so as not to be tagged immediately after play is stopped. (6 years and older)	Defensively, close and persistent marking are techniques practiced in this drill. Offensively, techniques for dribbling and maintaining control are practiced. This drill can also be used to enhance anaerobic conditioning.	1. Permit the defensive player to tackle the ball away and continue the drill until the signal is given. (6 years and older)
Center Circle Possession		A maximum of about 16 players are inside the center circle. All players except two are given a ball. The object of the game is to have possession of a ball when the coach signals to stop play. Upon a signal to start, the players not in possession of a ball try to dispossess another player of a ball. If, in the process, balls go beyond the line of the center circle, they are out of play. Players in possession of a ball at the end of the game score a point, and the game is repeated. (8 years and older)	The length of the game needs to be adjusted. This depends upon how many balls are being contested. The game should be stopped when the number of balls is approximately equal to one-half the number of players. It becomes somewhat dangerous for many players to pursue only a few balls. Players should be encouraged to make tackles where they can gain possession of the ball. This game is also very good for providing practice at shielding and protecting the ball.	1. Divide the groups into two teams. On each team, all players except one are in possession of a ball. After a period of time during which one team has lost about one-half of their balls, the game is stopped and the team with the most balls wins. (8 years and older)

DRILLS AND GAMES FOR DEFENSIVE TECHNIQUES

NAME	DIAGRAM	DESCRIPTION	KEY POINTS	VARIATIONS
Through Passes	10 yds	A 10-yard square is marked by four cones. One offensive player is positioned outside each of the sides of the square. Two defensive players are inside the square. One of the offensive players has a ball. Offensive players are permitted to make either diagonal passes (a pass from one side to an adjacent side) or through passes (a pass from one side to the opposite side). Offensively, the object of the game is to score a point for each through pass. Opportunities for these passes may be set up by quick diagonal passes. Defensively, the object of the game is to prevent through passes by responding to the position of the ball. One point is awarded to the defense for each pass that is intercepted. After a certain period of time, the defenders switch with two offensive players. (8 years and older)	This drill forces the defenders to respond quickly to each pass. There must also be communication and coordination in order for the defenders to be successful.	

DRILLS AND GAMES FOR DEFENSIVE TECHNIQUES

NAME	DIAGRAM	DESCRIPTION	KEY POINTS	VARIATIONS
Inside-Outside	(15 yds / 10 yds)	Four cones mark a 10-yard by 15-yard rectangle. One member of each team is positioned outside the narrow side of the rectangle. The other member of the team plays either within the rectangle or outside the space on the same side with his/her teammate. The opposing team has the same two options. A ball is thrown into the rectangular space to start the game. One player from each team attempts to gain possession of the ball and dribble it across the opponent's end line. A player can pass or dribble the ball outside his/her own end line where the opposing player is not permitted to mark. If both players are outside their own line, either player can enter the rectangle with or without the ball. Neither team can have two players in the rectangle at once. A team is awarded one point for each ball played over the side lines by their opponents or for errors in play in which two players from the opposing team are inside the rectangle at once. Two points are awarded each time a team dribbles over the opponent's line. After each score, the game is restarted. Teams can play to a certain number of points or for a designated time period. (10 years and older)	This is both an offensive and defensive game. Defensively, a player must continually respond to changing situations in determining where and who to mark.	1. Other combinations of offensive and defensive players, inside and outside the rectangle, as well as changes in the size of the rectangle could be used. (10 years and older)

Section V
INDIVIDUAL TECHNIQUES FOR SOCCER GOALKEEPERS

19

GOALKEEPING

Eugene W. Brown, Gary Williamson, and Joe Baum

QUESTIONS TO CONSIDER
- What are the six fundamentals of goalkeeping?
- What positioning should a goalkeeper use in response to various ball locations?
- How should a goalkeeper respond to a breakaway?
- What are appropriate progressions in teaching goalkeepers individual techniques?
- What are the four elements of catching?
- When should a goalkeeper deflect or punch a ball?
- What are the five components of a diving save?
- What progression is recommended to teach youth goalkeepers how to dive?
- What are the key elements, common errors, and variations of the individual goalkeeping techniques?

INTRODUCTION

The goalkeeper is the only member of the team who can legally use his/her hands to control the ball. This privilege is limited to the goalkeeper's own penalty area.

All players on a youth squad should be given a chance to practice and play the goalkeeper position during various practice sessions. However, consistent training for this position may need to be limited to a few players. In selecting players for this unique position, a coach should consider children who want to play the position as well as children who possess or are likely to develop greater than average stature, agility, courage, confidence, quickness, hand-eye coordination, physical strength, decisiveness, and kicking and punting techniques.

Generally, it is not appropriate to rotate several players into the goalkeeper position during the course of the game. This may place some children in potentially embarrassing and fearful situations as well as disrupt the flow of the game because of the repeated exchange of goalkeeper equipment. The easiest time to exchange goalkeepers is at halftime or at quarter breaks in youth games. It is equally inappropriate to encourage or permit the labeling of a youth player below the age of 13 years as "goal-keeper" and not to encourage these players to experience other field positions.

Purpose of Goalkeeping

The goalkeeper is the last line of defense in preventing balls from entering the goal. The goalkeeper is also the first line of attack in initiating offensive play after a save.

Fundamentals of Goalkeeping

- **Ready Position**

When the opponents have the ball close to the goalkeeper's goal, the goalkeeper should be in a ready position (see Figure 19-1), prepared if called into action. The goalkeeper should be mentally and physically alert. In the ready position, the knees and trunk are bent and the feet are approximately shoulder-width apart with weight forward on the balls of the feet. The arms are spread at waist height with the palms held out facing the play. The eyes are fixed on the ball, with concentration extended to players around the penalty area. In this position, the goalkeeper is less vulnerable to a quick shot and being caught off balance. Quick and well-coordinated movements can be carried out from this ready position. When there is no immediate threat on goal, a goalkeeper can maintain a moderate level of attention by jogging in place or moving around the penalty area near the arc.

Figure 19-1. Ready position.

Key Elements
- Position the feet shoulder-width apart.
- Bend the knees and trunk.
- Distribute the body weight forward and onto the balls of the feet.
- Position the hands in front of the body, palms facing play.

- Keep mentally alert.

Common Errors

- Positioning feet too far apart, resulting in delayed body movement
- Positioning feet too close together, resulting in instability
- Carrying hands at sides or placing them on the knees instead of in front of the body, resulting in delayed reaction
- Not concentrating on the ball and opposing players

● Positioning

Apart from set plays, such as a penalty kick or a free kick, the goalkeeper should not stand in a stationary position for a long time. A goalkeeper must change positions in the goal area by reacting to the play. A goalkeeper should move along an imaginary arc (see Figure 19-2) that decreases the opening to the goal for the player with the ball and also provides the best positioning to stop a shot on goal. This position is along an imaginary line that connects the ball and the center of the goal line. Before play, it is advisable for goalkeepers to create a mark, with their cleats, at the center of the goal line to use as a guide for proper positioning. As the ball approaches the goal, the imaginary arc should get closer to the goal. Note, if the ball is along the goal line and away from the goal (in a poor shooting position), the goalkeeper should retreat toward the far post.

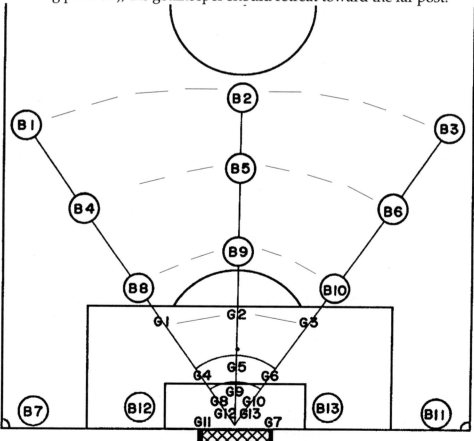

Figure 19-2. Goalkeeper positioning in response to ball position. The letters "B" and "G" with the same numerals designate corresponding pairs of ball positions and goalkeeper positions.

However, if the ball is brought toward the goal from the wing into a shooting position, the goalkeeper must come to the near post.

To be correctly positioned, a goalkeeper must face the ball. Movement sideways should involve small shuffle steps in which the feet do not cross one another. This will enable the goalkeeper to quickly transfer the body weight from one foot to the other. If a goalkeeper's weight rests for a considerable time on one foot, typical of long strides, the goalkeeper may be restricted in changing direction rapidly. Similarly, if a goalkeeper hops sideways, once the feet leave the ground it is impossible to change direction until contact with the ground is regained.

Key Elements
- Use an imaginary arc.
- Face the ball.
- Use short and quick shuffle steps.
- Keep body weight forward onto the balls of the feet.

Common Errors
- Moving too far off the goal line
- Remaining on the goal line
- Hopping sideways
- Crossing the legs
- Standing flat footed, with weight primarily on the heels

Progressions for Coaching

One of the first techniques youth soccer players should be taught about playing goalkeeper is how to correctly position themselves around the goal. Goalkeepers should be taught to:

1. position themselves correctly in response to each of several balls located outside and inside the penalty area (see Figure 19-2);

2. continually assume proper positioning in response to the changing location of a ball that is dribbled outside and inside the penalty area;

3. continually assume proper positioning in response to movements of a player dribbling, stopping, changing directions, and faking shots;

4. assume proper positions in response to players taking shots on goal from stationary positions to the left, center, and right of the goal; and

5. assume proper positions in response to attacking players receiving and shooting balls served to the left, center, and right of the goal.

● Narrowing the Angle on a Breakaway

The goalkeeper should maintain a pattern of positioning as suggested in Figure 19-2 with slight variations in response to anticipated passes to unmarked opponents in the penalty area. However, when a player with the ball is unmarked and has an open path to the goal without the chance of being marked by a defender, the goalkeeper should move into a position to maximize the possibility of making a save. To do this effectively, a goalkeeper should quickly advance, under control, along an imaginary line from the center of the goal line to the ball. This line bisects the shooting angle (see Figure 19-3). The goalkeeper should have his/her arms out to the sides of the body to reduce the visually open area of the goal (see Figure 19-1 and 2). As the goalkeeper advances in a balanced and controlled manner, the target area for the attacking player will become smaller (see Figure 19-3).

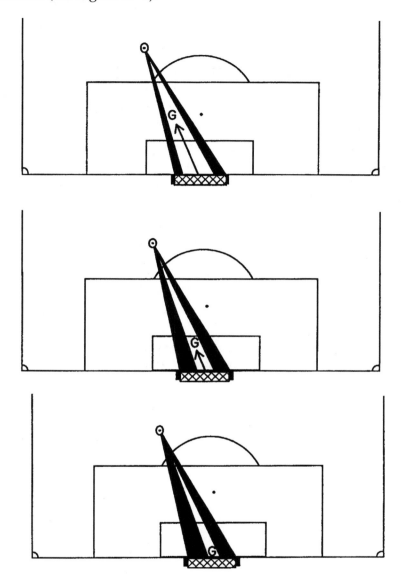

Figure 19-3. *Narrowing the angle. As the goalkeeper moves closer to the ball, the area of the goal that appears to be visually open, narrows, or decreases.*

The order of desirable outcomes (from most desirable to least) that the goalkeeper should attempt to achieve in stopping a breakaway is:

1. get the ball before the attacker shoots,

2. get to the ball as the shot is being taken, and

3. block the ball immediately after the shot is taken.

If the goalkeeper gets to the ball before the attacker, the goalkeeper can catch or dive and catch the ball in a variety of ways. However, if the goalkeeper arrives simultaneously as the shot is being taken, or slightly after the shot, the goalkeeper must quickly react by diving to the side of the intended shot. This is a potentially dangerous situation and goalkeepers must be taught how to protect themselves. Basically, a dive is made to position the goalkeeper in front of the attacker (see Fundamentals - Diving). The top arm must be positioned away from and in front of the face (see Figure 19-4). This positioning of the top arm is used to:

- permit a good view of the actions of the shooter,
- absorb the blow of a kick toward the face and head,
- enable the goalkeeper to react and protect the trunk, and
- aid in blocking or catching the shot.

When properly diving in front of an attacking player, the objective of the goalkeeper is to block the ball with the arms, body, or legs. The goalkeeper's stomach may be the most vulnerable body part. Therefore, strong abdominal muscles are important.

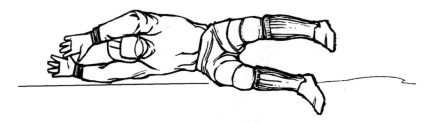

Figure 19-4. Body and arm position when landing, after the dive, in front of the kicker.

Key Elements
- Visualize a shooting angle. (Note, this can be practiced by connecting string from the ball to the goal posts.)
- Bisect the shooting angle.
- Move along the imaginary line quickly and under control.
- Before the shot is taken, momentarily assume a ready position.
- Present as big a barrier as possible.

Common Errors
- Giving the attacking player a larger target area on one side of the goal
- Staying on the goal line and not coming out to approach the ball
- Approaching the ball without maintaining controlled body movements
- Advancing too slowly or too quickly
- Running out from the goal to play an attacker who is being marked by a defender
- Not having the hands and arms extended toward the near post side

Progressions for Coaching

If goalkeepers are taught how and when to come out from their goal line in order to narrow the shooting angle of an attacking player, they will not feel as threatened in this potentially dangerous event. Goalkeepers should be taught to:

1. assume a proper positioning of the top arm while on the ground,

2. approach a ball placed on the ground and go down as if to make a save,

3. approach and stop a shot from an attacking player who has been instructed to kick softly at the ball, and

4. approach an attacking player, who is being pursued from behind by a defender, and attempt to stop the shot on goal (realistic break-away).

● Supporting the Defense

It is important for the goalkeeper to support his/her teammates at all times during the game. Supporting the defense involves correct positioning by the goalkeeper, as previously presented, and effective communication between the goalkeeper and the defense.

The goalkeeper is in an ideal position to assume or be assigned the responsibility of communicating with the defense (directing the defense) because play is usually in front of him/her and the entire field can be viewed. The goalkeeper should communicate in a loud and clear voice to prevent mistakes, misunderstandings, and lapses in concentration. A goalkeeper can tell teammates to "cover" or "mark" opponents, "pressure" a player with the ball, "shift" position on the field, and give a "support pass" back to the goalkeeper. By yelling "keeper" or "goalie" the goalkeeper is telling teammates not to play the ball, because the goalkeeper is in a better position to take charge of play. This type of communication must be given as early as possible so defenders have sufficient time to respond to the goalkeeper's commands. On the other hand, when a defender has good control of the ball and is not under immediate pressure, it is not appropriate for a goalkeeper to shout extraneous information, because this may unsettle the defender. Table 19-1 contains a list of several key words and short commands that can be used by the goalkeeper to direct the defense.

Key Elements

- Communicate with authority in a loud and clear voice.
- Instill confidence by communicating correct information to the defense.
- Communicate with short phrases and key words that are understood by the defense.
- Anticipate and communicate early in order to give the defense sufficient time to react.

Table 19-1. Key words and commands goalkeepers use to direct the defense.

Key words and commands used by goalkeepers	Meaning
"Clear!"	"Kick the ball far away from our goal, toward the opponent's goal, to relieve pressure that is being applied by the attack."
"(Teammate name), cover (number, position, or player description)!" "Mark" or "Guard" are alternate words for cover.	"Guard or mark (specified player) who by his/her position is challenging our goal." e.g., "Tom, cover the left wing!" "Mary, mark number 15!" "Chris, guard the tall player!"
"Goalie!" "Keeper!" is an alternate word.	"Do not play the ball. I am in a better position to play it."
"Man on!"	"While you have the ball (or are about to receive it), an opponent, that you may not see, is ready to guard you."
"Move up!" "Push up!" are alternate words.	"Move toward the opponent's goal to force play away from our goal or to possibly catch the other team offside." (Note, in playing an offside trap, secret words should be established that do not give away the team's intentions as "move up" does.)
"Outside!" or "To the outside!"	"Play the ball toward the nearest side line because there is pressure from opponents and a chance of losing possession of the ball."
"Support!"	"If you need help, I am open and ready to receive a pass back."
"(Teammate name), shift (direction)!"	"Move in the direction I specify." e.g., "Mary, shift right!" "Sam, shift back!"
"(Teammate name), (near or far) post!"	"Position yourself at the near (or far) post and be ready to assist me in playing any ball that gets by me." (Note that this command is associated with the positioning of fullbacks to defend against corner kicks or other free kicks taken from near the corner kick area.)
"Time!"	"You have sufficient time to receive the ball before opponents mark you."
"Wall!"	"Form a wall of players to defend against a free kick." (Note, that the goalkeeper could also specify the number of players wanted in the wall, e.g., "Four-man wall!").

Common Errors

- Communicating trivial information
- Giving mixed messages
- Giving too many messages
- Not taking charge

Progressions for Coaching

1. Establish a list of key words and short commands (see Table 19-1) and review their meanings with all players.

2. Have the goalkeeper shout appropriate information to unopposed defenders as a ball is kicked into the penalty area.

3. Have the goalkeeper direct three or more defenders against three or more attacking players.

4. Have the goalkeeper direct the defense in full-sided games.

5. Have the goalkeeper direct the defense in various restarts.

● Shot Stopping

Each shot on goal requires the goalkeeper to engage in a quick decision-making process.

First, the goalkeeper must judge the level of difficulty in stopping the shot. (In Table 19-2, several factors that influence the level of difficulty in shot stopping are presented. These factors can be manipulated by a coach to create appropriate challenges for goalkeepers in practice sessions.)

Second, the goalkeeper must decide whether to attempt to catch the ball or to punch or deflect it away from the goal. For shots that are relatively easy to stop, the goalkeeper should attempt to catch the ball. On the other hand, shots that are relatively difficult to stop should be punched or deflected away from the front of the goal area.

Finally, the goalkeeper must select which individual shot- stopping technique to use in either catching, punching, or deflecting.

Table 19-2. Factors influencing the level of difficulty in stopping shots on goal.

Level of Difficulty	Conditions of Play	Factors					
		Pressure	**Pace of the Ball**	**Weather Conditions**	**Point of the Kick**	**Location of Shot on Goal**	**Technique Selection**
Relatively easy	Practice-like	No pressure from attacking players	Slow	Calm, dry	Far from the goal	Close to the goalkeeper	Preselected by coach or goalkeeper based on predetermined path and pace of ball
Moderate		Passive pressure from attacking players	Intermediate		Intermediate distance		
Relatively difficult	Game-like	Pressure from attacking players	Fast	Windy, wet	Close to the goal	Away from the goalkeeper	Selection made by goalkeeper based on conditions of play at the time of the shot

There are two basic forms of catching used by a goalkeeper. They are underhand (scoop) and overhand catching (see Figures 19-5 and 19-6). Underhand catching should be used on balls that are received below the chest. Overhand catching should be used on balls received above the chest.

The chest is the region in which it is possible to use either form of catching. Generally, if the ball is received at the chest from a relatively steep arc, it should be caught with an underhand positioning. However, fast-moving balls with shallow trajectories should be received at the chest with overhand positioning.

Catching by a goalkeeper primarily involves the use of the fingers and palms of both hands to reduce the speed of the ball so that it can be sub-

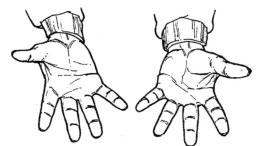

Figure 19-5. *Hand positioning for underhand catching.*

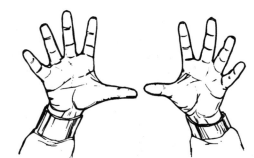

Figure 19-6. *Hand positioning for overhand catching.*

sequently controlled. For all catching in soccer, this process consists of four elements. These four elements are:

- Positioning

  From the ready position (see Figure 19-1), the goalkeeper must attempt to quickly position his/her body in line with the path of the ball. Positioning the body in this manner allows the goalkeeper to use various body parts as a second barrier behind the hands. If sufficient time is not available to position the body in line with the path of the ball, the goalkeeper should attempt to get as close to this position as possible to reduce the difficulty in catching the ball. One of the first techniques youth players should be taught about playing goalkeeper is how to position themselves correctly in goal. Moving to position may involve footwork and/or diving.

- Reaching

  The second element of catching involves reaching the hands toward the ball. This action positions the hands close together and in line with the approaching ball to form an initial barrier in its path. A full reach should be achieved before the ball contacts the hands.

- Controlling

  When the ball contacts the hands, they should be drawn back to reduce the pace of the ball. Control is enhanced if the hands contact the ball over a broad area (i.e., fingers spread) and if the pace of the ball is reduced over a relatively long period of time (i.e., drawing the hands back while in contact with the ball).

- Securing

  Once the pace of the ball has been reduced, it should not be left exposed to attacking players. If left exposed, this will entice attackers to kick at the ball and will endanger the goalkeeper.

  A ball caught from a standing or kneeling position should be secured by wrapping the hands and arms around it (see Figure 19-7). This should be done with the elbows close together.

  Balls controlled while the goalkeeper is on the ground should be drawn into the trunk with the arms wrapped around the ball and the top leg should be swung forward to protect the ball and goalkeeper from late kicks (see Figure 19-8). This positioning provides the goalkeeper with a view of the field of play and an opportunity to begin to decide upon which distribution technique to use.

Punching and Deflecting

If the goalkeeper is uncertain about his/her ability to catch a shot on goal, then the goalkeeper should attempt to punch or deflect the ball away from the goal. Attempting to catch a ball that is beyond the goalkeeper's ability to do so is a major error made by youth players. If the ball is missed, it may proceed into the goal or rebound in front of the goal where a second shot by an attacking player could occur. By punching or deflecting a shot, the goalkeeper is: preventing a goal, acquiring addi-

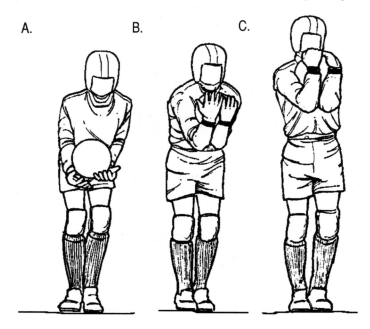

Figure 19-7. Securing the ball with the hands and arms.

A.   B.   C.

Figure 19-8. Securing the ball while on the ground.

tional time to react to subsequent play, and providing time for the defense to reorganize. Any shot that the goalkeeper cannot confidently catch should be punched or deflected away from the goal.

When punching a ball, the goalkeeper should attempt to project the ball far out of the penalty area and to the side of the goal. There are primarily two situations in which a goalkeeper should punch the ball. One occurs when the goalkeeper attempts to receive the ball among attacking players. Under these conditions, the goalkeeper may be bumped and catching is uncertain. This situation occurs often when high crosses and lofted balls are kicked in front of the goal. The second occasion in which punching is appropriate occurs when the goalkeeper must dive to stop a forceful shot on goal. In either case the goalkeeper should attempt to punch the ball with the knuckles of both fists (see Figure 19-9). However, when diving to stop a ball shot to the top or bottom corners of the goal, additional reach can be gained by using one hand.

Deflecting involves the use of the heels of the hands and fingers to redi-

Figure 19-9. Using both fists in punching.

rect the ball. As in punching, the goalkeeper should be taught to use two hands in deflecting the ball whenever possible. A deflection should be used when it is difficult for the goalkeeper to punch the ball sufficiently far from the goal. Deflections are used to redirect the ball: a) in bounds to either side of the goal where the angle for shooting is difficult; b) out of bounds to either side of the goal, giving up a corner kick; or c) out of bounds over the goal post, giving up a corner kick.

• Diving

A dive is used to quickly position the body to play a ball, which is relatively far from the goalkeeper, when sufficient time is not available to run to position. Through the use of good positioning, the goalkeeper minimizes the number of times he/she is called upon to have to dive to make a save. However, the goalkeeper must be ready at all times to respond by diving in an attempt to stop a shot on goal.

Components of a Good Save

There are five components of a diving save. These components are the takeoff, flight, save, landing, and cover-up.

• Takeoff

The takeoff is initiated from a ready position (see Figure 19-10A). The foot to the side of the intended dive is lifted. Simultaneously the opposite foot pushes the body to the side so a short side step is quickly taken onto the lifted foot (see Figure 19-10B-D). Throughout this movement the trunk must maintain a position facing the field of play, the arms are swung back, and the body should be lowered.

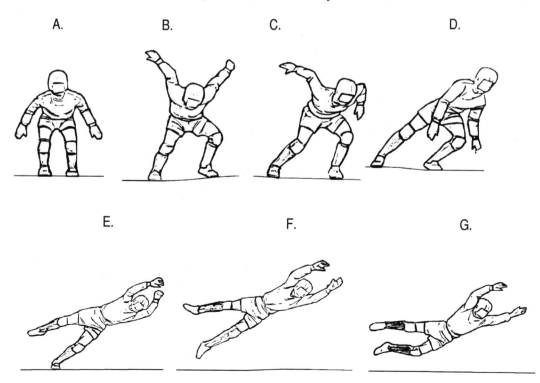

Figure 19-10. Diving—takeoff and flight.

From this position, the leading leg is forcefully extended while the trailing leg is lifted (see Figure 19-10D-F). This has been called the power step[1]. Simultaneous with the action of the legs, the arms are forcefully swung over the head. The leg and arm movements drive the body into the air.

- Flight

  The flight is the path of the body in the air. The path taken must be compatible with the location of the ball. The path, however, is determined at takeoff by the action of the legs and arms. Irrespective of the location of the ball, it is important that the body maintain a position with its shoulders, trunk, and hips parallel to the plane of the goal line (see Figure 19-10F-G).

- Save

  While in the air, the goalkeeper will attempt to catch, punch, or deflect the ball. Each of the diving saves will be presented in the section on Individual Techniques - Diving Saves.

- Landing

  Irrespective of the type of save used (catch, punch, or deflection), it is important for the goalkeeper to land safely. A safe landing is accomplished by a) distributing the blow over a broad area of the body, and b) absorbing the force of landing over a relatively long period of time. These two principles of safe landing are achieved by a goalkeeper who sequentially contacts the ground with segments of the side of the body. For dives used in saving rolling or low air balls, contact with the ground is sequentially made by the outside of the leg, hip, side of the trunk, shoulder, and finally the arm (see Figure 19-11A-C). An opposite sequence of contact with the ground is used to absorb the shock of landing from a medium-high to high air ball diving save.

If the ball is caught, it is important for the goalkeeper to maintain possession of the ball. The shock of landing, however, may jar the ball from the goalkeeper's hands. Two approaches to this problem have been suggested by experts. The first suggests that the goalkeeper should use the ball to help absorb some of the shock in landing. This technique is more appropriate when attempting to reduce the blow associated with a dive to catch medium and high air balls. The second approach argues that the very act of hitting the ball to the ground may jar the ball loose and, there-

A. B. C.

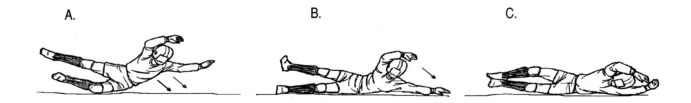

Figure 19-11. *Landing sequence from a diving save on a rolling or low air ball.*

fore, only the body should be used to absorb the force of landing. This technique is more appropriate when attempting to dive and catch a low shot on goal. This type of dive does not result in as great a lateral shock to the body as experienced in the dive for a high ball.

● Cover-up

When a ball is caught during a diving save and attacking players are near, the ball should be covered up. Covering the ball serves two functions. First, if properly performed, it protects the goalkeeper against foul kicks from attacking players. Second, covering the ball secures it and removes the ball from attackers tempted to kick at what might appear to be a loose ball.

The ball is covered up by bringing it into the stomach. As the ball is secured in the midsection of the body, the arms wrap around the ball and the hips flex (see Figure 19-8). The top leg is swung over the bottom leg, further hiding the ball and also forming a barrier to protect the body from errant kicks. The cover-up position permits the goalkeeper to clearly see the field of play and to think about how to distribute the ball.

Key Elements

- Start the dive from a ready position.
- Take a short and quick sidestep in the direction of the shot.
- Drive off the lead leg and quickly swing the trailing leg and arms upward.
- Face the field of play throughout the dive.
- Sequentially absorb the shock of landing.
- Cover up the ball when opponents are near.

Common Errors

- Not being ready to dive
- Taking a long sidestep with the foot pointed toward the goal post
- Taking a face down ("Superman") dive
- Landing on the back
- Abruptly absorbing force on landing
- Exposing a caught ball to onrushing attackers

Progressions for Coaching

When teaching the fundamentals of diving, it is very important for the coach to avoid exposing goalkeepers to potentially painful experiences. The technique of diving should be learned and practiced where the field is soft and void of exposed rocks and the grass is relatively tall. If available, gymnastic-type mats and high-jump pits provide an excellent tool for instilling confidence in the goalkeepers and removing the potential fear associated with landing from a dive. Goalkeepers should also be encouraged to wear extra clothing and padding (e.g., knee and elbow pads) to practice sessions.

A progression for teaching the dive involves the following sequence of activities over several training sessions. Teach your goalkeepers how to:

1. Form a "C" curve with their trunk, alternately to the left and right, while in a kneeling position (see Figure 19-12). Note that their buttocks should not be resting on their heels and their arms should be extended over their heads.

2. Fall from a kneeling "C" curve position, alternately to the left and right, and sequentially absorb the force of landing along the side of the body. Telling your goalkeepers to pretend their bodies are like the rockers of a rocking chair will help them to understand the sequencing of their falls.

3. Fall from a kneeling "C" curve position and receive and cover up balls alternately rolled to the left and right.

Figure 19-12. *"C" curve right with the trunk while kneeling and falling.*

4. Fall, alternately to the left and right, from a squatting position and sequentially absorb the force of landing along the side of the body (see Figure 19-13A-D).

5. Fall from a squatting position and receive and cover up balls alternately rolled to the left and right.

6. Take short dives, from a squatting position, to receive and cover up balls alternately rolled to the left and right.

7. Fall from a standing "C" curve position, alternately to the left and right, and sequentially absorb the force of landing along the side of the body.

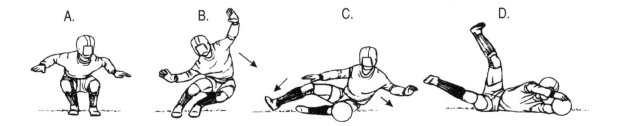

Figure 19-13. *Falling from a squatting position.*

8. Fall from a standing "C" curve position and receive and cover up balls alternately rolled to the left and right.

9. Take short dives, from a ready position, to receive and cover up balls alternately rolled to the left and right.

10. Take dives of short to intermediate length, from a squatting position, to grasp and cover up balls alternately held low to the left and right.

11. Take dives of short to intermediate length, from a ready position, to grasp and cover up balls alternately held low to the left and right.

12. Practice dives to catch and cover up, punch, and deflect balls kicked at various paces and heights (see Diving Saves).

INDIVIDUAL TECHNIQUES

Distribution

After securing the ball, the goalkeeper initiates an attack on the opponent's goal by either kicking or throwing the ball to teammates. Skill in distributing the ball is an essential element in effective goalkeeping.

● Bowled Ball (Underhand Pass)

This type of distribution is useful for passing the ball over short distances. The ball is rolled along the ground to the receiver, allowing easy control. The ball should only be passed to a player who is alert to the pass and has space and time to turn with the ball. It is important for the goalkeeper to support the receiver. If the receiver is pressured, it may be necessary for the receiver to pass the ball back to the goalkeeper.

To execute this underhand pass, the ball is held in front of the body with the palm and fingers of the passing hand. The opposite hand should be placed on top of the ball to maintain control (see Figure 19-14A). As the bowling arm swings back, the goalkeeper should initiate a forward step onto the opposite foot and keep the top hand in front of the body (see Figure 19-14B). This action results in a shifting of the goalkeeper's weight from the back foot toward the front foot while the bowling arm reaches the end of the backswing. Simultaneously with the start of forward swing of the bowling arm, the opposite foot makes contact with the ground (see Figure 19-14C). The ball is released with the hand, following through close to the ground to minimize the bounce of the ball, and in the direction of the intended pass.

Key Elements
- Support the ball in the palm of the bowling hand.
- Initially control the ball with the opposite hand placed on top of the ball.

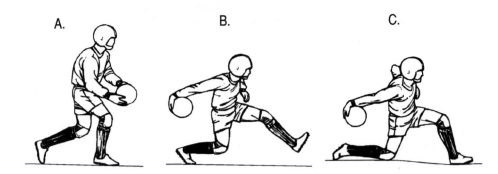

Figure 19-14. *Bowled ball.*

- Focus eyes on intended receiver.
- Step in the direction of the intended receiver.
- Release the ball close to ground.
- Follow through in the direction of the receiver.

Common Errors

- Bouncing the ball to the receiver
- Passing the ball too fast or too slow
- Bowling inaccurate passes
- Bowling to a marked player
- Not being prepared to receive a support pass

Progressions for Coaching

The easiest distribution technique to learn and execute is the bowled ball. In order to master underarm passes, teach your goalkeepers how to:

1. bowl the ball from a standing position to a stationary receiver,

2. bowl the ball from a standing position to a moving receiver,

3. bowl the ball, after taking a few steps, to a stationary receiver,

4. bowl the ball, after taking a few steps, to a moving receiver, and

5. bowl the ball under match-type conditions to stationary and moving receivers.

- **Sling Throw**

The sling throw can be used to pass the ball quickly over moderate to long distances. Tactically, the goalkeeper may use a sling throw to distribute the ball to the side of the field, opposite to a preceding attack, where there is apt to be more space and teammates may outnumber opponents. The sling pass may also be used to distribute the ball down field to initiate a quick counterattack. Because of the trajectory and pace of a sling pass, the goalkeeper should attempt to use it as a lead pass whenever possible. This will direct the receiving player into open space and ball contact with the ground will reduce the bounce and speed of the ball, making it easier to control. The sling throw can also be used to throw the ball over the head of attacking players who are positioned between the goalkeeper and intended receivers.

To perform the sling throw, one or more preparatory steps may be taken. This is followed by a cross-over step (see Figure 19-15B) or a hop in which the leg on the same side of the body as the throwing arm crosses behind the lead leg. The lead leg then steps in the direction of the intended target (see Figure 19-15C and D). During this preparation, the throwing arm is brought low and behind the body and the opposite arm is elevated in front of the body in the direction of the throw (see Figure 19-15C). When the final step is made onto the lead leg, an exchange of positions should take place between the arms as the throwing arm slings the ball forward (see Figures 19-15D and E). The ball should roll up the hand and be released by the tips of the fingers (see Figure 19-15E). This will result in backspin. The trajectory of the ball should be a moderate arc allowing for easy control in receiving the ball. It should be noted that the sling throw can also be performed from a side arm or ¾ arm position. The side arm throw, however, is not highly recommended because it tends to result in the ball taking a curved path.

Key Elements

- Hold the ball with the fingers, palm, and wrist.
- Turn the body with the side opposite to the throwing arm toward the target.
- Point the non-throwing arm in the direction of the target.
- Exchange arm positions by bringing the throwing arm forward and the non-throwing arm backward.
- Release the ball when the arm is straight and above the head.
- Impart backspin to the ball.
- Follow through by taking a step forward after the release.

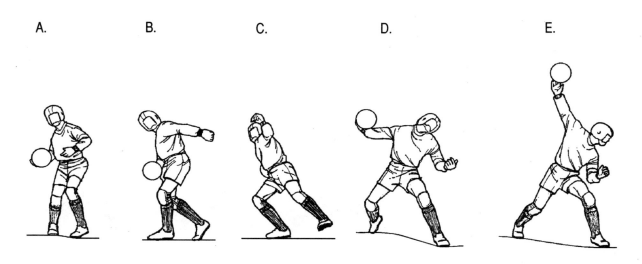

A. B. C. D. E.

Figure 19-15. *Sling throw with cross-over step.*

- Throwing with a bent arm
- Releasing the ball too early or too late in the arm swing
- Releasing the ball with the side of the hand, resulting in lateral spin
- Throwing the ball with too high an arc, permitting defenders time to mark the receiving player

Progressions for Coaching

Practice of the sling throw should follow the progressions for coaching outlined for the bowled ball.

● Baseball Throw

This type of pass provides maximum speed and good accuracy over moderate distances. The ball is held by one or both hands and lifted to head height (see Figure 19-16B and C). The palm and fingers of the throwing hand form a cup to support the ball from behind. The opposite hand can hold the front of the ball, to provide additional control, prior to drawing the throwing arm back. As the non-throwing hand leaves the ball, this hand should be elevated in front of the body and point in the direction of the intended target (see Figure 19-16D). Immediately after the rear leg drives the body forward, the throwing arm is rapidly brought forward and the opposite arm is swung back (see Figure 19-16D and E). As the ball is leaving the hand, the wrist and fingers flex for added power (see Figure 19-16F). The weight of the body, having transferred to the front leg, continues to move forward and is received by the rear leg, taking an additional step to aid in balance. This is a relatively difficult throw for children to perform because of their small hand size and relatively weak upper body, even though a size 3 or 4 ball is used.

Key Elements

- Hold the ball just above shoulder height.
- Cup the fingers and palm of the throwing hand behind the ball.
- Initiate the throw with a bent elbow.
- Turn the body sideways and point the non-throwing hand toward the target.
- Release the ball in front of the face and above the head.

Figure 19-16. Baseball throw.

Common Errors

- Throwing the ball inaccurately
- Stepping onto the foot that is on the same side of the body as the throwing arm
- Not stepping toward the target
- Failing to control the ball with the palm and fingers of the throwing hand
- Not following through with the throwing arm

Progressions for Coaching

Practice should follow the progressions for coaching outlined for the bowled ball.

Punt

The mechanics of kicking presented in Chapter 13 apply to all forms of kicking, including punting. Therefore, a review of these mechanics may be helpful in gaining a better understanding of punting.

Punting is very similar to the instep kick (see Figure 19-17). Both forms of kicking use one or more approach steps followed by a leap onto the support foot. The forward swing of the kicking leg is initiated at the hip by the thigh and followed by a whipping action of the lower leg in both kicks. In both kicks, the shoe laces make contact with the ball, with the ankle in a fully extended position (see Figure 19-17F). Similar to the instep kick with an angled approach, a variation exists in the punt. Additional leg and foot speed can be obtained by a slightly lateral swing of the kicking leg.

Punting differs from the instep kick in that, in punting, contact is made about knee height, the follow through of the kicking leg is higher, and the trunk tends to be more upright. It should be noted that the higher the ball is contacted above the ground and the greater the backward lean of the trunk, the steeper the arc of ball projection.

Control of the ball before the punt is an important factor in the success of the kick. Because of the relatively small hands of youth goalkeepers, two hands should be used. The arms should be extended and the ball dropped to the kicking foot, not tossed upward and outward. As the goalkeeper's hand size and ball control increase, he/she may begin controlling the ball with the hand opposite the kicking foot. This permits greater freedom of trunk and hip movement, which is important in the punt with a lateral leg swing.

The high trajectory and long distance that can be achieved with a punt enable teammates to move forward under the ball, while forcing opponents to retreat toward their own goal. However, possession of punted balls may be lost because: defenders have time to challenge for the ball, they are difficult to receive and control, and the punt may be inaccurate. This type of distribution is useful for relieving pressure or to initiate a fast

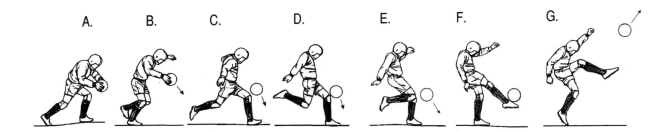

Figure 19-17. *Punt from a straight approach.*

break, turning defense into attack. In teaching this kick, it is important to remember that the rules allow a goalkeeper to take only four steps during each possession of the ball.

Key Elements

- Take one or more approach steps followed by a leap onto the support foot.
- Drop the ball from waist height with outstretched arms.
- Contact the center of the ball with the instep.
- Maintain visual concentration on the ball.
- Forcefully swing the kicking leg so the follow through lifts the body off the ground.

Common Errors

- Lacking approach and leap
- Contacting the ball off center
- Tossing the ball instead of dropping it
- Kicking primarily with the lower leg and not sequencing a forceful thigh swing followed by the swing of the lower leg
- At contact, looking where the ball is to be kicked instead of watching the foot contact the ball

Progressions for Coaching

In practice sessions teach your goalkeepers to:

1. Punt the ball into a goal from just inside the goal line. (Note that this provides the goalkeepers with an opportunity to concentrate on their form without having to be concerned with distance, accuracy, and chasing errant punts.)

2. Punt relatively short distances while concentrating on good form.

3. Punt relatively short distances to a stationary target.

4. Punt long distances to a stationary target.

5. Punt long distances to a moving target.

6. Repeat progressions one through five using one hand to control the ball and an angled approach.

• Drop Kick

This type of distribution results in the ball traveling with a relatively low trajectory. The drop kick (see Figure 19-18) is a useful technique when kicking into the wind. It is similar to a combination of the instep kick and the punt. When performing the drop kick, timing of the movements of the kicking leg is crucial. The foot should strike the ball with the shoelaces (instep) momentarily after the ball hits the ground. Note that if the surface of the field is very uneven, the drop kick should not be used.

Key Elements

- Contact the ball after it strikes the ground momentarily.
- Drop the ball close to the support foot.

Common Errors

- Kicking the ball before it strikes the ground
- Kicking the ball after it has bounced a considerable distance off the ground
- Dropping the ball on uneven ground

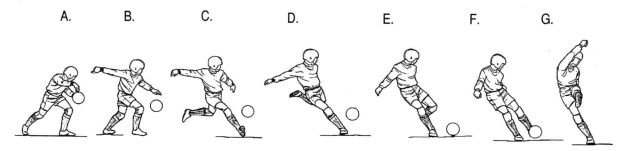

Figure 19-18. Drop kick with angled approach.

Progressions for Coaching

The same progressions for teaching the punt can be used in teaching the drop kick.

• Goal Kick

You should teach your goalkeepers how to perform an instep kick so they can take your team's goal kicks. If the goalkeeper can take the goal kick, this frees an additional player to get into position to receive the goal kick. (Review Chapter 13 for the mechanics of kicking, key elements, common errors, and progressions for coaching the instep kick.) After taking the goal kick, the goalkeeper must immediately recover and get into a good defensive position.

Saves

Technically, a save occurs when the goalkeeper prevents a ball from going into the goal. There are many individual saving techniques that can be used to catch, punch, or deflect a ball. These are described next.

● Scoop Catches

Scoop catches are performed with the hands in an underhand position (see Figure 19-5) . In all of the scoop catch techniques, the movement pattern of the hands and arms are similar. First, the hands absorb most of the force of the ball by retracting under its pressure. The arms, which are held together, then wrap around the ball in controlling and securing it to the trunk (see Figure 19-7). If the ball slips between the hands and arms, a second barrier to its path to the goal may be formed by the trunk or legs.

Standing Scoop Catch

This technique is used to secure rolling and bouncing balls that permit the goalkeeper sufficient time for positioning. In the standing scoop catch, the goalkeeper moves forward to meet the ball, positions himself/herself directly in line with the ball, straightens the legs, and bends the body forward at the waist (see Figure 19-19A). After the fingers and palms make contact with the ball, the trunk begins to straighten and the elbows bend to scoop the ball up to the chest so it can be held firmly (see Figure 19-19B-D). The arms and hands wrap around the ball to prevent it from bouncing off the chest. The movement of the arms in scooping the ball should occur with the elbows held close together. The ball should be trapped between the chest, forearms, and hands. Once the ball is secured, the goalkeeper can select and concentrate on a distribution technique.

Key Elements

- Position the body in line with the ball.
- Place the feet close together.
- Position the hands and arms close together behind the ball.
- Keep the head down with the eyes focused on the ball.
- Bring the ball to the chest by wrapping the arms and hands around it.

Common Errors

- Attempting to make a standing scoop catch on a ball to the side of the feet
- Positioning the legs and arms apart, which might permit the ball to pass through them
- Contacting the ball on the sides with the hands
- Not moving to meet the ball

Progressions for Coaching

The following sequences can be used to teach your players the standing scoop catch. Teach your players to start from a ready position and:

1. move to the right or left and mimic the standing scoop catch,

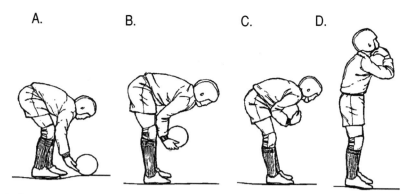

Figure 19-19. *Standing scoop catch.*

2. scoop balls rolled to the right and left,

3. scoop balls kicked to the right and left,

4. scoop bouncing balls kicked to the right and left, and

5. scoop rolling and bouncing balls under pressure of an attacking player.

Variations

There are five variations of the standing scoop catch. In each of these variations, the goalkeeper must be able to position his/her body in line with the path of the ball in order to properly use the scoop technique. Variation in the standing scoop is determined by the height and arc of the ball.

- Low Air Ball Scoop Catch

    The movement pattern to perform this technique is the same pattern that is used in the standing scoop catch on bouncing balls (see Figure 19-19). The only difference is that, in the low air ball scoop catch, the ball does not bounce before being caught.

- Waist High Air Ball Scoop Catch

    This technique varies from the low air ball scoop catch in two ways. First, in this technique, the trunk does not have to bend as far forward to scoop the ball (see Figure 19-20). Second, the legs do not have to be positioned close together because the trunk backs up the arms. It should be noted that balls slightly higher than the goalkeeper's waist can be caught with this technique if the goalkeeper jumps upward to properly elevate the body.

- Forward Diving Scoop Catch

    When attacking players are near, it is important for the goalkeeper to get to a low or waist high air ball before them. The forward diving scoop catch is a technique that can be used to beat opponents to the ball. In this save, a forward dive is made toward the ball. The ball is caught with a scooping action of the arms. The shock of landing is absorbed by the legs, hips, and forearms.

- **Chest High Air Ball Scoop Catch**

  This technique is used on balls with a relatively steep arc. The trunk is positioned more upright than in the waist high air ball scoop catch. The feet should be straddled forward-backward and spread laterally to aid in balance. As in all forms of the scoop technique, the ball is secured to the chest by the scooping action of the hands and arms.

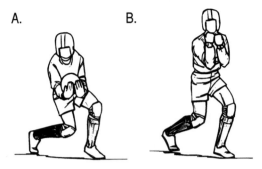

Figure 19-20. *Waist-high air ball scoop catch.*

Progressions for Coaching

Except for the variations in these catches, use the same progression that was suggested for the standing scoop save on a rolling or bouncing ball. After your goalkeepers know each of these variations, randomly change the nature of the ball fed to them in order to teach them proper selection of the appropriate standing scoop technique.

- **Kneeling Scoop Catch**

This technique is used to catch rolling and bouncing balls. It is generally used on balls that are moving relatively fast. To perform this technique, the goalkeeper must move quickly into a position in line with the oncoming ball so that his/her body is between the ball and goal. As the goalkeeper approaches the position where the ball is to be caught, the body should be lowering toward the ground (see Figure 19-21A to C). When in line with the ball, the goalkeeper lowers his/her body onto one knee at the last moment (see Figure 19-21D). If the goalkeeper goes down to receive the ball too early, he/she may not be able to sufficiently adjust the position in response to an errant bounce. This kneeling position is a relatively stable position that should be assumed just before catching the ball. Adjustments to movements of the ball should be made by the goalkeeper while still standing.

Proper body positioning is important in the kneeling scoop catch. For a catch to the goalkeeper's left, the knee of the right leg is positioned behind and close to the heel of the left foot (see Figure 19-21E). The toes of the right foot should be bent under the foot (see Figure 19-21E). Positioning the toes in this manner permits the goalkeeper to push off the back foot to dive and recover a ball that bounces off the goalkeeper's body. In the kneeling position, the trunk should face the path of the ball and the hands and arms should secure the ball as in the standing scoop catch. The arms should be held in front of the legs with the elbows close together so the ball may not go between them (see Figure 19-21E).

Two common errors occur in attempts at performing a kneeling scoop catch. The first involves the use of the wrong leg as the lead leg. The second occurs when the goalkeeper positions the arms on both sides of the lead leg. From this position, the ball is likely to bounce off the shin of the lead leg (see Figure 19-22).

A.   B.   C.   D.   E.   F.

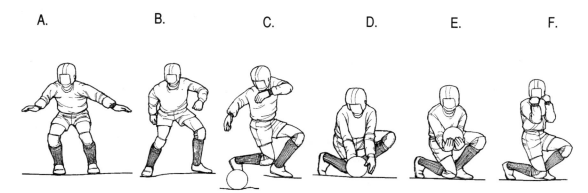

Figure 19-21. *Kneeling scoop catch.*

Key Elements

- Lower the body as the ball approaches.
- Position the body in line with the path of the ball.
- Assume the kneeling position at the last moment.
- Place the knee close to the heel of the lead leg.
- Bend the toes of the kneeling leg under the foot.
- Turn the trunk to face the path of the ball.
- Scoop the ball with the arms close together.

Common Errors

- Not positioning the body behind the ball
- Leaving a large gap between the knee of the trailing leg and heel of the lead foot
- Leaving a large gap between the arms
- Positioning the arms on both sides of the lead leg (see Figure 19-22)

Progressions for Coaching

Teach your goalkeepers to:

1. alternate assuming the kneeling position to the right and left side from a standing position,

2. alternate assuming the kneeling position to the right and left side following a short run,

3. make kneeling scoop catches on balls rolled close to them,

Figure 19-22. Improper arm positioning in the kneeling scoop catch.

4. make kneeling scoop catches on balls rolled away from them,

5. make kneeling scoop catches on balls kicked toward them, and

6. make kneeling scoop catches on balls kicked and subsequently pursued by an attacking player.

- Half-Kneeling Scoop Catch

Low air balls or bouncing balls can be caught in a half-kneeling position. The position of the trunk and arms are identical in the half-kneeling and kneeling scoop. However, the leg position is slightly different in these two catches. Because the ball is caught higher off the ground in the half-kneeling scoop, the legs are not as flexed as in the kneeling scoop.

● Overhand Saves

These saves are performed with the hands in the overhand catching (see Figure 19-6), punching (see Figure 19-9), or deflecting position. In some of the saving techniques, the goalkeeper must determine whether to complete the save by catching, punching, or deflecting the ball.

Chest-High Overhand Saves

A fast-moving ball with a shallow trajectory toward the chest should be received with the hands in the overhand catching position (see Figure 19-23A). The feet should be straddled forward-backward and spread laterally. The force of the ball is absorbed by a recoiling action of the hands and a shifting of the weight of the body from the front to the back foot (see Figure 19-23B-D). After catching the ball, it can be additionally secured by permitting the hands to slide around the sides of the ball and scooping it to the chest (see Figure 19-23D and E).

Head-High Overhand Save

A head-high save is performed similar to the chest-high save.

Above-Head Save

Balls kicked with a shallow arc, which are handled above the head of a goalkeeper, cannot be backed up with a second barrier. If they are mishandled, a goal is likely to occur. Therefore, it is important, if a catch is to be attempted, that the goalkeeper assume a good overhand catching position with the hands close together. Once the pace of the ball is reduced, it can

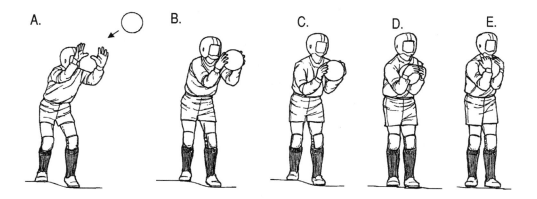

Figure 19-23. *Chest-high overhand catch.*

be brought into the chest and secured with the arms. If the goalkeeper is uncertain about catching a ball driven above the head, he/she should be instructed to punch or deflect the ball.

Balls that approach the goalkeeper with a steep arc are generally easier to control above the head than balls that are driven with considerable speed. The ball with the steep arc should be played in front of the goalkeeper (see Figure 19-24A and B). Thus, it can be backed up with the body. The steep arc also makes it easier to secure the ball into the chest by sliding the hands around the sides of the ball and lowering the ball into the scoop formed by the arms (see Figure 19-24E to F). However, if this type of ball is played in a crowd of attacking players, it may be necessary to punch it away.

Figure 19-24. *Above-head catch on a ball with a steep arc.*

Above-Head Jump and Save

An important factor that must be considered in playing the ball above the head is the positioning of opponents. If opponents are near enough to challenge the goalkeeper for the ball, the goalkeeper must attempt to play the ball high above their heads to remove the opportunity for them to jump and head the ball. This can be done by jumping upward to catch, punch, or deflect the ball. In preparation for the jump, the goalkeeper should take one to several steps in order to move into position to play the ball (see Figure 19-25A to C). The last step is lengthened and the opposite leg is swung forward and upward to aid the arms in lifting the goalkeeper up to reach the ball (see Figure 19-25D). Leaving the swing leg elevated protects the goalkeeper from charging attackers. The catch is completed in a similar manner to the above head overhand catch.

Figure 19-25. *Above-head jump and catch.*

• Diving Saves

A dive is used to position the body to make a save (catch, punch, or deflection) on a ball played away from the goalkeeper. The basic elements of diving have been described previously in Fundamentals of Goalkeeping - Diving. The remainder of this section will include descriptions of unique characteristics of the various individual techniques used to make diving saves.

Diving Save on a Rolling Ball

In this save, it is important that the goalkeeper quickly lower his/her body toward the ground. This is accomplished throughout the takeoff. The force of landing is absorbed over the down side of the body, progressing from the leg up through the arm (see Figure 19-11). If the goalkeeper does not quickly get the side of his/her body to the ground, the ball may pass under it or injury may occur to the ribs from landing on the ball.

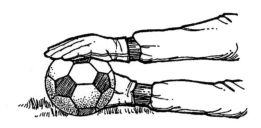

Figure 19-26. *Hand position in diving catch on a rolling ball.*

When attempting to dive and catch a rolling ball, the hand positioning is unique in comparison to all other diving catches. The lower hand should be placed behind the ball as a barrier and the upper hand should be placed on top of the ball to control it against the ground, which acts as a third hand in controlling the ball from beneath (see Figure 19-26).

Diving Save on a Low Air Ball

This save is similar to the diving save on a rolling ball. The save requires a slightly higher flight to the body than a diving save on a rolling ball and the standard overhand position is used when catching.

Diving Save on a Medium-High Air Ball

This save is similar to the diving save on a low air ball. However, depending upon the height of the flight, the blow of landing in this save is more likely to be sequentially absorbed from the upper body (and ball, if a catch is made) to the lower body.

Diving Save on a High Air Ball

This is a spectacular event in soccer, requiring a high level of skill and courage. The takeoff in the diving save on a high air ball is performed by a powerful extension of the lead leg, upward swing of the arms and trailing leg, and extension of the body.

Back Diving Punch or Deflection

A ball kicked over the goalkeeper's head and dropping under the cross bar may be difficult for the goalkeeper to handle. This situation is likely to occur in youth play because the goalkeepers have not reached full stature. In order to play this type of shot, the goalkeeper must take a drop step toward the goal from the ready position (see Figure 19-27A- C). In taking the drop step, the foot is positioned nearly parallel to the goal line and the body is rotated a quarter turn (see Figure 19-27C). Basically, this drop step sets the body and feet in position for takeoff as in other diving saves. From this position, the flight is initiated and the ball is punched or deflected with the upper hand (see Figure 19-27D and E). The ball should not be caught if the dive is going to carry the ball into the goal.

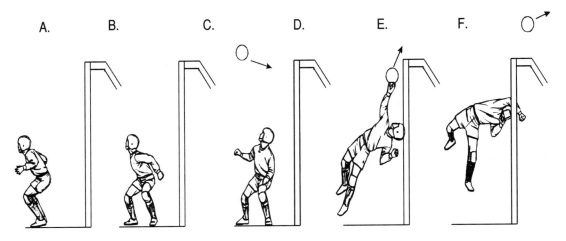

Figure 19-27. Back diving deflection.

Drop Dive Save

A drop dive is used on a ball that is driven low and slightly to the side of the goalkeeper's feet. Basically, the goalkeeper must collapse to the ground while quickly moving the feet away from the ball. The landing is completed as if the goalkeeper had taken a low dive.

SUMMARY

It is evident from the material presented in this chapter that the goalkeeper uses techniques that are different from those of the field players. Because of the goalkeeper's uniqueness and the importance of this position on the soccer team, youth coaches should not leave the development of goalkeeping skills to chance. Rather, practices must be planned in which goalkeeping techniques are an integral part.

REFERENCE

1. Machnik, J. (1982). *So You Want to Be a Goalkeeper!* Manhattan Beach, CA: Soccer for Americans.

SUGGESTED READINGS

DeWazien, K. (1986). *Fundamental Soccer Goalkeeping.* Clovins, CA: Fred Feathers.

Machnik, J. & Hoek, F. (1985). *So Now You Are a Goalkeeper.* New Haven, CT: Phoenix Press.

YOUTH SOCCER TECHNIQUES—GOALKEEPING
Difficulty Rating Form

Level of Player * Approximate Age *	Suggested Emphasis		
	Beginning 6-9 yrs.	Intermediate 10-13 yrs.	Advanced 14 yrs. & up
Fundamentals of Goalkeeping			
Ready position	X	X	X
Positioning	X	X	X
Narrowing the Angle on a Breakaway	X	X	X
Supporting the Defense	X	X	X
Shot Stopping			
catching	X	X	X
punching and deflecting	X	X	X
Diving (see Diving Saves)			
Individual Techniques			
Distribution			
bowled ball	X	X	X
sling throw	X	X	X
baseball throw		X	X
punt	X	X	X
drop kick		X	X
goal kick	X	X	X
Saves (catches, punches, and deflections)			
Scoop saves			
standing	X	X	X
low air ball	X	X	X
waist high air ball	X	X	X
chest high air ball	X	X	X
kneeling	X	X	X
half-kneeling	X	X	X
Overhand saves			
chest high	X	X	X
head high	X	X	X
above head	X	X	X
jump save		X	X
Diving saves			
rolling ball	X	X	X
low air ball		X	X
medium-high air ball		X	X
high air ball			X
forward diving			X
back diving punch or deflection			X
drop dive		X	X

*Note that Beginning, Intermediate, and Advanced does not always correspond with the age range given beneath it. Coaches should use this classification system as an approximation, adjusting the techniques to suit their players' ability levels.

GOALKEEPING DRILLS AND GAMES

NAME	DIAGRAM	DESCRIPTION	KEY POINTS	VARIATIONS
Ball Around the Body		The goalkeeper continually passes the ball from one hand to the next while moving it around the legs, trunk, head and neck. (7 years and older)	This drill is used to enhance the goalkeeper's hand control of the ball.	Walk, jog, run, or turn around while performing the hand passes. (7 years and older)
Toss and Catch		From a standing position the goalkeeper tosses the ball up, then catches it. (7 years and older)	Encourage the goalkeeper to use proper overhand and underhand positioning to perform chest high scoops; above head saves, punches, and deflections; and jump saves.	There are several variations to this basic drill. Each variation challenges the goalkeeper to quickly react to the ball by requiring the goalkeeper to perform additional activities. Some examples are: 1. Toss, sit down, get up and catch (7 years and older) 2. Toss, forward roll, get up and catch (9 years and older) 3. Toss, backward roll, get up and catch (11 years and older)
Back to Back Sideward Exchange		Two goalkeepers stand about 1 yard apart facing opposite directions. They twist their trunk from side to side, without moving their feet, and exchange possession of the ball. (7 years and older)	Each goalkeeper in receiving and handing the ball off should use the overhand catching position. The drill should be performed slowly to enhance trunk flexibility. If the goalkeepers are not stretching, have them move farther apart.	Back to Back Over and Under exchange —In this drill, the goalkeepers arch backward to exchange possession of the ball and then they exchange possession between their legs. (7 years and older)

GOALKEEPING DRILLS AND GAMES

NAME	DIAGRAM	DESCRIPTION	KEY POINTS	VARIATIONS
Back Arch Up Toss and Catch	≈2 yds	Two goalkeepers rock on their stomachs and pass a ball back and forth over each others head.(11 years and older)	This drill enhances flexibility, back strength, and overhand catching. The hands should only be used to catch the ball and should not be used to push against the ground and arch the trunk.	Side Arch Up Toss and Catch - A ball is tossed to a goalkeeper lying on his/her side on the ground. The goalkeeper then arches sideways in order to lift the trunk and hands upward to catch the ball. (11 years and older)
Wrestling for the Ball		Two goalkeepers take a secure grip on the ball by simultaneously wrapping their arms around it. On the command "wrestle" they each attempt to wrestle the ball away from the other. The goalkeepers should be encouraged to make twisting, turning and pulling movements, but must be cautioned against making quick forceful movements. Wrestling can continue while the goalkeepers are on the ground. (10 years and older)	The drill can be used to strengthen the arms, upper body and legs and to enhance a goalkeeper's ability to secure the ball.	
Sit-up, Toss and Catch	5 yds	Two goalkeepers perform synchronized sit-ups. When they sit up, one goalkeeper tosses the ball to the other, who catches it. (10 years and older)	This drill simultaneously develops overhand catching techniques and abdominal strength.	Sit-ups, Toss, Catch and Back Roll - After catching or tossing the ball, the goalkeeper begins a backward roll and stops when the feet touch the ground above the head. (10 years and older)

GOALKEEPING DRILLS AND GAMES

NAME	DIAGRAM	DESCRIPTION	KEY POINTS	VARIATIONS
Bowling Exchange	≈ 3 yds	In pairs, each goalkeeper simultaneously bowls a ball to his/her partner. Balls are received either by using a standing or kneeling scoop. (8 years and older)	The path of the two bowled balls should be separated. This prevents them from rolling into each other and forces the goalkeeper to alternately move right and left in performing a standing or kneeling scoop catch.	There are four variations to this basic drill. They each involve a different distribution technique and possibly different catching techniques. The distance between goalkeepers should vary with age and ability. 1. Sling Exchange (10 years and older) 2. Baseball Throw Exchange (10 years and older) 3. Punt Exchange (10 years and older) 4. Drop Kick Exchange (10 years and older)
Chest and Bounce Pass Exchange	≈ 2 yds	One goalkeeper makes a bounce pass while his/her partner provides a chest pass. This drill is similar to the bowling exchange drill except that the goalkeepers do not move from side to side. After several passes, the goalkeepers should switch the type of passes. (11 years and older)	Overhand and underhand catches should be used to receive the passes.	Low Chest and High Chest Pass Exchange (11 years and older)

YOUTH SOCCER: INDIVIDUAL TECHNIQUES FOR GOALKEEPERS

GOALKEEPING DRILLS AND GAMES

NAME	DIAGRAM	DESCRIPTION	KEY POINTS	VARIATIONS
Crab Walk, Dive, and Catch		One goalkeeper, in a crab walk position, moves backward while a second goalkeeper with a ball in his/her hands follows by walking. The ball is tossed to the right or left side of the crab walker who must extend the body to catch the ball. After several catches, the goalkeepers switch roles. (10 years and older)	The ball should be caught with an overhand positioning. The force of landing should be absorbed along the side of the body. After landing, the ball should be covered up.	1. Crab Walk, Dive, and Punch (10 years and older) 2. Crab Walk, Dive, and Deflect (10 years and older)
Turn Around and Save	≈10 yds, 8 yds	A goalkeeper faces toward the goal. On the signal "turn", a second player tosses the ball toward the goal. The goalkeeper quickly turns to face and react to the approaching ball by either catching, punching, or deflecting it. (7 years and older)	The level of difficulty is determined by the time permitted to the goalkeeper and the location of the toss. Goalkeepers should be instructed to react quickly and make the correct decision in selecting an appropriate save technique.	
Wall Rebound Saves	5 yds, 8 yds	A goalkeeper in a ready position faces a wall. A second player, positioned behind the goalkeeper, throws a ball at the wall. The goalkeeper reacts to catch, punch, or deflect the rebound and prevent it from going into the goal marked by two flags. (7 years and older)	See Turn Around and Save - Key Points.	

GOALKEEPING DRILLS AND GAMES

NAME	DIAGRAM	DESCRIPTION	KEY POINTS	VARIATIONS
One Hand Catch		Two goalkeepers toss the ball back and forth. The ball must be controlled and caught with one hand without touching the body before being thrown back. This drill can be made into a game by keeping score of the number of catches (or misses) by each of the two goalkeepers. (7 years and older)	This drill helps goalkeepers develop a sense of hand control and absorption of the force of the ball. Tosses should be made above and below the level of the waist to encourage overhand and underhand catches.	
Shuffle, Chest Pass, and Catch		Using a chest pass, two goalkeepers toss a ball back and forth while shuffling sideways across the field. (7 years and older)	Goalkeepers should be encouraged to shuffle while in a ready position and to catch and secure the ball with either overhand or scoop techniques.	
Rapid Fire		Four or more balls are positioned in an arc around the outside of the penalty area. A field player successively shoots each ball on goal attempting to score. After each shot, the field player must run around the flag before attempting another shot on goal. Simultaneously, the goalkeeper attempts to save each shot on goal. After each attempted save, the goalkeeper must touch either side goal post before getting ready to save the next shot. Score can be kept on the number of saves versus the number of goals. (7 years and older)	The fundamentals of the ready position, positioning, shot stopping, and diving as well as conditioning and quick reaction are incorporated in this drill. This drill also challenges the shooting skill of the field players.	On saves in which the goalkeeper catches the ball, punts or sling throws could be made to a target up field instead of touching either side goal post. Added points could be given for accurate distribution. (7 years and older)

YOUTH SOCCER: INDIVIDUAL TECHNIQUES FOR GOALKEEPERS

GOALKEEPING DRILLS AND GAMES

NAME	DIAGRAM	DESCRIPTION	KEY POINTS	VARIATIONS
Offense-Defense Exchange		Two field players stand at midfield shoulder to shoulder with their backs toward the goal. A ball is tossed over their heads. The player who gets the ball first is on offense and the other player is on defense. The object for the offensive player is to score a goal. If the ball is taken away by the defensive player, that player becomes the offensive player and attempts to score a goal. The two players' roles change as possession of the ball changes. The goalkeeper is responsible for stopping the shot by whomever takes it. (11 years and older)	The goalkeeper must continually adjust to changes in position of the ball and changes of possession. Directing the defense, shot stopping, positioning, diving, and narrowing the angle on a breakaway are all components of this drill.	Field players must shoot from outside the penalty area. (9 years and older)
Drive Back		The object of this game is to distribute the ball over the opponent's goal line. Two goalkeepers compete against each other on a field divided in half, lengthwise. The dividing line is marked by several cones. The game is started by a kick (punt or drop) or throw (sling or baseball) for maximum distance and accuracy from the 18 yard line. The opposing goalkeeper attempts to get to the ball and secure it as soon as possible to prevent the ball from going toward the goal line. After securing the ball, it is returned from where it was secured, with a kick or throw for maximum distance and accuracy toward the opponent's goal line in an attempt to gain a territorial advantage. If the ball goes out of bounds at either side of the field, the return kick or throw is taken from that point. The first goalkeeper to distribute the ball over the opponent's goal line wins the game. (7 years and older)	This game encourages goalkeepers to concentrate on distance and accuracy in distributing the soccer ball. Quickness in securing and distributing the ball as well as practice in stopping balls projected over long distances are components of this game.	This game could be played with two or three goalkeepers per side on a full field. (7 years and older)

GOALKEEPING DRILLS AND GAMES

NAME	DIAGRAM	DESCRIPTION	KEY POINTS	VARIATIONS
Goalkeeper-Striker		Two portable goals are placed approximately 20 yards apart. One goalkeeper defends each goal. The object of this game is to score on the opposing goalkeeper by kicking or throwing the ball into his/her goal. The ball must be distributed from the goal line. After each distribution, the defending goalkeeper becomes the striker, attempting to score a goal. One point is awarded for each goal scored. (7 years and older)	Both distribution and shot stopping techniques are practiced in this game. Goalkeepers should be encouraged to catch the ball when they can. Otherwise it should be punched or deflected away from the front of the goal.	
Back Diving Game		One goalkeeper, with a ball, stands outside the penalty area. The opposing goalkeeper is in a ready position at a cone approximately 3 yards from the goal line. A sling throw is made in an attempt to project the ball over the defending goalkeeper's head and under the cross bar into the goal. If warranted, the defending goalkeeper responds by making a back diving punch or deflection to prevent the goal. Five or more sling throws are made, then the goalkeepers switch roles. The goalkeeper who permits the fewest goals is the winner. Distance of the sling throw and ready position will need to be altered to match the abilities of the goalkeepers participating in this game. String may be hung from the goal as a boundary to limit the lateral range of throws that may count as a goal. This encourages back diving saves instead of lateral diving saves. (13 years and older)	The primary function of this game is to practice back diving saves and to develop an awareness of how far off the goal line a goalkeeper should stand in order to have a chance at making a save on a looping shot.	

GOALKEEPING DRILLS AND GAMES

NAME	DIAGRAM	DESCRIPTION	KEY POINTS	VARIATIONS
Over the Hill		A cardboard box, ball bag, or other comparable object is placed on the ground. A goalkeeper stands in a ready position to the side of the object on the ground. The coach tosses a medium-high to high ball on the opposite side of the object. The goalkeeper, in the ready position, dives to make the save (catch, punch, or deflection). Diving saves are made alternately to the right and left sides. (11 years and older)	Diving saves on medium to high balls are practiced in this drill. The object on the ground encourages the goalkeeper to lift his/her feet to get high off the ground. This drill should be practiced with goalkeepers dressed in full padding and in a location where the grass is high and the ground is relatively soft. A mat could also be used in the landing area.	
Catching Between the Legs		The goalkeeper starts in a semi-crouched position with legs spread, holding a ball with both hands in front of the knees. From this position, the ball is tossed backward between the legs and caught by both hands behind the knees. (7 years and older)	This drill is used to enhance the goalkeeper's hand control of the ball. Goalkeepers should attempt to quietly catch the ball with "soft hands" and not slap the ball.	Hold the ball between the legs with one hand in front of the knees and the other behind the knees. Toss the ball slightly upward, switch hand positions, and recatch the ball. (7 years and older)
Side Arch-up		The goalkeeper lies on his/her side on the ground. A ball is tossed so that the goalkeeper must lift the trunk and arms to catch. (7 years and older)	This drill should be practiced from both sides. It is used to acquaint goalkeepers to making catches from this position at the end of a dive.	

Section VI
BASIC STRATEGIES OF SOCCER

TACTICS OF PLAY

Eugene W. Brown and Gary Williamson

QUESTIONS TO CONSIDER
- What are the four fundamental principles of offense?
- What are the four fundamental principles of defense?
- What are the advantages and disadvantages of zone and player-to-player methods of defensive play?
- How and when should the fundamental principles and individual tactics of offense and defense be taught to youth players?
- What is a system of play?
- What are the advantages and disadvantages of various team formations?
- How should a team attack from or defend against various restarts?
- What drills can be used to teach youth players the fundamental principles and individual tactics of offense and defense?

INTRODUCTION

The objective of the game of soccer is very simple—score more goals than your opponent. The process of accomplishing this task, however, can be very complex. In order to provide you with an understanding of this process, offensive and defensive tactics of play will be presented and integrated with the concepts of team play.

Definitions

Individual techniques such as receiving and controlling the ball with the chest, kicking the ball with the outside of the foot, and marking an opponent in possession of the ball become *skills* when they are used under game conditions. Offensive and defensive skills, whether performed by one player, in combination with a few teammates, or by an entire team, become *tactics* when they are used with the intent to create a strategic advantage in play.

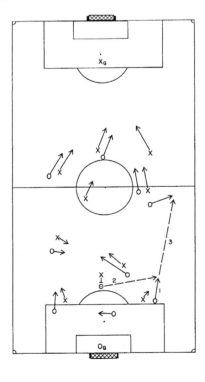

Figure 20-1. *A fullback making a penetrating pass, after regaining possession of the ball. Note that with this one penetrating pass defenders are no longer in goal-side marking positions.*

Figure 20-2. *Delay in penetration to achieve an opportunity for a safer forward pass.*

FOUR FUNDAMENTAL PRINCIPLES OF OFFENSE

All offensive tactics are used to help a team maintain possession of the ball to score a goal. Even though each of the many offensive tactics has the same ultimate objective, the principles by which they assist the team in achieving this objective may be different. Penetration, support, mobility, and width are the four fundamental principles of offense which encompass all offensive tactics. These fundamental principles of offense achieve their common objective by increasing the *time* and *space* players have to dribble, pass, receive and control, and shoot the ball.

1. Penetration

The first fundamental principle of offense is penetration. At the moment a team regains possession of the ball, players should attempt to exploit the offensive positioning of their opponents and the delay in the opponent's change from offensive to defensive tactics. Successful penetration is usually associated with quick movement of a ball toward an opponent's goal through long and accurate passes to teammates in open spaces behind defenders. Upon regaining possession of the ball, a long penetrating pass can be used to put several defenders on the wrong side of the ball (see Figure 20-1). The attacking team should attempt to advance the ball as quickly and as far as possible with each pass without losing possession. However, if the counterattack starts with dribbling and support, square, and crossing passes, the attacking team is delaying itself and helping defenders to recover.

Penetration is not effective if possession is lost. Players should be coached to decide whether to quickly advance the ball forward or to delay the attack until a safer forward pass can be made (see Figure 20-2). Penetrating down the middle of the field is more desirable than penetrating down the flanks. However, because of the tendency for defenders to funnel toward their own goal, opportunities for safe penetrating passes down the middle of the field may be limited. Penetration tends to become more difficult as an attacking team moves the ball closer to the opponent's goal. At this point, however, the potential for scoring a goal after a penetrating pass may be worth the risk of losing possession.

2. Support

The second fundamental principle of offense is support. Upon regaining possession of the ball, attacking team members near the ball must support the player with the ball, if long penetrating passes to teammates are likely to be intercepted. This assistance is intended to reduce defensive pressure on the player with the ball by increasing time and space to play the ball.

Positioning and *movement* of players near the ball are two categories of offensive support. The use of the terms positioning and movement is not intended to imply that positioning occurs without any movement. These categories of support tactics differ in that for positioning, the location of players is of primary importance; and for movement, the process of changing locations is important.

● Positioning Near the Ball

Positioning tactics should be initiated by players in the vicinity of the ball and should progress to players away from the ball. The player who regains possession of the ball is often in a position to be closely marked by an opponent. If teammates near the point of attack (near the ball) can attain open space, possession of the ball may be maintained through short forward, square, or support passes to these players. The delay resulting from these passes may provide additional time for other attackers to find space in advanced positions to which subsequent long penetrating passes can be made. Two positioning tactics used to achieve offensive support are depth and wall passes.

Depth

Increasing the spacing of players from goal line to goal line increases the depth of positioning. If possible, offensive players should take up positions both in front of and behind the ball. A player in an open space in front of the ball can reduce the pressure on the player with the ball by receiving a pass or drawing a defender away from the point of attack (see Figure 20-3A and B). Even though it is less desirable to pass the ball backward, offensive support from behind the ball may be needed to maintain possession and increase time and space for subsequent play (see Figure 20-4).

If players reduce their depth of attack by taking up positions across the field and alongside the player with the ball, it becomes easier for the defense to mark the point of attack and intercept square passes. In fact, one defender may be able to prevent a square pass to any of the attackers lateral to the player in possession of the ball (see Figure 20-5).

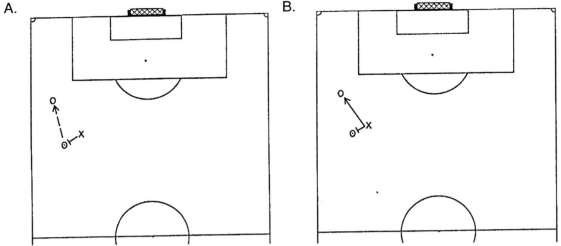

Figure 20-3. *Reducing pressure at the point of attack by positioning in front of the ball (depth in front of the ball). A. Offensive player in open space receiving a forward pass (left). B. Offensive player in an open space drawing a defender (right).*

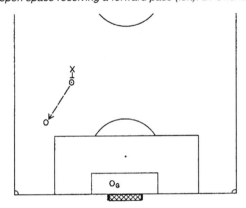

Figure 20-4. *Reducing pressure at the point of attack by supporting from behind the ball (depth behind the ball).*

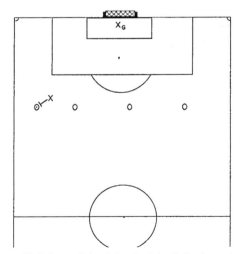

Figure 20-5. *Loss of depth in attack by flattening out across the field. Note that one defender may be able to prevent a square pass to any of the attackers lateral to the player in possession of the ball.*

There are two common reasons why players flatten out across the field. First, inexperienced youth players with specific positions in their team's formation will often literally take their assignments to the fullback, halfback, or forward "line." The second reason is that offensive players move into forward positions but are limited by the possibility of being offside.

Wall Pass

A one-touch return pass to a player who sprints into an open space to receive the ball back is called a wall pass or a give and go pass. This type of pass requires an offensive numeric advantage (two attackers versus one defender—2 v 1) at the point of the attack. This simple numeric advantage occurs often and in various regions of the field. Therefore, if players learn how to use the wall pass to exploit the defense, there will be many opportunities during a game to use this tactic to create time and space and to beat defenders.

When opportunities occur, a wall pass can be made backward to a supporting player to reduce pressure at the point of the attack (see Figure 20-6), or it can be made to a player in a lateral position, exploiting space behind a defender (see Figure 20-7). In either case, for a wall pass to be effective, the player making the initial pass must immediately sprint to an open space after kicking the ball and the ball must be quickly returned. The initial pass usually draws the defender's attention and may prompt the defender to attempt an interception. The success of the wall pass is determined during this defensive diversion of attention from the passer to the ball.

If the player acting as the wall is ahead of the ball, the give and go pass becomes risky. The defender may be in a good position to intercept the initial pass or an offside may result (see Figure 20-8).

● Movement Near the Ball

Offensive tactics associated with movement of attackers near the ball are very dynamic. Each movement of the ball, defenders, and attackers causes a change in the potential interactions of players in the vicinity of the ball. Checking runs, overlapping runs, and cross-over runs are three offensive tactics which can be effective in supporting the player with the ball.

Checking Run

An offensive maneuver consisting of a run in one direction followed by a quick change of direction to run in another direction is called a checking run. This type of run is used by an attacker not in possession of the ball to draw a tightly marking defender in one direction and then to break free of the defensive pressure by quickly changing directions (see Figure 20-9).

Direction and *timing* are two key elements of all checking runs. These runs can be made in any combination of directions. However, a checking run is successful only if the attacker frees himself or herself of the defensive mark and moves into an open space to receive a pass. In Figure 20-10A, this is accomplished. However, in Figure 20-10B, the attacker making the checking run is not in an open position to receive a pass and relieve pressure at the point of the attack. Defenders are more likely to release a close marking position on a player checking a run away from the goal under attack than they are to release an offensive player who completes a checking run toward the goal being attacked.

Players making checking runs must continually monitor the positioning of defenders and the movement of the ball so that they can make their runs at a proper moment. In Figure 20-11A, the attacker observed a change in direction in the dribble and then spontaneously checked his/her run into open space. In Figure 20-11B, the same checking run was made, but at a time and into a space in which the attacker with the ball was not free to pass. Players should be

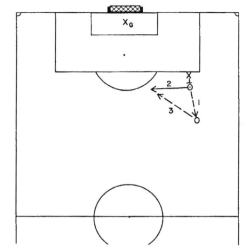

Figure 20-6. *A wall pass backward to a supporting player.*

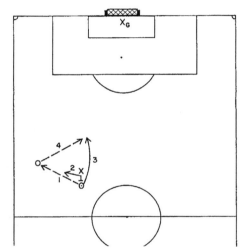

Figure 20-7. *A wall pass to a player in a lateral position.*

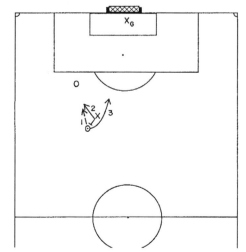

Figure 20-8. *Defender intercepting an intended wall pass to an attacker in advance of the ball.*

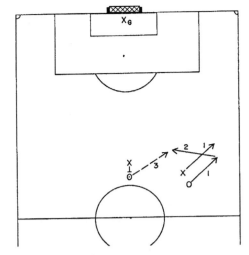

Figure 20-9. *Checking run.*

encouraged to continually look for opportunities to make checking runs. They should be informed that several changes in direction may be needed to free themselves from tenacious defenders.

Overlapping Run

When an offensive player runs from a position behind a teammate in possession of the ball to a position in advance of the ball, an overlapping run has occurred (see Figure 20-12). Often, offensive players behind the ball are unmarked. Therefore, when a player makes an overlapping run, problems are created for the defense, because an additional attacker comes forward and the defenders must reassess their marking responsibilities. Basically, an overlapping run by an unmarked attacker reduces the defensive pressure on the player with the ball by creating a "two against one" offensive advantage at the point of the attack.

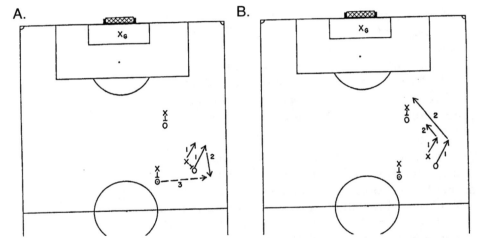

Figure 20-10. *Successful and unsuccessful checking runs. A. Checking run into open space (left). B. Checking run into closed space (right).*

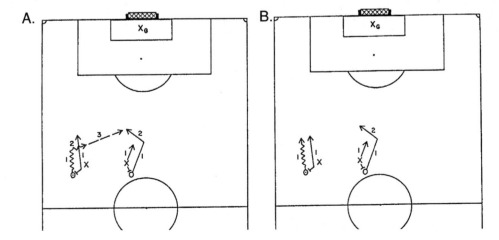

Figure 20-11. *A. Successfully and properly timed checking run, (left). B. Unsuccessfully and improperly timed checking run, (right).*

The attacker with the ball should be facing the defender during the overlap. If the attacker is unaware of the overlapping run from behind, the player making the run should shout, "overlap." This provides time for the attacker with the ball to prepare for options associated with the overlapping run.

Overlapping provides two offensive options, both determined by the response of the defender at the point of the attack. If the defender continues to mark the player with the ball and ignores the overlapping attacker, a lead pass should be made as the overlap occurs (see Figure 20-13A). If the defender moves to mark the overlapping player, the attacker with the ball is free to advance the ball by passing or dribbling (see Figure 20-13B).

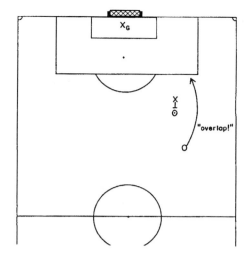

Figure 20-12. Overlapping run.

Cross-Over Run

When a dribbler and teammate run toward each other then pass side-by-side, they have completed a cross-over run. These runs can be effective against close player-to-player marking if they are properly performed. Basically, a player dribbles the ball toward an approaching teammate. The foot away from the defender should be used for the dribble so that the body of the attacker shields the ball. At the point the two offensive runs cross, two options are available to the attacking players. The dribbler may leave the ball for the approaching teammate to take over the dribble (see Figure 20-14), or the dribbler may maintain possession of the ball (see Figure 20-15). In either case, the attackers should attempt to create confusion in the defenders when the cross-over occurs, and then both attackers should accelerate their runs. The attacker without the ball should accelerate to possibly draw one or both defenders and the player with the ball should accelerate to beat the defense. If pos-

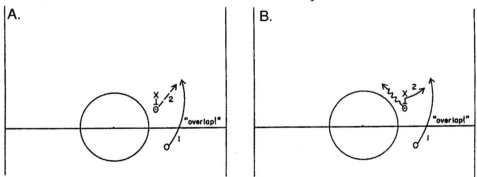

Figure 20-13. Offensive options for the attacker with the ball during an overlapping run by a teammate. A. Using a lead pass to beat the defender who persists in marking the player with the ball (left). B. Beating the defender who marks the overlapping attacker (right).

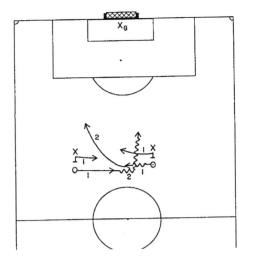

Figure 20-14. *Cross-over run in which possession of the ball is exchanged by the two attackers.*

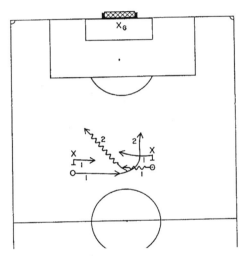

Figure 20-15. *Cross-over run in which possession of the ball is maintained by one attacker.*

session of the ball is to be exchanged by the two attackers, the initial dribbler should shield and leave the ball at the point of crossing. The ball should not be passed from close range in exchanging possession.

Cross-over runs are somewhat risky because the attackers may not communicate their intentions to one another. Cross-over runs should be limited to the middle and attacking thirds of the field. Cross-over runs can be made in a variety of directions; they do not have to be made across the field in order to be effective.

3. Mobility

The movement of players on offense may be associated with their reactions to movements of the ball, defenders, or other attackers. The fundamental offensive principle of mobility, however, is associated with self-initiated runs off the ball. Two mobility tactics are blind side and diagonal runs.

Players who engage in mobility tactics are usually physically fit and unselfish. Their creative runs off the ball do not necessarily result in them receiving a pass for a shot on the goal but may instead open a teammate for a chance to score.

Mobility of offensive players off the ball causes problems for defenders and tends to imbalance the defense. Attackers who continually interchange positions force defenders to decide whether to mark these mobile players or release them to other defenders. In the process of making these decisions, defenders may be drawn out of good defensive positions or may release attackers into open spaces where they can receive a pass.

- ### Blind-Side Run

A run by an offensive player in an area of the field away from the visual concentration of opponents is called a blind-side run. This type of run often takes place on the side of the field opposite to where the ball is located. Generally, attackers far away from the ball are not the focus of defensive concentration. Because these offensive players may be unmarked or only loosely guarded, they can run forward into advantageous positions behind the defense and not be noticed. A ball crossed in the air to the player making a blind side run creates problems for the defense (see Figure 20-16).

Defenders are responsible for concentrating on the ball and the player they are guarding. Occasionally their concentration is limited to watching the ball. When this occurs, blind side runs may even be made by attackers located close to the ball (see Figure 20-17).

● **Diagonal Run**

A curved run that begins on one side of the field and progresses simultaneously toward the opponent's goal line and opposite touch line is a diagonal run (see Figure 20-18). Diagonal runs may cut across the depth and width of the defense. In Figure 20-18, the diagonal run cuts across both the halfback and fullback lines (depth) as well as both flanks (width).

In comparison to a straight run toward the goal line, a diagonal run is more difficult to defend because: it provides a broader angle of passing opportunity to the player in possession of the ball (see Figure 20-19); it is easier to make a lead pass to a teammate crossing in front of the dribbler than to make a lead pass to a teammate running away from the dribbler; and defenders merely need to retreat (change in depth) to maintain a goal-side marking position in defense of a straight run toward their goal, whereas, they must also move laterally (change in width) in defense of a diagonal run.

Players should be cautioned about putting themselves in an offside position by making a diagonal run. The closer an attacker is to the second to last defender at the start of a diagonal run, the shallower the run must be (see Figure 20-20).

Diagonal runs tend to create confusion in the defense. The defender, marking the player making the diagonal run, must decide whether or not to run with the attacker. If the defender runs with the attacker, space may be created in the area vacated (see Figure 20-21). If the defender releases the attacker for others to mark, opportunities may be created along the run for the dribbler to advance the ball if supporting defenders fail to respond (see Figure 20-22). If supporting defenders respond by marking the player making the diagonal run, they may be releasing other attackers and permitting additional open spaces (see Figure 20-23).

Figure 20-16. Blind-side run on the side of the field opposite to where the ball is located.

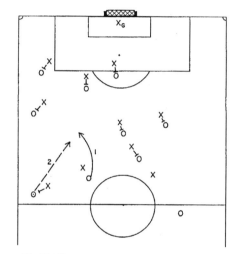

Figure 20-17. Blind-side run near the ball.

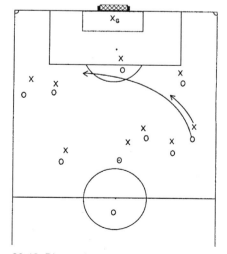

Figure 20-18. Diagonal run.

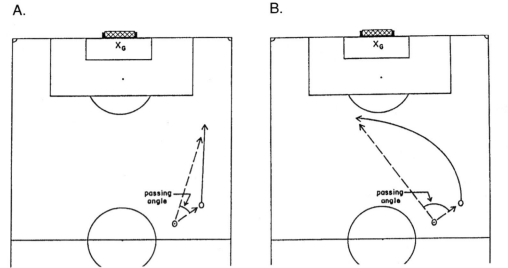

Figure 20-19. *Comparison of the angle of passing opportunity. A. Narrow angle of passing opportunity on a straight run (left). B. Broad angle of passing opportunity on a diagonal run. (right).*

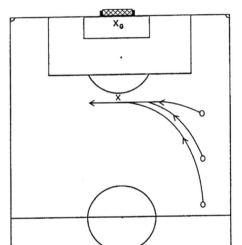

Figure 20-20. *Potential for depth in various diagonal runs.*

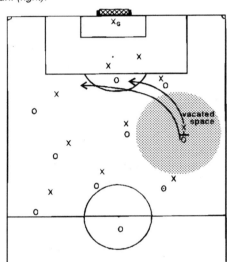

Figure 20-21. *Creating space with a diagonal run by causing a defender to vacate space.*

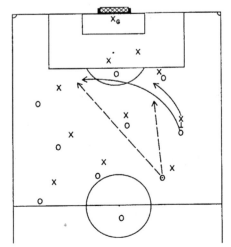

Figure 20-22. *Passing opportunities created along the path of a diagonal run by an attacker released from being marked.*

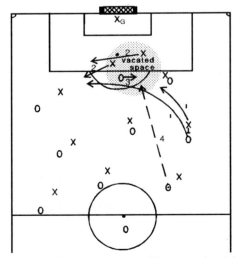

Figure 20-23. *Open space created by supporting defenders marking a player making a diagonal run.*

YOUTH SOCCER: BASIC STRATEGIES OF SOCCER

4. Width

The extent of spread of offensive players from touch line to touch line determines the width of attack. Width is a fundamental principle of offense that is used to counter defensive funneling and the concentration of defenders in the danger area. Similar to the fundamental offensive principle of support, width is achieved by the *positioning* and *movement* of attacking players. However, unlike support, width is achieved by positioning and movement of players off the ball.

● Positioning Off the Ball

When defenders mark attackers spread across the field, space is created between players and the potential for defensive support is reduced. As seen in Figure 20-5, width of positioning should not be achieved by a string of players lined up across the field. Rather, it should be achieved in combination with depth of positioning. In Figure 20-24, several players are needed to defend against the possibility of a square, support, or through pass; the ball being advanced by dribbling; or a shot being taken on goal.

In matches among youth and inexperienced players, there is a tendency for attackers to take positions near the ball. This results from the desire of players to become involved in play by personally having possession of the ball. It is difficult for these players to realize that by spreading out across the field they are indirectly involved in play because they are forcing the defense to open up spaces.

● Movement Off the Ball

Dummy Run

The one individual tactic specifically associated with movement off the ball to achieve width in offense is the dummy run. This is an offensive run intended to draw one or more defensive players away from a particular area of the field (see Figure 20-25A and B). A player making a dummy run should attempt to draw the attention of a defender by first running toward the defender. This approach is opposite to that used in a blind side run. In addition to drawing attention to a dummy run, the attacker must convince defenders that it is more important for them to follow and mark the run than it is

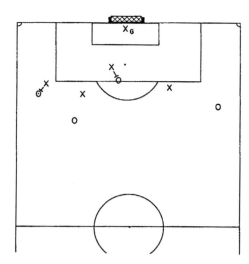

Figure 20-24. *Use of width and depth in the forward "line" to counter defensive funneling and the concentration of defenders in the danger area.*

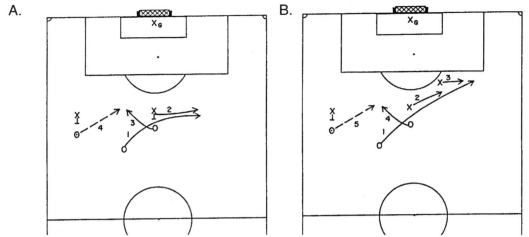

Figure 20-25. Dummy runs. A. Drawing a defender away from a close marking position (left). B. Drawing defenders away from an area of the field (right).

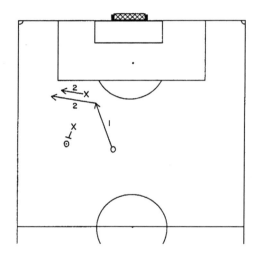

Figure 20-26. Dummy run to draw a defender out of a supporting position.

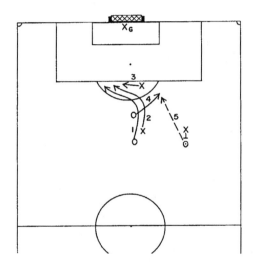

Figure 20-27. Dummy run to draw a defender out of a covering position.

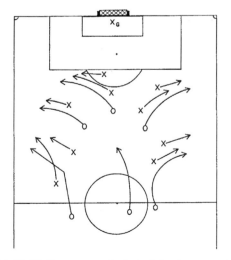

Figure 20-28. Dummy runs to draw defenders away from central retreating positions.

to guard other players or to cover other areas of the field. In other words, the attacker must "sell the dummy."

The function of a dummy run is to create time and space for the attack. Dummy runs can accomplish this in a variety of ways. They can be used to take defenders out of supporting positions (see Figure 20-26) and covering positions (see Figure 20-27). If several attackers make dummy runs toward the flanks, this may draw defenders away from central retreating positions (funneling) and open space in the danger area in front of the goal (see Figure 20-28).

FOUR FUNDAMENTAL PRINCIPLES OF DEFENSE

All defensive tactics are used to help a team regain possession of the ball while preventing opponents from scoring a goal. Even though each of the many defensive tactics has the same ultimate objective, the principles by which they assist the team in achieving this objective may be different. Delay, depth, balance, and concentration are the four fundamental principles of defense which encompass all defensive tactics. These four fundamental principles of defense achieve their common objective by limiting the *time* and *space* opponents have to dribble, pass, receive and control, and shoot the ball.

1. Delay

The first fundamental principle of defense is delay. When possession of the ball is lost, all members of a team should immediately switch from offensive tactics to defensive tactics.

Delaying tactics begin at the point of attack (at the ball) by the defender marking the player with the ball (first defender) and progress toward the goal that the defending team is guarding. If an attack can be delayed initially by some team members, additional time is provided for teammates to recover and eventually participate in other defensive tactics. Four delaying tactics used against the player with the ball are goal-side marking, recovering run, pressuring the ball, jockeying, and shepherding.

● Goal-Side Marking of the Ball

To effectively guard a player with the ball, a defender must mark from the defensive goal-side of the ball. When goal-side marking an attacker with the ball, the defender should be on an imaginary line from the ball to the center of the goal (see Figure 20-29A). A player who is marked from the "wrong-side of the ball" (see Figure 20-29B) is a threat to the defensive team because all offensive options to advance the ball (dribble, pass, and shoot) are not restricted.

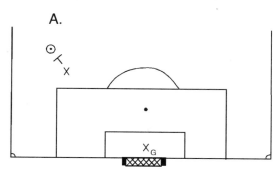
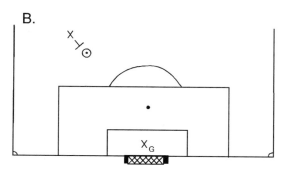

Figure 20-29. *Marking a player in position of the ball. A. Marking from the defensive goal-side of the ball (left). B. Marking from the wrong side of the ball (right).*

- ## Recovering Run

A defender on the wrong side of the ball when his or her team has lost possession, should make a recovering run to get into a goal-side marking position to restrict the attacker's offensive options. The recovering run should be toward the goal, intercepting the dribbler at a point as far away as possible from the goal (see Figure 20-30A). The location of this point is determined by the speed of both the dribbler and the defender. A judgment as to the path to take must be made by the defender and possibly adjusted during the recovering run. A defender who runs to a goal-side position too far ahead of the dribbler is not in a good marking position to delay the offense (see Figure 20-30B). If the defender is directly behind an attacker in possession of the ball, the recovering run should be made toward the center of the field (see Figure 20-30C) and not to the near touch line side of the field (see Figure 20-30D).

In general, defenders on the flank should be instructed to recover toward the near goal post. Recovering runs may also be made to mark other offensive players in advance of the ball to remove passing options for the player with the ball.

Figure 20-30. *Proper and improper recovering runs.*

A. A proper recovering run to cut off the attacker relatively far from the goal (top, left).

B. An improper recovering run allowing the attacker to approach relatively close to the goal (top, right).

C. A proper recovering run toward the center of the field from directly behind the attacker in possession of the ball (below, left).

D. An improper recovering run because it was made toward the near touch-line side of the attacker in possession of the ball (below, right).

A.
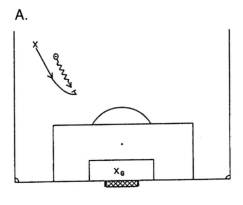

B.
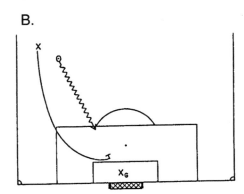

C.
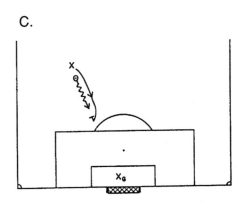

D.
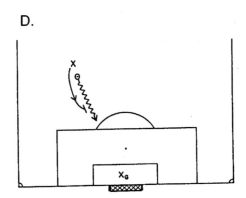

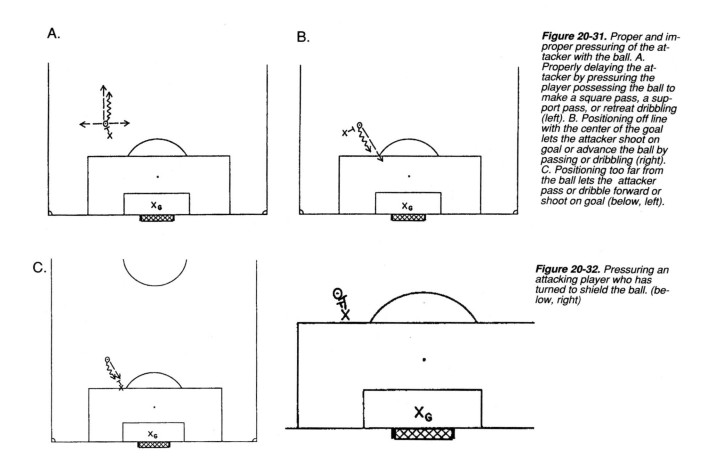

Figure 20-31. Proper and improper pressuring of the attacker with the ball. A. Properly delaying the attacker by pressuring the player possessing the ball to make a square pass, a support pass, or retreat dribbling (left). B. Positioning off line with the center of the goal lets the attacker shoot on goal or advance the ball by passing or dribbling (right). C. Positioning too far from the ball lets the attacker pass or dribble forward or shoot on goal (below, left).

Figure 20-32. Pressuring an attacking player who has turned to shield the ball. (below, right)

● **Pressuring the Ball**

When facing an attacking player who has possession of the ball, the defender must be close to the attacker (approximately two yards) and in a good goal-side marking position (see Figure 20-31A). By taking a position close to the player with the ball, the defender can delay the attack by forcing the offensive player to make a square or support pass or attempt to beat the defender by dribbling. If the defender is goal-side of the ball, but off line with the center of the goal (see Figure 20-31B) or too far from the ball (see Figure 20-31C), the attacker can easily advance the ball forward by passing or dribbling, or the attacker can shoot on goal.

If the dribbler turns his or her back toward the defender to reduce the pressure and shield the ball, the defender has succeeded in delaying the attack. At this point, the defender should move to make light body contact with the dribbler (see Figure 20-32) to further reduce the potential to advance the ball forward.

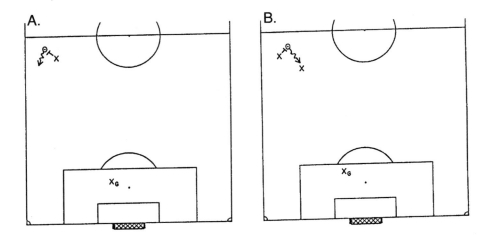

Figure 20-33. Defender shepherding an attacking player in possession of the ball toward the touch line (A., left), and shepherding an attacker toward a teammate (B., right).

- **Jockeying**

If a goal-side defender is outnumbered by the attacking team, ground may need to be given to the player with the ball in order for the defender to possibly mark or intercept passes to players in advance of the ball. In jockeying, a defender may repeatedly feint making a tackle and giving ground to disrupt advances of the dribbler and to provide defending teammates with time to recover.

- **Shepherding**

The position of the defender marking the player in possession of the ball may influence the direction that the ball is dribbled or passed. Shepherding is used to increase the predictability of the movements of the attacker with the ball. A defender can shepherd an attacker toward the touch line (see Figure 20-33A) or toward another teammate who is in position to tackle the ball away (see Figure 20-33B).

2. Depth

The second fundamental principle of defense is depth. Depth involves the use of defensive tactics in support of the player who is marking the attacker with the ball. These tactics are used to reduce the likelihood of the first defender being beaten and to take over for the first defender when beaten by the attacking player. Covering, supporting, and switching are three tactics associated with the fundamental defensive principle of depth.

- **Covering**

Closely marking players in advance of the ball is covering. A covering position that combines goal-side marking and a shift toward the ball (see Figure 20-34A) minimizes the opportunity for a marked player to receive a pass and increases the pressure on the player with the ball. Defenders,

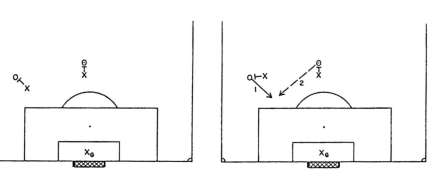

Figure 20-34. *Proper and improper covering position in advance of the ball.*

A. Proper position of goal-side marking and a shift toward the ball (far left).

B. Improper marking indicated by too much shift toward the ball (left).

however, must be careful not to position themselves alongside players in advance of the ball because they may be beaten by a through pass (see Figure 20-34B).

● **Supporting**

When defenders have a numerical advantage, a second defender can support a teammate who is marking the player with the ball. Distance and angle are two important factors which should be considered in selecting a supporting position.

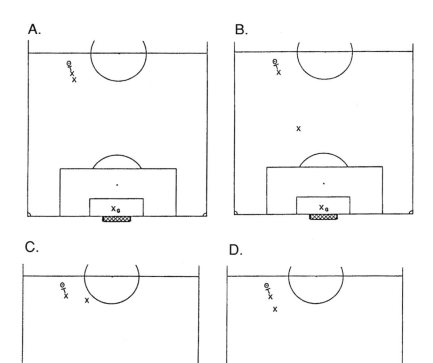

Figure 20-35. *Proper and improper distance and angle from which to provide support for the first defender.*

A. Supporting from too close (far left).

B. Supporting from too far (left).

C. Improper support from a position nearly square to the first defender (below, far left).

D. Supporting from an appropriate distance and angle (below, left).

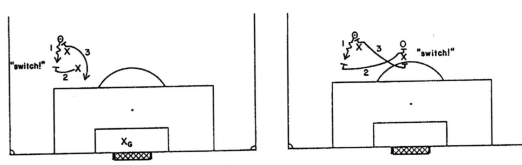

Figure 20-36. *Defensive switching. A. Defensive switch by supporting player (left). B. Defensive switch with a player in a covering position (right).*

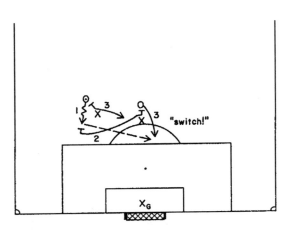

Figure 20-37. *Vulnerability of a defensive switch by a covering player.*

Distance

A distance of about five yards from the first defender is appropriate for providing support. It should not be too close, where an attacker can beat the first and second defender simultaneously (see Figure 20-35A), or too far, where the attacker has time to prepare for the second defender after beating the first defender (see Figure 20-35B).

Angle

If the supporting defender moves to the side of the first defender, both players may be caught square and beaten by a through pass (see Figure 20-35C). For youth players, a good angle of support is on an imaginary lie from the ball to the center of the goal (see Figure 20-35D).

● Switching

If a defender is beaten by a player dribbling the ball, another defender in a supporting position or in a near covering position may switch responsibilities with the beaten teammate (see Figure 20-36A and B). When performing a switch, the supporting or covering defender should call "switch" and proceed to mark the dribbler. The beaten defender should run directly toward the center of the goal in an attempt to regain defensive depth by getting into a supporting or covering position. This run is sometimes called a *defensive overlap*.

For a supporting defender, the switch should be made because of the numerical advantage that exists. For a covering defender, the decision to switch is more complicated because an offensive player in ad-

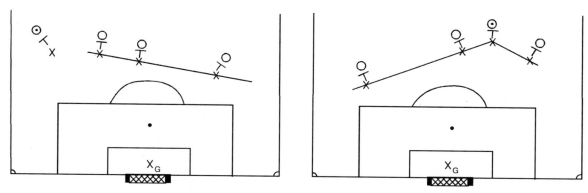

Figure 20-38. Diagonal coverages. A. Diagonal (left). B. "V" (right).

vance of the ball may become unmarked and free to receive a pass (see Figure 20-37). In this situation, the covering player must decide whether it is better to switch or maintain a goal-side marking position on an offensive player in advance of the ball.

3. Balance

Defenders who are not at the point of the attack, nor in positions to provide cover and support for their teammate who is marking the player with the ball, should be concerned about vital areas of the field away from the ball that can be exploited by the attacking team. In a balanced defense, emphasis is on the tight marking of players near the point of attack and on the marking of vital space, away from the point of attack. Diagonal coverage and shifting toward the ball are balancing tactics.

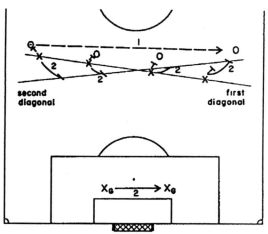

Figure 20-39. Shifting of the diagonal coverage in response to a cross-field pass.

• Diagonal Coverage

Defenders who are laterally far from the ball should have greater depth to their defensive positioning than those close to the ball. This principle results in a diagonal coverage for a ball near a touch line (see Figure 20-38A). When the ball is near the middle of the field, application of the principle of diagonal coverage results in an inverted "V" (see Figure 20-38B). The depth created by diagonal coverage permits defenders to cover for their teammate toward the ball and next to them. Greater depth is permitted away from the ball because this space can be closed during

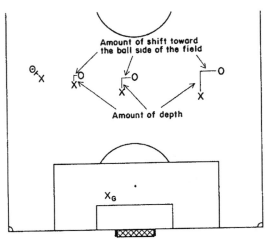

Figure 20-40. Defensive positioning based upon a combination of diagonal coverage (depth) and shifting toward the ball side of the field.

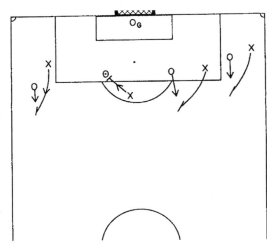

Figure 20-41. Immediately after losing possession of the ball in the offensive third of the field, the forward closest to the point of the attack marks the player with the ball while other forwards make recovering runs.

the time a pass takes to enter this area. A cross-field pass should result in a switching of the diagonal coverage (see Figure 20-39).

● **Shifting Toward the Ball**

Defenders who are laterally far from the ball should shift toward the ball. The amount of this shift should only be as far as they can recover during the time it takes for a player to receive a ball in the area they are assigned to defend. The greatest shifts should be made by players who have assigned positions farthest from the ball. An understanding of diagonal coverage and shifting toward the ball should help defenders establish their positions (see Figure 20-40).

4. Concentration

The fundamental principle of concentration is associated with the spread of defenders on the field. On defense, players who are not marking the attacker with the ball should attempt to achieve positions which do not spread them from touch line to touch line and from goal line to goal line. A defending team that is stretched in this manner permits considerable space for the attacking team to: pass the ball forward, play with only moderate defensive pressure, and attack its opponent's goal. Compactness, overloading, and funneling are three tactics associated with the fundamental defensive principle of concentration.

● **Compactness**

Offensively, teams attempt to spread the defense by having their players assume positions that are apart from each other. Upon loss of possession, immediate change to defense must occur. This requires a reduction in the space between the players (closing space) by narrowing the width (touch line to touch line) and depth (goal line to goal line) of their spread.

To achieve defensive compactness, forwards, halfbacks, and fullbacks must all make appropriate defensive responses upon loss of possession. If possession is lost in the offensive third of the field, the player with the ball should be marked by the forward who can most quickly achieve a close goal-side positioning, while other forwards make recovering runs (see Figure 20-41).

Upon loss of possession of the ball, half-backs and fullbacks must immediately cover attackers in advance of the ball and provide defensive support. Their switch fromoffense to defense and the establishment of compactness would be easier if they had moved forward when their team was in possession of the ball (see Figure 20-42A and B).

● Overloading

If the player with the ball is shepherded toward a touch line, or the ball has been dribbled or passed to the flank, other defenders can shift toward that side of the field to concentrate their team's defense. In Figure 20-43, the defending team has shifted toward the left touch line. The player with the ball is restricted in passing and dribbling by the closeness of the touch line, the defensive position of the marking player, and the compactness of the other defenders. In Figure 20-43, attackers who are away from the ball and in non-threatening positions have a numerical advantage in these areas of the field. However, attackers close to the ball are outnumbered by the defense on that side of the field.

● Funneling

Upon loss of possession of the ball, players who are uncertain about their defensive responsibilities should make recovering runs to get to positions on the goal side of the ball. This is especially true for halfbacks and fullbacks. Recovering runs should be toward the near goal post for defenders on the flanks and toward the penalty mark for central defenders (see Figure 20-44). This process is called funneling. It results in a concentration of defenders toward the center of the field and near the penalty area. A concentration of players in this manner reduces space and offensive opportunities in and near the danger area. Players making recovering runs toward their goal should assess their defensive responsibilities along the way. At some point, they may be able to engage in other defensive tactics such as marking, covering, or supporting.

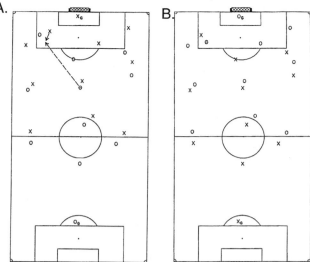

Figure 20-42. Maintaining compactness in transition from offense to defense from a depth that covers about one-half of the field.

A. Half-field spread (from goal line to goal line) of offensive players attacking opponent's goal (left).

B. Half-field spread of defenders immediately after losing possession of the ball (right).

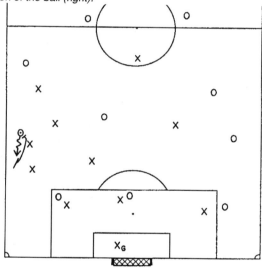

Figure 20-43. Shepherding the player with the ball toward the touch line and an overloading of the defense toward the ball-side flank.

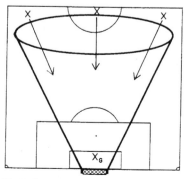

Figure 20-44. Lines of recovery associated with the defense tactic of funneling.

RELATIONSHIPS BETWEEN OFFENSIVE AND DEFENSIVE PLAY

Just as offense and defense are opposite to each other, the fundamental principles of offense are opposite to the fundamental principles of defense. The pairs of principles presented in Table 20-1 are opposite to each other. For example, upon gaining possession of the ball, the offensive team attempts to penetrate the defense by quick movement of the ball towards the opponent's goal. The defense attempts to delay this penetration by using tactics of goal-side marking of the ball, pressuring the ball, jockeying, and shepherding. In a similar manner, support and depth, mobility and balance, and width and concentration are opposing principles.

Table 20-1. Opposing principles of offense and defense.

Offense		Defense	
Objectives		**Objectives**	
Maintain possession of the ball to score a goal		Regain possession of the ball while preventing opponents from scoring a goal	
Fundamental Principles	**Tactics**	**Fundamental Principles**	**Tactics**
1. Penetration		1. Delay	• Goal-side marking of the ball • Pressuring the ball • Jockeying • Shepherding

2. Support	• Positioning near the ball
	  depth
	  wall pass
	• Movement near the ball
	  checking run
	  overlapping run
	  cross-over run
		2. Depth	• Covering
			• Supporting
			• Switching

3. Mobility	• Blind side run • Diagonal run	3. Balance	• Diagonal coverage • Shifting toward the ball
4. Width	• Positioning off the ball • Movement off the ball dummy run	4. Concentration	• Compactness • Overloading • Funneling

Even though the fundamental principles of offense and defense counter each other, characteristics essential for athletes to be successful in playing either offense or defense are the same. These characteristics are:

- an understanding of the fundamental principles and individual tactics of offense and defense,
- the ability to perform individual techniques to carry out offensive and defensive tactics,
- well-conditioned energy production and muscular systems to repeatedly respond to the demands of play,
- the ability to read the game and select appropriate tactics, and

- the ability to communicate intentions among team members to unify the effort of the players.

Thus, from a coaching perspective, the degree to which each of these individual characteristics is developed determines the level of success players will experience in both offensive and defensive play.

TEACHING THE FUNDAMENTAL PRINCIPLES AND INDIVIDUAL TACTICS OF OFFENSE AND DEFENSE TO YOUTH PLAYERS

Two problems in teaching youth players fundamental principles and individual tactics of offense and defense are the limited time available for practice and the natural tendency of players to be attracted to the ball. Information in this section is intended to assist coaches in overcoming these limitations through appropriate sequencing of instruction and efficient organization of presentations for practice.

Sequencing Instruction

Supplements 20-1 and 20-2 contain a listing of the fundamental principles and individual tactics of offense and defense. The supplements also contain a list of suggested emphasis, by ability level and age, to guide coaches in determining when to teach these principles and tactics to their players.

Instructional Model

In addition to the sequencing suggested in Supplements 20-1 and 20-2, coaches should follow a step-by-step systematic model of instruction (Chapter 5) for teaching their players. Specific steps that are appropriate for teaching fundamental principles and individual tactics of offense and defense follow.

- **Step 1: Establish Attention and Content Credibility**

Communicate the importance of what you are going to teach the players.

- **Step 2: Communicate Precisely
  What Needs to Be Learned**

To save practice time, your players should have previously reviewed handouts that clearly explain the principles and tactics to be covered in the practice. The handouts could consist of figures from this chapter with brief accompanying statements.

Communication during practice should begin with a chalk talk review of the fundamental principle and/or tactics to be learned. To carry this out, the coach must have a portable chalk board, chalk, and eraser, and the key points to be communicated listed on a practice plan. After the chalk talk, communication should continue through a demonstration.

- **Step 3: Provide for Practice and Feedback**

Activities used for practice should follow a simple to complex progression and should meet the players at their level of understanding and development. The progress of the players should be monitored and constructive feedback should be continually provided.

- **Step 4: Evaluate Results
  and Take Appropriate Action**

If the players are making good progress in learning, you should be pleased. If they are having difficulty learning the offensive and defensive principles and tactics you have selected to teach them, it may be the result of any of the following reasons:
- inappropriate instructional techniques were used,
- sufficient learning time was not provided,
- the tactics were too difficult for the members of the team, or
- the team members lacked the prerequisite individual techniques (e.g., if they cannot make a one touch pass, they will not be able to perform a wall pass).

Progression for Teaching

The following teaching progression is suggested:

1. Have your players mimic the principle or tactic being learned.

2. First, use drills in which passive pressure is applied. Progress to moderate pressure drills and finally full pressure drills (see Supplement 20-3). In some drills it is possible to simultaneously practice an offensive and a defensive tactic (e.g. defensive support and offensive overlap).

3. Use small group games (see Supplement 20-3). These games should progress from 2 v 1 to 5 v 5. All of the offensive and defensive principles and tactics can be used in these small group games and they

should be highlighted by the coach as being part of this type of practice. This will assist the players' understanding about how they are a part of full-sided games.

4. Include controlled scrimmages in your practices. Use these scrimmages to reinforce principles and tactics of play.

5. Schedule practice games. Provide feedback to your players that draws relationships between the offensive and defensive principles and tactics used by both teams.

SPECIAL DEFENSIVE TACTICS

Two team tactics that have not been presented, but are integral parts of defensive strategy, are the *defensive wall* and the *offside trap*.

Defensive Wall

A wall is a barrier formed by two or more defenders standing shoulder-to-shoulder to assist their goalkeeper in defending their goal against a free kick. When youth players achieve an intermediate level of ability and are 10 or more years of age, this team tactic can be introduced to them.

● **When to Form a Defensive Wall**

Distance

A defensive wall should be formed when the kicking team has a fair or better chance of scoring on a direct free kick from where the ball is placed, even though they may have been awarded an indirect free kick. As players mature and develop more powerful and accurate kicks, the farthest distance from a goal that a team should set up a defensive wall becomes greater. When free kicks are taken from beyond this distance, one defender should be positioned 10 yards from the ball on an imaginary line connecting the ball to the center of the goal (see Figure 20-45). This player can distract the kicker and pressure any short kick. However, as the distance of the free kick from the goal decreases, more defenders should be added to the wall (see Figure 20-46).

Figure 20-45. *Position of single defender on a free kick when the ball is placed beyond direct free kick scoring range.*

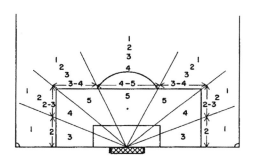

Figure 20-46. *General guide to determine the number of players in a defensive wall in relationship to distance and angle of the wall from the goal.*

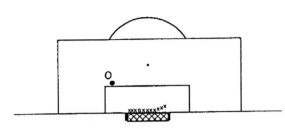

Figure 20-47. *"Packing the goal" as a defense against an indirect free kick from less than 10 yards from the goal.*

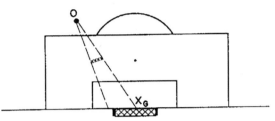

Figure 20-48. *The near post end of the defensive wall protecting an area just outside the near post.*

Angle

Figure 20-46 is provided as a general guide to determine how many players to use in the defensive wall. As the shooting angle becomes more and more acute, fewer and fewer defenders should be used in the wall.

- ## Number of Players in a Defensive Wall

Five is the maximum number of players most teams will employ in a defensive wall. If five players are used, five remaining field players are left to guard as many as nine attackers (all players except for the attacker taking the kick and the goalkeeper). Using more than five players in a defensive wall leaves too many attackers unmarked. One exception exists to the guideline of using five or fewer players in a defensive wall. This occurs when an indirect free kick is awarded to a team either on the opponent's goal area line or inside the opponent's penalty area at a distance of less than 10 yards from their opponent's goal. If this situation occurs, the defense is permitted to stand on its own goal line at a distance of less than 10 yards from the location of the indirect free kick. The defense should "pack the goal" with all of its members (see Figure 20-47). Their positioning on the goal line should start just inside the ball side goal post and fill in the goal mouth toward the far post. The line of players near the far post may be curved toward the ball and still remain 10 yards from the ball placed for the indirect free kick. The goalkeeper should select a position slightly toward the ball side of the center of the wall of players. As the ball is played, all defenders should rush forward as a unit to block the shot.

- ## Where to Form a Defensive Wall

Irrespective of the number of players in the defensive wall, players should stand 10 yards from the ball in a shoulder-to-shoulder formation. The near post end of the defensive wall should protect an area beginning just outside the near post to defend against a swerved kick (see Figure 20-48).

Mechanics of Forming a Defensive Wall

One defender should be designated to protect the near post. Another player, usually a forward or half-back, should be assigned the responsibility of directing the near post defender (see Figure 20-49). Note that the goalkeeper should not be responsible for directing the near post defender. When a free kick is awarded in which a defensive wall is needed, the player on the near post end of the wall should attempt to quickly assume a position that is close to 10 yards from the placed ball and on an imaginary line joining the ball and the near side goal post. The player designated to direct the wall should stand farther away from the goal than the ball and point (right or left) to help direct the player protecting the near post. While this is occurring, other players assigned to the positions in the wall should fill in shoulder-to-shoulder.

If the placement of the free kick is centered in front of the goal, a split wall is appropriate (see Figure 20-50). In this situation, the player assigned to direct the wall is responsible for aligning two players, one for each post. When they are in position, other defenders assigned to the wall take up positions toward the center of the goal and shoulder-to-shoulder with the two previously positioned defenders.

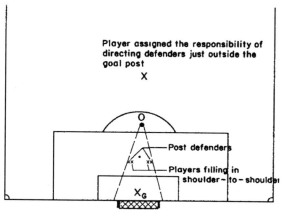

Figure 20-49. Mechanics of forming a defensive wall.

Figure 20-50. Mechanics of forming a split wall.

Orientation of a Defensive Wall

The defensive wall can be oriented perpendicular to an imaginary line joining the placed ball and the center of the goal or it can be oriented parallel to the goal line with the near post defender 10 yards from the placed ball (see Figure 20-51A and B). If the wall is oriented as in Figure 20-51A, the wall protects a

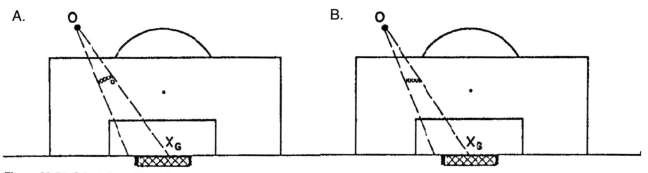

Figure 20-51. Orientation of the defensive wall. A. Defensive wall oriented perpendicular to imaginary line joining the ball and the center of the goal (left). B. Defensive wall oriented parallel to the goal line (right).

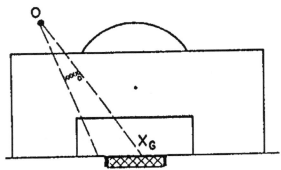

Figure 20-52. *Goalkeeper positioned to the wall side of the center of the open space.*

larger portion of the goal than the defensive wall orientation shown in Figure 20-51B. However, the orientation of the defensive wall shown in Figure 20-51A permits attackers to be behind the wall and not in an offside position. Coaches must decide which of these two orientations is best for their teams.

- ### Which Players to Use in a Defensive Wall

The least skilled defenders should be used in the defensive wall. The most skilled defenders should be responsible for marking the opponent's attackers. Also, there is some advantage to using tall players in the wall. This will make it more difficult for the attacking team to chip the ball over the wall and into the goal.

- ### Location of the Goalkeeper

When a defensive wall is formed, the goalkeeper is responsible for the area of the goal that is not protected by the wall. This includes the open area to the far post side of the goal as well as space vulnerable to chips over the wall. Thus, the goalkeeper should be positioned to the wall side of the center of the open space (see Figure 20-52). If a split wall is used, the goalkeeper should be positioned in the center of the open space (see Figure 20-50). In both cases, the goalkeeper has a clear view of the free kick.

- ### Position of the Remaining Defenders

Defensive players, other than those in the wall or playing the goalkeeper position, should have assigned responsibilities. The following set of guidelines should be helpful in positioning these players:

1. Assign one defender the responsibility of rushing toward any short pass. This player should be in line with the center of the goal and could be an extra player next to the defensive wall.

2. Defenders, if outnumbered, should mark attackers who are closest to the goal being attacked.

3. Player-to-player marking should be used.

4. Use one or two players up-field to draw offensive players away from the goal they are attacking because of their concern for a counterattack.

5. Marking positions should be on the goal side (as opposed to the touch line side) of the attackers being marked.

6. For walls formed within or near the penalty area, position the remaining defenders no closer to their goal than the players in the wall (see Figure 20-53A).

7. For walls formed beyond the penalty area, the remaining players may be positioned closer to their goal than the players in the wall. However, their positioning should restrict the attack from taking up positions within the penalty area (see Figure 20-53B).

- ## Defensive Responses

Table 20-2 provides a listing of desired defensive responses to a variety of free kicks.

Table 20-2. *Defensive responses to the taking of a free kick.*

Types of Free Kicks Taken	Proper Defensive Responses
• Direct shot on goal	• Players maintain integrity of the defensive wall • Defenders who are marking attackers prepare to clear the ball
• Short pass and shot on goal	• One assigned defender must rush the player receiving the short pass • Defensive wall must maintain its integrity and move as a unit toward the short pass • Defenders who are marking attackers prepare to clear the ball
• Ball chipped or passed behind the defensive wall	• Players in the wall or other defenders who are closest to the ball should attempt to get to the ball before attacking players • Goalkeeper should be prepared to come off the goal line and handle or kick the ball • Defenders who are marking attackers should maintain their guard or move to clear the ball
• Ball crossed to attacking player away from the defensive wall	• Defender closest to the player receiving the cross should mark this attacker • Wall should break up and these defenders should participate in player-to-player marking of attackers who are in the best scoring positions • Player assigned to rush the short kick should participate in player-to-player marking

Progression for Teaching Players When and How to Form a Defensive Wall

Players should achieve an intermediate level of ability and 10 or more years of age before they are taught the mechanics of forming a defensive wall. If your players have achieved this status, the following progression is appropriate.

1. A chalkboard should be used to initially explain to your team the mechanics of forming a defensive wall.

2. Distribute diagrams on when and how to form a defensive wall. Note that several figures presented in this section can be photocopied and distributed to your players to take home and study. This will reinforce what you explained to them using the chalkboard.

3. Divide the team into groups of six or seven (one near post defender, three to four other wall players, one player to direct the group, and one player prepared to rush a short kick). Have each group practice, with a goalkeeper in goal, quickly setting up a defensive wall on balls placed in front of the goal. Note that players should rotate assignments within their groups between trials to be exposed to each of the responsibilities in forming a defensive wall.

4. Place balls at varying distances and angles from the goal. Using groups of six or seven, as in step 3, assign each group the responsibility of defending against a free kick. Balls should be variously placed to elicit each of the following responses:

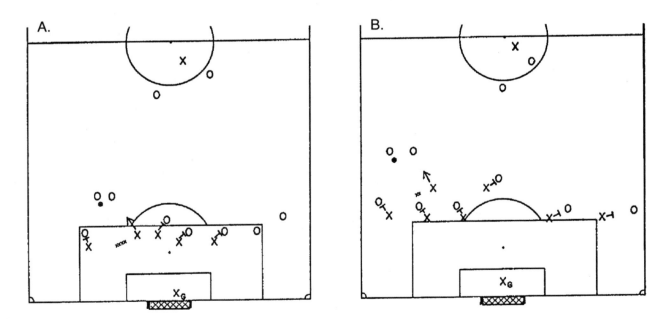

Figure 20-53. *Players in compliance with guidelines for defense against a free kick in which a wall is used. A. Wall formed within the penalty area (left). B. Wall formed beyond the penalty area (right).*

- one defender guarding against a short kick on a ball not requiring a defensive wall and the remaining players prepared to engage in player-to-player marking;
- depending on the location of the placed ball (distance and angle from the goal), two to five players in a defensive wall being directed by one player, one player positioned to rush a short kick, and any remaining defenders prepared to mark player-to-player;
- four or five players forming a split wall in defense against a ball directly in front of the center of the goal, one player directing two defenders on the outsides of the wall, and one player prepared to rush a short kick; and
- all players packing the goal, from the ball side goal position, in defense against an indirect free kick less than 10 yards from the goal line.

5. Add three attackers (one to take the free kick, one to receive a short pass or a through pass beyond the wall, and one away from the wall to receive a cross) to challenge the defensive arrangement described in step 4. Defenders should be encouraged to make the following appropriate responses:
   - On a short pass, one player rushes the ball and the wall moves toward the ball as a unit to block as much of the goal as possible.
   - If a through pass is made, players in the wall and closest to the passed ball should run to mark the attacker receiving the pass or attempt to clear the ball by getting to it first.
   - The wall should dissolve if a cross is made. At this point, the wall is no longer functional and defenders assigned to the wall must be prepared to mark attackers in scoring positions.
6. Practice defense against free kicks in a controlled scrimmage. Defensive players added to the arrangement described in step 4 are responsible for goal side player-to-player marking of attackers in the most threatening positions to score. These defensive positions should not be closer to the goal than the penalty area.

The keys to success in defense against any free kick is for all defenders to know what their assignments are and to quickly set up to fulfill these responsibilities.

Offside Trap

An offside trap is a defensive tactic designed to put attacking players offside. This usually involves fullbacks quickly moving away from their own goal to create a situation in which attackers are positioned illegally in advance of the ball (see Figure 20-54).

The most complex rule in soccer is the offside rule. Its complexity is derived from the contingencies and judgments associated with the application of the rule. According to the rules of play, two events must occur in order for a player to be illegally positioned in advance of the ball and be called offside. First, a player must be in an offside position. Second, the player must be seeking to gain an advantage from the position by attempting to either play the ball or hinder or distract opposing players. Even if these two events occur, an offside will not be called unless the referee sees and judges an offside to have occurred. Thus, the use of an offside trap to regain possession of the ball may be a risky tactic.

● **Failure of the Offside Trap**

If an offside trap fails, the result is likely to be an unmarked attacker advancing with the ball toward your goal. An offside trap will fail if:

- the referee does not judge an offside to have occurred,
- backs do not move away from their goal in unison, and
- an attacker passes the ball to a forward positioned player before the defenders make runs away from their goal.

● **Success of the Offside Trap**

If the offside trap is successful, the defending team receives an indirect free kick from the point of the violation. In addition, an offside trap has the following potential advantages.

- It may thwart attacking runs off the ball.
- It may cause attackers to hesitate runs forward on set plays.
- It may be used to clear attackers away from the danger zone in front of the goal and give the goalkeeper uncluttered space in which to work.

For an offside trap to be successful, it must be used unpredictably by a well-coordinated defense.

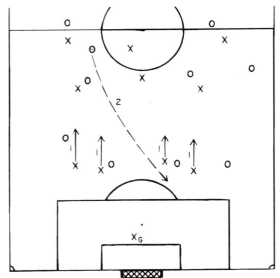

Figure 20-54. Offside trap caused by defenders quickly moving away from their goal before the attacking team's pass to its forwards.

The fundamental principles and individual tactics of defense must be employed in the two basic methods of defensive play. These methods are *zone* and *player-to-player* defense. These two methods of defensive play can also be integrated into a *combination* defense.

Zone Defense

In a zone defense, players are assigned to protect a particular area of the field. They are responsible for marking any player who enters their assigned zones. Note, that adjacent zones overlap each other (see Figure 20-55). These zones may vary somewhat, depending on the location of the ball and attacking players. A team in a 4-3-3 formation that loses possession of the ball on attack is likely to have its players up field. The zone responsibilities of these defenders at this time are also up field (see Figure 20-55A). As the defensive team retreats, the areas that its players are assigned to protect retreat with them (see Figure 20-55B). Similarly, if the attacking team plays the ball near a touch line, the zones should shift toward the touch line (see Figure 20-55C). Note, that as the defensive team retreats towards its goal, the zones should get smaller and more compact. This arrangement is compatible with the fundamental defensive principle of concentration.

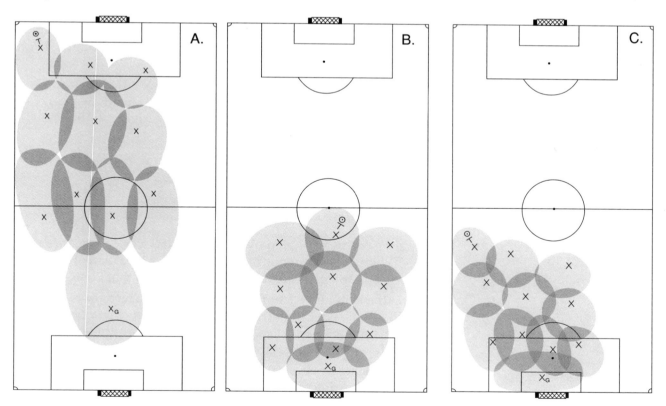

Figure 20-55. *Examples of zone responsibilities in a 4-3-3 team formation. A. Zone responsibilities upon loss on possession in the attacking third of the field (left). B. Zone responsibilities as a team retreats to its defensive half of the field (middle). C. Zone responsibilities in response to a ball near the touch line (right).*

- **Advantages of Zone Defense**

  - Players are assigned to protect vital areas of the field. Protection of the field around the penalty area may be the responsibility of several defenders.

  - Zone defense is flexible. Throughout the course of a game, a player responsible for a particular zone is likely to mark several different attackers.

  - In a zone defense, defenders are more concerned with the ball than they are with following an attacker around the field.

  - It is more advantageous to play a zone defense on a relatively small field. On small fields, it is less likely that there will be space unprotected. As field size decreases, the space that defenders can cover tends to overlap more.

  - It is advantageous to have relatively unfit players use a zone defense. In a zone defense, they are responsible for their assigned areas and not for following a fit attacker all over the field.

  - Zone defense is compatible with the individual defensive tactics of shepherding, covering, supporting, switching, diagonal coverage, shifting toward the ball, compactness, overloading, and funneling. Player-to-player defense is not compatible with these tactics.

  - In comparison to player-to-player defense, it is easier to make a transition from offense to defense using a zone defense. In a zone defense, players know the location of their assigned zones. However, when a transition from offense to defense occurs for a team using player-to-player defense, the location of assigned attackers is unpredictable.

  - Players are more likely to participate in attack if their team uses a zone defense. With a player-to-player defense, team members may be more concerned about where their assigned opponents are than they are about their team's offense.

  - A zone defense is a balanced defense.

  - Zone defense is easier for beginning players to learn.

- **Disadvantages of Zone Defense**

  - Any zone can be exploited by an attack that overloads a particular zone. When more than one attacker occupies a particular zone, a numeric advantage is created for the offense in that zone.

  - When attackers move from one zone to an adjacent zone, defenders will often have difficulty passing on defensive responsibility to the teammate in an adjacent zone. Good communication between players is essential for an effective zone defense.

  - From a coaching perspective, it is more difficult to pinpoint breakdowns in zone defense and make adjustments than it is to see problems and make appropriate changes in player-to-player defense. Individual mistakes can be more easily hidden in a zone defense. Zone defense allows more unencumbered movement of attackers than player-to-player defense.

- Players tend to be less motivated when playing a zone defense because they must be concerned with any attacker who enters their zone and not the personal challenge of one-on-one marking.
- In a zone defense, players may be more concerned about protecting an assigned space, when no attackers are present, than in assisting teammates who may need help in adjacent zones.

Player-to-Player Defense

In a strict player-to-player defense, each field player is assigned one attacker (one-on-one) to mark. This type of marking is basic to all methods of defensive play. Even in a zone defense, one-on-one defensive techniques of marking (player in possession of the ball and player not in possession of the ball) and tackling (front block tackle, pivot tackle, and slide tackle) are used (see Chapter 18 for details of individual defensive techniques).

When a team using a player-to-player defense loses possession of the ball, its members must quickly make a transition to defense by seeking out the players they were assigned to mark. It is important for the player assigned to mark the attacker in possession of the ball to rapidly close space to prevent or hinder a quick and deep penetration.

● Advantages of Player-to-Player Defense

- An excellent attacker may be nullified by a good defender. It is easier to defend, not having possession of the ball, than it is to attack with the ball.
- When being defended one-on-one, an attacker may work harder than usual in trying to get free and, therefore, become tired.
- In a player-to-player defense, each defender has a clearly defined responsibility.
- Tight marking tends to demoralize some attackers. They tend to become frustrated because they may be denied access to the ball.
- From a coaching perspective, one-on-one marking permits a matching of players by ability, speed, size, fitness, and strength. With a zone defense, the match-ups are determined by the attacking team.
- Player-to-player defense is motivating because the level of performance of each opponent on attack is a direct measure of success of each player on defense.
- It is easier to detect where breakdowns in player-to-player defense occur and to make adjustments.

- **Disadvantages of Player-to-Player Defense**
  - Defenders can be pulled away from vital areas of the field. Thus, the attack can easily imbalance the defense.
  - Once a defender is beaten, the attack has a free player to exploit the defense.
  - Upon loss of possession of the ball, it is more difficult for defenders to track down the player they are assigned to mark in a player-to-player defense than it is to retreat to their assigned zones in a zone defense.
  - It is physically tiring to mark one-on-one, especially when the attacking player does not have possession of the ball and can make unpredictable runs.
  - Player-to-player defense requires higher levels of fitness in both the energy production and muscular systems of the body than does zone defense.
  - When using player-to-player defense, there is a loss of team play. Player-to-player defense relies on individual defensive play. In zone defense, there is an integrated effort of players that fosters team cohesiveness.
  - If an attacker cannot be covered effectively by one defender, the attacker will continually create problems for a player-to-player defense.
  - In a player-to-player defense, defenders become too concerned about the attacker they are marking and lose track of the ball's location.

Combination Defense

Combination defense is the integration of zone and player-to-player defense. In combination defense, some players are given zone assignments and others are given the responsibility of marking specific players.

This is an effective method of defensive play because combination defense can maximize the advantages and minimize the disadvantages of zone and player-to-player defense.

SYSTEM OF PLAY

Definitions

- ### Style of Play

The nature of play demonstrated by an individual player or a team is called the style of play. The following terms are some examples of descriptors of style: short passing, long passing, deliberate play, aggressive play, finesse, counterattacking, defensive, and offensive.

- ### Team Formation

The general organization of players to prescribed positions on the field is called team formation. It is noted by a numerical grouping of 10 field players proceeding from those closest to the goalkeeper to those closest to the opponent's goal (e.g., a 4-3-3 is a formation that uses 4 fullbacks, 3 halfbacks, and 3 forwards, as well as a goalkeeper).

- ### System of Play

The amalgamation of style of play and team formation forms a team's system of play. Note that two teams, using the same team formation, may demonstrate a drastically different system of play because of the differences in their styles of play. Similarly, the overall systems of play of two teams using different formations may be relatively alike.

Building a System

- ### Players

The task of determining a system of play for advanced youth players requires considerable thought by the coach. The coach must consider the players' physical characteristics, level of fitness, ability to perform individual techniques, tactical knowledge of the game, and personalities, as well as the coach's ability to modify these characteristics through practice and game experiences. At the advanced level of play, coaches should build upon the current abilities of their players.

The style of play and team formation selected should be relatively compatible with the existing characteristics of the players. For advanced youth players, the system of play should be molded to the players, rather than requiring the players to change for a particular style and team formation.

Coaches of beginning and intermediate level players have a more difficult task and a greater responsibility in determining a system of play for their team than their colleagues who coach advanced level players. Coaches of younger players must place greater emphasis on teaching and providing developmental experiences in laying the foundation for them to play within various systems of play. It is inappropriate to label and train a field player below the age of 14 years for a particular position. Coaches should expose these young players to the techniques and tactics of playing a fullback, halfback, and forward position, as well as the goalkeeper position, to bring out their best.

● Positions

In a full-sided game, 11 players from each team compete against each other (10 field players and one goalkeeper). The laws of the game do not place any restrictions on where the field players are to be located (other than on the field). Freedom in positioning and the creativity of coaches has resulted in a wide variety of positions and positional names. All of the field player positions, however, can be grouped into three general categories: backs, midfielders, and forwards. Table 20-3 contains a listing of positional names, and offensive and defensive technical and tactical strengths which youth players should develop to become successful at the various positions.

As seen in Table 20-3, there is some differentiation among the four categories of positions. Among the field players, greater emphasis is placed upon the development of defensive technical and tactical abilities in the backs. In the forwards, greater emphasis is placed upon the development of offensive technical and tactical abilities. The midfielders, however, need to equally develop their offensive and defensive technical and tactical abilities.

In the 1974 World Cup, the Dutch national team introduced its "total football" system of play. This system requires all players to possess a high level of both offensive and defensive techniques and tactics because players freely change positions and responsibilities during a match. This trend is continuing. The boundaries differentiating desirable strengths among field players is becoming cloudy. Therefore, coaches of young athletes must provide players with a broad exposure to all techniques and tactics of the game.

	Goalkeeper*	Backs**	Midfielders**	Forwards**
POSITIONAL NAMES	• goalie • keeper	• fullback • sweeper • stopper • defender • libero • freeback	• halfback • linkman	• striker • winger • attacker
DESIRABLE TECHNICAL STRENGTHS Offense	• distribution (throws, kicks, punts)	• long passes • accurate passes • clears • receiving and redirecting the ball into space • shielding • advancing the ball quickly with the dribble • heading while on the ground • heading while in the air	• all offensive techniques	• one-touch passing • one-touch shooting • accurate kicks • finishing • quick reception and control • interpassing • close control of the dribble • body feints • ball feints • shielding • heading while on the ground • heading while in the air
DESIRABLE TECHNICAL STRENGTHS Defense	• ready position • shot stopping (catching, punching, deflecting) • diving	• marking player in possession of the ball • marking player not in possession of the ball • front block tackle • pivot tackle • side tackle • slide tackle • heading while on the ground • heading while in the air	• all defensive techniques	• marking player in possession of the ball • front block tackle • pivot tackle • side tackle • slide tackle
DESIRABLE TACTICAL STRENGTHS Offense	• communication • support of the backs • positioning on set plays • initiate counterattack	• reading opposing defense • initiating penetration • depth • overlapping runs • support the midfielders	• penetration • supporting forwards • depth • wall passing • checking runs • overlapping runs • cross-over runs • blindside runs • diagonal runs • positioning off the ball • dummy runs	• improvisation • reading opposing defense • wall passing • checking runs • overlapping runs • cross-over runs • blindside runs • diagonal runs • positioning off the ball • dummy runs
DESIRABLE TACTICAL STRENGTHS Defense	• positioning • narrowing the angle • communicating • supporting the defense • positioning on set plays	• goal-side marking of the ball • recovering runs • pressuring the ball • jockeying • shepherding • covering • supporting • switching • diagonal coverage • shifting toward the ball • compactness • overloading • funneling	• goal-side marking of the ball • recovering runs • pressuring the ball • jockeying • shepherding • covering • supporting • switching • diagonal coverage • shifting toward the ball	• goal-side marking of the ball • recovering runs • pressuring the ball • jockeying • shepherding

*For additional information on goalkeeping techniques, see Chapter 19.
**For addtional information on field player techniques, see Chapters 11 and 15.

• Team Formation

The freedom to position the 10 field players has often fostered confusion in beginning coaches. It is not uncommon for a beginning coach to ask, "Where do I position my players?" The response to this question could be "Anywhere you want to." However, this response would not be very helpful.

To provide some structure from which coaches can organize their teams, the following line of thinking is appropriate. Most teams use four backs and a minimum of two midfielders and two forwards. Based on this premise, decisions need to be made about the two remaining field players. This results in only three possible formations for field players: 4-4-2, 4-3-3, and 4-2-4. This may be a simplistic approach for determining team formation. However, the remaining material associated with team formation in this chapter will relate to the three formations derived from our premise. Once you understand team formation, you can be creative in positioning your players "anywhere you want to."

Irrespective of which formation coaches select for their teams to play, no formation can make up for players who lack fitness and technical and tactical ability and knowledge.

Fitness, techniques, and tactics are the foundation of all formations.

4-4-2

The 4-4-2 is a defensive-minded formation (see Figure 20-56). When defending, a team has eight defenders. When attacking, the midfielders attempt to move forward to support the two strikers. This formation is based on a compact defense and quick transition to offense through long penetrating passes. Upon losing possession of the ball, a team playing this formation usually retreats to form a compact defensive unit in front of its own penalty area.

The 4-4-2 requires: players in defense who can mark zone or player-to-player; midfielders who have good defensive skills, speed to run the ball forward on a fast break, and a high level of fitness to move from one end of the field to the other; and two central strikers who can pressure the opposing fullbacks to slow their opponent's attack, giving their teammates time to recover, and who have one-on-one offensive ability to take on defenders and shield the ball until support arrives from their midfielders. Some teams will switch to a 4-4-2 formation late in the game to protect a one goal lead.

Advantages
- Compact defense
- Numeric advantage on defense
- Space behind opposition to attack
- May be effective in protecting a lead late in the game

Disadvantages

- Difficult to overtake an opponent who is ahead by one or more goals
- Territorial advantage given up during defensive retreat
- Central strikers will likely be outnumbered
- Central strikers may have to attack alone
- Lack of width on the forward line
- Attack outnumbered by opponent's defense

4-3-3

This formation (see Figure 20-57) provides more balance between offense and defense when compared to the 4-4-2. The additional striker results in a forward line with a central attacker and two wing forwards. The central striker could play slightly behind the wing forwards and serve as a link player between the midfielders and wingers. The four backs and three midfielders will usually provide a numeric advantage in defense against most opposing formations. Offensively, the two outside backs may be called upon to participate in the attack by making runs forward and possibly overlapping the midfielders. Similarly, the midfielders may need to support the forwards.

This team formation requires: four skillful backs, two of whom are capable of supporting the attack by running down the flanks; three midfielders who are capable of defending and attacking by covering a lot of ground; and three forwards who can pass, receive and control the ball, maintain close control in the dribble, shield the ball, and turn and go for goal.

Advantages

- Compact defense
- Usually a numeric advantage on defense
- Relative balance between offense and defense
- Central striker playing deep, who may be difficult to mark

Disadvantages

- Defensively oriented formation
- Attack is usually outnumbered by opponent's defense

4-2-4

This is a balanced system (see Figure 20-58). When in possession of the ball, the two midfielders aid in the attack. When opponents possess the ball, the two midfielders assist the four backs in defense. Hence this for-

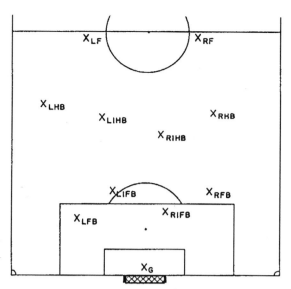

Figure 20-56. A 4-4-2 formation.

Figure 20-57. A 4-3-3 formation.

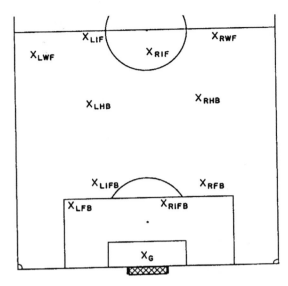

Figure 20-58. A 4-2-4 formation.

mation results in a balance of six field players on attack and six field players on defense. In this formation a numeric disadvantage exists in the midfield where two players must move forward in attack and back on defense, as well as move to the flanks.

The 4-2-4 requires: two outside fullbacks who can run forward and assist in the midfield; two central backs who can support the midfielders as well as the outside backs; two midfielders who are physically fit and very skilled to be able to aid the team in attack and on defense and be able to cover the center of the field from one flank to the other; two wing forwards who can bring the ball toward the goal from the corner, cross the ball from the flank, and delay the opponent's attack by harassing their backs; and two inside forwards with good skill to receive, control, dribble, and shoot the ball and who have better than average height to take advantage of air balls crossed in front of the opponent's goal.

Advantages

- Balance between offense and defense
- Attack on a broad front
- Ball may be able to be moved quickly from defense to offense

Disadvantages

- Vulnerable to counterattack
- Numerical inferiority in midfield
- Risk in losing the ball when making passes from the backs to the midfielders
- Demands placed upon the two link players

A.

B.

Figure 20-59. Use of a stopper in front of the fullbacks.

A. A 4-1-3-2 formation (far left).

B. A 4-1-2-3 formation (left).

Variations in the Four Back Formation

- Stopper

Some teams have removed one member from either the halfback or forward line and placed a stopper in front of the fullback line (see Figure 20-59). The resulting formation is either a 4-1-3-2 or a 4-1-2-3.

The responsibility of the stopper is to guard the central path to the goal and to mark the opposing center forward. The stopper also creates additional depth in defense and possibly provides a challenge to the attacker with the ball before the remaining backs. When using a stopper, the fullbacks, especially the central backs, take on a more supportive role.

- Sweeper

Some teams place a sweeper behind the fullback line (see Figure 20-60). If four fullbacks are used with a sweeper, the resulting formation is either a 1-4-3-2 or a 1-4-2-3. The sweeper is responsible for providing defensive support to all the backs. The sweeper marks any attacker with the ball who penetrates the fullback line. As a free back to support the fullbacks, the sweeper relieves the backs of the responsibility of being the last defender before the goalkeeper. With a sweeper, the backs can concentrate more on marking opposing players.

Figure 20-60. Use of a sweeper behind the fullbacks.

A. A 1-4-3-2 formation (right).

B. A 1-4-2-3 formation (far right).

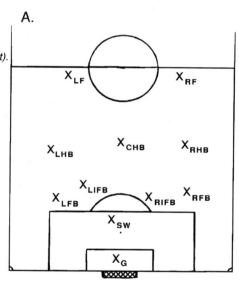
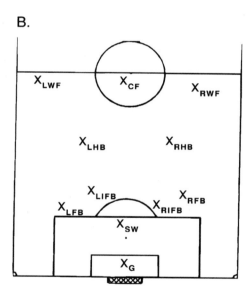

- Sweeper and Stopper

Some teams will use both a sweeper and stopper (see Figure 20-61). This is usually accomplished by combining three backs with a sweeper and stopper. The resulting team formation is either a 1-3-1-3-2 or a 1-3-1-2-3. This combination of sweeper and stopper adds structured depth to the defense and increases the number of "lines" of players across the field. This is an excellent approach to add depth to a youth team.

Figure 20-61. *Use of a sweeper and a stopper.*

A. A 1-3-1-3-2 formation (right).

B. A 1-3-1-2-3 formation (far right).

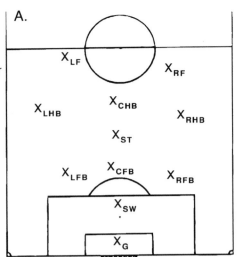

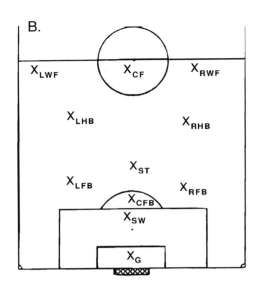

SET PLAYS (RESTARTS)

This section will include the offensive and defensive tactics and strategies associated with six restart situations (kick-off, goal kick, penalty kick, corner kick, free kick, and throw-in). Material that is pertinent to team formation will use the 4-3-3 as an example. If your team employs a different formation, make positional assignments based upon your team's formation in order to use the sample set plays that are provided.

Simplicity is one key to success in set plays, especially with youth players. The samples that are provided in this section require a few passes to complete. In addition, general and specific guidelines to teaching and performing the sample set plays are given. A second key to success in attacking with or defending against a set play is quickness of deployment.

Obviously, the percentage of goals scored as a result of set plays in different age and ability groups varies. This percentage may be as high as 40 percent in some leagues. It is, therefore, an important aspect of offense and defense. Coaches should take the time to plan set plays, develop handouts, instruct athletes on how to carry out set plays, and integrate set plays into practice plans.

Kick-Off on Offense

A kick-off is used to start play at the beginning of the game, after half time, and to restart play after a goal has been scored. This set play is unique in that both teams are confined to their own half of the field until the ball is kicked forward.

Relatively few goals are scored as the direct result of a set play on the kick-off. Given the choice, most teams forego selecting the kick-off at the start of the game in favor of the advantage provided by wind conditions, sun position, and field conditions. However, the kick-off is important. At the start of the first or second half, the kick-off may set the psychological tone of play that follows. During the game, a team takes a kick-off after its opponents have scored a goal. Under these circumstances, a set play may be used to refocus the team on the game and not on the opponent's goal.

Maintaining possession to start an attack should be the primary objective of the kick-off. Many youth teams violate this objective by kicking the ball as far as they can toward the opponent's goal on the first touch of the ball. Their objective is to gain a territorial advantage by regaining possession of the ball down field. This approach, however, should be discouraged because possession is immediately lost. Possession of the ball should be maintained to give teammates time to make runs down field and penetrate the opponent's defense. Most teams accomplish this by a short pass forward, followed by a support pass, and then a penetrating pass if a teammate is in an open position down field.

On the kick-off, most defending teams position themselves in the formation they will be using during play. Therefore, open space in the opponent's defense may be seen and exploited by runs into the gaps in their formation. Runs off the ball, including blind-side, diagonal, and dummy runs, can be effective. Players making deep runs must be careful that they are not running into off-side positions.

● Kick-Off Set Plays

Overload Right (see Figure 20-62)

Description—The ball is passed forward to the center halfback. After the pass is initiated, the center forward, right wing, and right halfback make runs toward the target area. The left wing forward attempts to draw attention by making a dummy run down the left flank. After giving a support pass to the left halfback, the center halfback runs forward to support the players in the target area. If a teammate is open in the target area, the left halfback makes a long penetrating pass into this space. If this pass is made, the fullbacks move forward and shift toward the right side of the field to support the attack. Successful reception and control of the ball in the target area may result in an opportunity for a shot on goal or possibly a cross to the left wing. If no player in the target area is open, the left halfback maintains possession of the ball and the fullbacks provide support.

Overload Left

Description—This set play is the same as the overload right except players change roles and the ball is played to a target area on the left side.

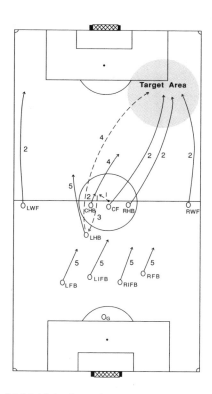

Figure 20-62. Kick-off set play—overload right.

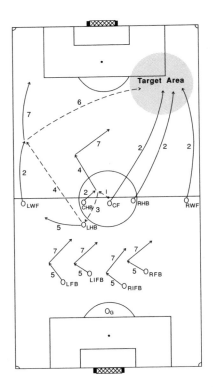

Target Area

Figure 20-63. *Kick-off set play—cross to overload right.*

Cross to Overload Right (see Figure 20-63)

Description—This set play is similar to the overload right except the left halfback makes a pass to the left wing forward on the flank and runs to support the pass. This pass may draw attention away from the blind side runs into the target area. The left wing crosses the ball into the target area if teammates are open there. The fullbacks should shift toward the left flank to support the left wing and left halfback and then toward the right flank if the ball is passed into the target area. Once the cross is made to the target area, the left wing should continue to run down the left flank into open space. If a team is unfortunate and has more than one kick-off in the game, the cross to overload set play can be alternated with the overload set play to confuse the defense.

Cross to Overload Left

Description—This set play is the same as the cross to overload right except players change roles and the ball is played to the right flank before being crossed to the target area on the left side.

Defense Against the Kick-Off

When defending against a kick-off, a team may show its opponents a formation different than the one planned for use during the game. As the ball is kicked forward, the defending players move quickly to assume responsibilities and positioning associated with the formation to be played. This defensive strategy may counter the kick-off play that may have been selected to exploit the original formation shown by the defense. Because some coaches adjust their team's tactics, strategy, and formation in response to their opponent's positioning, showing a different formation at the start of a kick-off may also confuse the attacking team.

The defensive team initially has a total numerical advantage on its half of the field when the opponents take a kick-off. Therefore, if the defenders adhere to the fundamental principles of defense and fulfill positional responsibilities, it is unlikely that their opponents will score on a kick-off play. The defenders can add pressure to the attack by closely marking offensive players making runs and by sending one or more forwards into the opponent's half of the field to pressure any support passes made by the attack (see Figure 20-64).

Goal Kick On Offense

The goal kick is used to restart play after the offensive team has played the ball out of bounds over its opponent's goal line. The ball is placed anywhere within the half of the goal area nearest to where the ball crossed the goal line. Players defending against the goal kick must remain outside the penalty area until the ball passes out of the penalty area. A set play on the goal kick is not likely to score a goal because of the distance from the kick to the opponent's goal. The object of the goal kick should be to maintain possession of the ball and penetrate deeply into the opponent's half of the field with a minimum number of passes.

Any player on the attacking team can take the goal kick. The kick, however, is usually taken by either the goalkeeper or one of the fullbacks because this frees halfbacks and forwards to make runs down field into open spaces and to draw defenders away from the goal kick. The goalkeeper should take the goal kick because this forces the defenders to attempt to mark one additional field player. Some coaches, especially in youth play, prefer a fullback to take the goal kick so the goalkeeper can focus on defending the goal in case the kick is intercepted by the defense. Irrespective of who takes the goal kick, the kicker must be able to make accurate short or long passes that are unlikely to be intercepted.

There are two general types of goal kicks: short and long. The short kick is played to an open teammate just outside the penalty area. From that point, it can be returned to the goalkeeper who can handle the ball (see Figure 20-65A) or it can be played down field (see Figure 20-65B). The short kick is usually

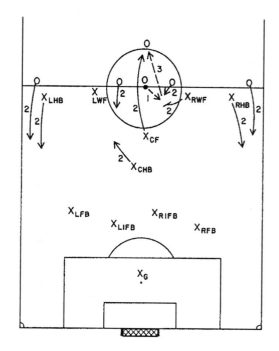

Figure 20-64. *Defense against the kick-off.*

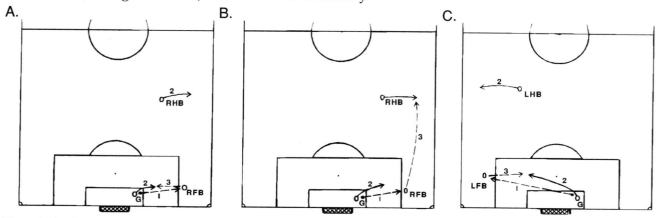

Figure 20-65. *Short goal kicks. A. Return pass to the goalkeeper (left). B. Ball passed down the field (middle). C. Ball passed out the far side of the penalty area; more likely to be intercepted (right).*

made to an open fullback on the same side of the penalty area as where the goal kick is taken. A short kick to the opposite side takes more time for the ball to be received and requires more accuracy from the kicker (see Figure 20-65C). Therefore, a ball kicked out the opposite side of the penalty area is more likely to be intercepted and is not recommended for youth teams.

For the same reasons as were given for the short goal kick, the long kick is usually played to the target area on the same half of the field as where the kick is taken (see Figure 20-66). Attackers on the flank are more often open than central attackers because defenders tend to funnel toward their own goal. For the offensive team, it is more desirable for a central attacker to receive a long pass down field than for an attacker on the wing to receive the ball (see Figure 20-67A and B). However, if the goal kick is to be intercepted by the defense, it is more desirable for this interception to occur on the flank then in the center of the field in front of the goal from which the goal kick was taken. Therefore, a player taking a long goal kick must weigh the offensive advantage of playing the ball down the middle of the field against the disadvantage of the goal kick being intercepted in front of the goal. Another factor to consider in taking a long goal kick is the direction and force of the wind. If the wind is blowing forcefully into the face of the kicker, the short kick may be essential.

Irrespective of whether a long or short kick is taken, the three keys to set plays on a goal kick are:
- quickly set up and take the kick before the defense can set up,
- make an accurate pass that can be handled by an open teammate, and
- be prepared to switch to defense if the pass is intercepted.

These keys to success are especially important in beginning youth players who may not be able to kick the ball in the air much farther than the edge of the penalty area. In this case, delay in taking the goal kick usually

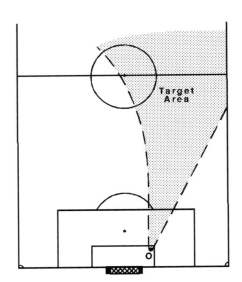

Figure 20-66. Target area for a long goal kick.

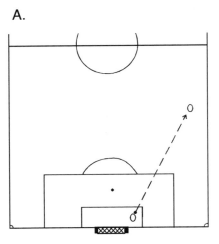

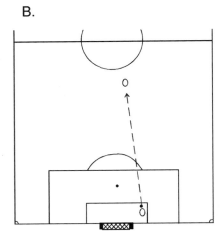

Figure 20-67. Long goal kicks. A. Pass down the flank (above left). B. Pass down the center (above right).

results in a gathering of defenders immediately outside the penalty area, waiting to intercept a short pass. If such a pass occurs, attackers can play the ball before it exits the penalty area and receive a rekick. This play may also receive a warning from the referee.

Other factors that may aid in the achievement of a successful goal kick relate to positioning and movement of attackers. Fullbacks prepared to receive a short kick can run to open spaces around the penalty area or make checking runs away from and then back toward the location of the kick. Halfbacks and forwards can also make various runs to take defenders away from the goal kick or to achieve open space down field.

Defense Against the Goal Kick

When defending against a goal kick, players should attempt to minimize the advantages of the attackers. This can be accomplished by:

- quickly setting up to defend against the kick,
- tightly marking players in the target area which may force a risky pass across the front of the goal,
- having forwards mark fullbacks in the vicinity of the penalty area, and
- having halfbacks and fullbacks mark attackers down field.

Penalty Kick On Offense

It is not a certainty that a goal will result from a penalty kick. Therefore, kicks from the penalty mark, as well as the responsibilities of other team members, should be practiced. For the kick, accuracy is of primary importance and velocity of the ball is of secondary importance. An inaccurate kick will not go in the goal, but a ball kicked slowly on target has a chance. This philosophy should be instilled in youth players because most penalty kicks that fail to score are the result of shots missing the goal and not the result of saves by goalkeepers. Therefore, when taking a penalty kick, the velocity of the kick should be directly related to the player's accuracy.

Figure 20-68. Use of string, hung from the cross bar, to make targets for practicing penalty kicks.

One approach to practice accurate kicks is to hang two strings from the cross bar on both sides of the goal (see Figure 20-68). These strings form two targets. The width between each pair of strings and the location of these strings can be adjusted to challenge the kicker. As the ability of the kicker improves, the strings can be moved laterally toward the goal posts and the target can be narrowed. Players should eventually practice penalty kicks without the strings by picking a target on the net.

In addition to excessive velocity, another factor that tends to result in inaccurate penalty kicks is an improper approach to the ball. An improper approach is usually characterized by too many steps and a run that is too fast. Sufficient approach velocity of the kicker's body can be achieved by a controlled run of four or fewer steps. As the approach distance increases, accuracy in the placement of the support foot decreases and inaccurate kicks tend to result. Approach footwork and kick should be established and practiced to enhance the potential of scoring a goal from the penalty kick.

As kickers become more skillful, they should attempt to take a straighter approach to the ball and also develop shots from this approach that can be played to either the right or left of the goalkeeper. If the kicker is unable to do this, the goalkeeper may be able to read the kick and obtain an advantage. After the kicker determines the type of kick to be attempted, this choice should not be changed during the approach to the ball. The kicker must maintain concentration and confidence in the kick that was selected before the approach.

Attackers not taking the penalty kick should vie for key positions outside the penalty area and arc. The two most advantageous positions are located at the intersection of the arc and penalty area (see Figure 20-69). These are the closest positions to the goal. Players achieving the inside positioning here can shield opponents off a ball that rebounds in front of the goal. Generally, on both sides of the arc, attackers should challenge for inside positioning on their opponents. Other positions that are desirable are along the sides of the penalty area. These are also relatively close to the goal. However, a rebound does not present as good a shot on goal because of the poor shooting angle.

The kicker and other teammates should be ready to move to play a rebounding ball. Those attackers not taking the kick should not cross the lines marking the penalty area and arc before the ball is kicked into play. Encroachment will result in a retake of the kick if the ball goes into the goal and may result in a caution for encroaching players. The kicker cannot play the ball again until it first has been played by another player. Therefore, the kicker should be alert for a ball rebounding off the goalkeeper, defenders, and teammates.

Defense Against the Penalty Kick

The odds of preventing a goal when defending against a penalty kick are not very good. However, if a team successfully defends its goal against a kick, not only does it prevent a goal, but it usually receives a psychological lift that may enhance its subsequent play. Because of these benefits, practicing defense against the penalty kick is worthwhile. The key elements to defense against the penalty kick are:

- the goalkeeper must be alert before signaling the referee to permit the kick,
- defenders must challenge for desirable positions around the penalty area and arc (see Figure 20-69), and
- defenders must be ready to move into the penalty area and arc, as soon as the ball is put into play, to clear any rebound.

Defenders should be instructed not to enter the penalty area too soon because encroachment results in the retaking of a missed kick and possibly cautions to the encroaching players. Defenders who have an opportunity to play a rebound should attempt to clear the ball to a teammate down field. However, if this is not likely, their second choice should be to kick the ball over either touch line and give up a throw-in. Defenders, however, may have to give their opponents a corner kick by kicking a rebound over the end line to reduce pressure on the goal.

Corner Kick On Offense

A corner kick is an ideal scoring opportunity. The kick is taken from relatively close to the opponent's goal and set plays from this location can usually deliver the ball into the danger area in front of the goal.

● Formations

There are two basic formations used by attacking teams when taking a corner kick: scattered formation and grouped formation (also known as echelon formation).

Scattered Formation

A scattered formation involves the positioning of attackers spread around and inside the penalty area (see Figure 20-70). When the corner kick is taken, each of these players has an assigned responsibility associated with his or her positioning. Attackers may, however, make timed checking runs away from and back to their assigned positions to confuse the defense.

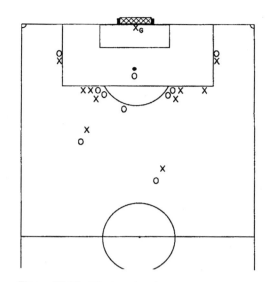

Figure 20-69. *Attackers in advantageous positions for the taking of a penalty kick.*

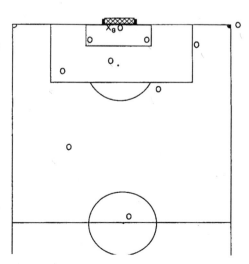

Figure 20-70. *Attackers in a scattered formation for the taking of a corner kick.*

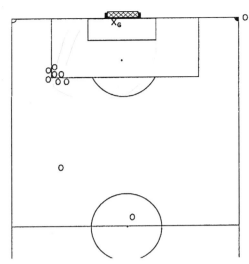

Figure 20-71. *Attackers in a grouped (echelon) formation for the taking of a corner kick.*

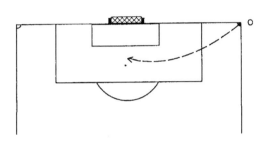

Figure 20-72. *Long corner kick—inswinger.*

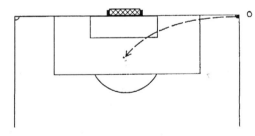

Figure 20-73. *Long corner kick—outswinger.*

Grouped (Echelon) Formation

In this grouped formation, several attackers gather near the far corner of the penalty area (see Figure 20-71). This arrangement tends to attract defenders away from their goal and create space deep in the penalty area. From an echelon formation, additional confusion may be caused in closely marking defenders if the attackers make checking and dummy runs in various directions before the corner kick is taken. Attackers, however, are responsible for timing a run into a designated location in front of the goal to assume an assigned responsibility associated with a set play that has been called.

- ### Entry Pass

There are two types of entry passes used for the corner kick: long and short.

Long Pass

If possible, the long pass should be delivered to the area between the penalty kick mark and the edge of the goal area. The long pass can be either an inswinger or outswinger. The inswinger curves toward the goal line and is easier for defenders to clear (see Figure 20-72). However, if it is delivered toward the near post it has a chance of going directly into the goal and may be out of reach of the approaching goalkeeper. The outswinger curves toward the attacking players and is easier for the attackers to deflect or shoot on goal (see Figure 20-73). The outswinger may also lure the goalkeeper out from the goal into a vulnerable position.

Short Pass

Because the corner kick is a free kick, defenders must be positioned 10 or more yards away from the kick. Thus, a short entry pass gives the attacking team a numerical advantage close to the point of the kick. This advantage can be exploited in moving the ball toward the goal for either a shot or a short chip into the penalty area. The short corner kick is very useful for beginning youth teams whose players may not have the strength and skill to kick a long corner kick into the penalty area.

- ### Corner Kick Set Plays

Right Long Corner Kick from Scattered Formation (see Figure 20-74)

Description—A long corner kick (inswinger or outswinger) is made from the right corner. The left wing forward takes up a position in front of the goalkeeper to distract the keeper's vision and movement toward the ball. A tall player in this position can do a better job of blocking the goalkeeper's vision. If the ball is received in the air, a tall player has the advantage to head the ball on goal. The center halfback, center forward, and right halfback make runs into different areas in front of the goal to play a ball kicked to them or to be in position to play a ball deflected into their area. The left halfback is responsible for any long corner kick which manages to reach the far side of the goal. Fullbacks may make runs forward. However, they must be concerned with opposing forwards who make runs to receive a penetrating pass if the corner kick is intercepted. The goalkeeper on the attacking team moves up field to provide support for the fullbacks.

Left Long Corner Kick from Scattered Formation

Description—This set play is the same as the right long corner kick from scattered formation except players change roles and the ball is kicked from the left corner.

Right Long Corner Kick from Grouped Formation

Description—The responsibilities of the players are the same as those for the right long corner kick from scattered formation (see Figure 20-75). The only difference in these two corner kicks is that in this corner kick a grouped formation is used and players must time their runs with the player taking the kick to get to their assigned positions as the ball arrives.

Left Long Corner Kick from Grouped Formation

Description—This set play is the same as the right long corner kick from a grouped formation except players change roles and the ball is kicked from the left corner.

Right Short Corner Kick from Scattered Formation (see Figure 20-76)

Description—The set-up for this corner kick is the same as that used for the right long corner kick from a scattered formation (see Figure 20-74). This short kick differs from the long kick in that the right halfback runs to the corner to receive a short pass from the right wing forward. After the short pass, the right wing forward overlaps the right halfback who either returns the pass (see Figure 20-76A) or dribbles toward the goal (see Figure 20-76B). Whoever has the ball at this point can cross it to the onrushing attackers or shoot it on the goal. On this play, the right fullback should move up the flank to support the right wing and right halfback. A short corner kick will often draw defenders away from their goal toward the corner and open space for attackers running to the goal from the far side. The right short and long corner kicks mutually disguise each other.

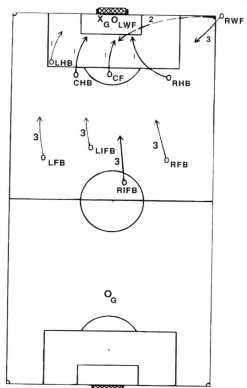

Figure 20-74. *Right long corner kick from a scattered formation.*

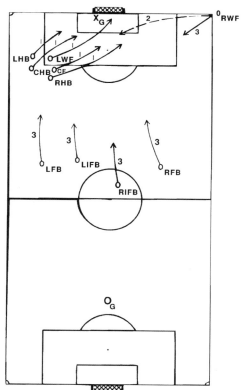

Figure 20-75. *Right long corner kick from a grouped (echelon) formation.*

445

TACTICS OF PLAY

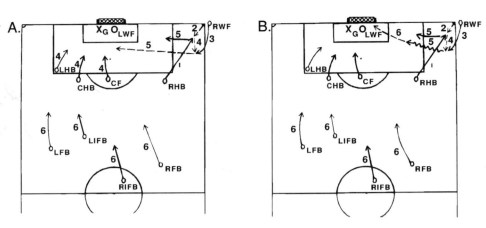

Figure 20-76. *Right short corner kick options from a scattered formation.*

A. Right wing forward overlaps the right halfback to receive a return pass for a shot on goal or a centering pass (right).

B. Right wing forward overlaps the right halfback to receive a return pass, then dribbles toward the goal for a shot (far right).

Left Short Corner Kick from Scattered Formation and Right and Left Short Corner Kicks from Grouped Formation

Description—These corner kicks are the same as the right short corner kick from scattered formation except for the change in corner and formation.

Defense Against the Corner Kick

When defending against a corner kick, a zone or combination (zone and player-to-player) defense is usually used. In both of these defenses, a minimum of four players are usually given specific zone responsibilities (see Figure 20-77). In a 4-3-3 formation, the right and left inside fullbacks should be positioned to the inside of the goal post on their respective sides. Their responsibilities are to mark the area immediately in front of the goal and to guard the goal if the goalkeeper runs out away from the goal to play a ball. One player should be responsible for guarding the area near the corner kick. In our sample 4-3-3 formation, this could be the outside halfback on the ball side of the field. This player should stand 10 yards from the ball and in line with the predicted path of the ball in a long corner kick. The responsibilities of this player are to guard against a short corner kick and to distract the kicker during a long corner kick. The positioning of the outside halfback should be farther from the goal line for an inswinger than for an outswinger. The goalkeeper is the fourth person assigned a zone responsibility. Before the kick, the goalkeeper should be positioned about a yard off the goal line and about two yards inside the far post. From this position, the goalkeeper can most easily move forward, backward, or out away from the goal to catch, punch, or deflect the ball. For beginning players, the goalkeeper may move closer to the kick if it is unlikely that the kicker can project the ball to the far post.

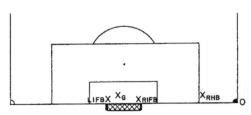

Figure 20-77. *The four minimum assigned zone responsibilites in either a zone or a combination defense against a corner kick.*

If the remaining players in the 4-3-3 formation are assigned zone responsibilities, they may be positioned as in Figure 20-78. Each player is responsible for defending the area in their immediate vicinity. If a short corner kick is taken, the outside fullback on the ball side should assist the outside halfback. The wing forward on the ball side covers the zone vacated by the ball side halfback and the remaining two forwards shift toward the ball side. They should, however, be ready to break down field to receive a penetrating pass if their team regains possession of the ball. If a combination defense is used, you should assign one of your best defenders to mark the best attacker and assign players who are tall and skilled at playing balls out of the air against opposing players of like ability.

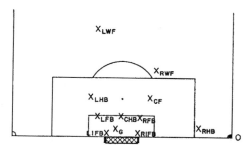

Figure 20-78. Zone defense against a corner kick using a 4-3-3 team formation.

There is a hierarchy of desirable outcomes when defending against a corner kick. Players should be instructed about this hierarchy to aid them in making decisions and to provide goals for their play. Outcomes, from most to least desirable, are listed below.

Hierarchy of Outcomes When Defending Against a Corner Kick (from most to least desirable)

1. Clear the ball up field to a teammate.

2. Clear the ball up field.

3. Kick the ball out of bounds up field.

4. Kick the ball out of bounds near your goal line.

5. Play the ball over your goal line.

6. Give up a goal.

Free Kick On Offense

Your team can be awarded a free kick from any location on the field, except within your opponent's goal area. Figure 20-79 is provided to add some structure to the planning of free kicks from six different areas of the field. Note that the size of these areas should vary with the age and ability of your players.

● Zone 1

A free kick from zone 1 should be played as if it was a goal kick. Use your restart plays which have been planned for the goal kick (see Section on Goal Kick on Offense and Figures 20-65 to 20-67).

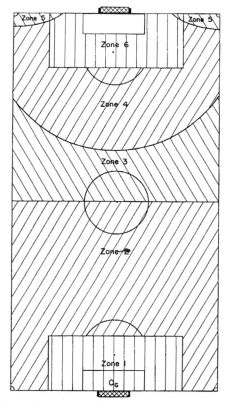

Figure 20-79. Zones for structuring free kicks on offense.
Zone 1. Unlikely to score directly or indirectly.
Zone 2. Unlikely to score directly or indirectly.
Zone 3. Unlikely to score directly, may score indirectly.
Zone 4. Good chance of scoring directly or indirectly.
Zone 5. Unlikely to score directly, good chance of scoring indirectly.
Zone 6. Good chance of scoring indirectly.

- ## Zone 2

  If the ball is placed near zone 1, the free kick may be played back to the goalkeeper. Other free kick options in zone 2 are to initiate the attack by making a short pass or by making a long penetrating pass to an unmarked teammate up field. In general, offensive players should be making runs near and away from the kick to get into open space. The best restarts from zones 1 and 2 are quickly played balls.

- ## Zone 3

  Free kicks from this location can be played as if they were kick-offs, but players are not restricted to their half of the field as they are for a kick-off. Thus, the delaying initial kicks used for the kick-off restart, which provide attackers with sufficient time to get to forward positions, should not be used. Attackers can move to position before the free kick or can make a variety of runs to get to position to receive the ball. A free kick from zone 3 will also differ from a kick-off in that the kick will usually be taken by a halfback, fullback, or a team member with the ability to make accurate long passes. This allows more attackers to move forward to pressure the defense. Players running to advanced positions, however, need to be cautious about putting themselves in an offside position beyond the loosely organized wall of fullbacks.

  Examples of free kicks from zone 3 follow. It should be noted that these are variations of kick-off plays.

Overload Right (see Figure 20-80)

Description—A long pass is played into the target area either in front of or behind the defensive backs. The right and center halfbacks and forwards time their runs into the target area to receive the ball as it arrives. From this location they attempt to get a shot on goal. The wing forward on the opposite side of the field should be ready to run behind the defense to retrieve an errant shot on goal and also to spread the marking by the fullbacks. The left halfback moves to receive a short pass and is in position to defend the center of the field against a counterattack. The fullbacks also are positioned around midfield to defend against a counterattack.

Overload Left

Description—This set play is the same as the overload right except players change roles and the ball is played to a target area on the left side.

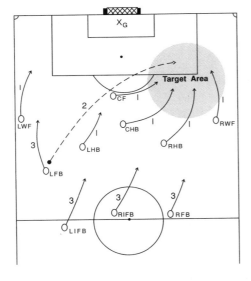

Figure 20-80. Free kick set play from zone 3— overload right.

Cross to Overload Right (see Figure 20-81)

Description—This set play is similar to the overload right except the initial pass goes to the left wing forward. This may draw attention away from the players overloading the target area. The left wing forward then crosses the ball into the target area. Because this cross is taken from a point relatively near to the opponent's goal line, the wing forward will more likely be able to project the ball behind the defense. Players running into the target area must carefully time their runs so as not to be caught offside. After making the cross, the wing forward should run forward to be in position to play an errant shot on goal.

Cross to Overload Left

Description—This set play is the same as the cross to overload right except players change roles and the ball is played to the right flank before being crossed to the target area on the left side.

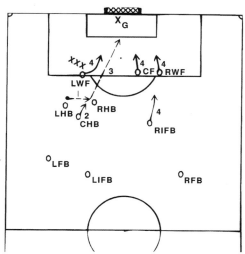

Figure 20-81. Free kick set play from zone 3—cross to overload right.

• Zone 4

From zone 4 there is a good chance of scoring either directly (direct free kick shot on goal) or indirectly (direct or indirect free kick passed before a shot is taken on goal). Players 10 years of age and older are capable of setting up a defensive wall to protect their goal against this offensive opportunity. If the free kick is located near the touch line, the attacking team should attempt to score indirectly by playing the ball toward the goal or middle of the field first before shooting on goal. If the free kick is taken from in front of the goal, a shot directly on goal is warranted. If the defenders have the path to the goal covered, a pass should be made to circumvent the defense or defensive wall before shooting on goal. With any free kick taken from zone 4, attackers must be cautious about running or standing in offside positions.

Examples of free kicks from zone 4 follow. In each of these set plays a pass is made before a shot is taken on goal. If a direct free kick is awarded and the player taking the kick sees a good opportunity to score directly from the kick, this player should be allowed to take the shot on goal.

Pass Right, Trap, and Shoot (see Figure 20-82)

Description—The left halfback makes a short and accurate pass to the right halfback who traps the ball with the sole of the foot. The center halfback runs forward to kick the ball on goal from its stationary position. The kick must be made with the right foot of the center halfback or a collision may occur between the center and right halfbacks. If

Figure 20-82. Free kick set play from zone 4—pass right, trap, and shoot.

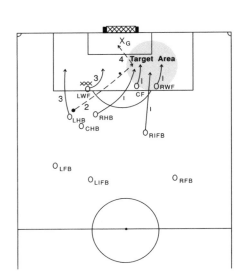

Figure 20-83. *Free kick set play from zone 4—overload right.*

the defense sets up a wall, the left wing stands in front of the wall to distract the defenders. The left wing could arrive at this position after running at the ball and feinting a kick. The center forward and right wing may make various dummy runs to draw defensive attention to themselves. At the time the kick is taken, they should be just on side and prepared to move forward to play the ball if it rebounds from the goal or players. One of the fullbacks may run forward to draw some defensive attention. The remaining fullbacks should be prepared for a counterattack.

Pass Left, Trap, and Shoot

Description—This set play is the same as the pass right, trap, and shoot except players change roles. It should be noted that a left footed shot on goal is to be taken to avoid a collision with the player making the trap.

Chip to Overload Right and Shoot (see Figure 20-83)

Description—The positioning of players for this set play is similar to the pass right, trap, and shoot restart. In this set play, the left halfback chips the ball into the target area. The center forward, right wing forward, right halfback, and right inside fullback time their runs into the target area to receive the chip and then head or kick the ball on goal. As the chip is made, the left wing, right halfback, and center halfback move forward to become involved with play. The use of this set play can be very effective if the pass right, trap, and shoot was previously used. Performing one of these two set plays and then the other confuses a defense that expects the attackers to repeat their initial free kick.

● **Zone 5**

A free kick from either of the zone 5 areas is unlikely to score directly because of the poor shooting angle. Free kicks from these areas should be played offensively as if they were corner kicks (see section on Corner Kick On Offense and Figures 20-70 to 20-76).

● **Zone 6**

A free kick from zone 6 will be either a penalty kick (see section on Penalty Kick On Offense) or an indirect free kick from outside the goal area. For an indirect free kick, it is important for the attacking team to quickly set up to take the kick. This may catch the defenders disorganized and unprepared for a shot on goal. The defense will usually set up a wall and bring all of its players back to defend against a free kick this close to their goal. Therefore, a quick kick may catch some of the opponent's halfbacks and forwards out of good goal side positions. For ball placements less than 10 yards from the goal line, the defenders may stand on their goal line. Not setting up quickly to take an indirect free kick from short range (less than 10 yards from the goal line) will give the defense time to "pack the goal" with defenders. Under these conditions it is somewhat difficult to shoot through all the bodies.

If the defenders set up quickly, an indirect free kick can be shot into the crowd of defenders in hopes that a deflection will go into the goal. This is a risky choice for an indirect free kick from zone 6. A better choice of set play, irrespective of defensive preparation, is the pass right, trap, and shoot (see Figure 20-82) or the pass left, trap, and shoot restart described for zone 4. These two set plays can be simplified to a pass and shoot restart (see Figure 20-84). In this set play the ball is passed just far enough toward the center of the goal to put it back into play (a distance equal to the circumference of the ball) and then it is shot on goal by another attacker.

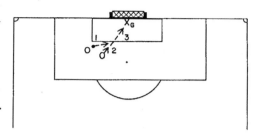

Figure 20-84. Free kick set play from zone 6— pass and shoot.

Defense Against the Free Kick

The defense's response to the placement of the ball for the taking of a free kick should vary with ball location (see Figure 20-85). The following descriptions are suggested defensive responses to free kicks taken from various locations on the field.

● **Zone 1**

Forwards should be prepared to defend against the short free kick that an attacker plans to return to his/her goalkeeper (see Figure 20-86). Thus, forwards should closely mark the attacking fullbacks in the vicinity of the goal. In beginning level youth games, forwards will often have an opportunity to intercept a short kick just outside the penalty area. Halfbacks should mark players on the ball side of the half way line. They should shift slightly toward the ball side of the field to entice the kicker to play the free kick across the front of the goal. Fullbacks should not be caught too far up field where a long penetrating free kick may go beyond them to an attacking forward. Thus, fullbacks and halfbacks, to some extent, must judge the ability of the kicker to plan the depth of their positioning.

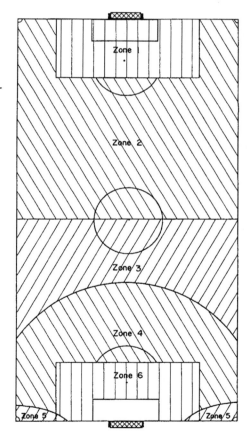

Figure 20-85. Zones for structuring defenses against free kicks.

● **Zone 2**

If the ball is placed close to the attacking team's penalty area, the free kick may be played directly to its goalkeeper (see Figure 20-87). Forwards need to be alerted to this op-

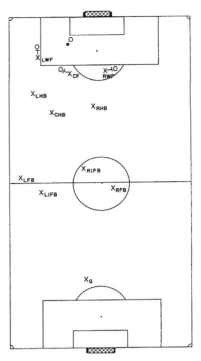

Figure 20-86. *Defense against a free kick from zone 1.*

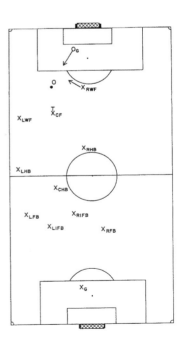

Figure 20-87. *Defense against a free kick from zone 2.*

tion because carelessness on attack may permit interception of this type of pass. The forward positioned in the vicinity of the free kick should move to within 10 yards of the ball to distract the kick and possibly intercept a short pass. Other forwards drop back to defend against the attacking team's midfielders. Fullbacks mark opposing halfbacks and forwards who take up or run to advanced positions. On defense, the fullbacks should not be caught too far up field and beaten by a long penetrating free kick.

● **Zone 3**

Defense against a free kick from zone 3 should be played similarly to the defense used against a kick-off. The defense of the free kick differs in that attackers will move into positions ahead of the ball before the kick is taken and the defenders will not have the numerical advantage on their half of the field that they experience when their opponents take a kick-off. A forward in the vicinity of the kick should move to within 10 yards of the ball to distract the kick and possibly intercept a short pass. Other defenders should adhere to the fundamental principles of defense and fulfill positional responsibilities. Defenders can add pressure to the attack by closely marking offensive players making runs.

● **Zone 4**

Because there is a good chance for the offense to score either directly or indirectly from this area of the field, the defenders should set up a wall to assist their goalkeeper in blocking the path to the goal (see Special Defensive Tactics - Defensive Wall). In addition to the defensive wall, one defender should be assigned to rush a short pass to disrupt any set plays evolving from a short pass. Players should not dissolve the wall to play a short pass because this leaves the goalkeeper vulnerable to shots through the wall. The wall should be dissolved if the ball is passed behind the wall or a long pass is made away from the wall which renders the wall ineffective. The remaining defenders may engage in zone, man-to-man, or combination defense. They should not, however, take up positions behind their team's wall. Because of the number of defenders used in the wall, the attacking team may have players whom the defense can only loosely mark. Attackers in the immediate vicinity of the goal must be marked closely. A sufficient number of defenders may not be available to mark attackers away from the goal.

Beginning level youth players (6 to 9 years of age) who have not learned how to set up a defensive wall should be instructed to concentrate their defense in the danger area in front of their goal to assist their goalkeeper in defending against free kicks from zone 4. One player should be assigned the responsibility of marking an attacker who receives a short kick. The hierarchy of outcomes previously presented in the section on Defense Against the Corner Kick is appropriate for the defense against free kicks in zone 4. This will provide the beginning youth players with a set of goals to direct their performance.

- **Zone 5**

Defenses used against free kicks from zone 5 should be the same as those used against corner kicks (see section on Defense Against the Corner Kick and Figures 20-77 and 20-78).

- **Zone 6**

Defense against an indirect free kick from zone 6 should be played in a similar manner to that used against kicks from zone 4. However, more than four players may be needed in the defensive wall. If the free kick is awarded at a point closer than 10 yards from the goal line, all defenders should "pack the goal" by standing between the goal posts on the goal line (see Figure 20-47). Their positioning on the goal line should start on the ball side goal post and fill in the goal mouth toward the opposite post. The line of players near the far post may be curved toward the ball and still remain 10 yards from the kick. The goalkeeper should select a position slightly toward the ball side of center of the wall of players. As the ball is played, all defenders should rush forward as a unit to block the shot.

Throw-In On Offense

As players' skills and understanding of the game increase, several factors should be considered in determining who should take the throw-in. Some examples of situations and considerations are presented in Table 20-4. As you become more familiar with the game and the ability of your players, you will begin to make other strategic decisions about the throw-in.

COMMON TACTICAL ERRORS AND THEIR CORRECTIONS

A listing of tactical errors in the throw-in and probable corrections is given in Table 20-5.

• Set Plays for the Throw-In

When play is restarted by a throw-in, the strategy for putting the ball back into play may be spontaneous or it may be preplanned (set play). Selection of an appropriate set play should be based on the ability level of the players and location of the throw-in (see Figure 20-88). Table 20-6 includes examples of set plays that may be helpful to your team.

Table 20-4. Throw-in strategy.

Situation	Consideration
• **Awarded a throw-in on the offensive third of the field near corner kick area**	Have the outside halfback on the throw-in side of the field take the throw-in to increase the number of forwards available to receive the ball.
	or
	Have a field player who can throw the ball the farthest take the throw-in. A long throw toward the opponent's goal from this location can be as effective as a corner kick. You may even use a set play developed for corner kicks.
• **Awarded a throw-in near midfield**	Have the outside fullback on the throw-in side of the field take the throw-in. This should move your halfbacks and forwards upfield to put additional pressure on the defending team. This may be considered when you have relatively skilled fullbacks and the opponents are not likely to counterattack quickly, or when you are trailing by one or two goals late in the game.
• **Awarded a throw-in on the defensive third of the field near the corner kick area**	Have the outside fullback on the throw-in side of the field throw the ball to your goalkeeper in the penalty area. The goalkeeper will be able to advance the ball by punting or throwing it.
	or
	If your team only uses two or three fullbacks or if your opponents have been dominating the play, you may not want to move one of your fullbacks away from your goal and weaken your defense. Therefore, you may want to have an outside halfback on the throw-in side of the field take the throw-in.

Defense Against the Throw-in

Quickly marking attackers is the primary defense against a throw-in. In addition to marking offensive players in the vicinity of the throw, one defender should guard the player making the throw-in.

As players mature, they develop strength and skill to project the ball long distances on the throw-in. Thus, it is important for defenders to have an understanding of the approximate distance the thrower may project the ball and to mark players tightly in this area. A throw-in from a player who has the potential to project the ball into the goal area may be defended as a corner kick (see section on Defense Against the Corner Kick).

SUMMARY

A considerable amount of strategy associated with offensive and defensive play is included in this chapter. This material is presented to provide insight into the tactical aspect of the game of soccer. In order for this material to be functional, coaches must select, modify, and teach strategies that are appropriate for their teams.

Table 20-5. *Tactical errors in taking the throw-in.*

Throw-in Error	Discussion and Probable Correction
• **Taking too much time to take throw-in**	This usually results in teammates being closely marked. Teammates should make fast runs into open spaces with quick changes in directions. or Players should know who is responsible for taking a given throw-in, quickly set up to take the throw-in, and be prepared to execute a set play.
• **Player receiving the throw-in is quickly marked and is forced to dribble around opponent**	Teammates should move to open space so they can receive a pass after the throw-in is performed. or Quickly set up to take the throw-in. This should leave some players unmarked. or Often the player taking the throw-in is not marked. After the throw-in, this player should quickly come back onto the field to receive a return pass.
• **Good throw-in, but the ball cannot be controlled by intended receiver**	The direction, velocity, and distance the ball is thrown are important factors in determining whether or not an intended receiver can control the pass. When practicing throw-ins, the importance of these three factors should be pointed out. Players should be encouraged to make good throw-ins that can be received and controlled by their teammates.

Figure 20-88.
Scheme for assigning beginning level players to take the throw-in.

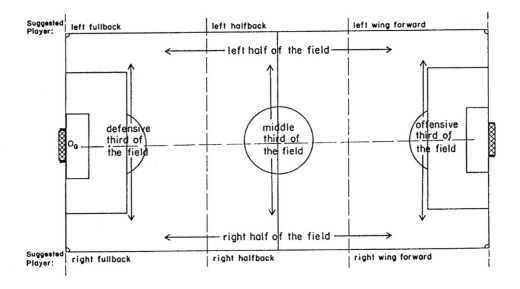

Table 20-6. *Examples of set plays for the throw-in.*

Set Play	Age/Ability Level	Comments/Diagrams
Return pass	8 years and older/beginning and above	The player taking the throw-in is usually unmarked. Therefore, a quick return pass can be effective.
Throw-in to goalkeeper	8 years and older/beginning and above	When your team has throw-in close to the goal you are defending, faking a down-the-line throw-in followed by a throw-in to your own goalkeeper can be effective. This should be done with caution, because if it is intercepted, it puts the goalkeeper in a difficult position. However, if caught by the goalkeeper in the penalty area, the ball can be punted or thrown clear of your goal.
"Who takes the throw-in?"	6 years and older/beginning and above	Players below the age of 9 tend to bunch around the ball. Therefore, it is important for young players to know who should take the throw-in and to quickly put the ball back into play (see Figure 20-88). If beginning level players take a long time, they may not be able to throw beyond the crowded space in front of them.

Table 20-6. continued.

Set Play	Age/Ability Level	Comments/Diagrams
"Down the line"	6 years and older/beginning and above	Have a player break free and run along the touch line toward the opponent's goal. This is especially useful to beginning players in advancing the ball. Note that a player who receives a ball directly from the throw-in is not offside.
Checking runs	10 years and older/intermediate and above	Have players run quickly in one direction and immediately change the direction of their run (e.g., run away from the person taking the throw-in, then toward the thrower). The intent of these checking runs is to fake the defender. However, if unprepared, the thrower may fall for the same fake. Thus, players making checking runs must communicate their intentions to the thrower.
Corner kick throw-in	12 years and older/intermediate and above	When a team has a throw-in close to its opponent's goal, a long throw-in may be taken like a corner kick. The set play could be the same as the set play the team uses for the corner kick.
Switch positions	12 years and older/intermediate and above	Selected offensive players make fast runs in order to exchange positions. Defenders who are cautious about getting out of position may stop marking these players. Thus, some attackers may be free to receive the throw-in.

FUNDAMENTAL PRINCIPLES AND INDIVIDUAL TACTICS OF OFFENSE
Difficulty Rating Form

Level of Player* Approximate Age*	Suggested Emphasis		
	Beginning 6-9 yrs.	Intermediate 10-13 yrs.	Advanced 14 yrs. & up
Penetration	X	X	X
Support			
Positioning near the ball			
depth	X	X	X
wall pass	X	X	X
Movement near the ball			
checking run	X	X	X
overlapping run		X	X
cross-over run		X	X
Mobility			
Blind side run	X	X	X
Diagonal run		X	X
Width			
Positioning off the ball	X	X	X
Movement off the ball			
dummy run		X	X

*Note that the Beginning, Intermediate, and Advanced does not always correspond with the age range given beneath it. Coaches should use this classification system as an approximation, adjusting the techniques to suit their players' ability levels.

FUNDAMENTAL PRINCIPLES, INDIVIDUAL TACTICS, SPECIAL TACTICS AND METHODS OF DEFENSE
Difficulty Rating Form

Level of Player* Approximate Age*	Suggested Emphasis		
	Beginning 6-9 yrs.	Intermediate 10-13 yrs.	Advanced 14 yrs. & up
Delay			
Goal-side marking of the ball	X	X	X
Recovering run	X	X	X
Pressuring the ball	X	X	X
Jockeying	X	X	X
Shepherding		X	X
Depth			
Covering	X	X	X
Supporting	X	X	X
Switching		X	X
Balance			
Diagonal coverage	X	X	X
Shifting toward the ball	X	X	X
Concentration			
Compactness	X	X	X
Overloading	X	X	X
Funneling	X	X	X
Special Defensive Tactics			
Defensive wall		X	X
Offside trap		X	X
Basic Method of Defense			
Zone	X	X	X
Player-to-player	X	X	X
Combination	X	X	X

*Note that the Beginning, Intermediate, and Advanced does not always correspond with the age range given beneath it. Coaches should use this classification system as an approximation, adjusting the techniques to suit their players' ability levels.

DRILLS AND GAMES FOR OFFENSIVE AND DEFENSIVE PRINCIPLES AND TACTICS

NAME	DIAGRAM	DESCRIPTION	KEY POINTS	VARIATIONS
Wall Passing Assists		Approximately half of the players on the team stand scattered within a designated space. The remaining players each dribble a ball among their standing teammates and make wall pass to them. Players must call out the name of the teammate to whom they are passing before initiating the wall pass. Wall passing and dribbling continues until the coach stops the drill. The players then switch roles. (6 years and older)	1. Wall passes should be kept on the ground. 2. The player making the first pass should sprint into an open space to receive a return pass. 3. One touch return passes should be encouraged. 4. Return passes should be good lead passes.	1. Add one or more chasers who attempt to tackle the ball away. If a player loses a ball to a chaser, both players switch roles. (7 years and older)
Checking Runs Assists		Approximately half of the players on the team stand scattered within a designated space with a ball at their feet. The remaining teammates call out the name of a player they want to pass the ball to them after they make a checking run. A player receiving a pass then makes a pass to a teammate making a checking run and calling their name. The drill continues until stopped by the coach. (6 years and older)	1. Passes should be kept on the ground. 2. The player making the checking run should quickly change direction and sprint into an open space. 3. Return passes should be good lead passes.	1. Add one or more defenders who mark players making the checking runs. Defenders intercepting passes switch roles with the player who made the checking run. (7 years and older)

DRILLS AND GAMES FOR OFFENSIVE AND DEFENSIVE PRINCIPLES AND TACTICS

NAME	DIAGRAM	DESCRIPTION	KEY POINTS	VARIATIONS
2 v 1 Keep Away		Two players attempt to maintain possession of the ball by passing and dribbling in an area approximately 10-yards by 10-yards. One defender attempts to gain possession of the ball by tackling it away or intercepting a pass. Whenever possession of the ball is lost or the ball is played out of bounds by an offensive player, the defender switches roles with the offensive player who lost possession and the drill continues without interruption. (6 years and older)	This drill promotes the individual defensive techniques of marking and tackling and the individual offensive techniques of dribbling, shielding, passing, and receiving and controlling. In addition, players may be exposed to offensive tactics (wall passes, checking runs, cross-over runs, blind side runs, and positioning and movement off the ball) and defensive tactics (pressuring the ball, jockeying, and shepherding).	1. By increasing the number of offensive and defensive players (2 v 2, 3 v 2, 3 v 3, 4 v 3, etc.) additional offensive and defensive tactics may be introduced into these drills. Note that as the number of players increases, additional space is needed for these drills. (7 years and older) 2. 3 Touch Keep Away - Each time the ball is passed, the player receiving the ball must pass it to a teammate within 3 touches of the ball or possession is lost to the opposing team. (10 years and older) 3. 2 Touch Keep Away (11 years and older) 4. 1 Touch Keep Away (12 years and older)

DRILLS AND GAMES FOR OFFENSIVE AND DEFENSIVE PRINCIPLES AND TACTICS

NAME	DIAGRAM	DESCRIPTION	KEY POINTS	VARIATIONS
2 v 1 With Two Single Cone Goals		Two players compete against one player. Each team defends one goal and attempts to score on the opposite goal. Goals are scored each time the ball makes contact with a cone. Teams can play to a selected score or for a designated period of time. Note that boundaries to limit the space are not needed. (6 years and older)	See 2v1 Keep Away. Because goals are included in this game, additional offensive and defensive tactics (overlapping run, goal-side marking, recovery run, covering, supporting, switching, and diagonal coverage) become part of the competition.	1. By increasing the number of offensive and defensive players (2 v 2, 3 v 2, 3 v 3, 4 v 3, etc.) additional offensive and defensive tactics may be introduced into these drills. (7 years and older) 2. Use pairs of cones to make two small goals. (6 years and older) 3. Permit scoring from either side of the small goals described in 2. (6 years and older)

DRILLS AND GAMES FOR OFFENSIVE AND DEFENSIVE PRINCIPLES AND TACTICS

NAME	DIAGRAM	DESCRIPTION	KEY POINTS	VARIATIONS
Jockey and Recover		Two attackers (one in possession of the ball) outside the center circle attempt to beat a defender, jockeying from the goal-side of the ball, and a goalkeeper. One additional defender starts outside the opposite side of the center circle and attempts to make a recovery run to participate in the defense. Attackers attempt to score a goal and defenders attempt to prevent a goal by gaining possession of the ball. After each goal or loss of possession, players return to the opposite line. Note that two drills may be going on one field. (7 years and older)	1. The jockeying player should attempt to delay the attack to permit the recovering player to participate in the defense, should maintain goal-side marking, and could use an offside trap to gain possession of the ball. 2. The recovering player should sprint toward the center of the goal and get to a goal-side marking position as soon as possible. 3. Attacking players should advance the ball quickly to prevent the defense from recovering. 4. The goalkeeper should communicate with the defense and be prepared for a shot on goal.	

DRILLS AND GAMES FOR OFFENSIVE AND DEFENSIVE PRINCIPLES AND TACTICS

NAME	DIAGRAM	DESCRIPTION	KEY POINTS	VARIATIONS
Offense vs Defense		Assign players to two teams. One team, designated as offense, has forwards and halfbacks in positions normally used by your team. The other team, designated as defense, has a goalkeeper, fullbacks, and halfbacks in positions normally used by your team. The offense attempts to score. The defense attempts to gain possession of the ball and clear it through either pair of flags positioned at midfield. The defense is given one goal for five clears. Offense and defense compete to score the most goals. After the ball is passed beyond the halfway line or a goal is scored, the offense restarts play at midfield. (7 years and older)	This half field scrimmage provides an opportunity to practice virtually all offensive and defensive tactics of play. The coach can interject various restarts even though they may not be called for by the rules, to provide team practice on offense and defense. This game also encourages quick transition from defense to offense and offense to defense.	

DRILLS AND GAMES FOR OFFENSIVE AND DEFENSIVE PRINCIPLES AND TACTICS

NAME	DIAGRAM	DESCRIPTION	KEY POINTS	VARIATIONS
Defending Against the Overlap		In groups of three, two attackers attempt to beat one defender by using an overlapping run. If the ball is tackled away, the defender switches roles with one of the attackers and the drill is repeated. If the ball is not tackled away, the attacker with the ball starts the drill again as the player at the point of attack. (10 years and older)	1. In this drill, both goal-side marking of the ball and overlapping are practiced. 2. The player making the overlap should call out "overlap" to alert the player with the ball. 3. If the defender continues to mark the ball, a pass should be made to the overlapping player. 4. If the defender marks the overlapping player, the player with the ball should advance the ball by dribbling.	1. Add a support player, behind the defender, who guards whichever player is not marked after the overlap occurs. (10 years and older)
Cross-Over Assists		Approximately half of the players have a ball to dribble. They make cross-over runs with their teammates and either exchange or retain possession of the ball. The activity is continuously repeated with different pairs of players crossing paths. (10 years and older)	1. If the ball is to be exchanged, it should be left for and not passed to the crossing teammate. 2. After crossing, both teammates should accelerate their runs.	1. Add one or more defenders who attempt to tackle the ball away. Defenders, who intercept the ball, switch roles with players who lose possession. (11 years and older)

DRILLS AND GAMES FOR OFFENSIVE AND DEFENSIVE PRINCIPLES AND TACTICS

NAME	DIAGRAM	DESCRIPTION	KEY POINTS	VARIATIONS
Neutral Zone	(field diagram with Attack Zone, Neutral Zone, Attack Zone)	Form three teams of four to six players. Each team should wear different colored scrimmage vests. Use cones to form a neutral zone 20-yards wide across the center of the field. The game is started with one team in each attack zone and one team in possession of the ball in the neutral zone. The team in possession of the ball attempts to score a goal against a team in an attack zone. Standard rules of play are used except: a. If the attacking team scores, they maintain possession of the ball and are given unobstructed movement of the ball back to the neutral zone from which they begin their attack against the defending team in the opposite attack zone. b. If the defending team gains possession of the ball and advances it under control back to the neutral zone, they become the attacking team and may attempt to score on the opposite goal. c. The attacking team may relieve defensive pressure by returning to the neutral zone where defenders are not permitted.	In this game, all offensive and defensive tactics may be encountered. It encourages a mid field buildup of attack and back passes to the neutral zone to relieve defensive pressure. It also provides time for each defensive unit to reorganize and prepare for the attack.	

DRILLS AND GAMES FOR OFFENSIVE AND DEFENSIVE PRINCIPLES AND TACTICS

NAME	DIAGRAM	DESCRIPTION	KEY POINTS	VARIATIONS
Neutral Zone (continued)		d. If the ball is played without control (as judged by the coach) into the neutral zone by the defending team, possession is given back to the attacking team and they continue their attack. At the end of the game, the team that has scored the most goals and the goalkeeper who has permitted the fewest goals are the winners. (10 years and up)		

DRILLS AND GAMES FOR OFFENSIVE AND DEFENSIVE PRINCIPLES AND TACTICS

NAME	DIAGRAM	DESCRIPTION	KEY POINTS	VARIATIONS
2 Ball Small-Sided Game		Two teams compete using two balls. Either team may be in possession of both, one, or neither ball. Standard rules of play are followed. After a goal is scored, the ball is put back into play by a goal kick by the team scored against. (10 years and older)	This type of game adds complexity to the strategy of play. When players revert to competition in which one ball is used, they can more easily handle the tactics of play.	1. 3 Touch (10 years and older) 2. 2 Touch (12 years and older) 3. Score from either side of goal (boundaries not needed) (12 years and older) 4. Assign one ball for each team. Only permit scoring by a team with its assigned ball. (11 years and older)
Keep Away Score		Two small sided teams compete against each other. During the first period, one team attempts to maintain possession of the ball without shooting on their opponent's goal while the other team attempts to score as many goals as possible. During a second period of equal time to the first period, the teams reverse roles. The team scoring the most goals wins the game. Period length (generally up to 4 minutes), number of players per side (generally 4-8), and size of the field must be determined by the coach. This game can be played with a small or full size goal and with or without goalkeepers. If goalkeepers are used, they must play keep away with their feet when not defending a goal. (10 years and older)	This game emphasizes both offensive and defensive tactics. When a team is not attempting to score, it tries to regain and maintain possession of the ball. Once this team has possession, it employs many of the individual and team tactics to create time and space to make it easier to maintain possession. When a team is attempting to score, it must regain and maintain possession to attack their opponent's goal.	1. 3 Touch Keep Away-Score (12 years and older) 2. 2 Touch Keep Away-Score (13 years and older)

DRILLS AND GAMES FOR OFFENSIVE AND DEFENSIVE PRINCIPLES AND TACTICS

NAME	DIAGRAM	DESCRIPTION	KEY POINTS	VARIATIONS
3 Sided Soccer		Three teams of 4 to 6 players compete simultaneously. Team 1 defends its goal from team 3 and attempts to score on team 2. Team 2 defends its goal from team 1 and attempts to score on team 3. Team 3 defends its goal from team 2 and attempts to score on team 1. A ball that goes out of play over a goal line is thrown back into play by the team defending the goal on that goal line. After a goal, the ball is put back into play from a goal kick by the team scored upon. (12 years and older)	See key points for 2 Ball Small-Sided Game.	1. 3 Touch (12 years and older) 2. 2 Touch (13 years and older) 3. 3 Sided Soccer with two balls (14 years and older)

SECTION VII
SPORTS MEDICINE AND TRAINING

21

CONDITIONING YOUTH SOCCER PLAYERS

Jeanne Foley, Paul Vogel, and Eugene W. Brown

QUESTIONS TO CONSIDER
- What are the energy production systems and how important are they to performance in soccer?
- What are muscular strength, power, endurance, and flexibility and how important are they to performance in soccer?
- What are the five principles of training that should be used when conditioning youth soccer players?
- What are interval training, circuit training, and weight training and how can they be used to enhance the conditioning of your athletes?

INTRODUCTION

Aerobics, anaerobics, strength, power, and endurance are some of the many terms that may lend confusion to your understanding of sport conditioning. The goals of this chapter are to provide you with an understanding of the basic principles of conditioning and how these principles apply to soccer. In order to provide you with a more detailed understanding of the process involved in conditioning, so you can appropriately apply these concepts to your players, this chapter will address several factors associated with conditioning youth soccer players.

Sport conditioning is the participation in physical activity, intended to enhance the energy production and muscular systems of the body, which may supplement and improve the performance of learned sport skills in future play.

ENERGY PRODUCTION SYSTEMS

Anyone who has played or watched soccer knows that a lot of energy is required to participate in the game. Sport scientists have discovered that the body can produce energy for physical activity by two different systems—*aerobic system* and *anaerobic system*. Muscle cells, which use the energy, can only store enough energy for about 10 to 30 seconds of all-out exercise. When this immediate energy supply is used up, new energy is generated by one of these two energy "refill" systems.

Aerobic System

The aerobic system is called the "endurance" system. In this system, food, the body's fuel, is converted into energy in the presence of oxygen. The aerobic system functions during long duration, low intensity exercise. This type of activity allows the body plenty of time to replace the oxygen that is used up during the production of energy in working muscles.

The aerobic system is very efficient because it converts fuel into energy with relatively little waste and produces little unnecessary heat. The aerobic system can function for extended periods of time because it can produce energy from fats, carbohydrates, and protein.

Protein is not a major source of energy for exercise except in cases of extreme starvation.

Carbohydrates are stored in a limited supply in the muscles and liver and can be used for both aerobic and anaerobic work.

Fats can be used *only* by the aerobic system. The virtually unlimited supply of this fuel, stored as adipose tissue or fat, is the basis for the long-term functioning of the aerobic system.

Conditioning the aerobic system is a necessary base for energy system conditioning in soccer. The reasons for this are twofold:

- *Soccer has an endurance component.*

  The soccer player with a well-conditioned aerobic system is not as susceptible to fatigue toward the end of a contest. The delayed onset of fatigue in an aerobically fit athlete can also be a factor in determining how much high quality work can be accomplished during lengthy practice sessions and games.

- *The body learns to "spare" carbohydrates.*

  As the aerobic system is trained, the body learns to use more fat for fuel and to conserve carbohydrates for the high intensity (anaerobic) activities.

Anaerobic System

High speed or sprint-type activities require a refilling of the muscle cells' energy supplies at a faster rate than is possible by the aerobic system. In this situation, energy production switches over to a special, faster operating system that converts carbohydrates into energy without using oxygen. This system is called anaerobic, meaning "without oxygen." As with any emergency procedure, there are trade-offs that must be made. In order to gain the advantage of quicker replenishment of energy supplies, the anaerobic system suffers two limitations.

- *Reduced efficiency*

  For each sugar (carbohydrate) unit consumed, the anaerobic system can produce only three basic energy units. On the other hand, the aerobic system can produce 39 units from the same fuel source. The aerobic system is therefore 13 times more efficient than the anaerobic system. This explains why the body uses the anaerobic system only in emergency conditions when the body has to produce energy faster than it can supply oxygen for the aerobic system.

- *Oxygen debt*

  The anaerobic system produces a byproduct called lactic acid that is not produced by the aerobic system. This chemical quickly builds up in fast-working muscles, causing temporary fatigue, discomfort, and impaired performance. The only way the body can get rid of lactic acid is to slow down and use the aerobic system to convert the lactic acid into usable fuel. In other words, using the anaerobic system leaves the body with an "oxygen debt" in the form of lactic acid buildup. This debt must be paid off by slowing down and taking in enough oxygen to remove the lactic acid by using the aerobic system. This explains why the term "catching your breath" makes sense from a scientific as well as a practical viewpoint.

The anaerobic system can produce energy at high speed for about 30 to 90 seconds or at a moderate speed for about 90 seconds to three minutes before the oxygen debt forces the body to slow down so it can switch to the aerobic system. After a recovery period, during which the oxygen debt is paid back, the anaerobic system can be turned on again to give another short burst of high speed work. This alternating of sprint work and recovery periods can be continued only until the body's stores of carbohydrates are used up or until the lactic acid removal system can no longer keep up with the rate of anaerobic work.

The energy production system responds to anaerobic training in three major ways:

- *by learning to tolerate larger amounts of lactic acid.*

  This adaptation can be understood by thinking of an anaerobically conditioned body as one that has earned a larger "oxygen credit line" and therefore being allowed to build up a larger oxygen debt before having to start paying it back. Thus, the body can adapt in order to maintain high intensity work for longer periods of time.

- *by reducing the recovery period.*

  The body can adapt and pay back the oxygen debt more quickly thereby reducing the recovery time required before the anaerobic system can be used again.

- *by increasing the rate at which the anaerobic system can operate.*

This adaptation affects the speed at which the system can produce energy.

A summary of the two energy production systems is presented in Table 21-1.

Table 21-1. *Energy Production Summary*

Energy Production Systems	Characteristics
Aerobic	• produces energy from fuel with oxygen • efficient • no lactic acid produced • slow rate of energy production • can use fats, carbohydrates, or protein as fuel
Anaerobic	• produces energy from fuel without oxygen • inefficient • produces lactic acid as a by-product • fast rate of energy production • can only use carbohydrates for fuel

USE OF THE ENERGY SYSTEMS IN SOCCER

Now that the basic principles of the energy production systems have been presented, let's take a look at the sport of soccer and determine where its requirements fit on the energy scale from aerobic to anaerobic. In analyzing the relative importance of the two energy systems in soccer, the main concept to keep in mind is that *performance time and effort determine the extent to which the aerobic, anaerobic, or both systems are called upon.*

Is soccer primarily an aerobic or an anaerobic sport? The extent of importance of each of the energy systems in soccer is influenced by the age and skill level of the players as well as the position they play. For example, the work rate of a beginning youth player should not be expected to equal that of a paid professional player. Similarly, the energy requirements to play the goalkeeper position are considerably different than the energy requirements to play a midfield position. However, soccer can be generally considered as a sport that places a relatively high demand on both the aerobic and anaerobic systems (see Figure 21-1). It consists of endurance activity, all-out sprints, and even rest periods. During all-out sprints, the anaerobic system is called upon. The aerobic system is used during recovery, to pay back the debts piled up by the less efficient anaerobic system, and during longer periods of low-level work. Thus, it is important to condition both of these energy systems to meet the specific soccer demands associated with age, skill, and positional play.

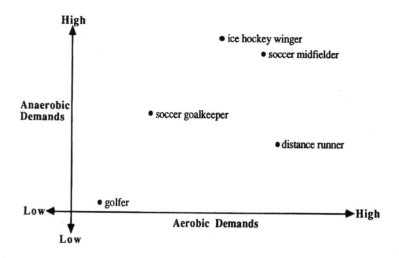

Figure 21-1. Graph, with examples by sport and position, of the aerobic/anaerobic continuum.

MUSCULAR SYSTEM

Besides requiring large amounts of energy to play soccer, the sport also demands a lot of muscular force. Shooting the ball, accelerating to outrun a defensive player, jumping to head the ball, and a long throw-in are only some of the many examples of forceful actions in soccer.

Muscles can produce force only by shortening or contracting. All muscle forces, therefore, are pulling forces and not pushing forces. For example, if you forcefully bend (flex) your knee, the muscles in the back of the thigh (hamstrings) are active. On the other hand, forceful straightening (extension) of the knee, is caused by contraction of the muscles in the front of the thigh (quadriceps). Almost all muscles in the body operate in this paired fashion. As one muscle (or muscle group) shortens to pull a body part in a particular direction, the paired muscle (or muscle group) relaxes and allows the movement to take place. To cause movement in the opposite direction, the muscles simply reverse their roles. If it is desirable to hold a body part in a fixed position, both muscles in the pair exert force to stabilize the joint.

When planning to condition the muscular system for soccer, several factors need to be addressed. In addition to the "muscle pair" concept, the components of muscular power, endurance, and flexibility; age and ability level of the players; and the specific muscular needs for participation in the sport must be carefully considered. These factors are covered in the following sections.

Muscular Power

The force that a muscle can apply is called muscular strength. In soccer, many of the movements not only require large muscular forces, but these forces must be exerted during short periods of time. This concept of rate of application of muscular force is called muscular power.

Muscular Endurance

Power is the high intensity component of muscular conditioning. There is also a low intensity aspect, the muscular endurance component. Muscular endurance refers to the ability of a muscle to exert a sub-maximal force for a prolonged period of time.

Scientists have shown that there are actually different types of muscle fibers within a muscle. Some of these fibers, called fast-twitch or white fibers, are used primarily for brief, powerful muscular movements. Other fibers, called slow-twitch or red fibers, are mainly used for longer, low-intensity movements. As with the aerobic and anaerobic energy systems, the power and endurance components of the muscular system require different types of conditioning.

Flexibility

Flexibility refers to the range of motion of a joint or the range through which the muscle groups can move the bones of a joint without causing injury.

Stretching exercises, used as part of a conditioning program to maintain or increase flexibility, are often ignored by coaches and athletes. However, flexibility exercises are an important component of a soccer conditioning program. They may reduce the occurrence of certain injuries and enhance the performance of certain techniques.

- *Reducing injury potential*

  When muscles are worked hard, there is a temporary breakdown in their tissue. This breakdown is quickly repaired, but the muscle fibers become shortened unless they are stretched. A shortened, inflexible muscle on one side of the joint won't be able to readily stretch when its muscle pair on the opposite side of the joint fully contracts. The result may be a muscle tear (strain) or damage to the connective tissues of the joint (sprain). Flexibility exercises may reduce the occurrence of these types of injuries.

- *Enhancing performance*

  Lack of flexibility may inhibit or prevent the performance of certain techniques. For example, limited trunk flexibility may retard a player's ability to make a long throw-in. Similarly, a player may not be able to receive and control a high air ball with the inside of the foot because of a lack of flexibility in the hip joint. These are only two of the many examples of the influence of flexibility on performance.

USE OF THE MUSCULAR SYSTEM IN SOCCER

Picture again a typical game of soccer. How would you rate the three muscular factors of power, endurance, and flexibility in terms of their importance to successful performance? (See Figure 21-2.) Clearly, most of the actions in soccer can be characterized as powerful movements. Along with powerful, high-force actions comes a high risk of injury, so flexibility should also be a high priority in conditioning for soccer. Finally, for the same reasons aerobic fitness is necessary in conditioning the energy systems for soccer, a muscular endurance base is required by the repetitive nature of the movements.

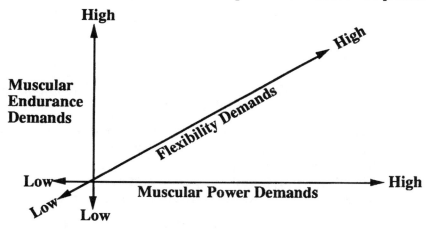

Where should the various positions in soccer be placed?

Figure 21-2. *Graph showing the continuum of the muscular system demands.*

How to Condition for Soccer

Now that we have examined conditioning, we can turn to the problem of how to develop programs to promote the kind of conditioning needed for soccer.

You should now have a basic knowledge of the underlying concepts of conditioning. The contrasts between the aerobic and anaerobic ends of the energy production continuum have been described. Three critical aspects of the muscular system continuum (power, endurance, and flexibility) have been explained. Both the energy production systems and the muscular system have been analyzed in relation to their specific applications to soccer. Now we come to the practical application of this information. How can you as a coach use the discoveries of the sport scientists to develop better soccer players?

Five Principles of Training

The following five principles of training should be used as guidelines for conditioning both the energy production and muscular systems.

1. Warm-Up/Cool Down

Before beginning a training session or game, jogging with the ball, calisthenics, soccer-specific exercises, and stretching should be used to prepare the body for more strenuous activity. A program for accomplishing this goal, as well as cooling down the body after strenuous exercise, is outlined in Supplement 1 later in this chapter. Warm-up activities increase the breathing rate, heart rate, and muscle temperature to exercise levels. Warm-up also causes cartilage pads in the joints to absorb fluids, thereby increasing their shock-absorbing capabilities. It is a period in which the athlete becomes more aware of his/her surroundings (field conditions, space, position of the sun, structural hazards, etc.) and gradually reacquainted with the demands of more vigorous activity to follow. Providing the opportunity for your athletes to become aware of their surroundings and sensitive to the demands of the sport are important factors in reducing the potential for injury.

Proper warm-up can thus improve performance and reduce the likelihood of injury to the athlete. Note that the warm-up should **not** be used as a conditioning period. Having your players exercise too hard during warm-ups defeats the purpose of this period and may cause, rather than prevent, injuries. Stretching exercises are appropriate **after** a warm-up.

As the age of the athlete group increases, a greater amount of time is needed to warm-up for exercises. Seven year olds may only need five minutes to warm up, whereas, 18 year olds may need as much as 10 to 15 minutes of warm-up exercises. It is, however, important to include a warm-up interval before practices and games even with the youngest athletes, because this proper approach to training may persist as they grow older.

After a workout session or game, the body should be cooled down. This process should include light, aerobic activity (e.g., jogging with the ball) to help the body clear out any remaining lactic acid from the muscles and to reduce the pooling of blood in the extremities. This will reduce soreness and speed the recovery process in preparation for the next day's activities. The cool down should also be followed by stretching exercises, as emphasized earlier, to help maintain flexibility.

2. Overload

In order to cause a change to take place in the energy production and muscular systems, a stress must be applied to these systems. Repeatedly demanding more than usual of a bodily system causes the system to respond by changing to a state in which it can more easily handle that stress. Overload does **not** mean placing an impossibly heavy work load on the system, but rather, asking the system to work harder than it is normally accustomed to doing, without reaching a work load at which injury may occur.

Regulation of the overload is the basis
of all conditioning programs.

There are five factors that can be manipulated to produce an exercise overload within a workout:

- *Load*

  This is the resistance to muscular force. It can be the body, a body part, or any object, such as a weight, which is to be moved. Systematic variation of resistance (load) can be used to create an exercise overload to enhance the development of muscular strength.

- *Repetitions*

  This is the number of times muscular force must be applied in attempting to move a load. Conditioning of the aerobic energy-production system and enhanced muscular endurance result from progressively increasing the number of repetitions of muscular contraction.

- *Duration*

  This is the length of time muscular force is applied in performing a set (bout) of repetitions. Similar to a systematic increase in repetitions, increasing duration of exercise can be used to enhance the aerobic energy-production system and muscular endurance.

- *Frequency*

  The rate of exercise (number of repetitions for a given time unit) is the frequency. As frequency increases, exercises shift from having a conditioning effect on the aerobic energy-production system and muscular endurance to having a conditioning effect on the anaerobic energy-production system and muscular power.

- *Rest*

  The recovery interval between bouts of exercise, during which a muscle or muscle group is moderately inactive to inactive, is the rest period. Note that rest for the anaerobic system also may occur when the frequency of exercise is reduced so the demands of the exercise are placed upon the aerobic system.

3. Progression

The overload principle must be applied in progressive stages. Conditioning must start with an exercise intensity the body can handle, allowing time for recovery from the physical stress, before progressing to an increased work level. Overloading your athletes too rapidly or failing to allow sufficient time for them to recover between workouts can cause injury or illness rather than enhance their fitness.

A good example to keep in mind is the method by which muscles get stronger. A training overload actually causes a temporary breakdown of the muscle fibers, which are then repaired to an even stronger state. If the muscles are overloaded again before the repair period is over, the result may be further damage instead of adaptation. Coaches should be familiar with the signs of overtraining as outlined in Chapter 23 (Prevention of Common Soccer Injuries) and should monitor their athletes closely to make sure they are progressing at a rate their bodies can handle.

4. Specificity

In order to activate the energy production systems, the muscular system must also be activated. Even though this relationship exists, it is important to carefully consider the desired nature of conditioning when selecting physical activity to achieve these goals.

Physical exercises have specific conditioning effects. Stretching the hip joints will have little, if any, influence on increasing the power of the muscles that move these joints. Exercises to strengthen the calf muscles will not increase the strength of the stomach muscles. Similarly, a well-conditioned gymnast is not likely to possess the type of fitness required for soccer. Thus, when planning a conditioning program, it is important to first assess the demands of soccer on your players in order to select exercises and manipulate the overload factors to help condition your players to meet these specific demands.

The specific components of the energy and muscular systems can be conditioned by application of the following general guidelines to overload these systems. However, these guidelines must be applied in conditioning the energy and muscular systems associated with the specific demands of soccer.

Training the Energy Production Systems

- Aerobic system—endurance activities involving moderate exercise intensity of large body segments or the whole body. Some examples include running and dribbling the soccer ball, swimming laps, running, and bicycling long distances. Running and dribbling the soccer ball is more desirable for soccer than the other aerobic activities because it has a more specific training effect for the sport.

- Anaerobic system—"sprint" type activities involving very intense exercise of large body segments or the whole body. The same exercises, as listed for aerobic training, are appropriate activities for anaerobic training. However, distances must be reduced and the intensity increased. This results in sprint dribbling, swimming, running, and bicycling. Again, sprint dribbling would have a more specific training effect for soccer. By dribbling, players would be concomitantly developing their techniques along with anaerobic conditioning.

Training the Muscular System

- Power—exercises, by specific muscle groups, involving the rapid application of relatively large forces and few repetitions.

- Endurance—exercises, by specific muscle groups, involving the application of relatively small forces and many repetitions.

- Flexibility—repetition of slow and sustained (six to 30 seconds) stretching of specific muscle groups to the point of slight discomfort.

5. Reversibility

It is not enough to plan and carry out a developmental conditioning program. Once an athlete's body attains a certain fitness level, a maintenance program is necessary to prevent the conditioning benefits from being lost.

Studies on athletes have shown that even starting players will experience a decrease in fitness level during the competitive season unless provisions are made to maintain conditioning throughout the season. The maintenance program does not have to be as frequent or as intense as the build-up program, but without a minimal program of this type, the hard-earned fitness will gradually be lost.

METHODS FOR CONDITIONING

Regulation of the exercise overload is the basis for all conditioning programs. As previously stated, this can be accomplished by manipulating the factors of load, repetition, duration, frequency, and rest. There are three distinct training methods that can be used to effectively manipulate these factors to enhance conditioning. These methods are *interval training, circuit training,* and *weight training.*

Interval Training

This type of training was first used in training runners. Interval training, however, has been used in many sports, including soccer. Interval training involves a period of vigorous exercise followed by a recovery period. It functions by using aerobic and anaerobic activities to condition the energy production systems. By gradually increasing the duration, intensity, and number of exercise bouts and by decreasing the rest interval between bouts, an overload can be achieved.

Interval training can be adapted to soccer by alternating bouts of intense practice on basic skills, such as dribbling, with recovery periods. In fact, a series of practice sessions can be structured with an interval training basis. The first session would consist of relatively low intensity exercises of short duration with relatively long rest intervals; whereas, in subsequent practice sessions, the exercise intensity and duration would be increased and the number and duration of rest intervals would be decreased. It should be noted that in interval training, rest periods can be used for rest, water breaks, strategy sessions, team organization, and light aerobic activity.

The specific conditioning components enhanced by an interval training program depend upon the nature of the exercises included in the program. A systematic interval training program can improve the energy production systems (aerobic and anaerobic) as well as the strength and endurance of specific muscle groups that are exercised. A year-round interval training program for highly skilled and motivated players who are 14 years of age or older is included in Supplement 2.

Circuit Training

This type of training involves participation in a variety of activities in rapid succession. These activities are conducted at various locations (stations) around the soccer field. The team is divided so about an equal number of players are at each station. When the circuit begins, all players attempt to perform their best at the tasks assigned to each station within a set time. Successive stations should differ in the demand they place on the body. For example, an intense leg exercise should not be followed by a dribbling drill. Recovery occurs as the groups rotate, within a specified time interval, to the next station and as subsequent stations differ in their demands upon the body.

In circuit training an exercise overload is produced by:

- increasing the number of stations in the circuit,
- increasing the number of repetitions or work intensity at one or more stations,
- increasing the time for exercise at each station,
- increasing the number of times the circuit is completed, and
- decreasing the recovery period between stations.

The variety of activities that can be included in a circuit provides the opportunity to be flexible in creating different and specific exercise overloads as well as simultaneously enhancing skill. Supplement 3 contains an example of a soccer training circuit and recording form, which can be photocopied as is, as well as a blank form upon which you can implement your own training circuit to meet the specific needs of your players.

Weight Training

This type of training involves the lifting of weights to produce an exercise overload. In weight training, a variety of sub-maximal lifts are performed to produce increased strength, power, and endurance in the specific muscle groups that are exercised. In general, weight training involves applying the Five Principles of Training to produce increases in muscular strength.

Following the Five Principles of Training, the first part of a weight training routine is the *warm-up* and *stretching* program. The weight resistance is the *overload,* which is increased in a *progression* as the athlete's workout record indicates gains in strength. Analysis of the strength requirements of soccer (*specificity*) has resulted in the list of exercises outlined in Supplement 2. The *cool down* and post-lifting stretching routine decreases muscle soreness and prevents loss of flexibility. Finally, once strength gains are achieved, the maintenance program must be used to avoid *reversal* of strength increases acquired during the developmental program.

In weight training, an exercise overload can be produced by varying the:

- exercise load,

- number of repetitions per set,

- frequency of exercise during each set,

- number of sets, and

- length of rest interval between exercise sets.

The exercise load determines the number of repetitions of an exercise an athlete can perform during each set. Generally, no fewer than eight repetitions per set of each exercise are recommended when attempting to increase muscular strength for soccer. However, if increased muscular endurance is the goal of a particular weight training exercise, a) the load should be decreased to permit a much greater number of repetitions, b) the number of sets should be increased to three or more, and c) the rest intervals between sets should be decreased. On the other hand, if increase in muscular power is the goal, this can be achieved by rapidly and repeatedly lifting a relatively heavy load eight to 12 repetitions per set.

It should be noted that it is possible to train some muscle groups to increase power and others to increase endurance. The degree to which either component increases depends upon the specific nature of the overload condition.

Several factors should be carefully considered before engaging your players in a weight training program. These factors include:

- *Age of the athletes*

    A weight training program for soccer is not recommended for players under 14 years of age.

- *Level of interest*

  A weight training program is not an essential element for participants in a recreational league. However, a weight training program can be beneficial to highly skillful players who are interested in participating in a very competitive league.

- *Availability of facilities and equipment*

  Sites and equipment for weight training may not be accessible. Before encouraging your athletes to participate in a weight training program, some investigation of availability is needed.

- *Availability of qualified adults*

  Before encouraging your players to participate in a particular weight training program, a qualified adult must be available to supervise the weight room and to provide instruction in proper spotting and performance techniques for each of the suggested exercises.

Because of the great variety of weight training equipment and the availability of many books and guides to weight training, only general guidelines are presented here. A suggested program of weight training exercises appropriate for the highly skilled soccer player who is 14 years of age or older is included in Supplement 2. These exercises can be done using either free weights or weight machines. The guidelines given cover training schedules and how to fit a weight training program into the overall plan of the season. Specific techniques and explanations of weight training exercises can be found in manuals available in most local bookstores. Some references are:

- *Shape Up for Soccer* by Rich Hunter and Pete Broccoletti (Icarus Press, 1981). Specifically designed for the training of soccer players.

- *Strength Training by the Experts* by Daniel P. Riley (2nd edition, Leisure Press, 1982). Covers a variety of equipment, including free weights, Nautilus, and Universal. Explains which muscle groups are used in each exercise.

- *Weightlifting for Beginners* by Bill Reynolds (Contemporary Books, 1982). Designed primarily for free weights and at-home weight training.

Economical Training

The relative importance of conditioning for soccer must be put into perspective with the importance of meeting the cognitive, psychosocial, strategy, and sport techniques needs of your players. As a soccer coach, you must address all of these needs, to varying degrees, during practices and games. However, because of the limited amount of time available to meet the needs of your players, whenever possible, you should plan activities that simultaneously meet needs in more than one area. This approach is referred to as economical training. If practice sessions are carefully planned, it is possible to devise activities that simultaneously meet needs in more than one area. For example, the intensity, duration, and structure of a dribbling drill could be organized to enhance components of conditioning and strategy, as well as techniques of dribbling.

---

*It is easier to get 14-year-olds in condition to play
than it is to make up for the years in which
they were not taught the techniques of the game.*

The concept of economical training is presented here because many coaches erroneously set aside blocks of time within their practices for conditioning-only activities. Push ups, sit ups, sprints, and distance running are typical of what is included in these conditioning-only blocks of time. With youth players who have not achieved a high level of mastery of the techniques of the game, conditioning-only activities are not recommended. Practice time needs to be spent on learning the techniques and strategies of the game of soccer, with conditioning an accompanying outcome as the result of planned economical training. As players develop a higher level of mastery of the techniques of soccer, conditioning-only activities could be included in practices. However, they should be made as closely related to soccer as possible.

SUMMARY

In this chapter you have learned how the energy and muscular systems work, how they are used in soccer, and how to condition these systems. Although separate conditioning-only workouts were not recommended for the under-14 age group, guidelines were given for incorporating the principles of training into the regular practices for the double purpose of skill improvement and enhanced conditioning (economical training). Athletes begin to require and benefit from supplementary programs for conditioning the energy and muscular systems around the age of 14. Examples of such programs have been provided, with guidelines for varying the training at different points in the year. Suggested schedules and workout routines to guide this training are provided in the supplements.

A basic knowledge of the scientific principles of physical conditioning will help you design effective practices and training sessions. It will also help you communicate to your athletes the importance of each type of conditioning activity you use. Conveying this understanding to your players will not only make them more knowledgeable, but will also help them develop good lifelong habits and attitudes towards exercise and fitness.

SUGGESTED READINGS

Fox, E.L. (1979). *Sports physiology*. Philadelphia: W. B. Saunders.

Lamb, D.R. (1984). *Physiology of exercise* (2nd ed.). New York: Macmillan.

Sharkey, B. (1984). *Physiology of fitness* (2nd ed.). Champaign, IL: Human Kinetics Publishers.

Stone, W.V. & Knoll, W.K. (1978). *Sports conditioning and weight training*. Boston: Allyn and Bacon.

WARM-UP, COOL DOWN, AND STRETCHING ACTIVITIES FOR SOCCER

The players' preparation for each practice and game should begin with a warm-up session and should be followed by a cool down period. Warm-up and cool down activities should be conducted at light to moderate intensities and should be followed by stretching exercises.

Warm-up

Warm-up activities should be performed to increase the breathing rate, heart rate, and muscle temperature to exercise levels. These are done to prepare the body for the demands of subsequent strenuous activities. Additionally, warm-ups enhance the players' awareness for their surroundings, especially as it relates to the condition of the field. Warm-ups can also be used as a valuable introduction in setting the tone of the players' attitude toward the activity to follow. Warm-ups for sport should involve the regions of the body upon which more intense exercise demands will be placed during training for and participation in the sport. Thus, with soccer, virtually all regions of the body should be prepared. The following categories included some examples of warm-ups that can be used for soccer.

- **Light Aerobic/General Warm-ups**

  - Jogging
  - Jogging in place
  - Jumping jacks

- **Light Aerobic/Soccer-Specific Warm-ups**

  - Dancing with the ball—Alternating touching the ball with the right and left foot to the top of the ball.
  - Jogging and dribbling the ball
  - Independent dribbling—Individual, free-lance dribbling and maneuvering of the soccer ball is performed.
  - Independent passing—Partner, free-lance dribbling, maneuvering, and passing of the soccer ball is performed.
  - Juggling the soccer ball
  - Seated juggling—The ball is juggled with the feet, while the player maintains a seated position on the ground.

- **Body Region-Specific Warm-ups**

  - Neck rolls—The head is rolled from shoulder, to chest, to opposite shoulder, and the procedure is reversed and repeated.

  (Note: Do not make complete head circle. There is potential for compression of the vertebrae when the neck is hyperextended.)

  - Shoulder circles—With arms horizontal and to the side of the body, small circular rotations of the arms are made. These circles are gradually increased. This pattern is then repeated; however, the arms are rotated in the opposite direction.

  - Trunk circles—While standing with the feet shoulder-width apart and the hands on the hips, the trunk is moved in a circular manner.

  (Note: Avoid an excessive arch of the low back by keeping the head in an upright position.)

Stretching

Stretching should be performed by *slowly and gently extending each muscle group and joint to the point of slight discomfort.* This position should be held for six to 30 seconds. The stretch should then be released and repeated in the same manner two or more times. *Bouncing or fast, jerky movements are inappropriate* in that they activate the muscles' stretch reflex mechanism and, therefore, limit rather than enhance flexibility.

Stretching exercises, used as part of a soccer conditioning program to maintain or increase flexibility, may reduce the occurrence of certain injuries, such as muscle strains and joint sprains, and may enhance performance of certain techniques. Because soccer involves virtually all major muscle groups and joints of the body, a variety of flexibility exercises, targeted at these regions, should be a part of each pre- and post-practice and game. The following flexibility exercises are some examples that are appropriate for soccer.

- Calf stretch—With the legs straddled in a forward-backward alignment, the knee of the back leg is bent while the entire sole of the back foot maintains contact with the ground. By switching the position of the feet, the other calf is stretched.

- High road-low road (hamstring stretch)—In a seated position with the knees straight, players roll a ball on the ground around their feet, legs, and back.

- Kneeling quad stretch—From a kneeling position, the hip is pressed forward. By switching the positions of the legs, the other quadiceps muscle and hip joint are stretched. Note that this exercise also stretches the trunk.

- Seated straddle (groin stretch)—From a seated position with the legs straddled, the trunk is moved forward. The head should be kept upright to reduce pressure on the lower back.

- Butterfly (groin stretch)—In a seated position, place the soles of the feet together with the knees bent no more than 90 degrees. Grasp the ankles with the hands and apply pressure with the elbows to the inside of the legs to rotate the legs outward. Keep the back straight with the head in an upright position.

- Trunk and hip stretch—From a supine position, both arms are placed 90 degrees from the trunk. The head is turned toward one of the outstretched arms while bringing the opposite leg (90 degrees from the trunk) over the midline of the body and toward the ground. This exercise should be performed on both sides.

- Shoulder stretch—Bend the elbow and position the arm behind the head. The hand of the opposite arm grasps the bent elbow and slowly pulls it toward the midline of the trunk. To stretch the other shoulder, the roles of the arms are switched.

Cool Down

The importance of cooling down has not received sufficient emphasis among coaches of young athletes. Cool down sessions are infrequently used to end a practice session and are rarely used following a game. A cool down period helps to:

- clear out lactic acid accumulated in the muscles,

- reduce the pooling of blood in the extremities, and

- prevent the loss of flexibility that may accompany intense muscular exercise.

Like the warm-up, cool down activities should include movements similar to those included in the practice or game. Thus, the warm-up and stretching activities, previously listed, are appropriate for the cool down. Have your athletes perform the cool down exercises first, then the stretching activities.

YEAR-ROUND CONDITIONING PROGRAM

This supplement contains information on a year-round conditioning program. It is directed at conditioning the energy production systems through a program of interval training, and the muscular system, through a weight training program. *This year-round program is appropriate for the highly motivated player who is 14 years of age or older.* It is for players who have chosen to concentrate on soccer and wish to maximize their performance through enhanced conditioning on a year-round basis. *This program is NOT for beginning players and/or players below the age of 14 years* who would derive greater benefit by devoting their time to learning and perfecting the techniques of soccer.

Interval Training Program

Interval training is a method for developing the anaerobic energy-production system while maintaining and/or enhancing a previously established base of aerobic fitness. This type of training uses alternating periods of short duration, high-intensity anaerobic ("sprint" type) exercises with longer periods of moderate- to low-intensity aerobic exercises.

The training outlines provided in this supplement can be used with different modes of exercise, depending on individual preference and the availability of equipment and facilities. Dribbling, jogging and running, and/or bicycling are modes of exercise suggested for interval training in soccer. Specific distances are not indicated in this supplement because of the variety of exercises possible and because of variations in individual fitness. All players should maintain, however, a record of distances covered on individual forms provided in this supplement so their progress can be assessed. Distance records can be kept in yards, meters, miles, kilometers, blocks, or laps.

An important concept to keep in mind, when planning an interval training program, is that the program should progress to a point where it places a similar aerobic and anaerobic demand on the athlete as that of a hard-played game of soccer. This type of work load, in an interval training program, conditions the athletes to the demands they will be confronted with during competition. *Regulation of the duration and intensity of exercise, as well as the rest intervals, are the components of an interval training program that can be manipulated to achieve the desired exercise levels.*

The interval training program included in this supplement is divided into five phases. These phases are briefly described and followed by forms that can be used by athletes to keep records of their progress.

- *Pre-Season Aerobic/Anaerobic Transition Program*—This four-week program is used to prepare athletes for high intensity anaerobic conditioning after they have developed a good aerobic fitness base (see Chart 21-1S).

- *Pre-Season Anaerobic Developmental Interval Training Program*—This is an eight-week program to be started 10 weeks before the first game. The program should be preceded by anaerobic training and the four-week Aerobic\Anaerobic Transition Program (see Chart 21-2S).

- *In-Season Anaerobic Maintenance Program*—This program should be completed once a week, starting two weeks before the first game and continuing through the end of the season (see Chart 21-3S).

- *Post-Season Aerobic Program*—This program involves rhythmical, low-intensity aerobic activities such as dribbling, jogging, running, and bicycling for three days per week to enhance aerobic fitness (see Chart 21-4S).

- *Post-Season Anaerobic Maintenance Program*—This program should be done once a week to maintain anaerobic fitness levels during the aerobic phase of off-season conditioning (see Chart 21-4S).

Weight Training Program

Weight training for soccer should focus on the development of muscular power, or the ability to quickly exert large muscular force. The load should be lifted explosively, then returned to the starting position slowly. Generally, the larger muscle groups should be exercised first. Also, the same muscle groups should not be exercised in succession. Table 21-1S contains weight lifting exercises that can be used to meet the specific requirements of soccer. They are arranged in an appropriate order.

Since the weight training exercises listed can be done using a variety of equipment, details of technique and an explanation of procedures for each exercise will not be given here. Many good guides for weight training are available in local bookstores. A few examples of such guides that contain explanations of correct technique and details for each specific exercise are:

- *Sports Conditioning and Weight Training* by William J. Stone and William A. Kroll (Allyn & Bacon, 1978). This book is designed to offer sound, systematic training programs for those who wish to apply strength and conditioning techniques to specific sports.

- *Strength Training by the Experts* by Daniel P. Riley (2nd edition, Leisure Press, 1982). This book covers a variety of lifting equipment, including free weights, Universal equipment, and Nautilus equipment, and explains which muscle groups are used in each exercise.

- *Weightlifting for Beginners* by Bill Reynolds (Contemporary Books, 1982). This book is designed primarily for free weights and at-home weightlifting.

Chart 21-1S

PRE-SEASON AEROBIC/ANAEROBIC TRANSITION PROGRAM
(To be started 14 weeks before the first game)

Name_____

The information at the top of each week's schedule specifies a suggested duration and intensity of the workout for that week. Space is provided for a coach or player to write an alternate workout for each week. The frequency of workouts is three per week, on an every-other-day basis. Each workout should be preceded and followed by stretching exercises. Work intensity is specified in terms of percentage of effort as follows:

LM = Light to Moderate	**50%** of maximum effort*
H = Hard	**80%** of maximum effort
S = Sprint	**100%** of maximum effort

For example, 3x(2:H,2:LM) means do three sets of (two minutes at 80% of effort followed by two minutes at 50% of effort). For each workout completed, record the date and total distance covered.

Pre-season Aerobic/Anaerobic Transition Program

WEEK		Day 1	Day 2	Day 3
1		[9:LM,3x(2:H,2:LM),9:LM]	alternate workout: [	]
	Date:			
	Distance:			
2		[7:LM,4x(2:H,2:LM),7:LM]	alternate workout: [	]
	Date:			
	Distance:			
3		5:LM,5x(2:H,2:LM),5:LM]	alternate workout: [	]
	Date:			
	Distance:			
4		[3:LM,6x(2:H,2:LM),3:LM]	alternate workout: [	]
	Date:			
	Distance:			
	TOTAL TIME FOR EACH WORKOUT = 30 MINUTES			

* If the intensity of the hard and sprint portions of the exercise intervals cannot be maintained, the athlete should reduce the intensity of the light to moderate intervals.

Chart 21-2S

PRE-SEASON ANAEROBIC DEVELOPMENTAL INTERVAL TRAINING PROGRAM
(To be started 10 weeks before the first game)

Name_____

The information at the top of each week's schedule specifies a suggested duration and intensity of the workout for that week. Space is provided for a coach or player to write an alternate workout for each week. The frequency of workouts is three per week, on an every-other-day basis. Each workout should be preceded and followed by stretching exercises. Work intensity is specified in terms of percentage of effort as follows:

LM = Light to Moderate	**50%** of maximum effort*	
H = Hard	**80%** of maximum effort	
S = Sprint	**100%** of maximum effort	

For example, 4x(:20S,2:LM) means do four sets of (20 seconds at maximum effort followed by two minutes at 50% of effort). For each workout completed, record the date and total distance covered.

Pre-season Anaerobic Developmental Interval Training Program		
WEEK		**Day 1** / **Day 2** / **Day 3**

Week 1: [4:LM,2x(1:H,2:LM),4x(:20S,:40LM),4:LM]
alternate workout: [ ]
Date/Distance:

Week 2: [4:LM,2x(1:H,2:LM),5x(:20S,:40LM),4:LM
alternate workout: [ ]
Date/Distance:

Week 3: [4:LM,2x(1:H,2:LM),6x(:20S,:40LM),4LM]
alternate workout: [ ]
Date/Distance:

Week 4: [4:LM,2x(1:H,2:LM),7x(:20S,:40LM),4:LM]
alternate workout: [ ]
Date/Distance:

Week 5: [4:LM,3x(1:H,2:LM),8x(:20S,:40LM),4:LM]
alternate workout: [ ]
Date/Distance:

Week 6: [4:LM,3x(1:H,2:LM),9x(:20S,:40LM),4:LM]
alternate workout: [ ]
Date/Distance:

Week 7: [4:LM,3x(1:H,2:LM),6x(:10S,:20LM),2:LM,6x(:10S,:20LM),4:LM]
alternate workout: [ ]
Date/Distance:

Week 8: [4:LM,3x(1:H,2:LM),8x(:10S,:20LM),2:LM,8x(:10S,:20LM),4:LM]
alternate workout: [ ]
Date/Distance:

* If the intensity of the hard and sprint portions of the exercise intervals cannot be maintained, the athlete should reduce the intensity of the light to moderate intervals.

Chart 21-3S

In-Season Anaerobic Maintenance Program
(To be started two weeks before the first game)

Name_____

A suggested workout is provided at the top of the In-season Anaerobic Maintenance Program form. Space is provided for a coach or player to write an alternate workout. The frequency of workout is one per week. Workouts should be completed at the end of a practice, but not on a day before a game. Each workout should be preceded and followed by stretching exercises. Work intensity is specified in terms of percentage of effort as follows:

LM = Light to Moderate	50% of maximum effort*
H = Hard	80% of maximum effort
S = Sprint	100% of maximum effort

For example, 3x(2:H,2:LM) means do three sets of (two minutes at 80% of effort followed by two minutes at 50% of effort). For each workout completed, record the date and total distance covered.

In-Season Anaerobic Maintenance Program						
[2:LM,2x(1:H,2:LM),2x(20S,:40LM),8x(:10S,:20LM),4:LM]						
alternate workout: [			]			
MONTH		**WEEK**				
		1	**2**	**3**	**4**	**5**
1	Date:					
	Distance:					
2	Date:					
	Distance:					
3	Date:					
	Distance:					
4	Date:					
	Distance:					
5	Date:					
	Distance:					

* If the intensity of the hard and sprint portions of the exercise intervals cannot be maintained, the athlete should reduce the intensity of the light to moderate intervals.

Chart 21-4S

POST-SEASON AEROBIC AND ANAEROBIC PROGRAM
(To be started two to four weeks after the last game)
AEROBIC PROGRAM

Aerobic capabilities should be developed during the post-season to provide the base for building the more intense anaerobic work capacity required for top performance during the season. Aerobic work combined with muscular strength/power work on alternate days is a good variation from the typical season routine. In the post-season time period, the development of aerobic capacity and muscular strength/power become primary, rather than secondary, objectives.

Begin three days of aerobic activity (dribbling, jogging and running, bicycling, or rythmical, low intensity, long duration activities) alternated with three days of weight training. Progress up to 40 minutes of continuous aerobic activity and then work on increasing the speed or intensity at which the 40 minutes of work is done. Each workout should be preceded and followed by stretching exercises. Record the date and workout time on the Year-Round Conditioning Checklist in the portion of the checklist devoted to Post-Season.

ANAEROBIC MAINTENANCE PROGRAM

A suggested workout is provided at the top of the Post-season Anaerobic Maintenance Program form. Space is provided for a coach or player to write an alternate workout. The Post-season anaerobic maintenance program should be done once a week. It should not be completed on the same day as an aerobic workout. Each workout should be preceded and followed by stretching exercises. Work intensity is specified in terms of percentage of effort as follows:

LM = Light to Moderate	50% of maximum effort*
H = Hard	80% of maximum effort
S = Sprint	100% of maximum effort

For example, 4x(:20S,:40LM) means do four sets of (20 seconds at maximum effort followed by 40 seconds at 50% of effort). For each workout completed, record the date and total distance covered.

Post-Season Anaerobic Maintenance Program
[4:LM,2x(1:H,2:LM),4x(:20S,:40LM),4x(:20S,:40LM),4:LM]

alternate workout: [   ]

MONTH		WEEK				
		1	2	3	4	5
1	Date:					
	Distance:					
2	Date:					
	Distance:					
3	Date:					
	Distance:					
4	Date:					
	Distance:					
5	Date:					
	Distance:					

* If the intensity of the hard and sprint portions of the exercise intervals cannot be maintained, the athlete should reduce the intensity of the light to moderate intervals.

Table 21-1S. *Weight training exercises for field players and goalkeepers.*

Order	Exercise	Comment
1	Neck flexion	This can be done on specially designed weight machines or can be accomplished by wrapping a towel around the forehead and having a partner provide resistance.
2	Squat lift	The angle at the back of the knee should not become less than 90 degrees. The head should stay upright, and the back should be kept as close to vertical as possible throughout the lift. Trained spotters must be used. If using free weights, wrap a towel or foam pad around the center of the bar to lessen the discomfort of the bar across the back of the neck.
3	Bench press	Trained spotters must be used.
4	Bent knee sit-ups	A weight can be held high on the chest and/or the sit-up can be done on an incline to increase resistance. The feet should be held down by a partner or restraining structure.
5	Finger flexion*	Grip strength exercises can be done with a spring hand gripper.
6	Hip abduction	This exercise can be done on a specially designed weight machine or by having a partner provide resistance. Both legs should be exercised.
7	Bent-over row	The head should be supported, and the back should be in a horizontal position.
8	Neck extension	This exercise can be done on specially designed weight machines or can be accomplished by wrapping a towel around the head and having a partner provide resistance.
9	Hip adduction	This exercise can be done on a specially designed weight machine or by having a partner provide resistance. Both legs should be exercised.
10	Toe rise	If using free weights, wrap a towel or foam pad around the bar to lessen the discomfort of the bar across the back of the neck. Trained spotters must be used. A block of wood can be used under the toes to increase the range through which the muscles must exert force in lifting the body.
11	Arm curl	A rocking motion of the body should NOT be used to aid the arms in lifting the resistance.
12	Knee flexion	
13	Lat pull-down	Keep the hips extended and do not use hip flexion to aid in the pull-down motion.
14	Back hyperextension	A partner or restraining structure is needed to hold the legs down.
15	Knee extension	
16	Reverse forearm curl*	

*Additional exercises for goalkeepers.

Year-round conditioning for muscular power can be divided into three parts: pre-season (developmental), in-season (maintenance), and post-season (developmental). Pre-season and post-season workouts have improvement in muscular power as their goals. In-season workouts are done less frequently and should be used to maintain the muscular fitness developed during the off-season.

● Pre-Season Weight Training Development Program

Athletes new to weight training should start a development program at least three months before the first competition. Overloaded muscles require about 48 hours to repair and recover sufficiently, so a lifting schedule of three days per week with a minimum of one day off between workouts will give best results.

For the first one to two weeks, the athlete should do one exercise eight to 12 times (*repetitions*), then move on to the next exercise until each exercise in the weight training program has been covered. This series of repetitions of each exercise is called a *set*.

The appropriate weight load, or *resistance,* is a load the athlete can lift properly a minimum of eight times, but is not so light that it can be lifted more than 12 times. Some experimenting with weight loads will be necessary to determine correct starting weights for each exercise. Once these weight loads are determined, they should be recorded on the Weight Training Program Checklist included in this Supplement (see Chart 21-5S).

During this first phase of the weight training program (two weeks), the athlete should master the proper lifting technique and work through the initial muscle soreness that accompanies learning the correct weight loads. After this initial phase, the work can be increased to two sets while maintaining the initial weight levels for eight to 12 repetitions per exercise. Two sets of the same exercise are completed before the next exercise is done. This second phase also lasts two weeks.

In the third phase, three full sets are done during each workout. Three full sets of eight to 12 repetitions on an exercise are completed, then the next exercise is done. This phase should last for eight or more weeks and should end about two weeks before the first competition. It is during this third phase that weight levels are adjusted upward as strength increases. This information is summarized in Table 21-2S.

When 12 repetitions of a given exercise have been completed for each of the three sets for two successive workouts, the weight load for that exercise can be increased to the next level for the following workout. The athlete should be able to do a minimum of eight repetitions for each of the three sets at the new weight level. If this is not possible, a small weight increase is indicated.

Chart 21-5S

WEIGHT TRAINING PROGRAM CHECKLIST

Name _____

INSTRUCTIONS:
- Record the weight load only when there is a change in load.
- Record the number of repetitions for each set (example: 12/10/10)
- Increase the weight load when you have done 12 repetitions for each of three sets for two consecutive workouts.
- Use a smaller load increase if you cannot do a minimum of eight repetitions per set at a new load.

Date		Neck flexion	Squat lift	Bench press	Bent knee sit up	Finger flexion*	Hip abduction	Bent over row	Neck extension	Hip adduction	Toe rise	Arm curl	Knee flexion	Lat pull down	Back hyperextension	Knee extension	Reverse forearm curl*
	WT.																
	REPS.	/ /	/ /	/ /	/ /	/ /	/ /	/ /	/ /	/ /	/ /	/ /	/ /	/ /	/ /	/ /	/ /
	WT.																
	REPS.	/ /	/ /	/ /	/ /	/ /	/ /	/ /	/ /	/ /	/ /	/ /	/ /	/ /	/ /	/ /	/ /
	WT.																
	REPS.	/ /	/ /	/ /	/ /	/ /	/ /	/ /	/ /	/ /	/ /	/ /	/ /	/ /	/ /	/ /	/ /
	WT.																
	REPS.	/ /	/ /	/ /	/ /	/ /	/ /	/ /	/ /	/ /	/ /	/ /	/ /	/ /	/ /	/ /	/ /
	WT.																
	REPS.	/ /	/ /	/ /	/ /	/ /	/ /	/ /	/ /	/ /	/ /	/ /	/ /	/ /	/ /	/ /	/ /
	WT.																
	REPS.	/ /	/ /	/ /	/ /	/ /	/ /	/ /	/ /	/ /	/ /	/ /	/ /	/ /	/ /	/ /	/ /
	WT.																
	REPS.	/ /	/ /	/ /	/ /	/ /	/ /	/ /	/ /	/ /	/ /	/ /	/ /	/ /	/ /	/ /	/ /
	WT.																
	REPS.	/ /	/ /	/ /	/ /	/ /	/ /	/ /	/ /	/ /	/ /	/ /	/ /	/ /	/ /	/ /	/ /
	WT.																
	REPS.	/ /	/ /	/ /	/ /	/ /	/ /	/ /	/ /	/ /	/ /	/ /	/ /	/ /	/ /	/ /	/ /
	WT.																
	REPS.	/ /	/ /	/ /	/ /	/ /	/ /	/ /	/ /	/ /	/ /	/ /	/ /	/ /	/ /	/ /	/ /
	WT.																
	REPS.	/ /	/ /	/ /	/ /	/ /	/ /	/ /	/ /	/ /	/ /	/ /	/ /	/ /	/ /	/ /	/ /
	WT.																
	REPS.	/ /	/ /	/ /	/ /	/ /	/ /	/ /	/ /	/ /	/ /	/ /	/ /	/ /	/ /	/ /	/ /
	WT.																
	REPS.	/ /	/ /	/ /	/ /	/ /	/ /	/ /	/ /	/ /	/ /	/ /	/ /	/ /	/ /	/ /	/ /

*Additional exercise for goalkeepers.

Table 21-2S. Pre-season development weight training program.

Phase	Duration	Reps	Sets	Days/Week	Comments
1	2 weeks	8-12	1	3	Maintain starting resistance level.
2	2 weeks	8-12	2	3	Maintain starting resistance level.
3	8 or more weeks	8-12	3	3	Increase resistance levels as strength gains are made.

● In-Season Weight Training Maintenance Program

Strength improvement is the goal of the pre-season weight training developmental program. Maintenance of the increased strength is accomplished by a scaled-down in-season weight training program that should begin about two weeks before the first game. If weight training is done only during the pre-season period, the strength gains will gradually be lost as the season progresses. Research has shown that a weight training maintenance program of one to two workouts per week will prevent the reversal of strength gains. Performance will not be hampered by in-season weight training if three general rules are followed:

- Lifting should be limited to once or twice a week, with two to three days between weight training workouts.

- Do not schedule weight training workouts for the day before or the day of a game.

- Maintain the resistance at the last load level where 12 repetitions for all three sets could be done. *Do not increase weight loads during in-season workouts.* Use pre- and post-season periods for strength improvement with strength maintenance as the goal of the in-season workouts.

The workout program itself remains the same as in Phase 3 of the developmental program. The same series of exercises is followed, with eight to 12 repetitions per exercise, for a total of three sets. As long as the athlete lifts at least once every four days and does not increase the weight load, there should be no muscle soreness or undue fatigue that will interfere with performance during games.

● Post-Season Weight Training Development Program

Once the competitive season is over, players can again focus on achievement of higher strength levels. A post-season break from training of at least two weeks can be followed by a return to the program outlined in Phase 3 of the pre-season developmental program (see Table 21-2S). Three-set workouts, three times per week, can be continued throughout the off-season months. The Weight Training Program Checklist can be used to determine when weight loads should be increased. After the first year in which players build up gradually through the one-set and two-set phases during the pre-season developmental program, Phase 1 and 2 should not be needed.

Year-Round Conditioning Program

The year-round conditioning program contains two components. They are: a) an interval training program for conditioning the aerobic and anaerobic energy-production systems, and b) a weight training program for conditioning the muscular system (see Chart 21-6S through 21-8S). These components are integrated into a year-round conditioning program (see Table 21-3S and Figure 21-1S).

Chart 21-6S

YEAR -AROUND CONDITIONING CHECKLIST

Name_____

(Mark the date of each completed workout in the box.)

PRE-SEASON

	AEROBIC/ANAEROBIC TRANSITION PROGRAM AND WEIGHT TRAINING PROGRAM (Phases 1 and 2 or 3)					
WEEK	TRANSITION WORKOUT	WEIGHT TRAINING	TRANSITION WORKOUT	WEIGHT TRAINING	TRANSITION WORKOUT	WEIGHT TRAINING
1						
2						
3						
4						

PRE-SEASON

	DEVELOPMENTAL INTERVAL TRAINING PROGRAM AND WEIGHT TRAINING PROGRAM (Phase 3)					
WEEK	INTERVAL TRAINING	WEIGHT TRAINING	INTERVAL TRAINING	WEIGHT TRAINING	INTERVAL TRAINING	WEIGHT TRAINING
5						
6						
7						
8						
9						
10						
11						
12						

After 12th week, begin in-season maintenance programs (intervals once per week, weights one to two times per week).

Chart 21-7S

YEAR-AROUND CONDITIONING CHECKLIST

Name_____

IN-SEASON MAINTENANCE PROGRAMS

Place a check in the box corresponding to the month and week for each time you complete the interval and weight workout.

WEEK

Month	1		2		3		4		5	
	Wts.	Interval	Wts.	Interval	Wts.	Interval	Wts.	Interval	Wts.	Interval
1										
2										
3										
4										
5										
6										

Chart 21-8S

POST-SEASON CONDITIONING CHECKLIST

Name_____

Mark the date of each workout in the corresponding box. For aerobic workouts, record the distance covered and the total time of the workout.

WEEK	Aerobic	Weights	Aerobic	Weights	Aerobic	Weights	Anaerobic Maintenance
1							
2							
3							
4							
5							
6							
7							
8							

Chart 21-8S (Continued)

POST-SEASON CONDITIONING CHECKLIST

WEEK	Aerobic	Weights	Aerobic	Weights	Aerobic	Weights	Anaerobic Maintenance
9							
10							
11							
12							
13							
14							
15							
16							
17							
18							
19							
20							
21							
22							
23							
24							
25							
26							
27							
28							
29							
30							

Table 21-3S. *Overview of year-round conditioning program.*

Time	Interval Training Activity for Conditioning the Energy Production System*	Weight Training Activity for Conditioning the Muscular System**
Pre-Season (start 14 weeks prior to first game)	• Complete the Pre-Season Aerobic/Anaerobic Transition Program (four weeks). • Complete the Pre-Season Aerobic Developmental Interval Training Program (eight weeks).	• New lifters complete the Pre-Season Weight Training Program by beginning with four weeks of introductory weight training (Phase 1 and 2) and then starting the Post-Season Weight Training Program (Phase 3). • Continuing lifters complete the Post-Season Weight Training Program.
In-Season (two weeks prior to first game until last game)	• Participate in interval training as part of regularly scheduled practices. • Complete the In-Season Aerobic Maintenance Program.	• Complete the In-Season Weight Training Maintenance Program.
Post-Season (two to four weeks after last game until 14 weeks before first game of next season)	• Complete three days/week of aerobic activity (dribbling, jogging and running, or bicycling). • Complete the Post-Season Anaerobic Maintenance Program.	• Complete the Post-Season Weight Training Program.

* Note that all conditioning sessions should be preceded by warm-up and stretching and followed by cool down and stretching (see Supplement 1).

** Descriptions of these activities are included in this supplement.

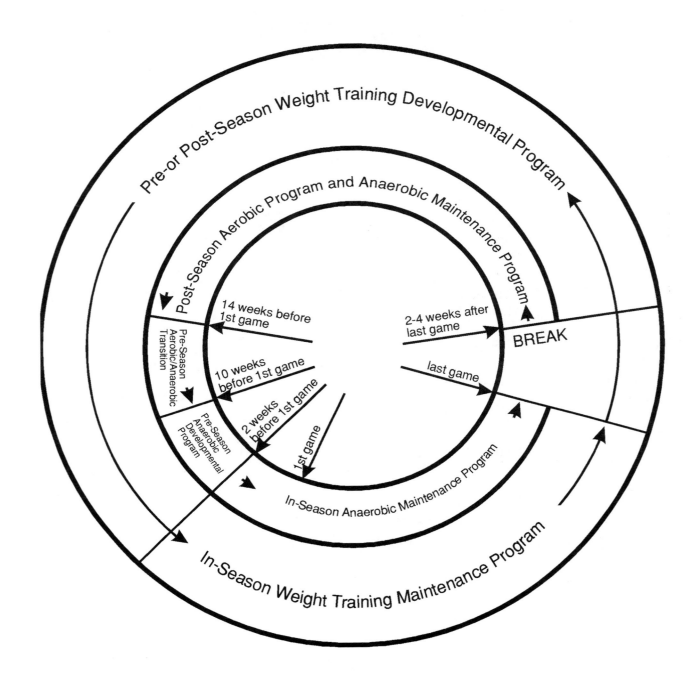

Labels within the figure:

Pre- or Post-Season Weight Training Developmental Program

Post-Season Aerobic Program and Anaerobic Maintenance Program

14 weeks before 1st game

2-4 weeks after last game

BREAK

Pre-Season Aerobic/Anaerobic Transition

Pre-Season Anaerobic Developmental Program

10 weeks before 1st game

2 weeks before 1st game

1st game

last game

In-Season Anaerobic Maintenance Program

In-Season Weight Training Maintenance Program

Figure 21-1S. *Year-round conditioning program.*

CIRCUIT TRAINING PROGRAM

This Supplement contains an example of a soccer training circuit and recording form for both field players and goalkeepers (see Figures 21-2S and 21-3S). These forms can be photocopied and duplicated on the front and back of a 5" x 7" card. Also included in this supplement is a blank form (see Figure 21-4S) upon which you can write your own training circuit to meet the specific needs of your players.

Using a Training Circuit

A training circuit can be implemented one to three time(s) per week during the season. The number of times per week you have your players engage in a training circuit should vary according to the number of games scheduled for a given week, the physical demands of an in-season interval training and weight training program, and other activities included in your practice. You should not have your players perform a circuit the day before or the day of a game.

The requirements for performance and scoring each station need to be thoroughly explained to the players. Players need to be informed that the correct performance of each station is as important as the number of repetitions. After all the players understand each of the items in the complete circuit, you may have them perform a partial circuit of four or five stations and then increase the number of stations by one on subsequent days until all stations of the training circuit are performed.

The prescribed time for exercise and for the rest interval, during which the players write their scores on their recording forms and rotate from one station to the next, should be controlled to create an exercise overload. The first day the team performs the entire circuit, 30 seconds of exercise and 20 seconds of rest between each station might be appropriate. This results in an eight-station circuit that can be completed in six minutes and 20 seconds. Gradually, the exercise interval should increase and the rest interval should decrease. You will need to judge what is the appropriate exercise/rest interval ratio for your players.

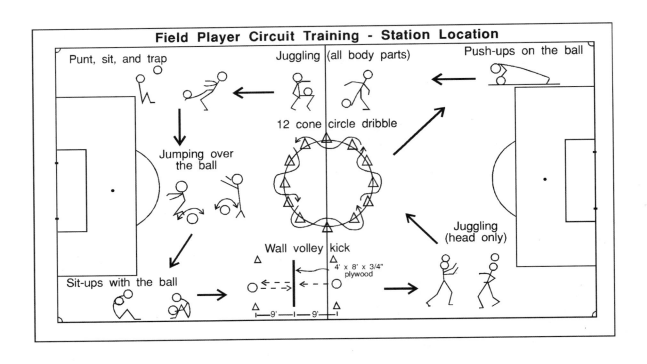

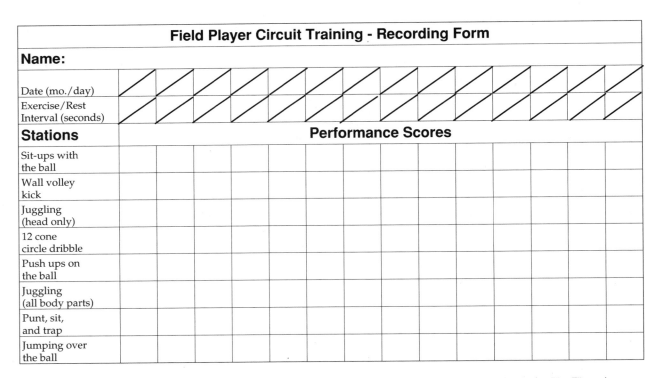

Figure 21-2S. *Example of an eight-station field player training circuit and recording form on two sides of a 5" x 7" card.*

Figure 21-2S. *(continued)*

Station	Description
Sit-ups with the ball	A bent knee sit-up is done with a ball held in the hands. In the upright position, a loop is formed with the arms and the ball is positioned in front of the shins. The number of sit-ups performed during the exercise interval is the score.
Wall volley kick	A 4' x 8' x 3/4" sheet of plywood is held in place vertically with the longest side in contact with the ground. On each side of the wall, a restraining line is marked on the ground parallel to the wall at a distance of nine feet. This permits two players to perform on a single wall. A ball is kicked and received behind the restraining line. The number of times this is successfully completed during the exercise interval is the score. You may specify the type of kick, whether the ball must be trapped before kicking it again, and the foot used.
Juggling (head only)	The number of times the ball is juggled with the head during the exercise interval is the score. Scoring could be changed to count only the greatest number of juggles in a row without a miss.
12 cone circle dribble	Twelve cones are equally spaced around the center circle. A zig-zag path is dribbled. The number of cones passed during the exercise interval is the score.
Push-ups on the ball	A push-up position is taken with the hands on the ball and the feet on the ground. The number of push-ups performed during the exercise interval is the score. This activity can be modified to meet the needs of the players with relatively weak arm strength by having them perform the push-up by supporting their weight on their hands and knees.
Juggling (all body parts)	The number of times the ball is juggled with all body parts, except the arms and hands, during the exercise interval is the score. Scoring could be changed to count only the greatest number of juggles in a row without a miss.
Punt, sit, and trap	A player must punt the ball into the air, sit down on the ground, stand up, and make a first-time trap of the ball. The number of successful first-time traps is the score. The difficulty of this station can be increased by substituting a forward or backward roll for the sit.
Jumping over the ball	A player jumps from side to side over a ball on the ground. The number of times this activity is completed is the score. The drill can be made to be more demanding by requiring the players to keep their hands on their hips. The activity can also be modified to a forward-backward jump over the ball. In this case, the feet must be kept together and not allowed to straddle and go around the ball.

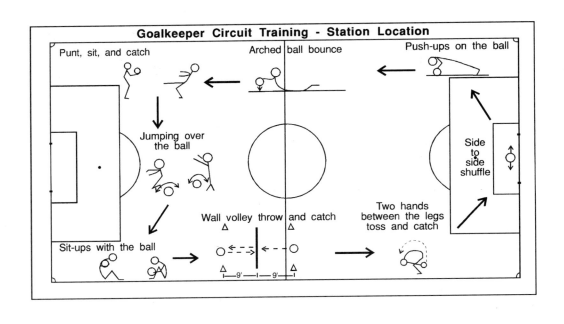

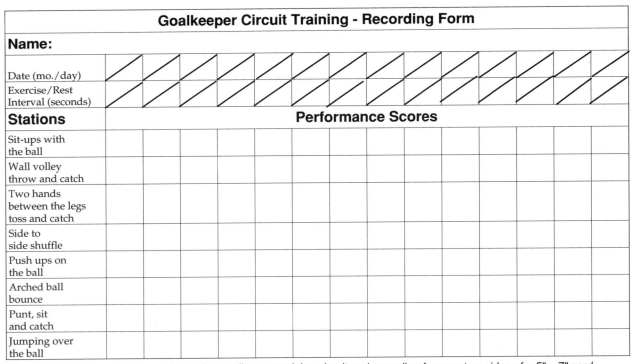

Figure 21-3S. *Example of an eight-station goalkeeper training circuit and recording form on two sides of a 5" x 7" card.*

Figure 21-3S. (continued)

Station	Description
Sit-ups with the ball	See description for field player circuit.
Wall volley throw and catch	A sheet of plywood is used as in the wall volley kick described in the circuit for field players. The ball must be thrown and caught behind the restraining line. The number of times this is successfully completed during the exercise interval is the score. You may specify the type of throw (underhand bowled ball, sling throw, baseball throw) and the type of catch. The drill could also be modified by substituting a drop kick for the throw.
Two hands between the legs toss and catch	With both hands between the legs, the ball is tossed upward and forward over the head. The goalkeeper must then catch the ball in front of the body before it strikes the ground. The number of successful completions of this activity during the exercise interval is the score. To increase the difficulty of this station, the goalkeepers can be instructed to perform additional activities between the toss and catch (e.g., clap the hands together a set number of times, kneel down and then stand up, turn completely around).
Side to side shuffle	The goalkeeper stands in a ready position facing the field of play with one hand touching a goal post. The goalkeeper then shuffles his/her feet without crossing the legs, and proceeds to touch the opposite post. This process is repeated, back and forth, while the goalkeeper continues to face the field of play. The number of times the goalkeeper crosses the goal mouth and touches the opposite post during the exercise interval is the score. Note that only one goalkeeper should be in a group. Therefore, more than one set of goal posts will not be needed.
Push-ups on the ball	See description for field player circuit.
Arched ball bounce	From a prone position on the ground, the back is arched so the knees, feet, head, shoulders, and elbows are off the ground. While maintaining that position, the ball is repeatedly bounced on the ground with both hands. The number of bounces performed, while in the correct body position, during the exercise interval is the score.
Punt, sit, and catch	A player must punt the ball into the air, sit down on the ground, stand up, and catch the ball. The number of successful performances of this routine during the exercise interval is the score. The difficulty of this station can be increased by substituting a forward or backward roll for the sit.
Jumping over the ball	See description for field player circuit.

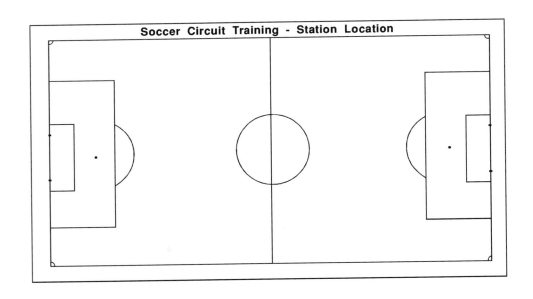

Soccer Circuit Training - Station Location

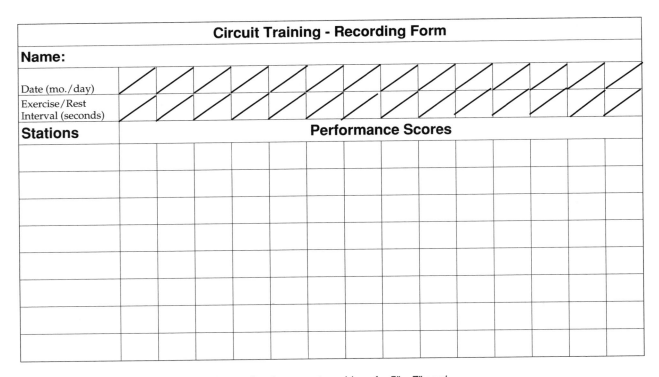

Circuit Training - Recording Form

Name:											
Date (mo./day)											
Exercise/Rest Interval (seconds)											
Stations	**Performance Scores**										

Figure 21-4S. *Blank circuit training and recording forms on two sides of a 5" x 7" card.*

22

NUTRITION FOR SUCCESSFUL PERFORMANCE

Elaina Jurecki and Wade Lillegard

QUESTIONS TO CONSIDER

- What is a proper diet for young soccer players?
- How much energy is required to play soccer?
- Do young athletes need protein, vitamin, and mineral supplements?
- Should the amount of water consumed before, during, and after games and practices be restricted?
- Should salt tablets be provided for the players during games?
- Are ergogenic aids important in improving soccer performance?
- When should a pre-game meal be eaten and what should it contain?

INTRODUCTION

All children have the same nutritional needs, but young athletes use more energy and, therefore, usually need more calories. Good performance does not just happen; it requires training sessions to improve techniques, increase endurance, and develop game strategies. Good nutrition is another important factor that affects each player's performance, but it is less frequently understood and practiced. Studies have shown that good overall eating habits are more beneficial to the athlete than taking vitamin or protein supplements or eating special foods at a pre-competition meal.

Food consists of all the solid or liquid materials we ingest by mouth, except drugs. Bread, meat, vegetables, fruit, as well as all beverages—even water—should be considered food, containing essential nutrients for the body. These nutrients include energy (calories from fat, protein, and carbohydrates), carbohydrates, protein (amino acids), fat (essential fatty acids), vitamins, salts (electrolytes), minerals, trace elements, and water. Yes, even water is considered an essential nutrient! Water constitutes more than half the body's weight and provides the medium within which other nutrients are delivered to different body parts to perform their important functions.

What impact could you have on your players' diets? How can you influence what your players eat when you do not cook their meals? When you meet with the team's parents during an orientation meeting, explain to them how good nutrition can aid their children's performance. This information can be reinforced by giving your players similar nutritional advice. Frequently, your players will listen more closely to your advice than that of their parents and use the tips you suggest on improving their diets because they believe these tips will also improve their performance.

PROPER DIET

A good diet is one that provides adequate energy (calories), protein, carbohydrates, fat, vitamins, minerals, and water in the amounts needed by the body in order to perform its normal daily functions. A variety of foods should be eaten to provide the 40 plus nutrients needed for good health. This can be achieved by eating a specified number of servings from each of the four food groups (see Table 22-1).

Calories

Calories are the energy content of food to supply the needs of the body so it can properly function. Foods vary in calorie and nutrient content. Foods to avoid are those that are high in calories and low in nutrient content. Foods that are high in sugar (candy, cakes, soda pop, cookies) or fat (fried foods, chips, salad dressings, pastries, butter) supply "empty calories," meaning they do not contribute to the essential nutrients discussed earlier, but do contribute many calories. These foods should be used with discretion.

Table 22-1. Recommended daily intake of each of the four food groups.

Dairy Products	• 3-4 servings (milk, cheese, yogurt) to provide calcium, phosphorus, vitamin D, protein, and energy.	• 1 serving = 1 cup of milk or 2 oz. of cheese
Protein Products	• 2 servings (meat, fish, poultry, or vegetable protein foods (i.e., beans and whole grains) to provide amino acids, B vitamins, iron, essential fatty acids, energy, and more.	• 1 serving = 2 to 3 oz. of meat
Fruits and Vegetables	• 4 servings (oranges, apples, pears, broccoli, carrots, green beans) to provide vitamin A and C, and electrolytes.	• 1 serving = 1/2 cup of vegetables or fruit
Grain Products	• 4 servings (bread, cereal, pasta, rice) to provide B vitamins and protein.	• 1 serving = 1 slice of bread or 1 cup of cereal, pasta, or rice

Table 22-2. Caloric expenditure during various activities.

Activity	Calories/minute*	Activity	Calories/minute
Sleeping	0.9	Basketball	5-7
Sitting, normally	1.0	Calisthenics	4
Standing, normally	1.2	Skipping rope	8-12
Classwork, lecture (listen to)	1.4	Running (10 mph)	16
Walking indoors	2.5	Soccer (game)	6-8

*Based on an average adolescent, 120 lbs. Add 10 percent for each 15 lbs. over 120, subtract 10 percent for each 15 lbs. under 120.

The energy cost—or amount of calories burned for energy—of a sport depends upon a) the intensity of the physical activity and b) the length of time of exertion. A young soccer player, about 120 pounds in body weight, burns approximately 430 calories per hour of practice. During a game or training session, ranging from 45 minutes to 1 and 1/2 hours, your players burn up to 25 percent of their total daily energy (calories) output. Hence, heavy training may require an additional 400 to 600 calories per day intake to compensate for the calories burned during the activity.

An average adolescent burns differing amounts of calories during the various activities listed in Table 22-2.

When your players reach exhaustion, most of their bodies' energy stores are depleted and their blood sugars decrease, causing fatigue. This is remedied with appropriate rest and calorie ingestion—preferably from carbohydrate sources since these foods can replenish energy stores more effectively.

Carbohydrates

Carbohydrates come from sugars and starches, and are widely distributed in foods. Carbohydrates cannot be stored in large amounts by the body and, therefore, should be an important part of the daily diet. These nutrients can be digested easily and quickly. Thus, they are the most readily available source of food energy.

Carbohydrates are easily digested and are the most readily available source of food energy.

Fat

Fat is the most concentrated source of energy. It contains twice as much energy (calories) per unit weight as either carbohydrate or protein. Fats have many important functions in the body including carrying vitamins A, D, E, and K to perform their necessary functions, building blood vessels and body linings, and providing a concentrated store of energy (calories).

Foods high in fat content are digested at a slower rate than foods high in carbohydrates or protein. If players have high fat meals (hamburger, fries, pizza, etc.) before their game, chances are good that such meals will not empty completely from their stomachs for three to five hours, and this may adversely affect their play. Foods having a high concentration of fat include butter, margarine, vegetable oils, peanut butter, mayonnaise, nuts, chocolate, fried foods, chips, and cream products.

Although some fat is necessary in the athlete's diet, a high fat diet is not recommended. In Figure 22-1, the percent of calories that comes from fat—versus protein and carbohydrates—from a portion of various food items are listed.

Protein

Protein is needed on a daily basis to maintain growth and promote normal functioning and repair of all body tissues—not just for muscles, but for skin, liver, kidneys, eyes, brain, nervous systems, blood and body fluids, bones, teeth, and other structural tissues. Protein in foods is the body's source of amino acids. The body needs certain amino acids to

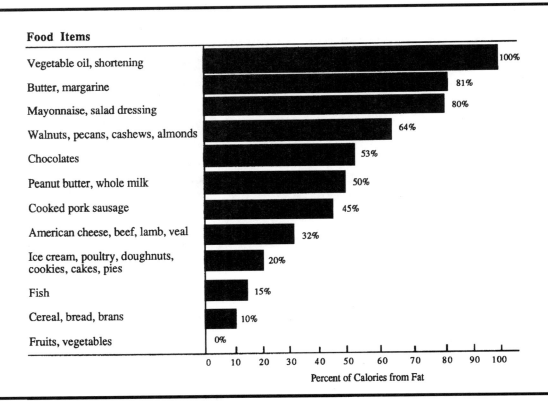

Figure 22-1. *Percent of calories from fat from specified food items.*

make the components required for normal functioning and repair of the body tissues mentioned. The body must obtain these amino acids from foods because the body is unable to make them itself. Therefore, they are called "essential amino acids."

Foods from animal sources (e.g., meat, fish, poultry, eggs, milk, and cheese) provide the body with all of the essential amino acids. Vegetable foods (dried peas, beans, nuts, cereals, breads, and pastas) are also important sources of protein, but most vegetables are lacking in certain essential amino acids. Therefore, a combination of foods from animal and vegetable sources assures meeting the needs of all essential amino acids, as well as other nutrients.

Because of an increased rate of muscle growth, athletes have a *slightly* larger protein requirement than non-athletes. Studies on the dietary habits of athletes show that this increased requirement can be easily met by the athlete's normal diet; no protein supplement is necessary. During training, at most, an additional nine grams of protein (which can be provided by one cup of milk or two ounces of meat or cheese) is sufficient to meet increased demands. In fact, too much protein is hard on the body!

Athletes do not need a protein supplement; too much protein is hard on their bodies.

Excessive amounts of ingested protein—greater than the body's needs—must be converted into body fat. The waste products from this conversion must be excreted by the kidneys, placing a greater strain on these organs. Water must be excreted with the protein-waste products in the urine. Thus, eating a high-protein diet could lead to dehydration of the body, which could actually decrease athletic performance.

It is a myth that building muscle requires a high-protein diet featuring large quantities of meat. One myth is that a steak dinner eaten before the event will help the team members improve their performance. This type of meal may actually work against them if consumed less than three or four hours before playing time. These meals, as well as any high protein meal, are also usually high in fat. Players cannot digest this type of meal as easily as a high-carbohydrate meal and may suffer from cramps and/or feel weighed down and sluggish.

Vitamins and Minerals

Vitamins and minerals are found in varying quantities in many different kinds of foods, from a slice of bread to a piece of liver. Vitamins and minerals are nutrients required by the body in very small amounts for a larger number of body functions. They do not contain calories or give the body energy. When an athlete feels "run down," *this is usually not caused by a vitamin deficiency.*

We need vitamins and minerals in only minute quantities. Requirements of most vitamins and minerals are in milligram (1/1000 gram) amounts. Vitamins taken in excess of the body's need will either be stored in the body or excreted in the urine. The extra amounts will not provide more energy or enhance performance.

Minerals and certain vitamins taken in excess can be toxic to the body. Vitamin and mineral supplements are of no value to the athlete on an adequate diet. Because of the increased requirements for energy (calories) of the athlete due to participating in the sport, additional needs for vitamins and minerals will be obtained through the extra calorie intake.

Vitamins and minerals do not supply energy; high levels of vitamins and minerals can hinder the athlete's performance.

Some vitamin and mineral supplements contain 10 or more times the Recommended Daily Allowance (RDA), which is sometimes just below the level of toxicity. If vitamin and mineral supplements are used, a single daily multi-vitamin/mineral, that provides 100 percent of the RDA or less for each nutrient is preferable to therapeutic level supplements providing greater than 100 percent of the RDA. Only those individuals with special nutritional problems may need a supplement. The RDA's of vitamins and minerals are listed in Table 22-3.

Water

Water plays a vital role in the health and performance of an athlete. Your soccer players can lose more than two percent of their body weight due to dehydration from playing a fast-moving game or during a long workout. A player's performance significantly deteriorates after dehydra-

Table 22-3. Recommended daily dietary allowances.*

Age (Years)	Children 7-10	Males 11-14	Females 11-14
Weight (pounds)	62	99	101
Height (inches)	52	62	62
Energy (calories)	2,400	2,700	2,200
(range of calories)	1,650-3,300	2,000-3,700	1,500-3,000
Protein (grams)	34	45	46
Vitamin A (υg RE)	700	1,000	1,000
Vitamin C (mg)	45	50	50
Calcium (mg)	800	1,200	1,200
Iron (mg)	10	18	18

*Adapted from Food and Nutrition Board, National Academy of Sciences — National Research Council, Revised, 1980.

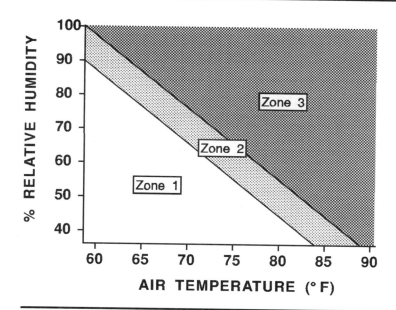

Figure 22-2. *Guide for preventing heat illnesses associated with participation in soccer under various conditions of temperatures and humidity.* [5]

tion of more than two percent of his/her body weight. Drinking plenty of water is necessary for soccer players who are physically active in hot, humid weather (see Figure 22-2).

Physical exercise increases the amount of heat produced in the body. If sufficient water is not available for perspiration, the body temperature may exceed safe limits. The individual will become tired more rapidly and in severe cases, heat exhaustion and heat stroke may result (see Chapter 24). A temperature guide for fluid and practice time is included in Table 22-4.

Athletes need plenty of liquids.

Feeling thirsty is not an adequate indication that the body needs water. In fact, by the time athletes feel thirsty, they may already be behind in replenishing body water. It takes several hours to achieve water balance once water loss has occurred. There is no physiological reason for restricting water intake before, during, or after athletic contests and practices. Players should drink eight to 16 ounces of water 30 minutes before the game and eight ounces every 20 minutes during the game.

Athletes should be encouraged to drink water before, during, and after each game and practice session.

Keeping enough drinking water available at the playing field may be difficult if a fountain is not within a reasonable distance, but access to plenty of fluids is an important key to winning performances.

If you are unable to carry enough drinking water to the field, ask the parents to help out by taking turns bringing in water or diluted fruit juice to practices and games. If you explain the importance of plenty of fluids in playing soccer, the players and their parents will be willing to help bring fluids to practices and games.

Table 22-4. *Temperature guide for taking precautionary action during practices and games.*

TEMPERATURE	PRECAUTIONS TO TAKE
Under 60° (F)	• No precaution is necessary.
61-65° (F)	• Encourage all players to take fluids. Make sure water is available at all times.
66-70° (F)	• Take water breaks every 30-45 minutes of playing or practice time.
71-75° (F)	• Provide rest periods every 30-45 minutes of playing time—depending on the intensity of exercise. During a game, substitute players in the game, so that they may receive appropriate rest and fluids.
76° (F) and up	• Practice in coolest part of the day. Schedule frequent rest breaks. Force water intake. Tell players to wear light, loose clothing that allows free circulation of air. Remove outer clothing when it gets wet since wet clothing reduces the skin's ability to cool.
	• Move to the shade if possible.
	• Drink water before, during and after practice sessions and competition.
Relative humidity greater than 90%	• Similar precautions should be taken as those listed for 76° (F) and up.

Salts and Electrolytes

Another common myth is that salt (sodium) tablets and electrolyte solutions (solutions containing the elements sodium, potassium, and chloride, which are needed by the body to maintain fluid balance) are needed by the athlete. These are not only unnecessary but can be harmful.

Salt tablets are irritating to the stomach and intestine and can increase the danger of dehydration by causing diarrhea when taken before a practice or game. Although the body needs to replace both water and sodium, the need for water is more critical.

Some coaches provide 0.2 percent salt solutions for drinking water during an athletic event, but research has shown that plain water is just as effective. The body needs water immediately to replace the water lost during a game or practice, but the need for sodium can easily be met by eating salted foods after the event. Most Americans get more sodium than they need from salt in their diet.

> *The best replacement fluid is water.*

Ergogenic Aids

Ergogenic foods are those substances that claim to "give you more energy," "improve your performance," "enhance your endurance," and much more. There is no scientific evidence supporting any of these substances' claims. Most of these foods and dietary practices are harmless to the athlete. The only danger these foods pose occurs when they replace necessary foods that the athlete needs for normal bodily functions. Some examples of these foods are bee pollen, pangamic acid, honey, lecithin, wheat germ oil, phosphates, alkaline salts (e.g., sodium bicarbonate, tomato or orange juice), and gelatin.

You could mention these substances to your players and explain that eating a healthy diet is the real key—contrary to what all of the advertisements claim—to improving their performance.

Steroids

The first athletes known to use anabolic steroids were Russian weightlifters participating in the 1954 World Powerlifting Championships. The number of athletes using these drugs has dramatically increased since then. In the 1983 Pan American Games, seven of the 19 athletes tested were disqualified for steroid use and many more withdrew from competition to apparently prevent detection.

Steroids are part of a large family of hormones with a similar chemical structure. Steroids have two general effects: anabolic and androgenic. "Anabolic" refers to tissue building by increasing muscle mass and decreasing muscle breakdown. "Androgenic" refers to a change in secondary sexual characteristics such as body hair and deepening voice.

The discovery of testosterone, an anabolic plus androgenic steroid, brought on attempts to separate the androgenic or masulinizing effects from the anabolic or tissue-building effects that are desired for improved strength and performance. Complete separation of these two effects has not yet been possible. Therefore, all anabolic steroids have androgenic side effects. These side effects are what most concerns the medical community, and they include the reversible and irreversible side effects described in Table 22-5.

> *The best prescription for increased strength and improved performance is hard practices, plenty of rest, a good diet, healthy eating habits, and plenty of fluids.*

Table 22-5. Harmful effects of anabolic steroids.*

Body System	Reversible Effects	Irreversible Effects
Cardiovascular (heart/blood vessels)	High blood pressure, changes in blood fats predisposing to heart disease, sticky platelets	Abnormal heart muscle, heart disease, stroke, heart attack
Skeletal	Minor changes in height	Early closure of the growth plates, making you shorter than you would be otherwise
Muscular	Increased water in muscle	Abnormal muscle cells, tendon rupture
Reproductive—male	Shrunken testicles, decreased sperm production, breast development, increased size of the prostate gland	Cancer of the prostate, increased breast development, abnormal testicles
Reproductive—female	Decreased breast size, increased body hair (facial also), menstrual problems	Increased size of clitoris, deepening of voice, baldness, use during pregnancy may cause fetal deformity or death
Liver	Increased leakage of liver enzymes, abnormal growth of liver cells, turning "yellow" from backup of bile in liver	Cancer of liver, blood-filled sacs in liver
Endocrine (hormones)	Too much insulin secreted, decreased thyroxine, decreases hormone secretion from pituitary gland in brain	Not known which effects are permanent
Skin	Acne, increased facial hair	Severe acne, baldness
Mental Attitude	Irritability, aggressiveness, mood swings, problems getting along with people, change in sex drive	Relationships with people damaged, possible personality changes
Immune	Decreased functioning of the immune cells and antibody formation	Serious infections, cancer

* This table comes from a paper titled "What the High School Athletes, Coaches, and Parents Should Know about Anabolic-Androgenic Steroids." This paper is available upon request from the Michigan State University Sports Medicine Clinic, Clinical Center, East Lansing, MI 48824

MEAL PATTERNS

Preadolescents and adolescents should eat at least three meals daily, or four or five smaller meals, adding snacks to the regular breakfast-lunch-dinner pattern. Most active youngsters tend to skip meals and grab quick-fix meals or depend on fast food restaurants and vending machines for meals on the run. This could lead to diets low in vitamins and minerals and high in fat and sodium (salt). For example, a meal consisting of a hamburger, fries, and soda would provide 571 calories or approximately one-third of the energy requirement of a 7- to 10-year-old child, but less than a tenth of the other nutritional requirements. Nutritional foods with proportional amounts of nutrients to calories are listed in Table 22-6. To maximize performance during periods of intense daily training, an athlete should consume approximately 500 grams (2000 Kcal) of carbohydrates per day.[6]

Pre-Game Meal

One of the biggest concerns of athletes and coaches is what the team members should eat for the pre-game meal. Unfortunately, there are no foods that contain any special, magical properties that could improve your soccer players' performances if eaten before the game. Performance during an event or workout is more dependent on food consumed hours, days, or even weeks before the event. The most important consideration should be to select foods that can be digested easily, tolerated well, and liked by the players.

Pre-game stress causes the athlete's stomach and intestine to be less active. Some food is recommended before vigorous exercise to delay feeling exhausted, but this should be eaten two or three hours before the competi-

Table 22-6. Nutritional snacks and their nutritional contribution.

Food	Amount	Calories	Vit. A	Vit. C	Calcium	Iron
Fresh orange	1 med. size	65	8%	150%	7%	5%
Orange juice	1 cup	110	14%	200%	3%	5%
Peanut butter	1 tablespoon	95	—	—	0.5%	3%
2% Milk	1 cup	120	14%	4%	37%	1%
Cheese and crackers	1 oz. cheese, 4 crackers	175	9%	—	27%	7%
Carrot sticks	8 or 1 carrot	30	70%	13%	3%	5%
Ice cream	1 cup	270	15%	2%	22%	1%
Fruit-flavored yogurt	1 cup	230	14%	2%	43%	2%
Raisins	1/4 cup pressed	120	—	—	56%	15%
Applesauce	1/2 cup	115	1%	3%	—	7%
Banana	1 med.	100	6%	27%	—	7%
Ready-to-eat cereal	1 ounce	110	29%	27%	—	36%

tion to give the stomach and intestines sufficient time to empty. Meals eaten before a practice session should be given the same general consideration as the pre-game meal, except there is no need to compensate for nervous stress.

Carbohydrate foods leave the stomach earlier and are digested more readily than either fats or protein. Foods that are easily digested include cereals, bread, spaghetti, macaroni, rice, potatoes (baked and not fried), and fruits. Foods high in fat take longer to leave the stomach and intestine. Examples of foods to be avoided include cake, peanut butter, nuts, luncheon-type meats, gravy, yellow cheese, butter, and ice cream. Gas-forming foods (e.g., cabbage, cucumbers, cauliflower, and beans) and foods high in fiber and roughage (e.g., whole wheat bread, bran cereal, and raw vegetables) may cause discomfort to the player if eaten the day of competition.

Those players who have difficulty digesting solid foods before competition may prefer a liquid meal. These products should not be confused with instant powdered meals or "instant breakfasts," which have too much fat, protein, and electrolytes to be eaten before athletic contests. Liquid meals have the following advantages: a) they leave the intestine rapidly, b) they provide substantial calories, and c) they are more convenient than preparing a meal. But, liquid meals do not provide greater benefits for improving performances than eating an easily digested, well-tolerated meal.

If the team usually practices and has its games in the afternoon, around 3:00 p.m., the pre-game meal could be eaten around noon. Possible choices for lunch include: spaghetti with tomato sauce; sandwich of white bread with a thin spread (e.g., two or three pieces of mozzarella cheese, only a thin spread of peanut butter and jelly, or two or three slices of lean roast beef, chicken, or turkey); chicken noodle or vegetable soup; low-fat yogurt or cottage cheese; fresh or canned fruits and fruit juices; crackers with white cheese or cheese spread; low-fat milk; baked potato sprinkled with white cheese and bacon bits (not real bacon but the soybean-flavored brand); or pizza—heavy on the tomato sauce and light on the cheese. If the team has an early morning practice or game, around 8:00 a.m., the pre-game meal should be eaten around 5:00 a.m. The team members should eat breakfast as soon as they wake up to ensure plenty of time to digest their breakfast before playing time. If they do not wish to eat breakfast that early, they could eat a lighter meal (e.g., liquid meals or juice and a piece of white toast with jelly—no butter or margarine) an hour before playing time. Eating a larger meal two or three hours before playing time would delay the feeling of fatigue and hunger and would be recommended when the team has to play a soccer tournament lasting more than four hours. Possible selection for breakfast would include: cereal with low-fat milk, pancakes, French toast, fruit juice, oatmeal or cream of wheat, white toast with jelly or cinnamon sugar, soft- or hard-boiled eggs, and fresh or canned fruit.

> **Pre-game meal:**
> - *Eat carbohydrate-rich foods*
> - *Avoid fatty foods*
> - *Avoid gas-forming and high-fiber foods*
> - *Eat three or four hours before the game*
> - *Drink plenty of fluids hourly*
> - *Avoid concentrated sweets*

Candy bars are not a good source of quick energy and will not help your players perform better. A candy bar eaten right before the game may give your players a sudden burst of energy, but this energy boost is only a temporary feeling. The body over- compensates for the increase in blood sugar that results from eating a simple sugar (such as candy), causing a rebound effect of feeling hungry and tired. Your players will be full of energy for only a short time, then they will become sluggish and slow down.

Nutritional Support During Competition

Intense prolonged activities such as soccer and distance running require significant fluid and energy replacement during the event. Water is the most important replacement, but performance and endurance will be enhanced with proper carbohydrate replacement.

In one study of elite soccer players,[4] muscle glycogen (carbohydrate) stores were assessed after a 90-minute soccer match. The group of players that drank one liter of a 7 percent sugar solution during the game had 63 percent more glycogen in their muscles than the group that drank plain water. In other words, the group that drank the sugar solution had much more "reserve."

A 7 percent carbohydrate solution can easily be made by dissolving 70 grams (2.45 ounces) of glucose (sugar) in one liter (34 ounces) of water. Athletes should drink about eight ounces of this mixture every 20 minutes during a match to maintain their blood glucose level. Many commercial carbohydrate replacement "sports drinks" are available with similar concentrations.

Post-Game Nutrition

For a tournament, it is important to maximize your players' energy stores after a game to enable them to perform well during the next game, which may be scheduled for a few hours later. A recent study[3] showed that drinking a 23 percent glucose solution immediately after exhaustive exercise resulted in a 300 percent increase in the rate of muscle glycogen syntheses and a tenfold increase in glycogen stored in the muscles. It has been shown that glucose solution should be ingested immediately after the match. At this time, the muscles are more sensitive to insulin and there is a relatively high rate of blood flow that allows for better delivery of glucose and insulin to the muscles. If the players wait two hours after exercise to drink the glucose solution, its effect will be reduced by approximately 50 percent.

In another study[2] on soccer players, one-half of a team was given a flavored solution containing 115 grams of carbohydrate and the other half of the team was given a similarly flavored water drink without the carbohydrate. Both groups of players ingested their assigned solutions after their first game. The performance in their second game that day was evaluated on the basis of two criteria: 1) the ratio of the yardage covered in their first and second games, and 2) the intensity of the players' movements (walking, jogging, cruising, and sprinting). The players who drank the glucose solution significantly increased their movement at the strategic (cruise and sprint) intensities and these players also covered 40 percent more field at these strategic intensities.

- ## Amount Needed

How much carbohydrates do your players need between games on the same day? According to a recent study[1], 0.68 grams per pound (1.5 grams per kilogram) of body weight should be ingested immediately after exercise, and the same amount should also be ingested two hours following exercise. Ingesting more than this has no additional benefit. (See Supplement 22-1 for an easy recipe for making the appropriate amounts for your players.)

- ## Form Needed

It does not matter whether players ingest carbohydrates between games in a liquid or a solid form. The critical factor is the amount. However, players tend to tolerate the liquid form better because it is less bulky.

Some commercially available "sports drinks" contain a glucose polymer. Carbohydrates in this form are not as sweet-tasting as a solution with equal concentrations of sugar and water. Thus, some players will be able to tolerate the glucose polymer better than the sugar and water solution.

WEIGHT LOSS AND WEIGHT GAIN

Each of your soccer players is different in height and build and, therefore, they have different ideal body weights. Rather than suggesting that your players weigh a specific number of pounds, you should work at improving their skill and physical fitness.

Weight Loss

Players who have too much fat will tend to be slower and tire more easily. For those individuals, some weight loss could improve their performance. In order to lose weight, energy output must exceed energy intake. Because of this, the more active athletes have an easier time losing weight than their less active peers.

One pound of fat is approximately 3,500 calories. Reducing food intake by 500 calories per day will result in a loss of about one pound per week. Athletes in training could lose more weight, or could decrease their intake by 300 calories per day to lose a similar amount of weight. Losing more than one or two pounds per week could result in a loss of body-tissue protein and not body fat, because fat cannot be lost at a faster rate than one or two pounds per week. Hence, crash diets are not recommended because loss of body fat from these diet plans is only slight.

Sauna baths, cathartics, and diuretics are methods used to lose weight by dehydrating oneself. These methods are **not** recommended because loss of body fluids reduces strength and endurance. In these methods, weight loss is from fluid loss and not body fat. The key to losing weight is to begin months before the season starts and follow a healthy diet—avoiding high-calorie foods, eating three balanced meals, and increasing activity level.

Important points to consider when attempting to lose weight:

- *Start early*
- *Lose at a slow pace*
- *Lose fat, not fluid or muscle*
- *Avoid excessive weight loss, especially during growing periods*
- *Avoid use of saunas, diuretics, or cathartics*

Weight Gain

The goal for athletes trying to gain weight is to add more muscle, rather than fat. Eating an extra 500 calories per day should result in gaining one pound of muscle per week. This increase in caloric intake must be accompanied with intensive exercise, at a level that is slightly less than full exertion. A good way to add those extra calories is by adding a daily snack such as dried fruit, nuts, peanut butter sandwich, juice, milk shake, or oatmeal-raisin cookies. Trying to gain weight at a faster rate will only result in more body fat in the wrong places, rather than muscle in the right places.

> *Important points to consider when*
> *attempting to gain weight:*
> - *Start early*
> - *Gain at a slow pace*
> - *Eat nutritious foods, and not foods high in fat content*

As a coach, you can give your players some tips on how to gain or lose weight properly — eating the right foods and gaining/losing weight at the proper pace. Encourage your players to eat a healthy diet because they should naturally achieve their ideal body weight by eating balanced meals and snacks, along with exercise. Most of your players will still be growing and will require additional calories to meet the demands of their growing bodies.

If you have players who are excessively over- or underweight, you may tactfully approach their parents and suggest that they seek medical attention for their child.

> *At the ideal body weight, the athlete performs best.*

Many teenagers eat a lot of junk foods—high in calories and low in nutrients—but the motivated athletes would prefer foods high in nutrients if they realize that these foods could help them in performing their best.

SUMMARY

Your group of soccer players is a motivated group of individuals who want to improve their performances to become a successful team. As their coach, you can provide them with the necessary information on how they can play their best. Providing your team with the nutritional advice presented in this chapter will assist them in obtaining maximum performance through eating a healthy diet.

REFERENCES

1. Foster, C., Thompson, N.N., & Dean, J. (1986). Carbohydrate supplementation and performance in soccer players. *Medicine and Science in Sports and Exercise.* 18(2), Supplement S 59, Abstract.

2. Ivy, J.L. (1988). Muscle glycogen storage after different amounts of carbohydrate ingestion. *Journal of Applied Physiology.* 65: 2018-2023.

3. Ivy, J.L. (1988). Muscle glycogen synthesis after exercise: Effect of time on carbohydrate ingestion. *Journal of Applied Physiology.* 64: 1480-1485.

4. Leatt, P.B., & Jacobs, I. (1986). Effects of glucose polymer ingestion on muscle glycogen utilization during a soccer match. *Medicine and Science in Sports and Exercise.* 18(2), Supplement S 6, Abstract.

5. Mathews, D., & Fox, E. (1976). *The physiological bases of physical education and athletics.* Philadelphia: W.B. Saunders.

6. Williams, M.H. (1983). *Ergogenic aids in sports.* Champaign, IL: Human Kinetics.

SUGGESTED READINGS

American College of Sports Medicine (1987). Position stand on the use of anabolic-androgenic steroids in sports. *Medicine and Science in Sports and Exercise,* 19(5): 534-539.

Clark, N. (1981). *The athlete's kitchen: A nutrition guide and cookbook.* Boston: CBI Publishing.

Darden, E. (1976). *Nutrition and athletic performance.* Pasadena, CA: The Athletic Press.

Food and Nutrition Board: Recommended Dietary Allowances. Rev. Ed., 1980. Washington, DC: National Academy of Sciences.

Higdon, H. (1978). *The complete diet guide for runners and other athletes.* Mountain View, CA: World Publications.

Katch, F.I. & McArdle, W.D. (1977). *Nutrition, weight control and exercise.* Boston: Houghton Mifflin.

National Association for Sport and Physical Education (1984). *Nutrition for sport success.* Reston, VA: American Alliance for Health, Physical Education, Recreation and Dance.

Smith, N.J. (1976). *Food for sport.* Palo Alto, CA: Bull Publishing.

Wadler, G.I. (1989). *Drugs and the athlete.* Philadelphia: F.A. Davis.

Williams, E.R. & Caliendo, M.A. (1984). *Nutrition, principle issues, and application.* New York: McGraw-Hill.

Williams, M.H. (1983). *Nutrition for fitness and sport.* Dubuque, Iowa: Wm. C. Brown.

Easy Recipe for Making Carbohydrate Replacement Drink*

Information

1. Players need 0.68 grams of carbohydrate per pound of body weight immediately after the first match and again two hours later.

2. Twenty tablespoons of sugar per quart of water yields a 25 percent carbohydrate solution.

3. A 25 percent carbohydrate solution has 7.5 grams of carbohydrate per ounce.

Formula

1. Athlete's body weight (lbs.) x 0.68 grams of carbohydrate per pound = grams of carbohydrate needed immediately after the first match and again two hours later.

2. Grams of carbohydrate needed divided by 7.5 grams per ounce of solution = ounces of solution to be consumed immediately after the first match and again two hours later.

Example: Amount of 25 percent carbohydrate solution needed for 130 pound athlete.

1. 130 pounds x 0.68 grams of carbohydrate per pound = 88.4 grams of carbohydrate needed immediately after the first match and again two hours later.

2. 88.4 grams of carbohydrate divided by 7.5 grams per ounce of solution = 11.8 ounces of solution to be consumed immediately after the first match and again two hours later.

---

* This recipe comes from an example presented in *Research Running News* (January-February 1989) Vol. 5, No. 1.

23

PREVENTION OF COMMON SOCCER INJURIES

Rich Kimball, Eugene W. Brown, and Wade Lillegard

QUESTIONS TO CONSIDER

- What role does equipment and apparel play in injury prevention?
- How can the facilities be made safer for soccer?
- What effect can warm-ups, cool downs, and conditioning have on preventing injuries?
- What role does teaching players safety, appropriate soccer techniques, and proper drills have in injury prevention?
- What commonly used exercises can cause, rather than prevent, injuries?
- What injury prevention techniques can be implemented over the course of a season?

INTRODUCTION

Soccer involves the application of large muscular forces and physical contact at all levels of the game. In spite of rule modifications for younger players, collisions between players and balls, goal posts, the ground, and other players are inevitable. Each collision presents an opportunity for an injury to occur. All of the muscular force and physical contact cannot be eliminated from soccer. However, if you follow several steps aimed at preventing injuries, you can make soccer a safer game.

As a youth soccer coach, you are responsible for doing everything reasonable to provide participants the opportunity to compete in an environment that is healthy and safe.

Equipment and Apparel

A properly equipped and attired soccer player is less likely to be injured. Included within Supplement 3-7, in Chapter 3, are guidelines for selecting essential protective equipment for all soccer players (ball, shin guards, shoes, and mouth guard) and goalkeepers (gloves, shirt, pants, helmet, and athletic supporter with cup, or athletic bra). Because most soccer injuries are minor contusions and skin abrasions to the legs and feet, good quality shin guards and properly fitting soccer shoes should be required to lessen the severity and number of injuries.

Parents should be informed during a pre-season parents' orientation meeting about appropriate soccer equipment and apparel for their children. They should be made aware that: a) if eyeglasses are essential for their child to play, they should be safety glasses worn with a safety strap; b) their child's soccer ball should not be too heavy (e.g., water soaked) or have dangerous protrusions (e.g., loose panels); c) their child's soccer shoes should not have any sharp edges (e.g., screw in cleat with sharp exposed metal); and d) jewelry is not appropriate at practices or games.

At the start of the first practice, you should reinforce what you told the parents about appropriate soccer equipment and apparel and determine if:

- all players have essential protective equipment,
- all players are properly attired,
- equipment is in good repair, and
- equipment properly fits.

This type of inspection should be carried out regularly. Extra shin guards, knee pads, and elbow pads should be included in the team's equipment bag for players who may occasionally forget their equipment.

Facilities

Inspection of a practice or game facility for safety hazards is the responsibility of the adults in charge. For practice, the coach is responsible. For games, both the officials and coaches are responsible. Therefore, you or your assistant must inspect the facilities before permitting your players to participate in practices and games. Whoever is responsible for inspecting the facilities should arrive approximately 10 minutes before the players to carry out the inspection.

If a safety hazard is present, it must be avoided by either relocating, rescheduling, restricting the activity, or removing the hazard.

There are three categories of safety hazards associated with facilities. These are field conditions, structural hazards, and environmental hazards. Safety hazards that are not easily rectified must be reported to the league and/or program administrators. If corrections are not made quickly, you should resubmit your concerns in writing.

● Field Conditions

Some fields are improper for soccer. They may have large ruts, rocks, and holes, which are dangers as well as detractors from the skill of playing the game. Other fields, which have playable conditions, can quickly change from one that is safe to one that is dangerous. These changing conditions are usually associated with an excessive buildup of water and mud from rain storms. Playing soccer when the field is excessively wet may not only be hazardous to the participant, but may also ruin the field for subsequent play. Broken glass bottles carelessly left on the field are another frequent safety hazard that can quickly cause a dangerous situation.

● Structural Hazards

Goals and corner flags are the two structures required by the rules of play. The goals must be soundly constructed with no sharp protrusions. Four of the six soccer-related fatalities reported in the United States from 1973 to 1980 to children from 5 to 14 years old resulted from a goal post falling on the victim.[1] The corner flags must be a minimum of five feet high with a non-pointed top. Flexible posts, which minimize the chance for impaling injuries, are recommended for corner flags. Other permanent and temporary structural hazards are often found around fields assigned to soccer play. Some common examples include: benches, bleachers, water fountains, vehicles, fencing, and poles.

● Environmental Hazards

Lightning is an environmental condition that can be extremely hazardous. No matter how important a practice or game may seem to be, it is not worth the risk of a fatality. Other extreme weather conditions, such as high winds, hail, high temperatures, humidity, cold, snow, and rain need to be cautiously evaluated as potential safety hazards.

Insufficient light is another environmental condition that could be hazardous. Playing under this condition is usually the result of poor scheduling and can be easily avoided.

Activity should not be permitted to continue under the threat of lightning.

Management of Practices and Games

Every physical activity that occurs during practices and games has some potential to result in an injury. Fortunately, in soccer, most practice and game activities have only a rare chance in resulting in an injury. Injuries that do occur are the result of interactions between the situation in which the activity occurs and the physical status of the player. In addition to having an influence over the equipment, apparel, and facilities in reducing the risk of injuries, you have a major influence over the physical activities of your players during practices and games. There are several steps you can take to properly manage the physical activities that occur at practices and games to reduce the rate and severity of the injuries. These steps include the following.

● Teaching Safety to Players

Whenever appropriate, inform your players about the potential risks of injury associated with performing certain soccer activities, and methods for avoiding injury. For example, a diving header can be a dangerous play if executed with the head low to the ground while other players are near. By informing your players of this danger and possibly establishing a team rule that permits diving headers only when a player is not being challenged by opponents, you will reduce the risk of injury to your players. There are many other examples that could be highlighted here.

The key to teaching safety to your players is to prudently interject safety tips in your instruction whenever appropriate.

● Warming Up

A warm-up at the beginning of your team's practices and before games provides several important benefits. If the field is not immediately available for your team's use, warm-ups can start in the space surrounding the field. Specific warm-up suggestions are included in Chapter 21 (Conditioning Youth Soccer Players) under the section titled Warm-Up, Cool Down, and Stretching Activities for Soccer. When warm-ups and stretching are completed, the skill-oriented drills on your practice plan or the formal drills before the game may begin. A warm-up period:

- increases the breathing rate, heart rate, and muscle temperature to exercise levels;
- reduces the risks of muscle pulls and strains;
- increases the shock-absorbing capabilities of the joints; and
- prepares players mentally for practices and games.

• Teaching Appropriate Techniques

The instructions you provide during practices on how to execute the skills of soccer have an influence on the risks of injuries to your players as well as their opponents. Teach your players the proper ways to perform soccer techniques, and avoid any temptation to teach how to intentionally foul opponents.

First, an improper technique often results in a greater chance of injury to the performer than the correct execution. For example, use of the side of the head (temple region) is not a correct technique to use in heading a soccer ball and has a much higher risk of injury than heading the ball with the forehead. Acceptable techniques in sports usually evolve with safety as a concern.

Second, techniques involving intentional fouls should never be taught or condoned. Coaches who promote an atmosphere in which intentional violent fouls are acceptable must be eliminated from the youth soccer program. You should promote fair and safe play in practices and games with strict enforcement of the rules to encourage skill as the primary factor in determining the outcome of the game.

• Selecting Proper Drills

Drills that you select or design for your practices and the ways in which they are carried out have an influence on the risks of injuries for your players. Drills should be selected and designed with safety as a primary feature. Before implementing a new drill into your practice, several safety questions should be considered.

- Is the drill appropriate for the level of maturation of the players?
- Are the players sufficiently skilled to comply with the requirements of the drill?
- Are the players sufficiently conditioned to handle the stress of participation in the drill?
- Are other, less risky drills available to achieve the same practice results?
- Can the drill be modified to make it less risky and yet achieve the desired training result?

• Conditioning

High intensity work is part of the game of soccer. How well your players can handle fatigue will determine how well they perform. Is there, however, any relationship between fatigue and injury? The following sequence of events draws an association linking fatigue with an increase potential for injury.

Athlete becomes fatigued

↓

Skilled performance is reduced

↓

Concentration becomes difficult

↓

Reactions slow down

↓

Judgment becomes impaired

↓

Faulty decisions are made

↓

Injuries may result

Figure 23-1. How fatigue is linked to an increased potential for injuries.

In addition to improving performance, every conditioning program should be designed to minimize fatigue and the potential for injury. Being "in shape" can postpone fatigue and its detrimental effects. By progressively intensifying your practices throughout the season, you can produce a conditioning effect that can be an important deterrent to injury. (See Chapter 21, Conditioning Youth Soccer Players.)

Coaches must also be aware that older players who engage in intense, frequent practices and games may need time off as the season wears on. It is possible to overtrain, and predispose to, rather than prevent, injuries. Injuries caused by overtraining have grown to represent an increased portion of reported sports injuries. Some telltale signs of overtraining include:

- elevated resting heart rate,

- poor performance,

- loss of enthusiasm,

- depression,

- higher incidence of injury, and

- longer time to recover from injury.

Antidotes to overtraining include time off from practice, shorter practices, alternating intense practices with lighter workouts, or any combination of these suggestions. Overtraining is not usually a problem when players are practicing two or three times a week, unless they are also: a) playing two or more games per week, b) playing on more than one soccer team, or c) playing on a different sport team during the same season.

● Avoiding Contraindicated Exercises

Over the past several years, researchers and physicians have identified a list of exercises that are commonly used by coaches but are potentially harmful to the body. These are called contraindicated exercises. This information has been slow in reaching coaches and their players. Table 23-1 contains a list of these exercises and how contraindicated exercises can be modified to eliminate their undesirable characteristics. Also included in Table 23-1 are substitute soccer exercises that accomplish the same purpose in a safer manner, with the added benefit of using the ball.

● Cooling Down

There are few feelings more uncomfortable than finishing a vigorous workout, sitting down for a while, then trying to walk. Muscles in the body tighten during periods of inactivity following hard work.

To minimize the stiffness that usually follows a workout, and the soreness the following day, take time to adequately cool down at the end of practice. A gradual reduction of activity (the reverse of the warm-up procedure) facilitates the dissipation of waste products associated with muscular activity. Letting the body cool off gradually may not prevent injuries, but the players may experience less discomfort and be better able to function at high levels during the next workout. (See Chapter 21, Conditioning Youth Soccer Players, the section titled Warm-up, Cool Down, and Stretching Activities for Soccer.)

Table 23-1. Contraindicated exercises.

EXERCISES	MUSCLES AND JOINTS AFFECTED	PROBLEMS	ADAPTATIONS	SOCCER EXERCISES
Toe touches	Hamstrings, lower back, knee	Puts excessive strain on lower back and overextends the knee joint	Seated straight-leg stretch	High road-low road
Straight leg sit-ups	Abdominals, lower back	Puts excessive strain on lower back throughout the exercise; strengthens muscles that contribute to pelvic tilt, thus promoting lower back problems	Abdominal curls: bent legs, arms across chest; curl 2/3 of the way up slowly	Bent leg sit-ups with the ball
Straight leg lifts	Abdominals, lower back	Same as straight leg sit-ups	Bent leg abdominal curls	
Deep squats	Quadriceps	Opens knee and stretches ligaments	Squat only until thigh is parallel to ground	Jumping over the ball
Hurdler's stretch	Hamstring (straight leg); knee joint (bent leg)	Stretches the ligaments of the bent knee	V-sit with legs spread 90° and both legs straight, or leave one leg straight and place the bottom of the foot of the bent leg up on the straight leg (next to knee)	High road-low road
Standing one-leg quad stretch	Quadriceps, knee of bent leg	Stretches the ligaments of the bent knee	Hold leg with opposite hand and extend the hip joint	

SUMMARY

This chapter has focused on three areas in which you can exert an influence to reduce the potential number and severity of injuries in soccer. The first area involves your insistence that your players wear appropriate protective equipment and apparel. Avoiding safety hazards associated with the soccer facilities (field conditions, structural hazards, and environmental hazards) is the second area. Management of practices and games is the third area. Proper management includes teaching your players safety, appropriate soccer techniques, and proper drills; and running practices with warming up, conditioning, and cooling down exercises; but exclude known contraindicated exercises. Safety and injury prevention should be a primary factor to consider in whatever plans you make for your soccer team. You will be more than compensated for the extra time and effort required to implement the suggestions found in this chapter by the comfort of knowing that you have done as much as you can to assure that your players will have a safe season.

REFERENCES

1. Rutherford, G., Miles, R., Brown, V., & MacDonald, B. (1981). *Overview of sports related injuries to persons 5-14 years of age.* Washington, DC: U.S. Consumer Product Safety Commission.

SUGGESTED READINGS

Agre, J.C., & Krotee, M.L. (1981). Soccer safety—Prevention and care. *Journal of Health, Physical Education, Recreation and Dance,* 52(5): 52-54.

American College of Sports Medicine, American Orthopaedic Society for Sports Medicine & Sports Medicine Committee of the United States Tennis Association (1982). *Sports Injuries—An Aid to Prevention and Treatment.* Coventry, CT: Bristol-Myers Co.

Estrand, J., & Gillquist, J. (1983). Soccer injuries and their mechanisms: A prospective study. *Medicine and Science in Sports and Exercise,* 15(3): 267-270.

Jackson, D., & Pescar, S. (1981). *The Young Athletes Health Handbook.* Everest House.

McCarroll, J.R., Meaney, C., & Sieber, J.M. (1984). Profile of youth soccer injuries. *Physician and Sportsmedicine,* 12(2): 113-115, 117.

Micheli, L.J. (1985). Preventing youth sports injuries. *Journal of Health, Physical Education, Recreation and Dance,* 76(6): 52-54.

Mirkin, G., & Marshall, H. (1978). *The Sportsmedicine Book.* Little, Brown, & Co.

Smodhaka, V.N. (1981). Death on the soccer field and its prevention. *Physician and Sportsmedicine,* 9(8): 101-107.

CARE OF COMMON SOCCER INJURIES

Rich Kimball, Eugene W. Brown, and Wade Lillegard

QUESTIONS TO CONSIDER
- Can you identify and provide first aid for the different medical conditions commonly associated with soccer?
- What items belong in a well-stocked first-aid kit?
- What procedures should you follow when an injury occurs?
- What information should you have about your players in case they become injured?

INTRODUCTION

Chris has the ball and one fullback to beat. A feint leaves the fullback out of the play. Only the goalkeeper is left on defense. As Chris sprints toward the goal, the goalkeeper begins to leave the goal area and approach the ball. Chris momentarily loses control of the dribble and everyone is uncertain as to who will get to play the ball first. Both Chris and the goalkeeper sprint full speed toward the ball and each other. They arrive simultaneously, neither backing off of the play. There is a violent collision, and Chris lies motionless on the ground. The referee, sensing the likelihood of injury, immediately signals Chris' coach onto the field to tend to the downed player.

Watching from the bench, the first, and normal, reaction of a coach is to be frightened by the possible outcome of this violent collision. The sinking feeling in the stomach and the "Oh, no" message sent out by the brain when Chris went down have been felt by most coaches at some point in their careers.

If this, or some similar situation confronted you, what would you do? Are you prepared to act appropriately? As a coach of a youth soccer team, it is your obligation to be able to deal with such an emergency. Before your first practice, you should:

- obtain medical information on your players,

- establish emergency procedures, and

- prepare to provide first aid.

You must not rely on the likelihood that a serious injury will not occur to the players on your team as an excuse for not being prepared to handle an emergency situation!

MEDICAL INFORMATION

The completed Athlete Medical Information (Supplement 3-5) and Medical Release (Supplement 3-6) forms in Chapter 3, Working Effectively with Parents, should be in your possession whenever your players are under your supervision. Hopefully, the need to use this information will never arise. But, if an injury does occur, the information on these forms will help you and qualified medical personnel respond quickly to an emergency.

EMERGENCY PROCEDURES

As the coach of an injured player, you are responsible for the actions taken until the player is placed in the care of competent medical personnel, parents, or guardians. Parents and players expect you to know how to proceed. The following sequential steps should be taken in an emergency:

1. Take charge of the situation.

2. Determine the nature of the injury.

3. Start emergency procedures if necessary.

4. Transfer care to a medical professional.

Step 1: Take Charge

Establish immediate control over the situation by having your assistant coach take charge of all uninjured players. If you do not have an assistant coach, send the players to a designated area within range of your voice and vision until the injury situation is resolved. This simple action establishes control, clears the area of potentially harmful distractions, and facilitates a quick response to emergency situations.

Step 2: Determine the Nature of the Injury

Upon reaching an injured player, you should perform a visual analysis of the situation. Is the player breathing? . . . conscious? . . . bleeding? Ask the player questions to find out what happened and where the pain is located. This information will help you determine whether the injury is serious and requires emergency measures or whether it is an injury that can be properly cared for without emergency procedures.

Step 3: Provide Emergency Care

Most emergency situations can be appropriately handled if you remember the ABC's of emergency care, as advocated by the American Red Cross. [1]

A = Airway

B = Breathing

C = Circulation

Remembering the ABC's will remind you of how to proceed in a life-threatening situation.

It is beyond the scope of this chapter to provide the complete information necessary to handle all emergencies. To familiarize you with what is involved and to encourage you to obtain appropriate first aid and CPR (cardiopulmonary resuscitation) instruction, the ABC's and bleeding are briefly outlined. More complete information on artificial respiration is available through your local chapter of the American Red Cross.

The ABC's

- Open the Airway

  Always check the airway to make sure it is free of any items that may impede breathing. In soccer, the mouth guard can obstruct the airway and should be removed immediately. The primary method advocated for opening the airway is the jaw thrust or chin lift method. The Red Cross provides materials and training for developing this skill.

- Restore Breathing

  Once the airway is open, check to see if the player is breathing. Is the chest moving up and down? Are there sounds of breathing? Can you feel exhaled air at the mouth or nostrils? If breathing is not taking place, begin artificial respiration. The procedures taught by the Red Cross are the standard to follow when attempting to restore breathing.

- Restore Circulation

  If the heart has stopped beating, circulation should be restored via CPR. Cardiopulmonary resuscitation is a valuable skill to learn and maintain because you are coaching a sport in which the temporary interruption of cardiopulmonary function could occur. The techniques of CPR are beyond the scope of this manual. You are encouraged to attend one of the many American Red Cross CPR courses that are regularly offered in nearly every local community that sponsors youth soccer.

Bleeding

If the player is bleeding profusely, you must still follow the ABC's. Stopping the bleeding will serve no benefit if the injured player cannot breathe.

Extensive bleeding should be controlled by applying direct pressure over the wound for 10 to 20 minutes without checking the wound. A sterile pad is preferred, but in an emergency, use whatever is available: a towel, a shirt, your hand, etc. The use of a tourniquet is ill-advised and should only be employed when one accepts the fact that its use may be trading the loss of a limb to save a life.

Step 4: Transfer Care to a Medical Professional

The usual culmination of providing emergency care is transferring that care to trained medical professionals (a physician and/or emergency medical technician, an EMT) and transporting the player to a medical facility. This action presumes knowledge of how this should be done.

We recommend that a call for assistance be made immediately upon determination that the injury is life-threatening. This should be completed by an assistant during the time that appropriate care is being administered to the player. To complete this important task, the location of a phone must be known, correct change must be available, and the telephone number must be readily available. If you have the completed Athlete Medical Information and Medical Release forms in your possession, you are prepared to act.

It is recommended that you contact parents as soon as possible. If the player's family cannot be contacted, you may need to accompany the injured player to the hospital because the Medical Release Form designates you to act in the place of the parents. The information on the Athlete Medical Information Form is useful to direct EMT's or others to the family's preferred physicians or hospitals. The Athlete Medical Information Form must accompany the injured player to aid the medical professionals in their diagnosis for treatment of the problem(s).

Rehearsing emergency care procedures can be invaluable.

Immediate treatment of life-threatening injuries is extremely important. Being trained in basic first-aid and emergency procedures is invaluable and will give you more confidence when dealing with any type of injury.

If the player is seriously injured, have your assistant coach, a parent, or a responsible player take the coins and the list of emergency telephone numbers from the first aid kit and call an ambulance. You should stay with the injured player until help arrives.

Aids for Proper Care

If the injury is less serious and does not require assistance from trained medical personnel, you may be able to move the player from the field to the bench area and begin appropriate care. Two important aids to properly care for an injured player include a first aid kit and ice.

● **First Aid Kit**

A well-stocked first aid kit does not have to be large, but it should contain the basic items that may be needed for appropriate care. The checklist below provides a guide for including commonly used supplies. You may wish to add and subtract from the kit on the basis of your experience and/or local policies or guidelines.

FIRST AID KIT CHECKLIST

_____ white athletic tape	_____ plastic bags for ice
_____ sterile gauze pads	_____ coins for pay telephone
_____ Telfa no-stick pads	_____ emergency care phone numbers
_____ elastic bandages	_____ list of emergency phone numbers
_____ Band-aids, assorted sizes	_____ scissors/knife
_____ foam rubber/moleskin	_____ safety pins
_____ tweezers	_____ soap
_____ disinfectant	

A good rule of thumb for coaches is, "If you can't treat the problems by using the supplies in a well-stocked first aid kit, then it is too big a problem for you to handle." You should be able to handle bruises, small cuts, strains, and sprains. When fractures, dislocations, back, or neck injuries occur, call for professional medical assistance.

- Ice

Having access to ice is unique to every local setting. Thus, every coach may have to arrange for its provision in a different way. Ice, however, is very important to proper immediate care of many minor injuries and should, therefore, be readily available.

Care of Minor Injuries

- R.I.C.E.

Unless you are also a physician, you should not attempt to care for anything except minor injuries (e.g., bruises, bumps, sprains). Many minor injuries can be cared for by using the R.I.C.E. formula.

R.I.C.E. Formula

The R.I.C.E. formula for care of minor injuries involves the following steps:

R = Rest: Keep the player out of action.

I = Ice: Apply ice to the injured area.

C = Compression: Wrap an elastic bandage around the injured area and the ice bag to hold the bag in place. The bandage should not be so tight as to cut off blood flow to the injured area.

E = Elevation: Let gravity drain the excess fluid.

Most minor injuries can benefit from using the R.I.C.E. formula for care.

When following the R.I.C.E. formula, ice should be kept on the injured area for 15 minutes and taken off for 20 minutes. Repeat this procedure three to four times. Icing should continue three times per day for the first 72 hours following the injury. After three days, extended care is necessary if the injury has not healed. At this time, options for care include:

- stretching and strengthening exercises,
- contrast treatments, and
- visiting a doctor for further diagnosis.

- Contrast Treatments

If the injured area is much less swollen after 72 hours, but the pain is subsiding, contrast treatments will help. Use the following procedure:

1. Place the injured area in an ice bath or cover with an ice bag for one minute.

2. After using the ice, place the injured area in warm water (100° - 110°) for three minutes.

3. Continue this rotation for five to seven bouts of ice and four to six bouts of heat.

4. Always end with the ice treatment.

Contrast treatments should be followed for the next three to five days. If swelling or pain still persists after several days of contrast treatments, the player should be sent to a physician for further tests. Chapter 25 of this section deals with the rehabilitation of injuries. Read it carefully, because proper care is actually a form of rehabilitation.

COMMON MEDICAL PROBLEMS IN SOCCER

Information about 23 common medical conditions that may occur in soccer is presented in this section. The information about each condition includes: 1) a definition, 2) common symptoms, 3) immediate on-field treatment, and 4) guidelines for returning the player to action.

ABRASION

Definition:

- superficial skin wound caused by scraping

Symptoms:

- minor bleeding
- redness
- burning sensation

Care:

- Cleanse the area with soap and water.
- Control the bleeding.
- Cover the area with sterile dressing.
- Monitor over several days for signs of infection.

Return to Action:

- after providing immediate care

BACK or NECK INJURY

Definition:

- any injury to the back or neck area that causes the player to become immobile or unconscious

Symptoms:

- pain and tenderness over the spine
- numbness
- weakness or heaviness in limbs
- tingling feeling in extremities

Care:

- Make sure the player is breathing.
- Call for medical assistance.
- Do not move neck or back.

Return to Action:

- with permission of a physician

BLISTERS

Definition:

- localized collection of fluid in the outer portion of the skin

Symptoms:

- redness
- inflammation
- oozing of fluid
- discomfort

Care:

- Put disinfectant on the area.
- Cut a hole in a stack of several gauze pads to be used as a doughnut surrounding the blister.
- Cover the area with a Band-aid.
- Alter the cause of the problem when possible (e.g., proper size and/or shape of the soccer shoes).

Return to Action:

- immediately, unless pain is severe

CONTUSION

Definition:

- a bruise; an injury in which the skin is not broken

Symptoms:

- tenderness around the injury
- swelling
- localized pain

Care:

- Apply the R.I.C.E. formula for first three days.
- Use contrast treatments for days four to eight.
- Restrict activity.
- Provide padding when returning the player to activity.

Return to Action:

- when there is complete absence of pain and full range of motion is restored

CRAMPS

Definition:

- involuntary and forceful contraction of a muscle; muscle spasm

Symptoms:

- localized pain in contracting muscle

Care:

- Slowly stretch the muscle.
- Massage the muscle.

Return to Action:

- when pain is gone and full range of motion is restored

DENTAL INJURY

Definition:

- any injury to mouth or teeth

Symptoms:

- pain
- bleeding
- loss of tooth (partial or total)

Care:

- Clear the airway where necessary.
- Stop the bleeding with direct pressure.
- Make sure excess blood does not clog the airway.
- Save any teeth that were knocked free; store them in the player's own mouth or a moist, sterile cloth.
- Do not rub or clean tooth that has been knocked out.
- Transport player to a hospital or dentist.

Return to Action:

- when the pain is gone (usually within two to three days)
- with permission of a dentist or physician

DISLOCATION

Definition:

- loss of normal anatomical alignment of a joint

Symptoms:

- complaints of joint slipping in and out (subluxation)
- joint out of line
- pain at the joint

Care:

- mild

  —Treat as a sprain (i.e., R.I.C.E.).

  —Obtain medical care.

- severe

  —Immobilize before moving.

  —Must be treated by a physician.

  —Obtain medical care. Do not attempt to put joint back into place.

  —R.I.C.E.

Return to Action:

- with permission of a physician

EYE INJURY—CONTUSION

Definition:

- direct blow to the eye and region surrounding the eye by a blunt object

Symptoms:

- pain
- redness of eye
- watery eye

Care:

- Have the player lie down with his/her eyes closed.
- Place a folded cloth, soaked in cold water, gently on the eye.
- Seek medical attention if injury is assessed as severe.

Return to Action:

- for minor injury, player may return to action after symptoms clear
- for severe injury, with permission of a physician

EYE INJURY—FOREIGN OBJECT

Definition:

- object between eyelid and eyeball

Symptoms:

- pain
- redness of eye
- watery eye
- inability to keep eye open

Care:

- Do not rub the eye.
- Allow tears to form in eye.
- Carefully try to remove loose object with sterile cotton swab.
- If object is embedded in the eye, have the player close both eyes, loosely cover both eyes with sterile dressing, and bring the player to an emergency room or ophthalmologist.

Return to Action:

- with permission from a physician

FAINTING

Definition:

- dizziness and loss of consciousness that may be caused by an injury, exhaustion, heat illness, emotional stress, or lack of oxygen

Symptoms:

- dizziness
- cold, clammy skin
- pale
- seeing "spots" before one's eyes
- weak, rapid pulse

Care:

- Have the player lie down and elevate his/her feet or have the player sit with his/her head between the knees.

Return to Action:

- with permission of a physician

FRACTURE

Definition:

- a crack or complete break in a bone [A simple fracture is a broken bone, but with unbroken skin. An open fracture is a broken bone that also breaks the skin.]

Symptoms:

- pain at fracture site
- tenderness, swelling
- deformity or unnatural position
- loss of function in injured area
- open wound, bleeding (open fracture)

[Note that, a simple fracture may not be evident immediately. If localized pain persists, obtain medical assistance.]

Care:

- Stabilize injured bone by using splints, slings, or bandages.
- Do not attempt to straighten an injured part when immobilizing it.
- If skin is broken (open fracture), keep the open wound clean by covering it with the cleanest available cloth.
- Check for shock and treat if necessary.

Return to Action:

- with permission of a physician

HEAD INJURY—CONSCIOUS

Definition:

- any injury that causes the player to be unable to respond in a coherent fashion to known facts (name, date, etc.)

Symptoms:

- dizziness
- pupils unequal in size and/or non-responsive to light and dark
- disoriented
- unsure of name, date, or activity
- unsteady movement of eyeballs when trying to follow a finger moving in front of eyes
- same symptoms as noted for back or neck injury may be present

Care:

- If above symptoms are present, player may be moved carefully when dizziness disappears. Players with head injuries should be removed from further practice or competition that day and should be carefully observed for a minimum of 24 hours.
- Obtain medical assistance.

Return to Action:

- with permission of a physician

HEAD INJURY—UNCONSCIOUS

Definition:

- any injury in which the player is unable to respond to external stimuli by verbal or visual means

Symptoms:

- player is unconscious
- cuts or bruises around the head may be evident

Care:

- ANY TIME A PLAYER IS UNCONSCIOUS, ASSUME AN INJURY TO THE SPINAL CORD OR BRAIN.
- If necessary, clear the airway, keeping the player's neck straight.
- Do not move the player.
- Call for medical assistance.

Return to Action:

- with permission of a physician

HEAT EXHAUSTION

Definition:

- heat disorder that may lead to heat stroke

Symptoms:

- fatigue
- profuse sweating
- chills
- throbbing pressure in the head
- nausea
- normal body temperature
- pale and clammy skin
- muscle cramps

Care:

- Remove the player from heat and sun.
- Provide plenty of water.
- Rest the player in a supine position with feet elevated about 12 inches.
- Loosen or remove the player's clothing.
- Fan athlete.
- Drap wet towels over athlete.

Return to Action:

- next day if symptoms are no longer present

HEAT STROKE

Definition:

- heat disorder that is life-threatening

Symptoms:

- extremely high body temperature
- hot, red, and dry skin
- rapid and strong pulse
- confusion
- fainting
- convulsions

Care:

- Immediately call for medical assistance.
- Immediately cool body by cold sponging, immersion in cool water, and cold packs.

Return to Action:

- with permission of a physician

LACERATIONS

Definition:

- a tearing or cutting of the skin

Symptoms:

- bleeding
- swelling

Care:

- Elevate area.
- Direct pressure with gauze (if available) to the wound for four to five minutes usually will stop bleeding.
- Continue to add gauze if blood soaks through.
- Clean the wound with disinfectant.
- Use the R.I.C.E. formula.
- If stitches are required, send to a doctor within 6 hours.

Return to Action:

- as soon as pain is gone, if the wound can be protected from further injury

LOSS OF WIND

Definition:

- a forceful blow to mid-abdomen area that causes inability to breathe

Symptoms:

- rapid, shallow breathing
- gasping for breath

Care:

- Check player to determine if other injuries exist.
- Place player in a supine position.
- Calm the player in order to foster slower breathing.

Return to Action:

- after five minutes of rest to regain composure and breathing has returned to normal rate

NOSE BLEED

Definition:

- bleeding from the nose

Symptoms:

- bleeding
- swelling
- pain
- deformity of nose

Care:

- Calm the athlete.
- Get the athlete into a sitting position.
- Pinch the nostrils together with fingers while the athlete breathes through the mouth.
- If bleeding cannot be controlled, call for medical assistance.

Return to Action:

- minor nosebleed—when bleeding has stopped for several minutes; if no deformity and no impairment to breathing, pack nose with gauze before athlete continues competition
- serious nosebleed—no more competition that day; doctor's permission if a fracture has occurred

PLANTAR FASCITIS[2]

Definition:

- inflammation of the connective tissue (fascia) that runs from the heel to the toes

Symptoms:

- arch and heel pain
- sharp pain ("stone bruise") near heel
- gradual onset of pain, that may be tolerated for weeks
- morning pain may be more severe
- pain may decrease throughout day

Care:

- Rest the foot.
- Stretch the Achilles tendon before exercise.
- Use shoes with firm heel counter, good heel cushion, and arch support.
- Use of a heel lift may reduce shock to the foot and decrease the pain.
- Use adhesive strapping to support the arch.[3]

Return to Action:

- when pain is gone

PUNCTURE WOUND

Definition:

- any hole made by the piercing of a pointed instrument

Symptoms:

- breakage of the skin
- minor bleeding, possibly none
- tender around wound

Care:

- Cleanse the area with soap and water.
- Control the bleeding.
- Cover the area with sterile dressing.
- Consult physician about the need for a tetanus shot.
- Monitor over several days for signs of infection.

Return to Action:

- with permission of a physician

SHOCK

Definition:

- adverse reaction of the body to physical or psychological trauma

Symptoms:

- pale
- cold, clammy skin
- dizziness
- nausea

- faint feeling

Care:

- Have the athlete lie down.
- Calm the athlete.
- Elevate the feet, unless it is a head injury.
- Send for emergency help.
- Control the player's temperature.
- Loosen tight-fitting clothing.
- Control the pain or bleeding if necessary.

Return to Action:

- with permission of a physician

SPRAIN

Definition:

- a stretching or a partial or complete tear of the ligaments surrounding a joint

Symptoms:

- pain at the joint
- pain aggravated by motion at the joint
- tenderness and swelling
- looseness at the joint

Care:

- Immobilize at time of injury if pain is severe; may use corner flag post as a splint.
- Use the R.I.C.E. formula.
- Send the player to a physician.

Return to Action:

- when pain and swelling are gone
- when full range of motion is reestablished
- when strength and stability is within 95 percent of the non-injured limb throughout range of motion
- when light formal activity is possible with no favoring of the injury
- when formal activity can be resumed with moderate to full intensity with no favoring of the injury

STRAIN

Definition:

- stretching or tearing of the muscle or tendons that attach the muscle to the bone (commonly referred to as a "muscle pull")

Symptoms:

- localized pain brought on by stretching or contracting the muscle in question

- unequal strength between limbs

Care:

- Use the R.I.C.E. formula.

- Use contrast treatments for days four through eight.

Return to Action:

- when the player can stretch the injured segment as far as the non-injured segment

- when strength is equal to opposite segment

- when the athlete can perform basic soccer tasks without favoring the injury

    [Note that, depending on the severity of the strain, it may take from one day to more than two weeks for an athlete to return to action.]

MAINTAINING APPROPRIATE RECORDS

The immediate care you provide to an injured player is important to limit the extent of the injury and to set the stage for appropriate rehabilitation. However, immediate care is not the end of prudent action when an injury occurs. Two additional brief but valuable tasks should be completed. The first of these is to complete an On-Site Injury Report Form (Supplement 24-1) and the second is to log the injury on the Summary of Season Injuries Form (Supplement 24-2).

On-Site Injury Report Form

It is important for you to maintain a record of the injuries that occur to your players. This information may be helpful to guide delayed care or medical treatment and may be very important if any legal problems develop in connection with the injury. Supplement 24-1 includes a standard form that will help guide the recording of pertinent information relative to each injury. These records should be kept for several years following an injury. You should check on legal requirements in your state to determine how long these records should be kept.

Summary of Season Injuries Form

Supplement 24-2, Summary of Season Injuries Form, lists each of the common medical conditions that occur in soccer and also provides a space for you to record when each type of injury occurred. At the end of the season, you should total the incidences of each injury type to see if there is any trend to the kind of injuries your team has suffered. If a trend exists, evaluate your training methods in all areas of practices and games. Try to alter drills or circumstances that may be causing injuries. Review Chapter 23, Preventing Common Soccer Injuries, for techniques that may help you prevent injuries. Perhaps your practice routine ignores or over-emphasizes some area of stretching or conditioning. Decide on a course of action that may be implemented for next season and write your thoughts in the space provided or note the appropriate changes you wish to make on your season or practice plans.

SUMMARY

This chapter attempts to acquaint you with various injuries associated with soccer and how you should be prepared to deal with these injuries. If you have prepared your first aid kit, brought along the medical records, and familiarized yourself with the different types of injuries, you should be able to handle whatever situation arises. Follow the steps that are outlined for you, and remember — you are not a doctor. If you are in doubt about how to proceed, use the coins in your first aid kit and call for professional medical help. Do not make decisions about treatments if you are not qualified to make them.

Remember, react quickly and with confidence. Most injuries will be minor and the injured players will need only a little reassurance before they can be moved to the bench area. Injuries will always occur in soccer. Therefore, you must prepare yourself to deal with whatever happens in a calm, responsible manner.

REFERENCES

1. American Red Cross (1981). *Cardiopulmonary resuscitation.* Washington, DC: American Red Cross.

2. Tanner, S.M., & Harvey, J.S. (1988). How we manage plantar fascitis. *The Physician and Sportsmedicine,* 16(8), 39-40, 42, 44, 47.

3. Whitesel, J., & Newell, S.G. (1980). Modified low-dye strapping. *The Physician and Sportsmedicine,* 8(9), 129-131.

SUGGESTED READINGS

American College of Sports Medicine, American Orthopaedic Society for Sports Medicine & Sports Medicine Committee of the United States Tennis Association (1982). *Sports Injuries—An Aid to Prevention and Treatment.* Coventry, CT: Bristol-Myers Co.

Hackworth, C., Jacobs, K., & O'Neill, C. (1982). *Prevention, Recognition, and Care of Common Sports Injuries.* Kalamazoo, MI: SWM Systems, Inc.

Jackson, D., & Pescar, S. (1981). *The Young Athlete's Health Handbook.* New York: Everest House.

Rosenberg, S.N. (1985). *The Johnson & Johnson First Aid Book.* New York: Warner Books, Inc.

ON-SITE INJURY REPORT FORM

Name _____ Date of injury _____
                    (Injured Player)   Mo   Day   Yr

Address _____
                    (Street)   (City)   (State)   (Zip)

Telephone _____
                    (Home)   (Other)

Nature and extent of injury: _____

_____

How did the injury occur? _____

_____

Describe first aid given, including name(s) of attendee(s) _____

_____

Disposition: _____ to hospital _____ to home _____ to physician

Other: _____

_____

Was protective equipment worn?   _____ Yes   _____ No

Explanation: _____

_____

Condition of the playing surface: _____

_____

Names and addresses of witnesses:

(Name)	(Street)	(City)	(State)	(Zip)	(Tel.)
(Name)	(Street)	(City)	(State)	(Zip)	(Tel.)
(Name)	(Street)	(City)	(State)	(Zip)	(Tel.)
(Name)	(Street)	(City)	(State)	(Zip)	(Tel.)

Other comments: _____

_____

_____
(Signed)   (Date)   (Title-Position)

SUMMARY OF SEASON INJURIES FORM

Injury Type	First 4 Weeks	Middle Weeks	Last 4 Weeks	Total
1. Abrasion				
2. Back or Neck Injury				
3. Blisters				
4. Contusion				
5. Cramps				
6. Dental Injury				
7. Dislocation				
8. Eye Injury—Contusion				
9. Eye Injury—Foreign Object				
10. Fainting				
11. Fracture				
12. Head Injury—Conscious				
13. Head Injury-Unconscious				
14. Heat Exhaustion				
15. Heat Stroke				
16. Lacerations				
17. Loss of Wind				
18. Nose Bleed				
19. Plantar Fascitis				
20. Puncture Wound				
21. Shock				
22. Sprain				
23. Strain				
24. Others				
25.				

Do you see a trend?   Yes   No

Steps to take to reduce injuries next season:

(1)_____

(2)_____

(3)_____

(4)_____

(5)_____

(6)_____

(7)_____

(Continued on reverse side)

SUMMARY OF SEASON INJURIES (cont.)

(8) _____

(9) _____

(10) _____

(11) _____

(12) _____

(13) _____

(14) _____

(15) _____

(16) _____

(17) _____

(18) _____

(19) _____

(20) _____

(21) _____

(22) _____

(23) _____

(24) _____

(25) _____

(26) _____

(27) _____

(28) _____

(29) _____

(30) _____

(31) _____

(32) _____

(33) _____

(34) _____

REHABILITATION OF COMMON SOCCER INJURIES

Rich Kimball, Eugene W. Brown, and Wade Lillegard

QUESTIONS TO CONSIDER
- What are the important components of a rehabilitation program?
- How can a coach tell when athletes are trying to "come back" too fast?
- What do recurring injuries tell the coach, athletes, and parents about the rehabilitation program?

INTRODUCTION

Decisions about the rehabilitation of injuries and reentry into competition must be made according to a flexible set of guidelines; not hard and fast rules. Every individual on your team and each injury is unique. Therefore, rehabilitation techniques and reentry criteria will differ for each injured player.

GENERAL PROCEDURES

Most injuries suffered by your players will not be treated by a physician. Therefore, you, the player, and the player's parents will determine when the player returns to action. It is prudent to seek the parents' written permission to return a previously injured player to practice activities and games. If a player has been treated by a physician, written clearance from the physician should also be obtained. Players, coaches, and parents realize that missing practices will reduce the player's ability to help the team. Pressure is often exerted on the coach to play injured players before they are fully recovered, especially if they are the stars of the team. If a player has been treated by a physician for an injury, written clearance by both the physician and the parents should be obtained before permitting the player to return to practices and games. Also, clarification as to any limitations on participation should be obtained from the physician.

Chances of an injury recurring are greatly increased if a player returns to action too soon. The following five criteria should be met, in order, before allowing an injured player back into full physical activity:

1. Absence of pain

2. Full range of motion at the injured area

3. Normal strength and size at the injured area

4. Normal speed and agility

5. Normal level of fitness

If a physician is not overseeing an injured player's rehabilitation, the task of rehabilitation will probably fall upon the coach. Stretching activities, calisthenics, and possibly weight training exercises form the basis of a rehabilitation program. Start with simple stretches. Presence of pain during movement is the key to determining if the activity is too stressful. The onset of pain means too much is being attempted too soon. When players can handle the stretching, then calisthenics and possibly weight training can be added to the program. The principles of training included in Chapter 21 (Conditioning Youth Soccer Players), should guide all phases of the rehabilitation program.

Absence of Pain

Most injuries are accompanied by pain, although the pain is not always evident immediately when the injury occurs. Usually, the pain disappears quickly if the injury is a bruise, a strain, or a minor sprain. For more serious injuries such as dislocations or fractures, the pain may remain for days or weeks. A physician should be consulted if the injury appears to be serious or if the problem doesn't seem to be normally resolving itself. Once the pain is gone, the player can start the stretching portion of a rehabilitation program.

The main goal of a rehabilitation program is to reestablish range of motion, strength, power, and muscular endurance at the site of the injury. As long as players remain free of pain, they should proceed with their program. If pain recurs, they should eliminate pain-producing movements until they are pain-free again. The athletes should be in close contact with their physicians during any rehabilitations from injury.

The chance of an injury recurring is greatly increased if a player returns to action too soon.

Full Range of Motion

Injuries generally reduce the range of motion around a joint. The more severe the injury, the greater the reduction in range of motion, particularly when the injured area has been immobilized. As soon as they are able to move an injured area without pain, players should be encouraged to progressively increase the range of movement until a normal range is achievable. For example, if the player has strained a groin muscle, a fairly common injury early in the season, the muscle should be stretched as much as possible without causing pain. Initially, the movement may be slight if the injury was severe. With stretching, the full range of motion will eventually return. The athletes' physicians must be involved at this stage of rehabilitation. Physicians often prescribe specific exercises to safely increase range of motion. When the player can move the injured joint through its normal range, strengthening exercises should begin.

Normal Strength and Size

After a body part has been immobilized (by cast, splint wrap or disuse), muscles become smaller and weaker than they were before the injury. Just because a physician removes a cast and the injuries have "healed," does not mean that players are ready to practice or play at full speed. Loss of muscle mass means a loss of strength. Letting players resume a normal practice schedule before their strength has returned to pre-injury levels could lead to re-injury. Strengthening the injured area should be done conservatively and under a physician's direction. If weights are used, start with light weights and perform the exercise through the entire range of motion. If the exercise causes pain, then lighter weights should be used. To determine when full strength and size has been regained, compare the injured area to the non-injured area on the opposite side of the body. When both areas are of equal size and strength, then the players may progress to the next phase of recovery.

Your goal is to have the players regain full strength through the entire range of motion before allowing them to return to competition.

Normal Speed and Agility

When a physician gives written clearance for a player to return to practice, incorporate progressively greater levels of intensity of activity. You should be careful to gradually challenge the previously injured body part. In your observation of injured players, try to detect any favoring of an injured part or inability to smoothly perform a skill at increasing intensities. When players can move at pre-injury speed and agility, they are almost ready to play.

The main goal of a rehabilitation program is to reestablish range of motion, strength, power, and muscular endurance to the injured area.

Normal Level of Fitness

Every extended layoff reduces the level of muscular fitness. While recovering, the player may be able to exercise other body parts without affecting the injured area. For example, someone with a sprained ankle may not be able to run and dribble the ball, but he/she may be able to swim. Someone with a broken wrist may be able to do a variety of lower body activities such as jog, dribble, receive and control the ball, and pass. Cautiously encourage this type of activity, because it helps to maintain portions of their pre-injury levels of fitness. Players who have missed long periods of time due to an injury should practice for several days after meeting the previous criteria before being allowed to play in a game. Their cardiovascular system and the endurance of the injured musculature need time to adjust to the demands of the game. The longer the layoff, the more conditioning work they will need.

SUMMARY

When the pain is gone, and the range of motion, strength, agility, and conditioning are back to normal, your player is ready to reinitiate play. The entire process may have taken two days for a bruise to 12 weeks or more and assistance from physicians for a fracture. In either case, if you have followed the general guidelines of this chapter, you know you have acted in the best long-term interest of the player. Participation is important, but only if participation is achieved with a healthy body. Resist the pressure and the temptation to rush players into a game before they are ready. Your patience will be rewarded in the games to come.

INDEX

A

Administration goals, 3
Aerobic/anaerobic post-season training, 497
Aerobic/anaerobic transition training, 494
Aerobic system, 474
Air ball, receiving, 253-262, 264
Anaerobic interval training, 495
Anaerobic maintenance training, 496-497
Anaerobic system, 474-476
Apparel, injury prevention, 532
Approach run throw-in, 321, 324
Assumption of risk, 8, 56
Athletes (see also Players)
    growth/development, 13
    medical information, 46-48
    training/conditioning, 13
    understanding drop-outs, 100
    understanding participation, 99-100, 102
Attitudes, improving, 103
Awards
    appropriate use, 109-113
    intrinsic, 111

B

Back-heel pass, 229
Backward heading, 301-302
Ball, 157
Ball controlling, 243-268
Ball in/out play, 167
Ball positioning, 395-400
Ball receiving, 243-268
    air ball, 253-262, 264
    difficulty factors, 263
    fundamentals, 244-245
    half volley, 251-253, 264
    rolling balls, 245-251
    teaching techniques, 262-268
Ball shifting, 412
Baseball throw, 368-369
Behavior, identifying, 120-121
Benefits, for participants, 1-2
Blind-side run, 400
Bowled ball (underhand pass), 365-366

C

Calendars, season planning, 14-16, 30

Carbohydrate replacement drink, 530
Cautionable offenses, 173
Change of direction dribble, 275-277
Change of pace dribble, 274-275
Checking run, 397-398
Checklists
    coaching effectiveness, 150-152
    weight training program, 500
    year-round conditioning, 502-504
Circuit training, 484, 507-512
Circuit training form, 512
Coach
    as role model, 131-132
    curricular objectives, 12-14
    duties of, 7-8, 55-56
    goals, 3-4
    legal liabilities, 6-14, 53-64
    misconceptions, 8, 56-57
    player evaluation form, 148-149
    qualifications, 7, 54-55
    responsibilities, 8-12, 54-55, 57
    role of, 3-5
Coaching
    effectiveness evaluation, 139-152
    medical/legal aspects, 12-13
    positive approach, 104-106
    psychological aspects, 13
    scientific basis, 12-14
    seasonal plans, 5-30
    techniques, 13-14
Code, sportsmanship, 121
Cognitive needs assessment, 70
Combination defense, 428
Communications, with players, 115-118
Competitive stress, dealing with, 108-109
Conditioning
    circuit training, 507-512
    cool down, 491
    interval training, 492-493
    methods, 483-487
    overload, 481
    progression, 482
    reversibility, 483
    specificity, 482-483

    stretching, 490-491
    warm-ups, 480, 489-490
    weight training, 493
    year-round, 492-507
Contraindicated exercises, 536-537
Cool down, 480, 491
Corner kick, 180-181
Corner kick defense, 446-447
Corner kick offense, 443-446
Covering, 408-409
Cross-over run, 399-400
Curricular objectives, 12-14

D

Defense
    corner kick, 446-447
    difficulty rating form, 340
    drills, 341-345
    free kick, 451-453
    goal kick, 441
    kick-off, 438
    marking, 330-331
    penalty kick, 443
    principle, 329
    principles and tactics, 460
    purpose of, 329
    relationship to offense, 414-415
    tackling, 331-339
    techniques, 329-345
    throw-in, 455
Defensive drills, 461-470
Defensive principles, 405-413
    balance, 411-412
    ball pressure, 407-408
    ball shifting, 412
    combination, 428
    compactness, 412-413
    concentration, 412-413
    covering, 408-409
    delay, 405-408
    depth, 408-411
    diagonal cover, 411-412
    free kicks, 421
    funneling, 413
    goal-side marking, 405
    jockeying, 408
    man-to-man, 427-428
    offside trap, 423-425
    overloading, 413
    player-to-player, 427-428
    recovering run, 406-407

shepherding, 408
supporting, 409-410
switching, 410-411
wall, 417-423
zones, 425-427
Diagonal cover, 411-412
Diagonal run, 401-402
Diet information, 513-530
Discipline, maintaining, 119-124
Diving head, 304-305
Diving saves, 378-380
Dribbling, 269-296
    change of direction, 275-277
    change of pace, 274-275
    control form, 285
    control techniques, 274-283
    drills, 286-295
    feinting, 278-283
    fundamentals, 270-272
    inside of the foot, 271-272
    instep, 272-273
    outside of the foot, 272
    purpose of, 269-270
    shielding, 275-277
    techniques, 271-273
Drills
    defense, 341-345
    defensive, 461-470
    dribbling, 286-295
    goalkeeping, 382-389
    heading, 311-315
    offensive, 461-470
    passing, 233-242
    receiving, 266-268
    shooting, 233-242
Drop ball, 166
Drop kick, 371
Drop-outs, reasons for, 100-102
Dummy run, 403-404

E

Early-season objectives, 10
Economical training, 486-487
Effectiveness evaluation, 139-152
    coaching checklist, 150-152
    conducting, 141-146
    data analysis, 144-147
    data collection, 142-143
    defining, 140
    objectives, 141
    second-party evaluator, 140-141
Emergency procedures, 540-542
Energy production systems, 473-476
    use in soccer, 476-477
Entry pass, 444
Equipment, 12, 49-51, 62-63, 160
    injury prevention, 532
Ergogenic aids, 521-522
Evaluation, coaching, 139-152
Exercises, contraindicated, 536-537

F

Facilities, injury prevention, 532-533

Federation Internationale De Football Association (FIFA), 155
Feinting dribble, 278-283
Field of play, 156-157
Field player circuit training form, 508-509
Field players
    equipment guidelines, 49-50
    objectives, 18-21
    weight training, 498
First aid, 543-545
First aid kit, 543
Fitness assessment, 69-70
Fitness objectives, 8, 27
Foot kicks, 214-229
    inside, 214-217
Formations, team, 429, 432-436
Forms
    circuit training, 512
    defense difficulty rating, 340
    dribbling control, 285
    field player circuit training, 508-509
    goalkeeper circuit training, 510-511
    goalkeeping difficulty rating, 381
    heading difficulty, 310
    medical history, 46-48
    medical release, 48
    on-site injury report, 557-558, 560
    player evaluation, 148-149
    season injuries, 558, 561-562
    throw-in difficulty rating, 326
Forward heading, 299-300
Fouls, 170-173
Free kick defense, 451-453
Free kick offense, 447-451
Free kicks, 174-175
    defending, 421
Front block tackle, 332-334
Funneling, 413

G

Game
    duration, 164-165
    starting play, 165-167
Glossary, 183-206
Goal kick, 179-180, 371
Goal kick defense, 441
Goal kick offense, 439-441
Goal-side marking, 405
Goalkeeper circuit training form, 510-511
Goalkeepers
    equipment guidelines, 49-51
    location in wall defense, 420
    objectives, 22-23
    weight training, 498
Goalkeeping, 349-389
    baseball throw, 368-369
    bowled ball (underhand pass), 365-366
    catching, 358-359
    cover-up, 363-365

difficulty factors, 357
difficulty rating form, 381
diving, 361-363
drills, 382-389
drop kick, 371
fundamentals, 350-365
goal kick, 371
key words, 356
narrowing breakaway angle, 352-355
positioning, 351-352
punching/deflecting, 359-361
punt, 369-370
purpose of, 350
ready position, 350-351
short stopping, 357
sling throw, 366-368
supporting the defense, 355-357
Goalkeeping saves
    diving, 378-380
    overhand, 376-378
    scoop catch, 372-376
Goals
    organization and administration, 3
    season, 6-12
    setting player, 106-108
    teaching and leading, 3-4
Guidelines
    control projection, 84
    environment, 81
    grouping players, 81-82
    instruction, 74, 79-84
    on-task time, 82-83
    progress monitoring, 83
    questioning players, 83
    realistic expectations, 79-81
    structure instructions, 80-81
    success rate, 83

H

Half volley, receiving, 251-253, 264
Hazards, 10, 59-60
Heading, 297-316
    backward, 301-302
    ball impact force, 305-306
    developmental concerns, 305-306
    difficulty form, 310
    diving, 304-305
    drills, 311-315
    forward, 299-300
    fundamentals, 298-299
    head movement control, 306
    jump heading, 302-304
    neck muscle strength, 306
    purpose of, 297
    sideward, 300-301
    spinal development, 306
    teaching progression, 308-309
    techniques, 299-305
Heel pass (back-heel), 229
Hop, step, and throw throw-in, 321-322

I

Injuries
    caring for, 539-562
    prevention, 61-62, 531-538
    rehabilitation of, 563-566
    sites of, 45
    types of, 44
Inside foot, dribbling, 271-272
Inside foot kicks, 214-217
Instep, dribbling, 272-273
Instep kicks, 217-226
Instruction guidelines, 74
Instruction planning, 67-98
Instructions, 8-9, 57-58
    guidelines, 79-84
    systematic model, 71-74
Interpersonal skills, 130-133
Interval training, 483-484, 492-493
Intrinsic awards, 111

J

Jockeying, 408
Jump heading, 302-304

K

Key words, goalkeeping, 356
Kick-off defense, 438
Kick-off offense, 436-437
Kicking, 209-242
    components of, 209-214
    factors of difficulty, 231
    foot kicks, 214-229
    individual techniques, 214-229, 232
    teaching components, 229-242
Kicks
    corner, 180-181
    free, 174-175
    heel pass (back-heel), 229
    inside foot, 214-217
    instep, 217-226
    outside foot, 226-229
    penalty, 176-177
    toe, 229
    toe poke, 229
Kits, first aid, 543
Knowledge objectives, 8, 24

L

Late-season objectives, 12
Laws of play, 156-182
Leadership goals, 3-4
Legal liabilities, 6-14, 53-64
    assumption of risk, 8, 56
Linesperson signals, 162-164
Listening skills, 117-118

M

Man-to-man defense, 427-428
Marking defense, 330-331
Medical history, 46-48
Medical information, 540, 557-558
Medical release form, 48
Meetings, orientation, 32-37
Mid-season objectives, 12
Misconduct, 170-173

Muscular systems, 477-479
    use in soccer, 479-483

N

Non-penal fouls, 172
Nutritional information, 513-530

O

Objectionable offenses, 173
Objectives
    early-season, 10
    field players, 18-21
    fitness, 8, 27
    goalkeepers, 22-23
    knowledge, 8, 24
    late-season, 12
    mid-season, 12
    personal, 9, 28
    practice, 12-17
    season, 6-12
    sequencing, 10-12
    skill, 8
    social skill, 9, 28
    tactics, 25-26
Offense
    corner kick, 443-446
    free kick, 447-451
    goal kick, 441
    kick-off, 438
    penalty kick, 441-442
    principles and tactics, 459
    relationship to defense, 414-415
    teaching principles, 415-417
    throw-in, 453-454
Offensive drills, 461-470
Offensive principles, 394-404
    ball positioning, 395-400
    blind-side run, 400
    checking run, 397-398
    cross-over run, 399-400
    diagonal run, 401-402
    dummy run, 403-404
    mobility, 400-402
    overlapping run, 398-399
    penetration, 394-395
    support, 395-400
    wall pass, 396-397
    width, 403-404
Offside rules, 168-169
Offside trap, 423-425
On-site injury report form, 557-558, 560
Organization goals, 3
Orientation meeting
    athletes responsibilities, 35
    emergency procedures, 35
    equipment needs, 35
    follow-up meetings, 38
    injury risks, 34-35
    introductions, 32-33
    organizing, 38
    parents responsibilities, 36-37
    scheduling parents, 37
    season schedule, 37
    team goals, 33-34

    understanding soccer, 34
Outside foot, dribbling, 272
Outside foot kicks, 226-229
Overhand saves, 376-378
Overlapping run, 398-399
Overloading, 413

P

Parents
    orientation meeting, 32-37
    responsibilities of, 36-37
    working with, 31-51
Passing drills, 233-242
Penal fouls, 170-171
Penalty kick, 176-177
Penalty kick defense, 443
Penalty kick offense, 441-442
Penetration principles, 394-395
Performance assessment, 69
Performance evaluation, 68-71
Personal assessment, 70-71
Personal objectives, 9, 28
Personnel, 10-11, 60-61
Pivot tackle, 334-335
Place kick, 165
Plans
    practice, 74-78, 86-98
    season, 5-30
Player evaluation form, 148-149
Player-to-player defense, 427-428
Players
    benefits for, 1-2
    communicating with, 68, 115-118
    conditioning, 473-512
    detriments for, 2
    emergency procedures, 540-542
    ergogenic aids, 521-522
    evaluating performance, 68-71
    first aid, 543-545
    injury care, 539-562
    injury prevention, 531-538
    injury rehabilitation, 563-566
    meal patterns, 523-526
    measuring maturity, 5-6, 54
    medical information, 540
    medical problems, 545-557
    motivating, 99-114
    number of, 158-159
    nutritional information, 513-530
    selecting, 12, 63, 429-430
    setting goals, 106-108
    weight loss/gain, 526-528
Positional names, 431
Positions, assigning, 430
Practice objectives, 12-17
Practice plans
    cool-down, 94
    equipment, 94
    evaluation, 95
    field player skill techniques, 93
    goalkeeping techniques, 93-94
    group games, 94

objectives, 92
organization/content, 86
sample, 86-98
set plays, 92-93
warm-up, 92
Practices, planning, 74-78
Punt, 369-370

R

R.I.C.E. formula, 544
Receiving
    air ball, 253-262, 264
    difficulty factors, 263
    drills, 266-268
    half volley, 251-253, 264
    rolling balls, 245-251, 263-264
    teaching techniques, 262-268
Recovering run, 406-407
Referees signals, 160-162
Responsibilities, coaching, 8-12, 54-
    55, 57
Rewards, understanding, 110-113
Risks, 10, 59-60
Role modeling, 131-137
Rules
    ball in/out of play, 167
    ball size, 157-158
    duration of game, 164-165
    equipment, 160
    field of play, 156-157
    fouls/misconduct, 170-173
    free kick, 174-175
    goal kick, 179-180
    linesperson signals, 162-164
    number of players, 158-159
    offside, 168-169
    referees signals, 160-162
    scoring methods, 168
    soccer, 156-182
    start of play, 165-167
    telephone tree, 42-43
    throw-in, 178-179, 317-318

S

Saves, goalkeeping, 372-380
Scoop catch save, 372-376
Scoring methods, 168
Season
    goals/objectives, 6-12
    injuries form, 558, 561-562
    organizing for, 1-4
    plan worksheet, 11, 29
    planning calendar, 14-16, 30
    planning for, 5-30
Self-esteem, developing, 126-129
Set plays (restarts), 436-456
Set plays, 457-458

corner kick defense, 446-447
corner kick offense, 443-446
entry pass, 444
free kick defense, 451-453
free kick offense, 447-451
goal kick offense, 439-441
kick-off defense, 438
kick-off offense, 436-437
penalty kick defense, 443
penalty kick offense, 441-442
throw-in offense, 453-455
Shepherding, 408
Shielding dribble, 275-277
Shooting drills, 233-242
Side tackle, 335-336
Sideward heading, 300-301
Signals
    linesperson, 162-164
    referees, 160-162
Skill objectives, 8
Skills
    improving, 102-103
    interpersonal, 130-133
    social, 125-128
Slide tackle, 336-339
Sling throw, 366-368
Soccer
    laws of play, 156-182
    medical problems in, 545-557
    tactics of play, 393-470
    terms, 183-206
Social needs assessment, 70-71
Social skills
    developing, 103, 125-138
    objectives, 9, 28
Sportsmanship code, 121
Sportsmanship, developing, 133-
    137
Stationary throw-in, 320, 322-323
Stress, dealing with, 108-109
Stretching, 490-491
Style of play, 429
Success, dealing with, 104
Supervision, 9-10, 58-59
Support principles, 395-400
Supporting, 409-410
Switching, 410-411
System, building, 429-436
System of play, 429-436
Systems
    energy production, 473-476
    muscular, 477-479

T

Tackling defense, 331-339
Tactics objectives, 25-26
Tactics of play, 393-470

definitions, 393
Teaching goals, 3-4
Team formations, 429, 432-436
Team roster, 41
Team rules
    defining, 120-121
    enforcing, 122-124
Telephone tree, 42-43
Terms, soccer, 183-206
Throw-in, 178-179
    approach run, 321, 324
    defense, 455
    difficulty rating form, 326
    errors in technique, 324-325
    fundamentals, 318-320
    hop, step, and throw, 321-322
    offense, 453-454
    plays, errors, 456
    purpose of, 317
    rules of play, 317-318
    set plays, 327
    stationary, 320, 322-323
    teaching progression, 322-324
    techniques, 317-328, 320-322
Toe kick (toe poke), 229
Toe poke, 229
Training
    circuit, 484, 507-512
    economical, 486-487
    interval, 483-484
    principles, 479-483
    weight, 485-486
Trophies, appropriate use, 109-113

U

Underhand pass (bowled ball),
    365-366
Unsportsmanship conduct, recog-
    nizing, 133-134

W

Wall defense, 417-423
Wall pass, 396-397
Warm-up, 480, 489-490
Weight training, 485-486, 493, 498-
    501
    program checklist, 500
Worksheets, season plan, 11, 29

Y

Year-round conditioning, 492-507
    checklist, 502-504
Youth sports, misconceptions, 8,
    56-57

Z

Zone defense, 425-427